D0076715

Comparative
Asian Politics

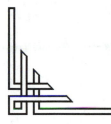

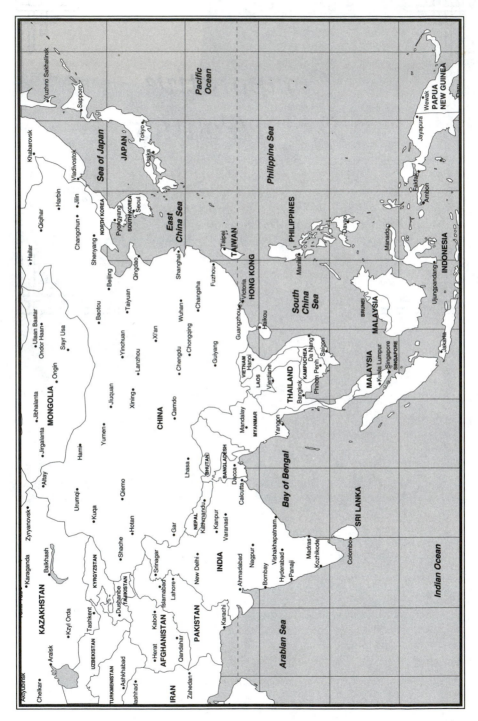

Comparative
Asian Politics

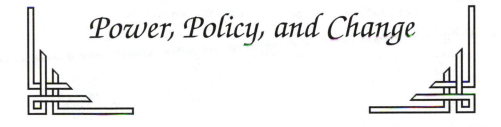

Power, Policy, and Change

James C. F. Wang

University of Hawaii at Hilo

 PRENTICE HALL, Englewood Cliffs, New Jersey 07632

Library of Congress Cataloging-in-Publication Data

WANG, JAMES C. F.
   Comparative Asian politics: power, policy, and change/James
   C. F. Wang
      p. cm.
   Includes bibliographical references and index.
   ISBN 0-13-155458-1
   1. Asia—Politics and government. 2. Comparative government.
   I. Title
   JQ22.W36   1993
   320.95—dc20   93-40378
                                                 CIP

Editorial/production supervision,
  interior design, and electronic page makeup: Kari Callaghan Mazzola
Acquisitions editor: Maria DiVencenzo
Cover design: Bruce Kenselaar
Production coordinator: Mary Ann Gloriande

 © 1994 by Prentice-Hall, Inc.
A Paramount Communications Company
Englewood Cliffs, New Jersey 07632

Printed in the United States of America
10 9   8   7   6   5   4   3   2   1

ISBN 0-13-155458-1

PRENTICE-HALL INTERNATIONAL (UK) LIMITED, *London*
PRENTICE-HALL OF AUSTRALIA PTY. LIMITED, *Sydney*
PRENTICE-Hall CANADA INC., *Toronto*
PRENTICE-HALL HISPANOAMERICANA, S.A., *Mexico*
PRENTICE-HALL OF INDIA PRIVATE LIMITED, *New Delhi*
PRENTICE-HALL OF JAPAN, INC., *Tokyo*
SIMON & SCHUSTER ASIA PTE. LTD., *Singapore*
EDITORA PRENTICE-HALL DO BRASIL, LTDA., *Rio de Janeiro*

Contents

5   Indonesia and the Philippines: The Archipelagic States   249

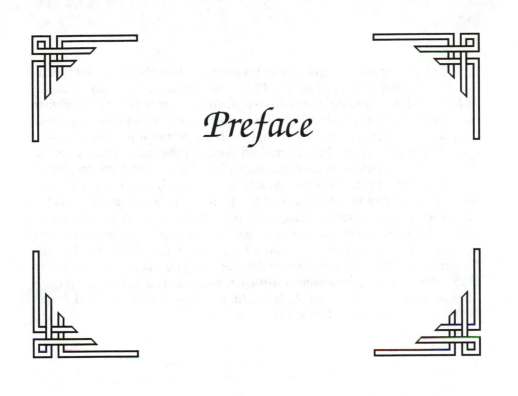

Preface

This book grew out of the frustration that many of us have experienced in teaching a course on Asian politics and government. A large part of the frustration has been the lack of suitable textbooks that present exclusively a comprehensive comparison of a representative number of Asian nations. To cover simply a selective number of nations from East, South, and Southeast Asia would mean a reading list of at least six to perhaps as many as twelve books, one on each of the Asian nations selected for study.

The mere selection of a group of Asian nations for a course would hardly solve the problem of providing a comparative framework for analysis and the most up-to-date information in a rapidly changing continent. Thus, this textbook offers at least three features for a course on Asian politics: (1) It provides the essential background information about each of the fourteen Asian nations studied without overburdening the students with details of historic facts; (2) it provides students with an up-to-date, comprehensive discussion of the political, economic, and social development for each of the fourteen Asian nations for East, South, and Southeast Asia; (3) it is probably the only attempt made so far in college textbook publishing to organize the vast material on Asian politics in a comparative framework in terms of historic background, political culture, political institutions and power, leadership recruitment and succession, political process and participation, group and military politics, and policy process and performance.

The preparation of this textbook would not have been possible without the help of a number of people. First, I must acknowledge my gratitude to Joseph Murray and Benjamin Nowell, field representatives of the Higher Education Group at Prentice Hall. They gave me the initial encouragement to approach the editors at Prentice Hall with the proposal for this textbook. Then Karen Horton and Julie Berrisford, former political science editors at Prentice Hall, provided encouragement and guidance during the preparatory stages of the book. I am also grateful to Nicole Signoretti for her assistance. I would like to extend special thanks to Kari Callaghan Mazzola for her patience and tolerance throughout the editorial-production process, as well as her editing, design, and page makeup skills. A word of thanks also goes to Catherine Tignac for research assistance and to Edith Morsencraft for her help with editing and typing the manuscript. Finally, I would like to thank the following reviewers for their input: Lawrence Ziring, *Western Michigan University*; Robert W. Hunt, *Illinois State University*; and Aruna N. Michie, *Kansas State University*.

Introduction

WHY STUDY COMPARATIVE ASIAN POLITICS?

To answer this question one must first ask, "Why study comparative politics at all?" Comparative study of politics is as old as Aristotle (384–322 B.C.), whose *Politics* was a comparative study of the Greek city-states. By comparing political and social structure of the ancient Greek city-states, Aristotle was able to determine how politics were made. Since the time of the Greek philosopher, students have been engaged in comparative study of nations or regimes.

There are two basic objectives to be achieved when engaging in comparative study of regimes. One is to seek understanding about other nations by gathering political knowledge and experience. Rolf Theen and Frank Wilson have this to say about the purpose of seeking understanding:

> The study of comparative politics offers help in gaining this understanding. The subject matter of comparative politics includes the political force, processes, institutions, and performance of foreign countries. In short, comparative politics is concerned with political experience in other cultural and historical settings. From the study of comparative politics comes the understanding of the historical and social background, the political groups and parties, and the political institutions that produce the events we read about in the newspapers.[1]

As explained by Gabriel Almond and Bingham Powell, Jr., comparative politics is an approach that helps to discover or explain "variations between the procedures and achievements of political systems."[2] Almond and Powell outline three steps in comparing institutions and processes: (1) description of assembled facts about the political system, such as legislatures, political parties, and bureaucracy; (2) classification of the phenomena into types—for example, those political systems with organized bureaucracies or interest groups and those without; and (3) examination of relationships between social and economic conditions in stable regimes versus those which are beset by civil disorder.[3] To Almond and Powell, the study of comparative politics is not only the "beginning of political science," but also "the beginning of political understanding and judgment."[4]

The study of comparative politics also enables us to better understand our own political system or "gain perspective on [our] own society."[5] As pointed out by Thomas Magstadt, some of the classical studies about American politics have been through foreign observers' eyes: Alexis de Tocqueville's *Democracy in America* and James Bryce's *The American Commonwealth*. Thus, in comparing other societies' political institutions and processes we gain a better understanding about ourselves.[6]

A fundamental approach in comparative politics is to have some accurate, descriptive information about how the individual political systems function. Then the task of comparative politics is to formulate generalizations about all these political systems. Needed next is a set of "criteria for analysis of the similarities and differences between countries."[7] These analytical criteria include the following: nature and quality of the regimes; how the governments perform the functions; the relationship between rulers and the people; and laws and rules that form the basis for government actions.[8]

A typical method of comparative analysis involves the application of theories or concepts which serve to explain what Almond and Powell termed as systems (political culture or beliefs), institutions of political structure (legislative bodies or parliaments), recruitment of leaders, political participation, political parties and interest groups, and policymaking or performance.[9] In other words, the whole gamut of inductive analysis that entails gathering relevant information, classifying the data assembled, comparing the similarities and differences, and finally reaching some conclusions from the facts or experiences shown in the comparative analysis.[10]

Now the answer to the question, "Why study comparative Asian politics?" There are a number of reasons. One, Asia is the largest of all continents. Its total land area is about 18.5 million square miles, or roughly 33 percent of the earth's total land surface. Its vast expanse stretches from its high mountains to the seas, bordering with Europe and Africa eastward to the Pacific; the region stretches from the Arctic shores of Siberia to tropical lands washed by the Indian Ocean. Asia contains more than half of the world's total population of 5.4 billion—the total population of Asia's most populous nations, China and India, constitutes about 2 billion. Asia has been the birthplace of the world's great religions and philosophies: Buddhism, Hinduism, Islam, and Confucianism. From Asia came the calendar, the numeral system, medicine, tea, silk, the compass, and gunpowder. It is a continent with numerous ethnic groupings, languages, and dialects. It is perhaps the most diverse continent in the world.

Today, Asia is characterized not only by enormous change as well as continuity, but by the presence of a remarkable economic dynamism. One now speaks about the future that lies in Asia and the Pacific. In 1980 U.S. trade with Asia surpassed its trade with Western Europe for the first time, $112 to $110 billion. In 1992 U.S. trade with Asia and the Pacific amounted to one-third of its total $422 billion. The Asian Development Bank (ADB) is predicting a 1993 gross domestic growth (minus foreign investment) averaging 7.3 percent for Asia's twenty-five developing countries. Today, from Beijing to Bengal and from Seoul to Saigon, Asia is undergoing rapid change accompanied by unprecedented prosperity for the region's once-impoverished millions. Political reform and democracy are on the rise for most of Asia. Even in communist Asia the free market system is preferred in the face of declining Marxist ideology.

While there has been a cascade of scholarly studies about Asia and its individual nations, in the main studies in comparative politics have been focused on the European political systems of England, France, Germany, Italy, the Soviet Union, and the Scandinavian countries. Occasionally a few—China, Japan, or India—have been selected to be part of the comparative politics as case studies.[11] In 1977 a pioneer work on Asian politics covering ten countries was done in one single volume by C. L. Kim and Laurence Ziring.[12] However, that study was essentially a country-by-country survey of events since World War II. Lucian Pye contributed to the study of development politics by focusing on power in the cultural dimension of a number of Asian countries.[13] Analysis of Asian nations in a comparative perspective gained ground with a study by Gary Gereffi and Donald L. Wyman on comparative industrialization in Latin America and East Asia (South Korea and Taiwan);[14] and with Thomas M. Magstadt's comparative study of three regions, including Asia (limited only to China, Japan, and India as case studies).[15] This brief survey indicates that there is a need in the extensive literature of Asian studies for a comparative political study of a representative group of Asian nations to reflect regional diversity, cultural patterns, various stages of economic development, and policy process and performance.

As an introduction to the study of comparative Asian politics, this textbook examines the political systems in fourteen countries: Japan, China, South and North Korea, Taiwan, and Hong Kong in East Asia; India and Pakistan in South Asia; Indonesia, Singapore, and the Philippines in the Pacific Rim states of Southeast Asia; and Vietnam, Laos, and Cambodia in mainland Southeast Asia. These fourteen countries have been selected on the basis of their geographic and cultural importance in the region, plus the fact that they are among the Asian countries most frequently discussed in the news and which occupy the attention of our policymakers. The list includes some of the most important powers in Asia and in the world scene. In most instances their political, cultural, and economic developments have shaped the course of events in the past, for the present and the future. The study of these fourteen Asian nations will permit us to introduce many of the key questions relating to the comparative study of politics. As a means of introducing students to the concepts of comparative analysis, this book pairs off the fourteen Asian countries into seven comparable groupings:

1. China and Japan: Modernization, Industrialization, and Contrast in Development
2. South Korea and Taiwan: Emerging Political Reform and Asian Models for Economic Success
3. Singapore and Hong Kong: Government Overregulation versus the Free Market
4. India and Pakistan: Diversity in Traditional Culture amidst Religious Fundamentalist Revival and Separatist Claims
5. Indonesia and the Philippines: The Archipelagic States
6. Vietnam and North Korea: Changes in the Two Nations That America Fought
7. Cambodia and Laos: Continued Battle for National Independence and against Foreign Interference

China and Japan are grouped primarily to illustrate not only the cultural influence of Confucianism, but also the contrast in the modernization process and development goals. China and Japan each represent different political patterns: one, Marxist-Leninist (now in the process of reform), and the other modeled on a Western democratic framework. In terms of economic development, Japan is a highly industrialized nation and an economic power in the world, while China is in the throes of becoming modernized.

The second comparison group consists of South Korea and Taiwan, for both share their colonial experience under Japan. For some time both were under military authoritarianism, which at the moment is emerging into civilian control through democratic reform and election. Economically, both South Korea and Taiwan are the shining examples of Asia's newly industrialized countries (NICs).

The third paired group consists of Singapore and Hong Kong, primarily because both had been prized British colonial possessions dominated demographically by ethnic Chinese. Here state paternalism is more pronounced in Singapore, but free enterprise, or laissez faire, has been a key feature for success in Hong Kong, which will be returned to China by 1997.

The fourth paired group for comparison consists of the southern Asian nations of India and Pakistan. India has been operating on the basis of the British parliamentary system with frequent elections. On the other hand, Pakistan has been ruled for the most part by military authoritarianism, interspersed with civilian rule and elections. An interesting comparative inquiry would be: Why have two parts of the same British colonial mold developed into quite different political patterns? Both India and Pakistan have been beset by ethnic conflicts and religious intolerance.

The fifth group of Asian nations to be compared consists of the island states of Indonesia and the Philippines. Their geography, consisting of thousands of scattered islands populated by diverse ethnic groups, is the common ground for comparison. Both Indonesia and the Philippines have experienced personal and military dictatorships.

The sixth comparative group consists of the two remaining Marxist-Leninist countries: Vietnam and North Korea. Both had been recipients of Soviet economic and military aid before the collapse of the Soviet Union in 1991, and both have allied with China. The political and economic adjustments that have taken place in the past few years may be instructive from a comparative viewpoint as to how highly ideologically controlled nations attempt to make pragmatic changes.

The seventh pair of countries to be analytically compared consists of Laos and Cambodia. Their development illustrates the tragic consequence of the international power struggle in Southeast Asia. The proximity and presence of China and Vietnam have made a tremendous impact on Laos and Cambodia. Their postwar struggle for independence has been thwarted by international rivalry.

The paired comparison scheme contains not only the features of a country-by-country case-study mode, but it places emphasis as well on the comparisons—the similarities and differences in their development. For each of the paired groups the comparative study will be organized along the following conceptual themes:

Political culture and political development
Locus of power
The political process
Political performance and public policy

POLITICAL CULTURE AND POLITICAL DEVELOPMENT

Contemporary Asian political systems have been influenced by history and cultural traditions. For all Asian nations—particularly China, Japan, and India—the past is ever present. In essence this fact compels us to recognize historic and cultural continuity as important factors in shaping the development of these nations in the contemporary world. For most American undergraduates it is sometimes difficult to appreciate the thousands of years of historic imprint on the Chinese or Japanese or Indian political traditions, institutions, and political behavior. For thousands of years China was able to develop its political traditions and institutions without challenges from the outside; the Chinese viewed their nation as the "center of the world," uncontaminated by foreign or alien influence. Japan, too, enjoyed hundreds of years of isolation under Tokugawa feudalism without contact from the outside world. Then came the Western demand for commerce and trade, which eventually forced China and Japan to open their doors to the West, ultimately bringing change, reform, and revolution. For many Asian nations Western colonialism also fashioned a lasting imprint on their contemporary political development. Since their independence at the end of World War II, many Asian nations have retained their institutions in education, bureaucracy, and military establishment introduced by the colonizers—the British, the French, and the Dutch.

In many ways political culture is also the legacy of the past. Almond and Powell define political culture as "a particular distribution of political attitudes, values, feelings, information, and skills."[16] What is involved here is the belief system about values and attitudes that are often associated with a particular nation: traditional views on politics and government, emotional commitment or loyalty toward a set of ideologies. Deference to and veneration for authority to rule are important parts of traditional political culture for China, Japan, and Korea. Whereas respect for authority may be highly pronounced under communist rule in China, that tradition has undergone some modification in Japan since 1947 as the authority of a popularly elected government has become accepted. However, in many parts of Asia today authoritarianism is still dominant in varying degrees.

In the first section devoted to discussions of political development and political culture, six specific thematic subtopics have been selected for comparison in each of the paired groups of countries:

1. *Historic Legacies*   A brief survey of the paired country group with emphasis on each nation's unique historic development.

2. *Political Belief*   A comparative look at each country's dominant belief and value system. How the general population and the leaders develop their feelings or attitudes that determine political behavior.

3. *Western Impact and Colonialism*   All Asian nations have experienced the impact wrought by contact with the West. Many Asian nations were ruled as colonies until World War II. Few of these nations have escaped from the colonial mold that has influenced their contemporary make-up as a newly independent nation.

4. *Nationalism and Independence*   With colonialism over time there arose the feeling of nationalism, a force that propelled each nation to strive

for political independence and territorial integrity. Nationalism binds the people who share common cultural, historic, and linguistic characteristics to produce collective loyalty for action. Nationalism in China is different from nationalism in Japan or the Indian sense of patriotism. For some Asian nations, nationalism implies self-determination as a people. For others, nationalism means rejection of Western influence and dominance.

5. *Striving for Modernization*   Modernization refers to the use of modern thinking and the acquisition of science and technology to build a new, powerful state. It is an ongoing process accomplished in stages, but with the ultimate goal of becoming a modern, industrialized society.

6. *Political Change: Reform and Revolution*   Here comparisons will be made to analyze the political change that has taken place after independence. Some Asian nations have experimented with the Western concept of democracy that has yielded unsatisfactory results. Others—China is an example—have embarked on revolutionary changes oscillating from ill-conceived radicalism to moderate orderly reform. For many in Asia political and economic reform have become the order of the day.

LOCUS OF POWER

The study of "where the power is" has been an established organizing concept in political science. David Easton writes that power is the allocation of values.[17] Power, or simply political power, is the allocation of authority in different institutions in a political framework. For instance, the major comparative difference between a parliamentary (British) and a presidential (American) political institution lies in the power relationship between the legislative and the executive divisions. Typically, the executive under the parliamentary form of government is elected by the legislature or the national assembly (as in the cases of Indonesia, South Korea, or Taiwan) or parliament (in the cases of Japan and India or Singapore). But in the presidential form of government, the executive is elected directly and independent of the legislature. Subthematic topics for this section are as follows:

1. *The Parliamentary versus Presidential Form*   In this section we first compare the advantages and disadvantages of parliamentary and presidential forms of government as experienced by some of the Asian countries selected for study and make appropriate application to any of the paired countries.

2. *Contrasting Federalism with Unitary States*   Here the question of power concentration or dispersion becomes the focus of comparison, appropriately applied to any of the paired countries.

3. *Leadership Style and Succession*   To determine the kinds of rulers, the comparative focus will be on recruitment of leaders and their socioeconomic background for a particular Asian nation. In other words, we make

comparisons not only with respect to the occupation, training, education, and social class of the leaders, but also how they acquired their leadership position and political power. Until very recently many Asian nations faced the challenge of making orderly and nonviolent transfer of power from one person to another—the political succession problem. Some Asian nations, such as Japan and India, have a well-established procedure for orderly succession. Others have been troubled but have recently resolved this issue— South Korea, Taiwan, Singapore, Pakistan, and the Philippines. For China or Indonesia it is still a problem to be resolved when the incumbent strong or paramount leader leaves the scene.

4. *The Bureaucracy*   A brief comparison will be made whenever it is appropriate or when information is available to contrast or to identify the similarities of the vast and too frequently complex organizational structure and those functionaries who staff government offices. The degree or extent for exercising bureaucratic power will also be discussed briefly and compared when information is available. So will be compared the character of the bureaucracy or civil service as to whether it is a merit system or one of patronage relying on partisan affiliation.

5. *The Justice System*   Brief comparisons will be made with respect to each nation's judicial system to identify similarities and differences in the dispensation of justice. The key question to be raised is, "To what extent is the judiciary system independent of political shifting winds, or how strong is its ability to maintain judicial integrity?"

THE POLITICAL PROCESS

Almond and Powell define participation as those political activities in which "the average citizen makes some attempt to influence policy making."[18] Of course, even in democratic states such as the United States, a majority of citizens give low priority to participation in political activities. In recent years, in most Asian nations (except Japan, India, Singapore, South Korea, the Philippines, and Taiwan) only a small proportion of the population has participated in organized political activities such as regular popular elections. For many Asian countries there are several obstacles that tend to prevent a higher degree of voluntary participation in political activities. These obstacles consist of low living standards, illiteracy (India's unique election system seems to have overcome illiteracy as an obstacle), geographic isolation, and clan, tribal, or religious loyalties.[19] Authoritarian regimes, such as China, often orchestrate mass participation in order to achieve the party's or leader's desire for conformity and against dissent, or for inducing political and social change. In some Asian countries there exists the patron-client relationship founded on "hierarchical interdependencies" whereby community members as clients serve the local patron (leader) by participating in political activities in order to receive material benefits.[20]

Subthematic topics used in this section for each of the paired countries include the following:

1. *The Electoral Process* It is useful for comparative politics to study how the electoral process works in Asian countries. In some countries election for representatives to national assemblies is based on functional representation, not on the equality of individual citizens. Indonesia and Hong Kong have adopted functional representation based on occupational groups or categories designated as such. In other countries geographic regions or ethnic/religious groups are entitled to specified representation. In some Asian countries the multimember constituency method is utilized. In these electoral systems a voter is permitted to choose more than one member. For such a system a proportional representation device is employed whereby seats are allocated to parties as in the case of the Japanese Diet upper house election since 1983.

2. *Political Parties* In a democratic system of government political parties are organized for the purpose of electing candidates to public office. In revolutionary socialist governments such as China, North Korea, and Vietnam, they are instruments for monopolizing political power. Michael Curtis suggests there are three types of political parties.[21] There are the representational ones, such as those in Western democracies and those Asian nations where democratic elections take place (Japan, India, Singapore, the Philippines, Taiwan, and South Korea in recent years). Representational political parties present platforms to the electorate and field candidates for public office who espouse the party's views. Then there are the traditional political parties that "reflect the social and economic control of a hereditary or oligarchic elite."[22] Many political parties in Asia contain some elements of "oligarchic elite" control. Finally, Curtis speaks of the mobilizing parties, such as the Communist party monopoly in China or Vietnam or North Korea.

3. *Interest Groups* David Truman pointed out that all politics is group politics and a conflict of various interest groups.[23] In developed, as well as developing societies, interest or lobbying groups can be organized to make demands on policymakers and for political power. Almond and Powell point out that interest groups are defined by their social base or goals.[24] Thus, groups organized for interest articulation can be tribal, racial, ethnic, religious, occupational, and issue oriented.[25] Interest groups can organize as formal institutional groups, such as business corporations, churches, or military officers' cliques, or the bureaucratic establishment. Or interest groups can be informally organized (unassociational or latent), such as the coffee-drinker consumer group or an ethnic group. As categorized by Almond and Powell, often anomic groups may spring up suddenly, for these are spontaneous interest groups formed to address certain frustrations

or disappointments.[26] Basic functions of interest groups are (1) to organize for gaining a share of the political power; (2) to influence government decisions; and (3) to help the effective implementation of policies—in most authoritarian political systems interest groups serve as "transmission belts."[27] It is not uncommon to discover that in some Asian nations formal interest groups are merely the mouthpiece and the muscle for the controlling elites. At any rate, it has been theorized that as "socioeconomic modernization" takes place in developing nations, there will be more and varied interest groups formed not only to articulate their interests or make demands but to influence policy decisions.[28] Thus, the impact of group politics is certainly a *must* topic for comparison in the study of Asian politics.

4. *Military Politics*   For a number of Asian nations the military plays an important, if not decisive, role. The Chinese military establishment is the dominant power in Chinese politics. For some periods in their contemporary history, South and North Korea, Taiwan, Pakistan, and Indonesia have seen the military establishment and its officers thrust into the center stage of domestic politics.

There have been many explanations for military intervention in politics in developing countries. One is the "agent of change,"[29] or the military as modernizer, the explanation of which states that military officers are better educated and are concerned with the traditional politics that often obstruct social and economic progress. As self-proclaimed agents for change, the younger officers become impatient and seize the opportunity to intervene in politics. Once in power, the military has the tendency for refusing to return to the barracks. In time the military officers take off their uniforms and assume the civil administration of the government. Another motive for military intervention may be the circumstance in a nation's development that has made the military the only viable cohesive force and institution for maintaining order and stability in the midst of protests and violent change. Or it may be a situation in which the internal police are not able to keep peace and order, so the military is called upon to provide internal security which ultimately and invariably paves the way for interference and control in politics. (In the cases of South Korea, Taiwan, and Indonesia real and alleged communist threats served as the rationale for military domination in politics.) Then the military as a political force in society may view its own interests, needs and security, or survival as more paramount than those of other competing groups in society. Thus, after having exerted pressure in vain on politicians to pay attention to military needs or demands such as increases in budgetary allocations, intervention in politics becomes a necessity to them. The result is a military coup.

For some Asian nations, the concern has been how to maintain the supremacy of civil authority over the military. For China it has been the question of following Mao's dictum of placing the military under party control. For Japan it has been the question of whether to limit the scope of the military within the boundaries of Japan and without violating the constitutional prohibition under Article 9 of the 1947 constitution. For South Korea, Taiwan, and Indonesia, or in Pakistan, it has been the matter of gradually replacing military control and dominance with civil authority. From a comparative viewpoint, one of the intriguing questions is: In contrast to the frequency with which the military in Pakistan has been able to topple civilian authorities through the use of martial law decrees, why has India been able to maintain its tradition of civil supremacy over the military since independence in 1947?

In each chapter for paired countries, we will see in what respect the military's role in politics has been placed under control of civil authorities.

POLITICAL PERFORMANCE AND PUBLIC POLICY

Political performance and public policy are intertwined and inseparable. Public policies are expressed goals from the elected leaders or the authoritarian rulers whose chances for reelection or retention of power depend to a large extent on how the policy goals have been achieved. In the United States, Bill Clinton's presidency and reelection in 1996 will to a large extent depend on the achievement of his promised goals of deficit reduction, health care reform, improved economy, and political reform in American politics. In comparative politics it is difficult to evaluate the performance of a particular political system because there are really no generally accepted universal standards for what constitutes a "good government."[30] In this section we employ Theen and Wilson's evaluation of performance of government policy in three specific areas: socioeconomic policies, political stability, and political dissent.[31] As argued by Theen and Wilson, there is general agreement among students of comparative government that all political regimes—democratic, oligarchical, and authoritarian—have established policy goals for the improvement of living standards for their populace. In the experience of most, if not all, Asian countries, economic material well-being can be obtained only under conditions of political stability and the absence of domestic disturbance or external threat. In the evaluation of a country's tolerance or intolerance of dissent or religious diversity, it is useful to compare the treatment of dissent in each Asian country.

Subthematic topics for political performance and public policy include the following:

1. *Economic Performance*   Emphasis is on the outcomes or accomplishments of political performance in terms of increases in gross or domestic national product, income distribution, and general economic performance. From a comparative standpoint, a brief review of a country's

modernization effort is analyzed and compared: Japan's economic miracle; the gains made by the newly industrialized countries: South Korea, Taiwan, Singapore, and Hong Kong; China's economic reform results; and so on.

2. *Government Role and the Corporate State*   For all Asian countries the government has intervened in the economy. Such interference varies from country to country: from centralized control to state manipulation and interference in the market economy to free-enterprise operation with minimal government interference (Hong Kong is the only example). Then there is the influence of bureaucracy on the economy, such as the role played by the Ministry of International Trade and Industry (MITI) in Japan. For a number of Asian nations, the initial government policy in land reform, which produced a basic foundation for subsequent economic change and take-off, is compared in order to gain some understanding about not only the role of government, but economic development as well.

3. *Influence of Big Business*   Big corporate formations, often with assistance and encouragement by government action, have played an important role in producing economic success for some Asian nations such as Japan, South Korea, Taiwan, and Indonesia. The similarities and differences of big corporate influence on a country's economic development are useful areas, not to mention the revelation aspect in politics, in comparative study.

4. *Education*   In the march for modernization and improvement of living standards, Asian nations place educational advancement as the most important goal to be attained by their leaders. Education is regarded not only as the key to individual and economic success, it is also the "effective agent"[32] for instilling national pride, and in the case of authoritarian political systems such as China, North Korea, and Vietnam, for enforcing conformity in political attitude. Some Asian nations, particularly Japan, South Korea, Taiwan, and Singapore, are educationally oriented and conscious. Here we make comparison in educational policies and goals, as well as government expenditures devoted to education. We also compare the results in terms of number of schools established for all levels of education and the number of students enrolled.

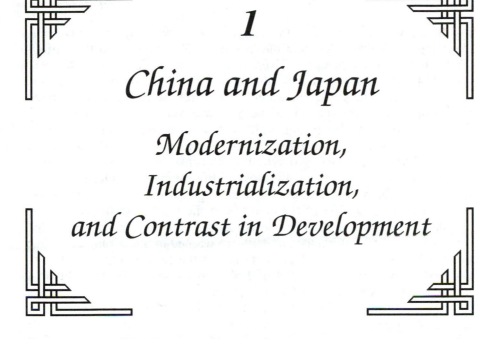

1

China and Japan

Modernization, Industrialization, and Contrast in Development

THE CASE OF CHINA (PEOPLE'S REPUBLIC OF CHINA)

A fundamental factor in understanding China is the relationship between the land and its people. China's total land area is about 3.7 million square miles, slightly larger than that of the United States. However, about 85 to 90 percent of China's more than 1 billion people live and work on only one-sixth of this area. The remaining land is mostly hilly and mountainous. Unlike the United States, only 15 to 20 percent of China's land area is cultivable, and much of this land has been used intensively for centuries.

In addition to the limited land area for cultivation, the climatic conditions compound the problem of food production for a vast population. The uneven rate of precipitation is one example. Rainfall comes to most parts of China in the spring and summer, usually in torrential downpours. It decreases from south to north. Average annual rainfall is about sixty to eighty inches for South China and less than ten inches for the northwest. The fertile Yangtze (Changjiang) River valley receives about forty to sixty inches, while most of northern China receives about twenty-five inches annually.

If the torrential downpours from the rainy season are not channeled into reservoirs, a serious water shortage may result, which can ultimately affect the livelihood of millions of people. The successive downpours during the rainy season can cause flooding in China's two major river systems, the Yangtze (3,900 miles) and the Yellow (3,600 miles) and their tributaries. The Yellow (Huanghe) River, known as "China's Sorrow" for centuries, has caused devastating floods. It has flooded 1,500 times in a period of 2000 years. The silt-laden waters of the Yellow River have changed course at least twenty-six times. The Yellow River normally carries fifty-seven pounds of mud per cubic yard; but when it rises after a torrential downpour its mud-carrying capacity can reach as much as 900 pounds.[1] In one flood, the Yellow River overflowed its banks in a northern province, inundating towns and cities with a loss of life estimated at close to 1 million. In 1981, heavy rains in late July and August caused the Yangtze River to flood over 65 percent of the counties in the southwestern province of Sichuan, leaving 1.5 million people homeless. Chinese scientists estimated that each year 250 million tons of earth are washed into the Yangtze's three main tributaries.[2] One study showed that for the period between 206 B.C. and 1911 A.D. there were a total of 1,621 floods and 1,392 droughts that brought endless sorrow to the Chinese people.[3]

With the factor of limited land for cultivation and the frequency of flood and drought added to the enormous population—over 1 billion by the official census—one can readily understand that China's primary problem is to mobilize its productive forces to feed its burgeoning population. This basic problem of the population pressure on the limited land for cultivation has plagued China throughout its history since ancient times. The functions of government and in many respects the very performance of government have involved what John Fairbank described as the control of "the land, the manpower, and the water supply" for this agrarian society.[4]

Population Control[5]

As expected by many demographers, the July 1982 national census showed that China's total population was over 1 billion with an annual growth rate of 1.5 percent. Of the total, 51.5 percent were male, and 48.5 percent were female. The far-ranging implication of this huge population for China's economic development is quite obvious. Former premier Zhao Ziyang told the 1982 National People's Congress (NPC) that "the execution of our national economic plan and the improvement of the people's living standards will be adversely affected" if population growth is not controlled.[6] This was certainly a most candid admission by a top Chinese leader that the Malthusian theory of population was valid, a theory that Mao Zedong never accepted as applicable to a socialist China.

How can China's population explosion be controlled? During the 1970s the much-publicized measure for population control was delayed marriage for the young. In addition, clinics were permitted to provide abortion services. Some birth control devices were disseminated in factories. Then, in 1977, the target became one child per family. As the 1982 census demonstrated, these measures were not able to check the enormous population growth. A major factor was the persistence of the traditional preference among the rural population for male offspring. While female infanticide was still an accepted practice in some rural areas, former premier Zhao condemned the practice.[7] The difficulty in controlling population growth is aggravated by the fact that 62 percent of the population in 1982 was under thirty-five years of age. As the young people reach the age of marriage and childbearing, the total number of births can be expected to rise dramatically—unless strict control measures are imposed. So far, the policy of one child per couple has been observed widely only in the urban areas. Under this policy the state imposes punitive measures, such as a 2 percent reduction in salary on a couple refusing abortion of their second child. Following the birth of the second child, a flat 15 percent salary reduction is imposed on the parents until the child has reached the age of seven. In urban areas couples have been encouraged to sign contracts pledging a one-child family in order to receive better and more spacious housing.[8] Obtaining general acceptance of the one-child-per-family policy among the peasants in rural China remains a Herculean task involving education, persuasion, and strong pressure from the state. Such efforts must be made, however, if China is to defuse its population bomb.

Unfortunately, resistance to the one-child family policy has been particularly prevalent in rural areas. There also have been "exceptions" granted in response either to "local conditions" or "hardships."[9] Exemptions from the policy have usually been granted to sparsely populated areas or in cases where the first child was a girl. The most common complaint in rural areas against the harshness of the one-child family policy is the desire for a son. Under rural reform, a one-child family pledge has been incorporated into the household contracts.[10] But the tradition for a son is as strong as ever.

Some final comments about the single-child policy are in order. The one-child family policy is not a national law for two obvious reasons: its controversial nature and the possible effect on recruitment for the military, which traditionally exempted one-child families. The single-child family policy is a temporary measure and is to remain so until the year 2000, when the Chinese population will remain at 1.2 billion.[11] China was able to hold total population growth for the first half of the 1980s to about 1.17 billion.[12] But by 1987, projections of demographic figures indicated a rising rate of growth. The total population could possibly reach 1.5 billion by the year 2025 if life expectancy increases.[13] And if the birthrate is maintained at more than 1.5 or up to 2.0 percent, China will have a population of two billion by the year 2030.

A national door-to-door census was taken in 1990; the result showed that China's total population was 1.13 billion. If the present trend of increasing population continues, there will be a growth of about 17 million people each year, or close to 2 billion by the year 2000. Of more significance, a large component of China's population will be age 65 and over, a possible 16 to 19 percent of the total by the year 2035.[14] This would mean a further financial burden on families in providing support for their aging parents. The 12.45 percent increase in population since 1982 also has raised doubt about the one-child family policy.

THE CASE OF JAPAN

The total land area of Japan is rather small (about 143,000 square miles, or 377,600 square kilometers) in comparison with China and the United States, which are 3.6 and 3.7 million square miles, respectively. But size is a relative measurement and can be misleading. In fact, Japan is larger than Italy, or the combined size of the New England states (minus Maine), or equal to the combined areas of New York, New Jersey, Pennsylvania, and Ohio. The Japanese archipelago stretches for a distance of about 3,800 kilometers from the Kurile Islands in the northeast axis to Okinawa (reverted to Japan in 1972) in the southwest axis of the East China Sea. The long-standing territorial dispute between Japan and the former Soviet Union over the Kurile Islands—the isles off the northeast tip of Hokkaido—remains to be resolved.

The geographic boundary of today's Japan is limited to the four major islands of Hokkaido, Honshu, Shikoku, and Kyushu, plus some 3,000 small islands, including Okinawa, Bonin, and Iwo Jima. The four major home islands are separated by narrow straits and the inland seas (between Honshu and Shikoku). Japan proper is connected to the Asian continent by a strait in the Korean peninsula, about 200 kilometers away. There are 500 miles of open sea that separate China and Japan, an important factor that kept Japan isolated from China's dominant influence.

On the whole, Japan is extremely mountainous, with only less than 20 percent of the total land area considered as plains level enough for cultivation. Mount Fuji, with an elevation of 3,776 meters, represents the highest peak of the mountain chain called the Japanese Alps. The plains are located mostly along the coast—the largest is the Kanto plain of 13,000 square kilometers in the Tokyo metropolitan area. Population concentration is found in the plains. There is a close relationship between people and land form or arable land. Throughout Japan's history people have reclaimed land from the sea, terraced the hilly terrain for rice cultivation, or razed the mountainsides for housing development.

Thus, there is a much higher degree of population density over the preciously limited land available for agriculture and urban development: 2,256 persons per square kilometer of arable land in the 1980s as compared to over 1,019 in Indonesia, 820 in West Germany, and 103 in the United States. In urban areas the crowding situation is even more acute: 20,000 persons per square kilometer in the Tokyo area.

While Japan is small in terms of land area in comparison with land masses such as China, the former Soviet Union, or the United States, it is large when measured by population and productive capacity.

Following the suggestion made by Edwin O. Reischauer[15] many years ago, Table 1.1 represents an updated and a more "meaningful measure" of Japan's size by comparing population, gross national product (GNP) and personal per capita income, besides the land area. In terms of population, Japan is small in comparison to China, India, the former Soviet Union, and the United States. Indonesia has about twice as many people as Japan. However, Japan's population today, about 124 million, is twice that of the United Kingdom (56 million), France (56 million), Italy (57 million), or West Germany (60 million). Also in terms of land area, Japan is larger than each of the Western European powers (except France). Japan is also larger than the Philippines in land area and twice its size in population.

Table 1.1 Comparative Indicators of Japan with Other Nations

	Size (sq. miles)	Population (millions)	GNP (trillion $)	Personal per Capita ($)	Steel Production (tons– millions)	Rate of Savings (%)
CHINA	3,705,390	1,100	0.270	258.00	59.2	—
France	220,668	56	0.764	13,046.00	19.1	8.6
West Germany	95,975	60	0.898	10,680.00	41.0	10.8
India	1,266,595	833	0.246	300.0	13.1	—
Italy	116,303	57	0.768	6,447.00	23.7	12.8
JAPAN	145,856	124	1.900	15,888.00	105.7	23.3
Philippines	115,831	62	0.034	598.00	—	—
USSR	8,649,496	289	2.540	3,000.00	163.0	—
United Kingdom	94,226	56	0.760	7,216.00	19.0	6.3
United States	3,529,289	248	4.860	19,800,00	90.0	4.2

Source: GIST, Bureau of Public Affairs, U.S. Department of State, March 1990; *New York Times*, 28 May 1990, p.23; and 30 January 1990, p. A-11; *World Almanac*, 1990.

Of more significance, when measured in terms of GNP, Japan is one of the leading economic powers of the world. Japan's GNP is $1.9 trillion, next only to the United States ($4.9 trillion) and the former Soviet Union ($2.5 trillion). Japan's GNP is more than twice as large as that of the United Kingdom ($760 billion), France ($764 billion), West Germany ($898 billion), or Italy ($768 billion). Per capita income for Japan is $15,888, next only to the United States ($19,800), France ($13,046), West Germany ($10,680), twice that of the United Kingdom or Italy, but five times that of the former Soviet Union.

The pressure of population over limited arable land for food production has plagued Japan in modern times. Japan's population was fairly stable, at about 30 million, for more than 200 years during the Tokugawa period (1602–1867). The Meiji Restoration in 1868, the beginning of Japan's industrialization, ushered in a rapid population increase so that by 1926 it doubled to over 60 million. It was this population pressure on land that led Japan to embark on a modern national policy of imperial expansion of land and sea that began with the defeat of China in 1895 and culminated in Japan's participation in World War II. When Japan was defeated in 1945, its population was more than 80 million. The defeat of Japan also limited its territory to the home islands, with the exception of Okinawa, which reverted back to Japan in 1972. The contemporary solution to the land-population problem now depends on advanced industrialization geared to export, plus social control in the form of family planning, amidst the continuance of chronic high population density in urban areas where 75 percent of the population resides. Furthermore, as birth control through family planning has reduced the birthrate, it has created a new set of social problems that result from a decline in the death rate and an increase in life expectancy.

POLITICAL CULTURE AND POLITICAL DEVELOPMENT

China: From Authoritarianism to Anarchy to Totalitarianism

Historic Legacies   THE DYNASTIC SYSTEM AND THE "EMPEROR CULT"
Historically, the Chinese emperor ruled absolutely over his subjects. His power and legitimacy to rule the empire were based on the mythological belief that he was the "Son of Heaven" with a divine mandate to rule the earth. The "mandate of heaven" was legitimate as long as the emperor ruled righteously and maintained harmony within Chinese society and between society and nature. Rituals and symbols were designed to perpetuate the prestige and charisma of the emperor, and also to symbolize the divine nature of imperial rule. Preferences for imperial symbols persisted long after the 1911 revolution, which ended the Chinese empire.

Attempts to cultivate a "personality cult" or "emperor cult" were evident in Nationalist China in the rituals and symbols devised for Sun Yat-sen and Chiang Kai-shek.[16] And one of the more interesting aspects of de-Maoization that is going on in China today has been the criticism made by the Chinese Communist party (CCP) under Deng Xiaoping's leadership that Mao engaged in a "personality cult" and ruled the state autocratically as though he were the emperor.[17]

Of course, an emperor could be overthrown. The right to rebel against a tyrannical ruler was a corollary to the "mandate of heaven" theory. Rebellion became accepted in Chinese history when the emperor failed to maintain harmony or when he failed to maintain adequate flood control and irrigation systems, resulting in famine. However, rebellion was legitimate only if it succeeded. Each successful regime became a new dynasty. Chinese history, the longest continuous recorded history in the world, is basically a record of twenty-four histories of imperial rule. Each dynasty was established either by a successful rebellion or through invasions by either the Mongols or the Manchus from outside the Great Wall. Rebellions were generally either peasant uprisings exploited by some military figure or direct military insurrections. Each of the twenty-four dynasties was said to have followed a pattern of development known as the dynastic cycle: (1) establishment of a new virtuous and benevolent rule; (2) a period of intellectual rejuvenation; (3) an era of corruption or misrule; (4) the occurrence of uncontrolled natural calamities, such as floods and/or droughts; and finally (5) overthrow of the regime by rebellion or invasions. The gigantic earthquake that shook Beijing in September 1976, prior to Mao's death, was viewed by many traditionalists as an omen of dynastic change.

SCHOLAR-GENTRY OFFICIALDOM: THE BUREAUCRATIC STATE   As the officially sanctioned ideology, Confucianism conditioned and controlled the minds of those who governed China; it became the undisputed "orthodox doctrine of the imperial state."[18] The teachings of the venerable sage served to legitimize the dynastic system. Traditional Confucian ideology made its greatest impact on the ruling elites. It left an "ideological vacuum" among the peasants, the bulk of the population then as now, who were more concerned with the burden of taxes levied by the rulers and the hardships of life than with theories of government.[19] The orthodox ideology was perpetuated by the Confucian education given to young men of means.

While the dynasties rose and fell, the actual administration of state affairs was vested in the hands of a civil bureaucracy. Under the imperial system, the government officials, the mandarins, dominated the political and economic life in China. The mandarins were those individuals who held positions of power and ruled the empire in the name of the emperor by virtue of imperial degrees obtained by successfully passing the civil service examination. A state civil service based on competence, merit, and professionalism was China's unique contribution to the world of bureaucracy. Much of the civil service examination for imperial degree candidates tested their knowledge and understanding of Confucian teachings. Three types of competitive examinations for the civil service were held at three intervals: the initial certification, the provincial examination, and the final imperial examination at the capital. Only successful candidates for the initial certification were permitted to take the provincial examination that qualified those who passed it to be appointed to lower-level government service. Only those who successfully passed the imperial examination were appointed to higher government posts as the emperor's ministers and counselors. Lucian Pye estimates that only 24,874 received the highest imperial degree during the 276 years of the Ming dynasty from 1368 to 1644.[20] Civil servants came almost solely from the wealthy landholding class who had the resources to provide extended education for their sons. Imperial appointments to positions of power and prestige enabled the mandarins to acquire fortunes in landholdings for themselves and their families. They constituted the small privileged upper class of Confucian scholars in the traditional Chinese agrarian society. The size of the civil service ranged from 10,000 to about 40,000.[21] These scholar-gentry officials wielded enormous arbitrary power over their subjects, the vast majority of whom were illiterate peasants living in the countryside.

Political Belief: The Confucian Orthodoxy   For over 2,000 years, Confucianism, China's orthodox ideology before the 1911 revolution, was "the chief subject of study" by scholars and the officialdom. As a body of political philosophy and social code of ethics, the term *Confucianism*, as pointed out by John Fairbank, is "as broad and various as Christianity." As an ideology it has undergone many changes during the 2,000 years of Chinese history. But in spite of its ups and downs and during the long course of China's cultural history, Confucianism remained pertinacious. Although China under communism has succeeded in inducing fundamental changes, many of the Confucian ideas of governance still influence this essentially agrarian society. Some argue that the personality worship of Mao, the code of behavior for the party cadres, and the institution of self-criticism are basically Confucian in nature.[22] During the decade of the Cultural Revolution (1966–76), Confucianism was fiercely denounced as the root of all evils in China. In the 1980s, Confucianism was regarded as a "valuable national legacy" that needed to be restudied. What are the basic tenets of Confucianism? To what extent have the Confucian traditions influenced China's political culture?

First, Confucianism stresses the cultivation of a moral or virtuous individual. Cultivation of the spiritual aspects of conduct applies to the ruler as well as the ruled. The emperor and the civil service are expected to set high moral standards of conduct and benevolence as examples for the populace to follow. Confucius and his disciples argued that when the ruler possesses impeccable virtues and moral standards the government need rely only on moral force; no coercive force would be needed to rule. This is the cardinal Confucian principle of "government by goodness" or "goodness produces power." As recently as 1982, the need for high moral standards was stressed as a force for shaping attitudes and conduct. Hu Yaobang, then the party's general secretary, called for the development of "socialist spiritual civilization" that embraces not only the raising of higher education and scientific training standards, but also of "ideological, political and moral standards."[23] Hu's definition of a "socialist spiritual civilization" is much closer to Confucianism than Marxism:

> In essence, it consists of, above all, revolutionary ideals, morality and discipline. All Party members and other advanced persons in our society must continuously propagate advanced ideas and set an example by their own deeds so as to inspire more and more members of our society to become working people with lofty ideals, moral integrity, education and a sense of discipline.[24]

Second, Confucianism is basically authoritarian. This orthodox ideology emphasizes the paramount need for accepting and obeying the established order, the centralized power of the emperor. Authoritarian rule is reinforced by the "mandate of heaven" theory, which provides that the emperor's rule is legitimate so long as it is good or unless things go wrong, signifying that heaven is angry by manifesting its displeasure in the form of flood or drought. Acceptance of authority is ingrained in the personality makeup of the Chinese through centuries of inculcation of this aspect of Confucianism.

Third, Confucianism proclaims that the "government of goodness" could come about if all citizens know their roles and how to conduct themselves accordingly. Confucianism is a set of ethical codes designed to regulate the relationships between ruler and subject, father and son, friend and neighbor, husband and wife, and brother and brother. Strict observance of the complex web of this social code promotes collective societal norms and conformity and de-emphasizes individuality. Thus, individual self-discipline is stressed at all times: One must be correct in one's moral conduct if others are to be expected to do likewise. This is the foundation on which social harmony rests.

Fourth, as an ideology, Confucianism is elitist. "Government by goodness" or "government by moral prestige" can only be transmitted through study and learning by those who have a superior intellect and financial resources and by those who hold positions of importance in society and government. From this notion there emerges the traditional concept of a ruling class, the Confucian scholar-gentry-officialdom. It is this class of elitists that not only perpetuates the orthodoxy, but actually governs the populace.

Western Impact   While the Manchu dynasty was confronting internal rebellions in the countryside, it had to deal with the demands of Western merchants and missionaries to keep China's door open for trade and diplomatic contact. Traditional Chinese policy toward Westerners was to keep them isolated in a corner of a port city, such as Canton, in order to restrict commerce and contact. Diplomatic relations on the basis of sovereign equality was considered unacceptable to the Chinese, who traditionally looked upon foreigners as "barbarians." The Mongol and Manchu invaders had not made any lasting impact on Chinese civilization. Instead, the conquerors were assimilated by the superior Chinese civilization. China under the Mongols and the Manchus was still governed and administered by the Confucian scholars in accordance with the sage's humanistic teachings. Until the 1840s, China did not feel threatened by the West and its dynamic civilization. But the Opium War of 1839–42, fought largely over cultural misunderstandings, not only paved the way for Western imperialism's entry into China, but also jolted Chinese civilization and encroached on the empire's territorial integrity. Thereafter, China was forced by superior Western firepower to sign a series of unequal treaties under which territorial concessions and spheres of influence were granted to European powers.

Nationalist Revolution   An eleventh attempt to overthrow the emperor, made on October 10, 1911, resulted in a successful uprising by discontented and dissatisfied provincial officials, merchants, and imperial army commanders. The Manchu emperor abdicated, and shortly thereafter the Chinese imperial dynastic system was ended.

After 1911 China was in a process of disintegration; it was a nation in utter chaos. The main pillars that had once supported Chinese civilization collapsed. There was no viable replacement for the Manchu imperial rule. The orthodox Confucian ideology was no longer the acceptable basis for legitimacy. The traditional civil service examination, the mechanism that had perpetuated the Confucian orthodoxy, was abolished in 1905 for its intellectual sterility and administrative corruption. The ancient Chinese civilization was beset on all fronts by the superior technology of the West.

The political turmoil in China provided the impetus for an intellectual awakening. In 1919 this intellectual ferment culminated in the May Fourth

Movement, instigated by high school and university students and their teachers to search for a model for building a new China. The May Fourth Movement led to reform in the written Chinese language, from the archaic classical style to the use of the vernacular. It also introduced the study of Western science, technology, and political ideologies, including Marxism. The movement was closely tied in with demonstrations by university students against foreign intervention in Chinese affairs and against warlordism. These activities gave impetus to the new nationalistic and patriotic feeling emerging from among the general population.

It was in this atmosphere of ferment and feelings of anger, humiliation, and disillusionment that a nationalist revolution took form. Sun Yatsen fled from the southern warlord in Canton to Shanghai in 1922. There he was contacted by Adolph Joffe, an agent of the Communist Third International, who offered assistance to the Chinese revolutionary movement. It was this alliance that enabled the new Chinese Nationalist forces to defeat the warlords. Then in March 1927 Chiang Kai-shek established the Nationalist government, which was recognized by most nations as the legitimate government of China in the 1940s. The remaining Chinese communists sought refuge in the mountainous regions of central China.

The Struggle for Modernization   During the decade of the Nationalists' rule from 1927 to 1937, modest progress was made in many areas of modernization, initiated by the Nationalists (Guomindang) under the leadership of Chiang Kai-shek and his Western-trained advisors and administrators. For the first time, China had a modern governmental structure. As soon as major provincial warlords were eliminated or co-opted into the system, the transportation and industrial facilities were improved and expanded in the area. Earnest attempts were made to expand elementary school education and to provide political indoctrination for the young. Most important from Chiang's point of view was the building of a more efficient and dedicated modern army for a host of purposes, including the eventual elimination of warlords and the communist guerrillas operating in mountainous areas of central China, as well as protecting China's borders from foreign attack.

There were glaring negative features in the Nationalist balance sheet. First, no real efforts were made to provide progressive economic and social programs to improve the lot of the people. Land-reform measures to alleviate the plight of the peasants remained mostly on paper. Second, the regime alienated the intellectuals with its repressive measures against them in the guise of purging any elements of communist influence from their ranks. Third, enormous expenditures from the national treasury were devoted to the "extermination" of the Chinese communists operating in remote mountain regions. The Nationalists steadfastly refused to seek a nonmilitary solution to the problem of communist insurrection. Nor were they willing to seek consultation with other political groups, let alone share political power with other elements of the Chinese society to pave the way for termination of their "tutelage rule." The Guomindang's modest accomplishments in nation building were soon obliterated by its obsession to eliminate all opposition.

Time was not on the side of the Nationalists. In 1931, when they had achieved some measure of national unification and modernization in the midst of waging encirclement campaigns against the communist guerrilla forces, the Japanese militarists annexed resource-rich Manchuria and made advances into northern China, inside the Great Wall. In the early 1930s the Nationalists tried to rapidly annihilate the communist guerrilla forces and then to face the Japanese. However, rising public sentiment, expressed in frequent demonstrations, demanded that the regime prevent further territorial losses to the Japanese, and in December 1936, Chiang was forced to join in a united front with the Chinese communists to fight the Japanese.

Political Change from Radicalism to Pragmatic Reform   Soon after Mao Zedong's guerrilla armies won the civil war against the Nationalists in 1949, the Chinese Communist party embarked on a confiscatory land-reform program that in 1953 redistributed some 113 million acres of land to some 300 million landless peasants.[25] Simultaneously China embarked on a program of rapid industrialization based on the Stalinist model of centralized planning and placing emphasis on heavy industry formation. By 1958 Mao was not content with this model of development, and he launched the radical alternative, known as the Great Leap Forward. To compensate for China's lack of capital goods, he mobilized its abundant human resources. This crash program brought disaster to China's economy and in 1959–60 was replaced by a return to the Stalinist model of development. From 1968 to 1976 when Mao died, this was followed by the Cultural Revolution, a drastic reversal of orderly development. With the arrest of Mao's radical disciples, in the fall of 1976, China was ruled by the pragmatic reformers led by Deng Xiaoping, who advocated a relaxation in ideology and the experiment for a new model of development, a mixture of planned economy and market socialism.

Most likely, Deng Xiaoping will be accorded a unique place in history as the man who engineered the "Second Revolution" in China during the decade after Mao's death, a period that ushered China into an era of economic and political reforms. Deng was the chief architect for change and the one who dared to make significant modification in China's experiment with socialism. He opened China's door to foreign investment and transfer of technology—thus ending its long isolation from the rest of the world, an isolation imposed mainly by Mao's ideological rigidity. Deng and his pragmatic reformers also introduced agricultural reform in the countryside: a profit-incentive or responsibility system that replaced the egalitarian commune system. (See the section on China in "Political Performance and Public Policy" in this chapter.) While the final verdict is not yet in, Deng's image has been damaged considerably as the result of his order and support for the military crackdown on the students in Tiananmen on June 4, 1989. His program of economic reform not only continued but gained ground when the delegates to the National People's Congress gathered in March 1993 to rewrite the 1982 constitution by pledging to "persevere in reform and opening to the outside world," a step tantamount to enshrine into law Deng's reform of building a "socialist market economy."

Japan: From Feudalism to Military Dominance to Constitutional Democracy

Historic Legacies   Chinese recorded history in the third century A.D. mentioned the appearance of a matriarchal society of numerous tribes engaged in farming and fishing for their main livelihood. It was evident that there were frequent cultural contacts between China and early Japan by way of the Korean peninsula in the fifth century A.D. Confucian texts of ethics and the Chinese written ideographs or characters had been brought over to Japan by the Koreans, who already had been under Chinese cultural influence. So was the importation of Buddhism, which came also by way of Korea to Japan in the mid-sixth century A.D.

The Chinese model of the centralized bureaucracy of the Tang dynasty characterized the reigns of Nara and Heian from 710 to 1185.

JAPAN UNDER FEUDALISM   Dominance over the imperial family by the Fujiwara clan, owners of vast tracts of private estates and a monopoly of state bureaucracy, produced a radical departure from the Chinese model of a centralized state system. Soon a system of local lords developed and expanded, so that by the end of the eleventh century the disintegrating central government was unable to collect taxes. This situation was exacerbated by the rise of locally armed fiefdoms and clan leaders with the samurai, the warrior caste, as their loyal retainers. For seven centuries, from 1185 to 1867, when the Tokugawa period ended, Japan became feudalistic, characterized by the rule of a military aristocracy or overlords and clan chiefs warring against one another's landed domains or banded together for mutual protection. Under feudalism the emperor delegated his imperial authority to the military government under a shogun who served as the emperor's chief general and ruled through his military headquarters.

Japan was a nation beset by civil war for much of the fifteenth and sixteenth centuries. Out of the widespread unrest and disintegration of the imperial system of government, there emerged attempts at unification by strong military commanders who became powerful shoguns: Hideyoshi (1536–98) and Tokugawa Ieyasu (1542–1616). The former was known for his failed attempts to conquer China in 1592 and 1598 by first invading Korea. Hideyoshi also was opposed to Christian missionaries; he banned their activities and executed their Japanese converts. His death in 1598 ushered in a 250-year feudal rule under Shogun Tokugawa, who was one of Hideyoshi's powerful commanders.

Tokugawa Ieyasu ruled feudal Japan by a political system of 260–295 daimyos—retainers of the shogun—who became local barons in their provincial fiefdoms with the right to levy taxes, but personally loyal to the shogun because of kinship, alliance, and submission. Many of the daimyos were given assignment to control strategic locations such as the Kanto plain, central Japan, and the Osaka region on behalf of the Tokugawa shogunate. To ensure the loyalty of the daimyos, the Tokugawa shogunate required the local lords to live every other year in their fiefdoms and Edo (the original name for Tokyo). While away from Edo, they were required to leave their families behind as hostage. Daimyos were not permitted to forge alliances among themselves or contact the emperor without authorization. They were not even permitted to communicate with one another.

Below the daimyo was the privileged elite caste of Samurai, salaried warriors and civil administrators, whose strict code, the bushido, demanded loyalty, bravery, and honor. The samurai caste constituted roughly 56 percent of Japan's total population of 30 million during the Tokugawa period. Sir George B. Samson wrote in his classical work on Japan that the bulk of the rice produced by the Japanese peasants was to meet the consumption demand of the samurai.[26]

While the Tokugawa shogunate made efforts to isolate the daimyos, it also kept the nation as a whole isolated from contacts with the outside world, so that by 1640 foreigners were expelled, except for a few Dutch and Chinese whose activities were restricted at Nagasaki. Isolation and internal peace during the Tokugawa period provided an opportunity for development in internal commerce and trade, transportation, flourishing of crafts and shipping, and urban growth. The samurai, no longer engaged in battles, became scholars and the backbone to the national and provincial bureaucracy. Some of the warrior class, however, became the "47 ronin," the wandering samurai about whom classical epics of their exploits were written. The Tokugawa period was marked for developments in art and literature, drama (kabuki and noh), the tea ceremony, and intellectual foment. Also, sectarian, rather than monastic, groups of Pure Land Buddhism and Nichiren, and most significantly the Zen Buddhism (imported from China with its emphasis on "meditation simplicity") were developed during the feudal period.[27] As Reischauer points out in one of his works, it was around Zen that "a whole esthetic system" of Japanese culture was built.[28]

Under feudalism, the Japanese society featured four distinct classes: the samurai, the peasantry, the artisans, and the merchants. "Centralized feudalism," the government under Tokugawa, was supported by peasants who carried a heavy burden of taxation, exacted by the daimyos. The requirement that the lords must maintain their establishments and residences at Edo meant that peasants in their domains must produce excess rice to enable the daimyos and the samurai to travel and to pay for their establishments. The samurai became the literati who staffed the bureaucracy at all levels and whose salaries were paid by the taxes exacted by the lords in their domains. On the bottom of the social scale under the Tokugawa feudalism was the urban merchant class, which was despised and taxed lightly. But peace and tranquility helped commerce and trade, and merchants prospered. According to Reischauer, by the seventeenth century giant merchant combines, such as the Mitsui, developed to provide trading outlets and manufacture of goods, as well as money lending.[29] Artisans were the secondary producers to the merchants.

Political Culture: The Loyalty and the Group   As a background for understanding Japanese political culture, we will discuss in some detail the characteristics of Japanese society. Traditionally speaking, the Japanese family, known as the *ie*, or household, participated in social and political life as "corporate entity."[30] The Japanese *ie* is a set of kinship relations that goes beyond blood ties as in the case of the Chinese family structure. The Japanese households extend to members who have no blood relationship. Membership in the household is often determined by "shared tasks," and succession to family hierarchy could be made not necessarily on the basis of blood-tie inheritance. It has been said the Japanese *ie* was a basic characteristic of Japanese political culture. In Japan, the *ie* was in many ways "the basic building block of its political system,"[31] unlike the Chinese family structure, in which the blood-related family clans constituted the separate local power base, often in conflict with central authorities.[32] In Japan, the ie was the basic social organization, which was legally a "corporate entity," and ideologically the agent of indoctrination of social values: An individual was required to register as a member of the household and obligated obediently to the will of the recognized household head, whose position and status in the hierarchy were not necessarily determined by blood relationship.

A persistent social value that characterizes the Japanese culture is a high degree of submissive attitude known as *Ko*, loyalty or obedience. Slave-like obedience to the parent or a superior came into the Japanese culture as part of the Confucian influence, embraced more pervasively by the samurai in the days of feudalism. Under conditions of constant warfare, it was necessary to require the fighting men to follow blind obedience. Thus, there was created the ethic of *bushido*, "death in life," which persisted until 1945 as an ideal social code. Out of the vertical superior-inferior relationship there developed also the *on* and *giri*, or reciprocal relationship, known as *oyabun-kobun*. Here a man of superior rank must provide adequate security and tangible rewards to the inferior in return for his obligation, *giri*, to be submissive.[33]

Another Japanese social value that helps to shape the Japanese political culture is the concept of harmony, *Wa*. It can be understood only in the group context: that each person knows his status in relation to others in society, and that as an individual he must think and behave in terms of the group and the goals of the group. *Wa* as a concept emphasizes the qualities of accommodation, amity, conformity, compromise, order, and unity.[34] Today *Wa* as a social value is frequently emphasized in industrial production settings and meetings, for it must be worked at constantly and at a sacrifice. Harmony, in turn, mandates the development of consensus. For many in the West, it is the national consensus that has made Japan an economic power among many other factors that have contributed to its success.[35]

GROUP EMPHASIS AND INDIVIDUALITY   Another important aspect of the Japanese political culture is the emphasis society places on group orientation. The social values discussed earlier focus on the pervasive influence of group orientation in a highly "collectivistic society" that characterizes Japan.[36] In Japan group orientation is highly valued. Moreover, loyalty to the group (or what Reischauer calls the "herd instinct") taking precedence over efficiency or any other consideration is as traditional as it is modern or contemporary. This is best described by the authors of the U.S. Army area handbook on Japan:

> ...Membership in a group gives one a social identity, provides a feeling of security, and enables one to receive the rewards of strong bonds of human interdependence. In traditional society the household or the village was the important group. In the 1980s colleagues at work, fellow students, neighbors, or family members are likely to constitute the groups from which one acquires social status and identity. This emphasis on the formation of groups is not confined to interpersonal relations but is important in other sectors of the society, such as industrial structure as well.[37]

Despite the strong group emphasis in Japan's cultural and social setting, there is also "a strong self-identity," according to Reischauer, who pointed out the clash between "individual self-expression" and "social conformity" from time to time, particularly in literature and the arts.[38] This conflict is more evident today among the young who have become more restive and rebellious. Nevertheless, the Japanese still prefer the group approach to fundamental human rights concerns as rights of "collectivity" in dealing with outsiders.[39] Laurence W. Beer's remark is instructive: "National groupism limits Japan's participation in international human rights efforts and sometimes gives rise to extreme social conformism."[40] It is a basic traditional Japanese social value that the individual must conform to the values of the group.

Western Impact   The greatest threat to Tokugawa rule was the forceful demand and pressure exerted by the West that Japan open its doors for commerce and trade. Its next door neighbor, China, had been forced by the British to open at the conclusion of the Opium War in 1842. As American trade expanded across the Pacific to China in the mid-nineteenth century, and as American whalers roamed the Pacific Ocean by sailing near the closed shores of Japan, it was inevitable that force might be necessary, so long as the Tokugawa shogunate refused to abandon its isolation policy. In 1853 Commodore Matthew C. Perry sailed into Edo Bay with his squadron of "black ships" and demanded port facilities for trade; this culminated in Japan's capitulation by concluding the unequal treaties of 1854 and 1858, followed by other awaiting European powers. The Tokugawa shogunate showed its internal weakness by seeking unprecedented consultation with the daimyos and the emperor at Kyoto in support of its open-door policies, and they responded negatively.

Now the unequal treaties and the extraterritoriality rights granted to the United States and other European powers angered and awakened the samurai elites who felt that Japan could be saved only by the reassumption of the emperor's rule with the slogan "Honor the Emperor and expel the barbarians." Young samurai, such as Yoshida Shonin of the western clan of Choshu, agitated for national unity under the emperor and for military preparedness. The outer daimyos in southwestern Japan had made contact with the Dutch and began military modernization; thus, they served as spearheads for revolt. Troops from Choshu and Satsuma defeated the forces of the Tokugawa shogunate in 1867, and the latter relinquished its power after 250 years of feudal rule.

But the irony of the restoration of imperial rule was that there was never the real intention of return to the absolute rule of the divinity-claimed emperor of the eighth century. What had occurred from 1868 to 1889 was that a new oligarchy of reformers, imperial nobles dominated by regional barons loyal to the Choshu and Satsuma clans from the south and southwest, aided by a corps of able and modernization-oriented leaders such as Ito Hirobumi and Inouye Tsuyoshi, had consolidated the control and moved toward modern industrial development.

The Meiji Restoration (1868) and Modernization   In April 1869, when the young emperor Mutsushito took the reins as Meiji ("the Enlightened rule") and moved his palace from Kyoto to a castle in the newly named capital of Tokyo, a new era, the Meiji Restoration, was ushered in. It was not a widespread revolution that resulted in the installation of a new Emperor. It was perhaps best described, at least at the conceptual level, as the return of the ultimate ruling legitimacy to the divine Emperor from the hands of the shogunate under the Tokugawa feudal rule. It was in essence a political movement by a new oligarchy, composed of the western tozamas, the "outer daimyos," and the literate samurai under the influence of their years of scholarship in Chinese Confucianism. Its purpose was to restore the Emperor as the center of political power and legitimacy on a theoretical basis modeled after the Chinese imperial system.

Scholarly studies of Confucianism by the samurai, who had acquired the leisure time to engage in such pursuits, brought out discussion about the Confucian precepts of men of merit, not birth or heredity, based on intellect, knowledge, and morality or goodness. In their study of Confucianism they embraced the Chinese model of the imperial system of rule which placed the emperor, the *tienzi*, as the source of legitimacy to rule handed down from "heaven," or the divine right to rule. The acceptance of this ideological orthodoxy of Confucianism by the scholarly samurai cast doubt as to the right of the shoguns and daimyos, the feudal barons, to rule in place of the emperor whose rule was absolute and divine in origin. Karel van Wolferen points out the advocacy of a return to Confucianism by the leading political thinker for the time.[41] The eighteenth-century intellectual movement paved the way for development of a maneuver toward supremacy of the emperor, a rather subversive idea to the Tokugawa feudal rule. The spread of these ideas was enhanced by the rise of academies for Confucian learning, many with persons of samurai origin as teachers.

During the first twenty years after the restoration of Meiji as the emperor, the daimyos returned their domains or lands registered to the emperor and, in return, received appointments as governors of their domains, which soon became new prefectures but administered by the central government. The feudal lords were compensated with government bonds to ensure their financial security. The hereditary samurai class gradually disappeared by 1876, with the institution of a pension for the class as a whole and abolition of their special privileges, including sword wearing. The central government was organized, modeled on Western nations of the time (Bismarck, of Germany). Modern economic institutions were adopted in banking, the monetary system, railroads, factories for producing modern weaponry, and mining. Western learning in the fields of science and technology accelerated, based on the country's suitable and appropriate needs.

The traditional social classes of samurai, peasant, artisan and merchants were abolished. This was the initial period of "change and experimentation."[42]

The most important change and experiment certainly was the inauguration of a constitutional system, the Meiji Constitution of 1889, which became the basis of Japan's government for about fifty-five years until 1945. The 1889 constitution made clear that the emperor was the symbol of national unity and that he was the direct divine descendant of the mystical sun goddess. While the Meiji constitution provided the emperor with ultimate power to rule, he was not to govern directly in practice. He merely gave approval or consent to actions taken by others who served and acted in his name and on his behalf. In fact, the emperor did not even possess the power to appoint the ministers. The power of appointment rested in the hands of a small group of advisors or the *genro*, "the elder statesmen," an informal group of leaders outside of the constitution. Members of the genro took turns to serve as prime ministers and perpetuate their authority. Thus, an oligarchy emerged which acted on the emperor's behalf. Members of the genro were former samurai and the original leaders of the Meiji Restoration. There was also the Privy Council appointed to advise the emperor on state affairs. Under the Cabinet, headed by a prime minister, was the establishment of a modernized civil service based on merit by examination, even though initially graduates of the Imperial Tokyo University dominated selection for the service.

The Meiji constitution of 1889 provided, as a limited concession to popular government, a bicameral national legislature, the Diet, with the House of Representatives and the House of Peers. It was not intended as a national parliament with law-making powers. The upper House of Peers was made up of hereditary feudal lords and appointive peers; while the lower House of Representatives was represented by any male who could pay a tax of 15 yen; thus, the electorate base represented about 1 percent of the total population at the time.

A unique aspect of the operation under the Meiji constitution was the emperor's authority in military matters. Theoretically, all military affairs officers—the army and naval ministers and their service general staffs—reported directly to the emperor. In practice the army and naval ministers were selected initially from the active duty list, subject to the authority of the supreme military command. The practice gave the military an enormous amount of power to bring about the downfall of the national government at any time when the army and naval ministers were recalled from active duty. The Diet, or the parliament, could control the military only through budget appropriation; thus there developed incessant conflicts between political leaders in the Diet and the military authorities which eventually paved the way for the rise of military domination and control over the government. In short, the Meiji oligarchy was characterized by its "Samurai background and martial tradition."[43]

Under the reign of Meiji Japan made significant inroads toward modernizing a society that was beginning to discard its feudal influences. First, compulsory education was promulgated under the Fundamental Code of Education, which abolished the feudal practice of reserving education as an exclusive privilege of the samurai class. Attendance of school-age children in schools was estimated to be at least 28 percent by 1873. By 1907 education was, in theory, free and for all on an equal basis up to the sixth grade at the elementary level—the beginning of a universal education in Japan. Technical education was emphasized at the secondary level and more elite in orientation. Educational modernization raised the literacy rate and opened up channels of communication and a search for ideas from the West.

Second, a system of military conscription was introduced through which, not only a new army was developed, but also a professional and aggressive military leadership emerged. The military's prestige and power were enhanced enormously by Japan's defeat of China in 1895 and Russia in 1904–05.

Third, under the Meiji reign, Japan made significant progress in industrialization so that by 1900 its gross national product was 1.9 billion yen, and by 1920 it increased to more than 11 billion yen.[44]

Fourth, with rapid industrialization a vigorous merchant class developed, which gradually exerted its influence in politics. The emergence of this merchant/business class was fostered and encouraged by the government. Many economic and industrial projects launched during the Meiji reign were financed by the government; they were then sold at bargain prices to families of pre-Meiji Restoration feudal daimyos and samurai who had already forged formidable alliances with the rising merchants through intermarriage. As a matter of practice former samurai were recruited into the rapidly developing activities of banking, commerce, manufacturing, insurance, shipping, and trade. Concentration of economic and commercial activities into family conglomerates known as zaibatsu, or "financial cliques," emerged between the period of the Meiji Restoration in 1868 to the war with Russia in 1905. These zaibatsu maintained close ties with the government. Some of the more well known family combines, such as Mitsui, Mitsubishi, and Sumitomo, carry the founders' names even to this date. As will be seen shortly, these financial and commercial family conglomerates established close connections with the political oligarchies and leaders of political parties that emerged just prior to Japan's entry into World War I.

The Rise of Military Control and Domination, 1926–1945   The brief interlude and image of liberalism under the Taisho democracy began to fade away when Emperor Showa, Hirohito, the grandson of Meiji, acceded to the throne in 1926. Within a decade Japan was deeply involved in a protracted war with China, and the government was soon controlled by the military, which eventually led Japan to disaster in 1945. The factors or causes that contributed to the rise of Japanese militarism were many and multifaceted. Some of these causes are discussed to provide understanding as to why Japanese militarists embarked on the road to total defeat at the end of World War II.

First, the men behind the Meiji Restoration were samurai class; their obsession was to make Japan modern, united, and powerful. This military tradition dominated the Meiji government and pervaded the society as a whole. The special position of the military under the Meiji constitution illustrates the point most clearly: that the military was not under the control of the civilian government, but under the direct command of the emperor. This absence of civilian control over the military placed the latter in a special privileged status. That special bias in favor of the military was magnified manyfold as the military won victories over China in 1895 and over Russia in 1905. By then, its prestige made a quantum leap upward in the eyes of the Japanese. More important, the fact that the military high command had direct access to the emperor and could disrupt the formation of the Cabinet made it a formidable contender.

Second, in the late 1920s there was a combination of worldwide economic depression and the end of a boom stimulated by the Meiji economic development, which caused the collapse of banks and social unrest. Hardest hit was the countryside, where half of Japan's population made their living. Prices for farm produce, particularly raw silk, a lucrative exportable item, plunged, causing a general panic. Since conscripts for the military came mostly from the countryside, their concern and fear of economic doom for Japan was shared by the young, restless officers of the army. As a result the targets of resentment were the zaibatsu—five of which became dominant—and the capitalist system nurtured by the government. Then the target was expanded to include party leaders and politicians in the Diet, for by then the Japanese political power was concentrated in the hands of an alliance between the political party politicians and the bureaucracy administering the national government. The alliance was "cemented and financed" by the zaibatsu.[45] The military also resented the reduction by the party politicians of funding for modernizing the army and navy, for this in turn affected their personnel and promotion.

Young army officers channeled their discontent and resentment through the formation of secret associations within the army, such as the Sakurakai (Cherry Blossom Society), which preached hatred toward the capitalist businessmen and the power-hungry party politicians.

Third, the catalyst for the military's rise to power and dominance in the 1930s was the conquest of Manchuria in China's northeast as a solution to both the overpopulation problem and the need for overseas possessions for resources and markets. The scheme for a Japanese colony by military conquest of Manchuria was made by the army general staff without consultation with the Cabinet. Recent studies have shown that offices of the Kwantung Army had drawn up plans for developing Manchuria as a base for possible war with either the then Soviet Union or the United States, and for a revolution by radical nationalists to create a "national defense state" devoid of zaibatsu and party politician influence.[46]

Japan's economic activities increased along the area of the South Manchurian Railway, a prize obtained by Japan at the end of the Russo-Japanese War. The Kwantung Army was stationed in Manchuria to protect the railroad and other economic interests. In order to make Manchuria a colony of Japan, an incident was staged on September 18, 1931, by the Kwantung Army—a bomb was planted and exploded on the railway—providing an excuse for the army to take complete control of Manchuria; then in February 1932, Manchukuo, a puppet state, was inaugurated by installing the last emperor of China, Henry Pu-Yi, to be the head. The Cabinet in Tokyo acquiesced to the Manchurian takeover because it could not really control the situation, and it feared that a possible military coup might occur if it had intervened.

Indeed, a coup attempt by the military officers had surfaced on May 15, 1932, when Prime Minister Inukai Tsuyoshi was shot to death at his residence. This followed by a wave of violence committed by other military officers who advocated political reform as an effective way of intimidating the party government and politicians. Thus, the seizure of Manchuria, which soon became an exclusive colony for the military as a new industrial base, and the uprising and assassinations staged by military officers created an atmosphere of tolerance and acceptance by the people, who believed the military had the right answers. Out of this general lack of control over the military by the civilian authorities in Tokyo there arose a power struggle between the factions within the military, culminating in the February 26, 1936, massive assassination attempt by young officers aimed at Cabinet officers. These actions resulted in dominance by the Control Faction of high-ranking officers of the army (among them General Tojo, who was tried as a war criminal at the end of World War II), who were responsible for the operation of the government and the economy.

Cabinet ministers appointed required the approval of the military. The military-controlled civilian Cabinet soon implemented the so-called national political innovation programs demanded by the officers for increases in armament, control in education, preparation for war, and support of the army in Manchuria. Japan had by then become a military-controlled authoritarian state. As war with China prolonged, with no end in sight, the economy became more restrained; this in turn meant rigid controls had to be imposed on the economy. By 1940 political parties were dissolved and practically disappeared from the scene.

American Occupation and Reform   With the protracted war in China and no end in sight, Japan sought to expand its hegemony from East Asia to Southeast Asia as major European powers were at war in the fall of 1939. First, Japan signed pacts of alliance with Nazi Germany and Fascist Italy. Then in early 1940, taking advantage of the European powers' preoccupation with war in that continent, Japan expanded its hegemony to Southeast Asia by the formation of the Greater East Asia Co-Prosperity Sphere. One of the main objectives of the envisaged scheme was to take possession of strategic resources, such as oil, tin, and rubber, in Southeast Asia by seizing Vietnam from the French, Malaya-Singapore from the British, and the Indonesian archipelago from the Dutch. These operations heightened the opposition of the United States, which instituted embargoes on shipment of vital materiel to Japan. Another aim of the Greater East Asian Co-Prosperity Sphere was to replace European colonialism with Japan as the new power in control of the rich resources of the region. The only power that posed an obstacle to Japan's imperial design was the United States, which initially sought a negotiated accommodation of each other's interests in the Pacific through diplomatic means. As a means of neutralizing U.S. forces posted in the Pacific to oppose Japan's march to seize the Dutch East Indies (now Indonesia), on December 7, 1941, Japan launched a surprise attack at Pearl Harbor, Hawaii, bringing the United States into the war. By November 1944, the United States had pushed the war to the home islands of Japan by systematically bombing its cities and crippling its industries. By August 1945, after the dropping of atomic bombs on Hiroshima and Nagasaki, Japan capitulated to the might of the Allied powers.

When Japan surrendered on August 15, 1945, after Emperor Hirohito ordered the acceptance of the American surrender terms, the country was in ruins both physically and spiritually. About 1 million soldiers had been killed and as many as 668,000 civilians were dead. Physical damage caused by Allied bombing included 80 percent of its shipping, 40 percent of buildings leveled in sixty-six major cities, and one-quarter of its national wealth destroyed.[47] It took almost a decade for Japan to restore its per capita production to the levels of the 1930s.[48]

The task of postwar reconstruction and reform for Japan was entrusted to the Supreme Command for the Allied Powers (SCAP), in accordance with the Potsdam Declaration of July 26, 1945. Although the occupation of Japan was supposed to be supervised on general policy matters by a Far Eastern Commission made up of representatives from the eleven nations at war with Japan and the Allied council of four (the United States, the Soviet Union, China, and the United Kingdom), the United States government had the exclusive right, under and through the command of General Douglas MacArthur, chairman of the Allied Council, to provide the actual direction and administration of SCAP.

The objectives of the American occupation were outlined in the Basic Initial Post-Surrender Directive from Washington:

> 1. To ensure that Japan will not again become a menace to the United States or to the peace and security of the world
> 2. To bring about the eventual establishment of a peaceful and responsible government which...should conform as closely as may be to principles of democratic self-government...

The basic objectives were commonly referred to as the twin goals of demilitarization and democratization of postwar Japan. Some of the specific programs launched by SCAP for realization of these goals are briefly summarized below.

First, the Japanese imperial military forces at home were demobilized and their war-making capacity destroyed. The Japanese ministries of the army and navy were abolished. Some 6.5 million Japanese troops and civilians who surrendered in East and Southeast Asia and the Pacific were repatriated home, adding further pressure to the widespread shortage of food and shelter in war-torn Japan.

Second, a purge was implemented to eliminate the ultra-nationalist influence. Military leaders responsible for the war and for committing atrocities during the war were tried as war criminals by an international tribunal in Tokyo and punished—seven military leaders and one civilian prime minister were executed. The purge of ultra-nationalists from public offices, conducted by the occupation forces, was more difficult and controversial. In the end, a total of 180,000 to 210,000 military and civilian personnel were screened for purge or removal temporarily from office. Available statistics seem to vary as to the exact number actually purged, but it is generally accepted that the actual purged number was about 1,500 military bureaucrats.[49] The purge was terminated in 1951, having deposed more than 70,000 persons.

Third, in the hope of reducing and eliminating the political influence and the monopoly of the big family business cartels, an attempt was made in the form of anti-monopoly policy to dissolve the zaibatsu by forcing them to sell their shares to the public, or by freezing their assets pending investigation of their ownership and control, or by breaking up their huge holdings into separate and competing units. The result was twofold: Zaibatsu lost family control of some 100 business concerns, and large amounts of securities, as well as administration or management of these enterprises, went into government hands.[50]

Fourth, as a way of strengthening democratic institutions, SCAP directives in 1946 called for the development of strong labor unions, with the right to collective bargaining, but then returned to a curb of the labor movement and prohibition of a general strike in 1947 in order to short-circuit communist influence and infiltration into the labor unions.

Fifth, land-reform measures were implemented by SCAP in December 1945, aimed at improving rural tenancy and land ownership. Under these reform programs, absentee landlords were required to sell their land to the government, and the resident landlords were limited to ownership of not more than 2.5 acres. Land purchased by the government was in turn sold to the landless tenants on long-term mortgage. Thus, land owned by the farmers increased from 53.7 percent to 86.9 percent by 1949, and the total number of farmers who owned land also increased from 36.3 percent to 61.6 percent by 1950.[51]

Sixth, a complete revision of the Japanese education system was ordered by SCAP, including a purge of teachers and textbooks. The American education system of six years of elementary school, three years of junior high, and three years senior high was introduced. As a way of counteracting the monopoly of higher education by a few prestigious universities, decentralized higher education was introduced at the prefecture (province) level.

The last reform measure that must be mentioned was the order by SCAP for a new free electoral law to allow all men and women who reached the age of twenty to vote. The first postwar election of the Diet took place in May 1946 with candidates from five political parties.

However, the most significant reform introduced during the occupation was the drafting by SCAP, and the acceptance by the Japanese people, of the constitution of 1947. The draft of the 1947 constitution was made initially by the staff at SCAP in secrecy as early as February 1946. It contained three specific planks for a political framework for Japan:[52] the renunciation of war and the abolition of armed forces, the limitation of the emperor's role as the symbol of the people of Japan, and the abolition of peerage. With some degree of coercion the Japanese Diet was persuaded to accept the American draft on November 3, 1946, after the draft was publicly announced jointly by MacArthur and the emperor on March 6, 1946. Six months after the Diet's adoption, the constitution came into effect on May 3, 1947. The new constitution began with the familiar American- inspired assertion that the sovereign power rests with the people of Japan, and that the emperor is no longer divine, but merely "the symbol of the State and the unity of the people." The Diet, which exercises the sovereignty of the people, is the "highest organ of the state power." The premier and the Cabinet must be responsible to the elected Diet, not to the emperor any more, and exercise control over the national bureaucracy. The judiciary power is vested in an independent supreme court, which has power to determine the constitutionality of any law enacted by the Diet or regulation by the bureaucracy. Finally, Article 9 declared that Japan renounces war forever as an instrument of national policy and will never maintain armed forces. In addition, the various reform measures discussed earlier were institutionalized as permanent features of the 1947 constitution.

Occupation of Japan was terminated by the Allied powers—except China—in April 1952, when a peace treaty was signed to restore national sovereignty to the Japanese people. China concluded the treaty of peace and friendship with Japan on August 12, 1978, terminating the long-standing animosity between the two nations.

LOCUS OF POWER: POLITICAL INSTITUTIONS, LEADERSHIP, AND THE BUREAUCRACY

China: Maximum Centralism and Leadership Succession

We are told that the 1982 constitution was the product of more than two years of work by the Committee for Revision of the Constitution, which was established in September 1980 by the Fifth National People's Congress. The constitution's revised draft was circulated within party and government circles for debate and discussion. Reportedly, over 7 million speakers commented on the draft at millions of meetings held across the nation. The review produced over 1 million suggestions for revision. The final version of the draft was adopted by the Fifth National People's Congress at its session on December 4, 1982. The new Sixth National People's Congress, which met in June 1983, was elected, organized, and conducted under the provisions of the 1982 constitution.

One major change in the 1982 constitution was the deletion of lavish praise for Mao and reference to the Cultural Revolution in the preamble. In its place, the 1982 constitution affirms adherence to the four fundamental principles of socialism: the people's dictatorship, Marxism-Leninism and Mao's Thought, the socialist road, and the leadership of the Chinese Communist party.

Articles 79–81 provided for the election of a president for the republic, a position that the 1975 and 1978 constitutions omitted in deference to Mao's long opposition to the idea of a chief of state in competition with the party chairmanship.

The 1982 constitution is said to have made a significant improvement over the previous constitutions because the role of the party has been restricted or downplayed in its powers and functions in the state organs. For example, Article 2 of the 1978 constitution stipulated clearly:

> The Chinese Communist Party is the core of leadership of the whole Chinese people. The working Class exercises leadership over the state through its vanguard, the Communist Party of China.

No such reference is found in the 1982 constitution. But this omission does not mean that the party's power has been reduced by the constitution. In fact, it may be greater, since the present state constitution fails to define the party's power in relation to the state organs. On the surface it is true that the 1982 constitution has disallowed the party to interfere in the decisions of the National People's Congress to appoint a premier and other members of the central government. But in practice it is highly questionable that the party plays no role at all in the choice of top government officials, since the party is the fountainhead and source of all political power in China. There cannot be any independent political power regardless of what the constitutional provisions state. One must bear in mind that the party controls and directs the machinery of state through an interlocking system of party personnel and a party structure parallel to that of the state organs.

It may be true that the interlocking system at present is as significant as ever. For example, Jiang Zemin, the party's general secretary, now holds the presidency of the Republic. The premier and his vice premiers for the State Council are also members of the Politburo. Politburo members are also in charge of major government ministries: state planning, restructuring the economic system, science and technology, and foreign trade. A majority of the state ministers and vice ministers are members of the party's Central Committee elected in October 1982.

The government of the People's Republic of China consists essentially of the following levels of structure:

1. A national parliamentary body known as the National People's Congress
2. A central government known as the State Council, which administers national affairs through a host of ministries and commissions, staffed by a huge bureaucracy or the cadre system
3. Provincial and local governments and people's congresses
4. A court system

The National Parliament: The National People's Congress   The National People's Congress is the highest government organ and has constitutional duties similar to those of many parliamentary bodies in other nations. It is empowered to amend the constitution, to make laws, and to supervise their enforcement. Upon recommendation of the president of the People's Republic, the NPC designates, and may remove, the premier and other members of the State Council and can elect the president of the Supreme People's Court and chief procurator of the Supreme People's

Procuratorate (equivalent to the combined role of a prosecutor and public defender).

Since 1964 eight National People's Congresses have been convened. The Eighth NPC, which convened in March 1993 had a total of 3,000 deputies. In accordance with the election law adopted by the Fifth NPC in December 1982, the Sixth NPC had a ratio of one deputy, or delegate, for every 1.04 million people in rural areas and one for every 130,000 people in the urban areas. Sparsely populated provinces and autonomous regions, however, were entitled to no fewer than fifteen deputies each.

The large size of the NPC was increased markedly from 1,226 members in 1954 to 3,459 in 1978. It then declined slightly to 2,978 in 1983. The Sixth NPC, for example, had the following occupational representation among its delegates: workers and peasants, 26.6 percent; intellectuals, 23.5 percent; cadres, 21.4 percent; democratic parties (officially recognized minor parties which accept CCP's leadership), 18.2 percent; soldiers, 9 percent; and overseas Chinese, 1.3 percent.[53] The enormous size of the NPC raises the question of whether the NPC was ever intended to be a genuinely deliberative body. The argument can be made that if the NPC was intended to be a "rubber stamp" for the CCP, then it might as well be very large and representative. However, the NPC cannot be totally dismissed as a rubber stamp. Delegates to the third session of the Fifth NPC (September 1980) demanded information from officials in the Ministry of Petroleum Industry about the 1979 capsizing of the offshore oil rig Bohai No. 2, which cost more than seventy lives. (The disaster was the result of many years of management neglect and disregard for safety measures in offshore oil drilling.)[54] Then there were numerous negative votes on the approval for the Three Gorges Dam project in 1993. However, the fact remains that the NPC generally enacts legislation of importance only after the CCP has made its wishes known within the party hierarchy.

The NPC is mandated by the constitution (1982) to meet at least once a year. Its annual session in the national capital in Beijing usually lasts for about two weeks. When it is not in session, its permanent body, the Standing Committee, acts on behalf of the Congress. The NPC's Standing Committee is comparable to the former Presidium of the USSR Supreme Soviet as the continuous functioning organ. The Chinese Standing Committee of the NPC has a membership of 133, a very large deliberative body when compared to the 39-member Presidium. Under the constitution (1982) the NPC's Standing Committee has the power to interpret the constitution, to enact or amend statutes, to adjust plans for national economic and social development, to annul local government regulations, to supervise the central government's administrative organs, and to appoint and remove court personnel as well as diplomatic envoys abroad.

The constitution also gave new power to the Standing Committee: to enforce martial law in the event of domestic disturbance. Article 67 states that the NPC's Standing Committee may declare martial law either for the country as a whole or for a particular province, autonomous region or municipality directly under the Central government. Measures for suppression of domestic disturbance can now be constitutionally instituted and enforced. The provision was used to suppress student demonstrations in Tiananmen in June 1989.

The State Council: Central Government's Executive Organs   The State Council, the nation's highest executive organ, administers the government through functional ministries and commissions. The constitution stipulates that the State Council be comprised of a premier, vice premiers, and heads of national ministries and commissions. The State council may also include others, such as vice ministers. The membership of the State Council has ranged from a low of 30 to over 100. As the government has expanded over the years, the number of ministries and commissions has grown to a peak of forty-nine just prior to the Cultural Revolution. Recent administrative reform has reduced the total number of ministries supervised by the State Council. The total number of ministries and commissions was reduced from ninety-eight to forty-five, mainly through merging of functions and staff. Staff personnel in the State Council were reduced from 49,000 to 32,000.[55] It was decided in March 1993 to reduce it by 20 percent. The new State Economic Commission was the product of a merger between at least six separate ministries and commissions: agriculture, machine-building, energy, building material, standards, and patents. The new Ministry of Electronics Industry was the result of a merger of the old Fourth Ministry of Machine-Building, the National Bureau of Radio and Television, and the State Computer Administration. The new Ministry of Foreign Economic Relations and Trade was an amalgamation of three former state agencies dealing with foreign economic relations, foreign investment, and export-import administration.

Since the full State Council is too large for effective decision making, this role has been assumed by an inner Cabinet of the premier and his vice premiers.[56] In 1982–83 the inner Cabinet consisted of a premier, four vice premiers, ten State Council senior counselors, and a secretary general for the office of the State Council.

A. Doak Barnett has aptly described the State Council as the "command headquarters" for a network of bureaus and agencies staffed by cadres who administer and coordinate the government's programs at the provincial and local levels.[57] The degree of centralization of authority has fluctuated over the regime's history. During the First Five-Year Plan, from 1953 to 1957, the ministries had enormous power over the provincial authorities in terms of quota fulfillment, allocation of resources, and management of such enterprises as factories and mines. The increasing complexity of coordinating the economy and the gravitation of power to the individual ministries, the "ministerial autarky," led to numerous problems and a continuing debate over centralization versus decentralization.[58]

In 1957, during the Great Leap Forward, decentralization was instituted by giving the provinces authority to administer and coordinate consumer-goods-oriented industries. The decentralization of the Great Leap Forward hampered central planning and resulted in inefficiency. Following the failure of the Great Leap, a modified version of centralization was adopted until the Cultural Revolution ushered in another period of decentralization.[59]

With the reestablishment of planning operations and emphasis on research and development under the Sixth Five-Year Plan (1981–85), approved by the Fifth NPC in December 1982, the pendulum once again swung back to more centralization. In his report to the Fifth NPC, former Premier Zhao Ziyang indicated that to execute the Sixth Five-Year Plan, the State Planning Commission would have to exercise strict centralized control over the volume of total investment in fixed assets. Investment in capital construction was to be placed under the centralized control of the Bank of Construction of China.[60]

Leadership Style: The Collective Leadership of Deng Xiaoping and the Succession   From 1980 to the end of 1986, China was, on the surface, under the collective leadership of three key people: Deng Xiaoping, Hu Yaobang, and Zhao Ziyang. This triumvirate controlled three main pillars of the Chinese political system: the military, the party, and the central government. However, some analysts held the view that the triumvirate was merely a facade to disguise Deng Xiaoping's role as the paramount leader. Power in China became consolidated under Deng beginning in 1978. The pragmatic reform measures launched since 1978 might be called "Dengism."

The student demonstrations of 1986–87 and 1989 had shaken the reform-oriented triumvirate that paramount leader Deng had installed. Within two and one-half years, Deng and his fellow octogenarians were twice required to remove their choice to head the party. In other words, the political leadership situation in China in the 1990s has been anything but stable. Following is a brief sketch of the top leaders who ruled China from 1980 until today.

DENG XIAOPING: ARCHITECT OF THE POWER TRANSITION   What type of person is China's paramount leader, and what are his views? Although a dedicated communist and Leninist, Deng has never been dogmatic. When China was experiencing economic recovery during the early 1960s following the disastrous Great Leap, Deng said, "It makes no difference if a cat is black or white—so long as it catches the mice." In 1975 he expressed his

disdain for a requirement that everyone spend long hours after work studying correct political thought. He called the practice "social oppression." A
pragmatist, Deng has advocated the line of profit-in-command, rather than
Mao's dictum of politics-in-command.

Deng was born in Sichuan Province in 1904. He was an early organiz-
er for the Chinese communist movement when both he and the late Zhou
Enlai were students in France under a work-study program. Before returning to China in 1927 to work in an underground party cell in Shanghai,
Deng studied briefly in Moscow. He joined Mao's guerrilla movement during the early 1930s and took part in the Long March. His rise in the party
hierarchy was rapid, and by 1955 Deng was elected to the powerful
Politburo and held the position of general secretary to the party. He
remained the party's general secretary until 1966, when he was purged by
the radicals during the Cultural Revolution.[61] In 1974 he returned to power
at the request of the then-ailing Zhou Enlai and Mao to introduce reforms
that would enable China to modernize its industry, agriculture, sciences,
and military defense. When the Tiananmen riot erupted in 1976, Deng was
again purged. Following the arrest of the Gang of Four, Deng was once
more returned to power to oversee China's modernization program as a
deputy premier and vice-chairman of the party.[62] The twice-purged Deng
realized that to fulfill his task as chief architect of modernization, he must
consolidate his power by replacing the remnants of Mao's followers with
his own people.[63] Deng, almost ninety years of age, has been the paramount leader for China since the 1980s. Although he holds no party or government position, he must be consulted regarding any major policy decisions.

LI PENG, THE PREMIER: A COMPROMISE CHOICE FOR A SOVIET-TRAINED
TECHNOCRAT   When Li was designated in late November 1987 as the act-
ing premier, several questions were raised about his elevation to succeed
Zhao at the State Council.[64] These questions or concerns seem to fall into
four major areas. One is his Soviet connection. His training as an engineer
from the Moscow Power Institute in the 1950s placed him in the "pro-
Soviet" camp. At an unusual press conference of China's vice premiers in
April 1987, Li defended his position by saying:

> The second question seems to ask whether I favor a pro-Soviet policy. Here I
> formally declare that I am a member of the Chinese government, and also a
> new young member of the Communist party's Central Committee. I'll faith-
> fully carry out the policies of the Central Committee and the government.[65]

Thus, it may not be fair to label Li as "pro-Soviet" on the grounds that
he received technical training in the Soviet Union. A number of Soviet-
trained technocrats, now members of the new Politburo, have supported

Deng Xiaoping and Zhao Ziyang and the reform programs; they have been given important positions in the party and government.

A second question raised about Li concerns the degree of his support for economic reforms, particularly urban reform and the open-door policy. Li is said to be under the influence of Chen Yun, who championed centralized planning and issued cautions on current economic reforms. Li's selection to succeed Zhao as premier was one of the compromises struck just prior to the Thirteenth Party Congress between Deng and the conservative hardliners at Beidaihe in the summer of 1987. Apparently Zhao's opposition to Li was based on two main considerations: their disagreements on some reform measures and Zhao's fear that Li's elevation to the premiership could lead to a takeover by the conservative hardliners. There is little evidence to document Li's open opposition to any of the economic reforms. On the day he was designated the acting premier, Li pledged to carry on both the economic reform and the open-door policies. However, at a general staff meeting of the State Council, he stated that the speed of economic reform might be "too fast."[66] For the foreseeable future Li seems to be committed to the reform policies.[67] But, in the long run, he may advance his own ideas, influenced perhaps by his Soviet training and the advice of his more conservative mentors.

Li disagreed with Zhao over the issue of how to handle the Tiananmen student demonstrations. By allying himself with the hardliners on the Politburo and Yang Shangkun, who was the president of the People's Republic of China and the then-permanent secretary for the Military Affairs Commission, Li proclaimed martial law on May 20, 1989. Since then, Li has emerged as one of the spokesmen for the hardliners and the target of attack and criticism by students, intellectuals, and those sympathetic toward political and economic reforms. Li Peng's image was somewhat tarnished when over 200 of the 2,573 delegates to the NPC in the March 1993 session voted against his reappointment, and 120 delegates abstained from voting.

JIANG ZEMIN: HIS PRECARIOUS POSITION IN THE POWER STRUGGLES[68]
Jiang Zemin was sixty-three years old in June 1989 when he was selected to replace Zhao Ziyang as the third party chief since Mao's death in 1976. His earlier work with the party was mostly in Shanghai factories manufacturing foodstuff, soap, and electrical machinery. In 1955 he went to Moscow as a trainee at the Stalin Automobile Factory, where he studied Russian. He returned after one year and was placed as deputy engineer at an auto plant in the northeast; in 1970 he rose to become the director of foreign affairs for the machine-building ministry. In 1982 he was a vice minister for the Ministry of Electronics Industry. In 1985 he became the mayor of Shanghai and its party chief; two years later he was elevated to membership in the Politburo, the apex of the party's decision-making hierarchy. By

then he had established wide contacts with diplomats and was able to speak several languages, including English, French, and Russian.

Jiang was obviously the personal choice of Deng Xiaoping, who selected Jiang to succeed the deposed Zhao as an acceptable compromise to the octogenarians in order to avoid a factional fight among the divided top leadership.[69] Other plausible reasons for Deng's backing of Jiang might be Jiang's handling of student protests in 1986–87, when he skillfully, but peacefully, terminated an otherwise dangerous situation. Deng also might have been impressed by Jiang's plans for developing Shanghai as the premier industrial giant—the two had a secret meeting in the spring of 1989 in Shanghai.[70] During the Tiananmen demonstration, Jiang acted decisively in support of the Center's desire to curb intellectual dissent and criticism by firing the chief editor of an outspoken Shanghai liberal economic journal. However, to some, Jiang's record in Shanghai was not by any means a distinguished one.

It is doubtful that Jiang is to be the successor to Deng even though the latter proclaimed that the newly appointed party chief must be "the core of the third generation of leaders."[71] Jiang lacks some essential factors to survive and ultimately win the inner party factional struggles. First, he does not have any previous military association or connection to inspire the military's support. He was recently appointed chairman for the powerful Military Affairs Commission after Deng stepped down in September 1990. As an outsider, it will take Jiang time to build up support and confidence among the military officers. Second, it is also doubtful that Jiang, as the party chief, possesses the real authority, in spite of Deng's backing, for collectively and individually the octogenarians exercise the real power. In this context, Jiang may be regarded as a figurehead, or a caretaker, until the next power struggle surfaces, and when some of the leading octogenarians "go to see Marx." Third, while the waiting game or the wake is in progress, Jiang needs to cultivate a support base, not only in the military, but also in the party and central government bureaucracy, which is the domain of Li, the premier. On the eve of convening the much-delayed seventh plenary session of the Thirteenth Party Congress, originally scheduled for October or November 1990, there seemed to be clear evidence that there was already some opposition building up against Jiang.[72] At the March 1993 session of the NPC, Deng engineered Jiang's move into the position of president of the People's Republic of China. This in effect made Jiang the head of state as well as the head of the party.

In short, without Deng's support, Jiang's position as Deng's successor is precarious indeed. Deng's track record on this score has been miserable, to say the least, considering the removal of Hu Yaobang and Zhao Ziyang within the short span of two years. Jiang may indeed be a transitory figure in the ever-changing and politically turbulent China.

Another succession contender may be Qiao Shi. Qiao is a serious contender for succession because of interlocking positions he holds in the Politburo's Standing Committee and his elevation as chairman of the NPC Standing Committee, in addition to his many years of organizational and security work within the party and behind the scenes. He has said that Deng instructed him to strengthen the NPC's legislative functions by recruiting legal experts from abroad to draft new economic laws for regulating reform measures such as foreign investment and stock markets.

There may be a fourth possible succession contender: Li Ruihuan. Deng Xiaoping elevated Li Ruihuan to the Politburo in August 1987, not only because he was, at age fifty-three, a relatively young leader, but also because of the reforms he had introduced while serving as mayor of Tianjin, an industrial city. Li was born of peasant background and trained as a carpenter at a construction company in Beijing in the early 1950s. In 1958, he had the opportunity to study at the Beijing Civil Engineering Institute. He joined the party in 1959 and by the 1960s was serving as a party secretary in the building material trade. He was purged during the early part of the cultural revolution. In 1971 he came to Beijing and engaged in party organizational work in the lumber and building material industries. He was also active in the trade union federation in Beijing, having served as a member of the executive committee for the All China Federation of Trade Unions, a mass organization.

In 1981 Li Ruihuan became the mayor of Tianjin. As mayor he introduced significant reform work in urban housing; he insisted on work efficiency. He is reform-minded and a key supporter of Deng's reforms. He is a crowd pleaser, speaking in a plain and clear manner with humor.

Li Ruihuan will be a wild card in the power struggle for succession if there is a deadlock among Jiang Zemin, Li Peng, and Qiao Shi. Li Ruihuan can use his new state responsibility as the chairman for the National Committee of the Chinese People's Political Consultative Conference (CPPCC) as a base for his succession contest. He has many friends in China's minor political parties and is acceptable to many intellectuals and industrial units without party affiliation. Also, he has wide support from overseas Chinese, particularly in Hong Kong and Macao, the economic boom areas crucial to economic development and investment in China.

Party/Government Bureaucrats: The Cadres   Chinese cadres, the *ganbu*—the bureaucrats who are in leadership or administrative positions in an organizational setup—are the elites. The top elites are senior cadres in the party and government. The intermediate-level bureaucrats are the middle-level functionaries who staff the various party and government offices. Then there are the basic-level cadres who must deal directly with the masses. On the basis of their employment, the cadres are divided into three broad general categories: state, local, and military. Each group has its own salary classification system with ranks and grades similar to civil service systems in noncommunist countries. Urban state cadres have a system with twenty-four grades, while local cadres have twenty-six grades. Local cadres at the commune level or below are paid directly by the organizations they work for. As in the former USSR, this ranking system also is associated with status, privileges, and the degree of upward mobility in the career ladder. A cadre's rank, particularly at the state level, is determined not necessarily by length of service or seniority, but frequently by educational background, expertise, or technical competence. Those cadres who have served the party since the days of the Long March and the war against Japan naturally command more prestige than those who joined after the liberation in 1949. During the Cultural Revolution the term *veteran cadres* was widely used to denote cadres who had acquired administrative experience in managing party and government affairs prior to the Cultural Revolution.

It is difficult to obtain precise figures for the total number of state, local, and military cadres in China today. We know that in 1958 there were about 8 million state cadres, or one state leader for every eighty persons in China. If we use the ratio 1:80 as a basis for a rough estimate, the total number of state cadres may now be over 20 million.[73] This figure does not include the millions of cadres at the local level and in the military, and it includes only some of the 52 million party members, many of whom are cadres. The leadership nucleus in China may well total between 50 and 60 million cadres. These are the Chinese elites who must provide leadership for the masses.

Cadres are a special class in Chinese society. Like their counterparts in the former Soviet Union, they enjoy special privileges. The acquisition of these special privileges sets them apart from the masses. Thus, we may generalize that China is still the type of society that is highly stratified in terms of "status and hierarchy" and submission to authority, in A. Doak Barnett's words. The special status and privileges accorded to the party/government cadres are in direct contradiction to the ideological stress for egalitarianism, a basic Marxist tenet. The problem of special privileges and material comforts for party and government cadres can best be seen by Chen Yun's talk at a high-level work conference:

> For transportation, we travel by car and do not have to walk; for housing, we have luxurious Western style buildings...Who among you comrades present here does not have an air conditioner, a washing machine, and a refrigerator in your house? Take the TV set, for example, please raise your hand if the one in your house is not imported from some foreign country.[74]

High cadres and members of their families not only have access to goods and services not available to ordinary citizens, but they also have access to foreign magazines and movies. Chen Yun also indicated that the children of higher cadres were the first ones to go abroad to study once the door was opened to the West in 1977. As a special privileged class, party and government cadres have been reluctant to give up any of these special prerogatives.

TRENDS IN THE CADRE SYSTEM   Over the past two decades, life for a cadre as an intermediary has not been easy. The cadre has not been able to please either those at the top of the party nor the masses at the bottom. Since all decisions have been subject to criticism from many directions, the wisest choice has frequently been to make no decision at all. The cadres who came from the intellectual class, but who possessed technical expertise, have been subject to special abuse as China's privileged "new class."[75]

The pendulum has now swung back to the moderation of the mid-1950s, when China's economic development demanded the rapid recruitment of capable, skilled persons as cadres to manage the nation's complex economic activities. Recently, deliberate attempts have been made to reform the cadre system. One key reform measure has been to place leadership positions in the hands of cadres who are "staunch revolutionaries, younger in age, better educated, and technically competent."[76] Efforts have been made since 1978 to upgrade the cadres' education and skills demanded by Deng's modernization and reform programs.[77] A rotation system for further education and training has been instituted for government cadres whose educational attainment is below the secondary level. But the task of upgrading cadres' competence seems formidable indeed when one considers the fact that a large number of cadres both at the center and in the provinces have only the equivalent of a primary-school education.[78]

As a part of the cadre management reform, the party's organization department published a detailed organizational management handbook setting forth guidelines, policies, and regulations for cadre management.[79] The 1983 handbook also established a Soviet-type *nomenklatura*, a comprehensive list of offices for party and state leaders in state enterprises and institutions, including scientists, professors, and even athletes. However, a study by Melanie Manion suggests the 1983 handbook reveals that little progress has been made since 1983 to improve the cadre management system because the party leadership lacks "an emancipated outlook and boldness in innovation."[80] In 1986, however, a set of rigid rules for cadre promotion was issued.[81] To curb the widespread abuse of nepotism, the rules called for a system of secret ballots to nominate capable cadres for promotion in work units, the *danwei*.[82] One rule stated that no candidate who received less than a majority vote was to be nominated for promotion. The rules also prohibited senior officials from attending meetings at which promotion decisions were to be made. The criteria for promotion evaluation was to be on the basis of candidates' "political awareness," ability, diligence, and merits—particularly their recent achievements.[83]

Closely related to the upgrading of cadres' competence is the problem of upward mobility for the middle-aged cadres. Prior to 1986, about 2 million of the 27 million cadres working for the Central Committee and the State Council were considered veteran cadres, having been recruited before 1949.[84] These veteran cadres, advanced in age, had clung to their posts in the party and government. A retirement system had been instituted to provide turnover in personnel. During 1981 and 1982 there were massive resignations of older cadres. In one machine-building industry ministry the 13 vice ministers and 269 cadres resigned or retired at the bureau level.[85] In 1981 some 20,000 aged cadres retired in one province.[86] By early 1986 more than half of the then 2.1 million aged cadres had been retired.[87]

There are two other serious problems in the Chinese cadre system: corruption and bureaucratism. Corruption is not a new problem, but since 1978 its scope and intensity have reached an unprecedented level. The mass media have been saturated with exposes of so-called economic crimes committed by cadres at all levels. Chinese leaders called these corrupt practices "obnoxious," citing lavish dinner parties with presents to the bosses, influence peddling for personal gain, and graft.

The use of bribery or favoritism to get scarce goods or to get things done by way of "back-door" dealings have been common practices.[88] The offspring of higher party and government cadres in Hong Kong have often served as "connections" for foreign merchants who desire to establish contacts for trade with China.[89] Also widespread is the practice of gift giving and wining and dining by cadres who do business with each other—Beijing municipal authorities have imposed a new prohibition against such practices.[90] In April 1982 the party Central Committee, the State Council, and the NPC Standing Committee enacted an order that demanded life sentences or death by execution for those cadres who were involved in graft or similar corrupt practices.[91] The party's theoretical journal, the *Red Flag*, called economic crimes such as embezzlement of public funds and smuggling new elements in the class struggle.[92] The number of economic crimes committed by the offspring of senior cadres also has been on the rise; one senior army officer agreed that his son should be punished for graft in an illegal timber sale scheme.[93] For the first six months of 1986, a total of 27,000 cases of economic crimes were investigated, an increase of 130 percent over the same period for 1985. Well over 31 percent of the total were considered "serious economic crimes, cases involving more than 10,000 yuan (about U.S. $2,700.)"[94]

Since 1980 bureaucratic practices have been under constant attack in China. One manifestation of bureaucratism is inertia and the inability to make decisions. This foot dragging is more evident at the middle and lower levels of the party organization and government structure. One senior leader made a lengthy speech charging that a few cadres have adopted a bureaucratic work style and have created a bad image for the party. She characterized the bureaucratic work style as follows:

> When there is a problem, they suppress it; when it is not possible to suppress it, they push the problem aside; when it cannot be pushed aside, they then procrastinate.[95]

Foreign businessmen stationed in China have given vivid pictures of the cadres' bureaucratic work style.[96] Deng Xiaoping charged that cadres seemed to be devoted to rules and regulations and to exhibit obstinacy, timidity, and an air of infallibility; they spent an enormous amount of time reading the interminable flow of documents and directives.[97]

The Courts: Functions and Structure The 1982 constitution provides that judicial authority for the state be exercised by three judicial organs: the people's courts, the people's procuratorates, and the public security bureaus. The Supreme People's Court is responsible and accountable to the NPC and its Standing Committee. It supervises the administration of justice of the local people's courts and the special people's courts. The local people's courts are at the provincial, county and district levels. The local people's courts at the higher levels supervise the administration of justice of the people's courts at lower levels. The local people's courts are responsible and accountable to the local people's congresses at the various levels of local government. Article 125 of the 1982 constitution stipulates that all cases handled by the people's courts must be open and that the accused has the right to defense.

When legal reforms were introduced in 1978, 3,100 local people's courts were established at four levels: basic people's courts at the district and county levels, intermediate people's courts at the municipal level, higher people's courts at the provincial and autonomous region levels, and the Supreme People's Court at the national level. Each of the basic people's courts has a civil and criminal division presided over by a judge. At the intermediate and higher levels, an economic division was added to help process cases that may involve economics and finance.

Alongside the court system is a parallel system of people's procuratorates, headed by the Supreme People's Procuratorate, which is responsible to the NPC and supervises the local procuratorates at the various levels. The system of procuracy is rooted both in Chinese imperial practices and in the Napoleonic civil code, which has been used in part by the Soviets and many other continental European nations in their legal systems.[98] The procurator serves the dual functions of prosecuting attorney and public defender during a trial. The procurator also is responsible for monitoring and reviewing the government organs, including the courts, to provide a legal check on the civil bureaucracy.[99] The procurator is responsible for authorizing the arrests of criminals and counterrevolutionaries. In other words, the procurator examines charges brought by the public security bureau (the police) and decides whether to bring the case before a court for trial.

As a part of political and economic reform in the post-Mao era, a criminal code and procedure was promulgated for the first time in 1980. The code contains some 192 articles over eight major areas. These were offenses concerning counterrevolutionary activities, public security, socialist economic order, rights of citizens, property, public order, marriage and the family, and malfeasance. Principal penalties for offenses include public surveillance, detention, fixed term of imprisonment, and death. The death sentence is reserved for adults who committed the most heinous crimes; an exception is made for pregnant women.[100] Productive labor and reeducation were to be stressed for detainees and prisoners.

Although the new criminal code represented China's effort to develop "a more predictable and equitable" criminal justice system,[101] the inclusion of counterrevolutionary as a criminal offense is a legacy of the Cultural Revolution. The code defines the term *counterrevolutionary* not merely as a thought a person might have at a given moment against the socialist system; it also must involve an "overt act." It should be pointed out that a large number of those placed under detention during the Cultural Revolution were accused of committing counterrevolutionary offenses under a law enacted in 1951 and in force today.[102]

The legal reforms introduced by the pragmatic leaders represent an attempt to establish a "creditable legal system," designed to restore the people's respect for law after more than a decade of lawlessness. But these efforts have been marred by the recent rash and ruthless treatment of criminals. Mass executions conducted periodically by the police throughout China raise serious questions, not only about China's legal credibility, but the human rights issue as well. Episodes of mass execution and arrest of criminals lead one to wonder about the willingness of the present regime to establish a "creditable legal system" in China. There were gross violations of human rights when student protesters and others demonstrated for political reform at Tiananmen Square in 1989. To this date many protesters have languished in jails and detention camps.

Japan: Change and Continuity of Tradition—The Workings of the Parliamentary System

The basic political framework for postwar Japan has been the constitution promulgated since 1947. The fundamental document for a new Japan provides, among many other things, five main political institutions: the emperor, the Diet, the Cabinet, the Judiciary, and the local government. The 1947 constitution contains 103 articles; about 54 articles, or 43 percent, deal with the exercise of power, or the limitation of such exercise, for these funda- mental political institutions. As discussed previously, although the constitu- tion was drafted by an alien power and imposed on Japan, the Japanese people have accepted it generally during the ensuing forty some odd years without any major alterations. From time to time proposals for constitution- al revision have been made informally by leaders of the political parties. One such proposed change concerned the status of the emperor, the focal institution of Japanese politics and culture, and the link to the past.

The Emperor   Having solemnly declared in the preamble to the 1947 constitution that the sovereign power resides with the people and that the government is a sacred trust of the people, Article 1 proceeds to de- mystify the emperor's deity by declaring:

> The Emperor shall be the symbol of the state and of the unity of the people, deriving his position from the will of the people with whom resides the sov- ereign power.

In one stroke Article 1 demolished the traditional concept of "imperial sov- ereignty." Now the emperor is not even the "chief of state," but merely "the symbol of the state." Then Article 4 states clearly:

> [T]he Emperor shall perform only such acts in matters of state as are provid- ed for in this Constitution and he shall not have powers related to govern- ment.

Articles 6 and 7 delineate ten specific acts of state that the emperor is per- mitted to perform, such as the appointment of the prime minister and chief judge of the Supreme Court as designated by the Diet, certain ceremonial acts with the advice and approval of the Cabinet: promulgation of laws and treaties, convocation of the Diet, proclamation of general elections for the Diet, awarding of honors, and receiving foreign ambassadors. In short, the emperor cannot perform these ritualistic and ceremonial functions of the state on his own initiative except with the consent and approval of the Cabinet and the Diet. As stated by John M. Maki, the intent and purpose of having the emperor perform purely ceremonial and meaningless functions was twofold: to "eliminate the imperial excessive powers" and to ensure that the throne would never be used politically by others.[103] Thus, Article 3 makes it clear that all acts of the emperor in matters of state must have the approval of the Cabinet, which shall be responsible therefor.

Thus, the emperor can no longer be the object of people's unques- tioned loyalty and absolute obedience. Under Article 9 there is to be no compulsory military service and the old concept of absolute obedience and obligation that prevailed before the war has been eliminated. However, the old controversy over the role, particularly during World War II, of Emperor Hirohito, who died on January 7, 1989, has been revived from time to time. Those Japanese on the Left, as well as the young, tend to favor the abolition of the emperor as an institution, and criticize the promotion of an overly reverent attitude toward him. The hardline Right wants to strengthen the role of the emperor to more than a figurehead, and has used the illness and death of Hirohito to revive some degree of emperor worship. The bulk of the Japanese people seem to reject both extremes so far as the role of the emperor is concerned; however, the shooting of Nagasaki's mayor in January 1990 for his criticism of Hirohito by a member of Japan's numerous right-wing extremist groups illustrates the intensity of the ongoing debate over the status of the emperor.

Under Article 2 of the constitution and the Imperial House Law passed by the Diet, succession to the throne is dynastic and limited to the eldest son of the emperor. In November 1989 Emperor Akihito, eldest son of the late emperor Hirohito, was installed as the new emperor of Japan in two formal ceremonies. One was his formal enthronement coronation as Emperor Heisei on November 12, 1989, at the Imperial Palace, located in the center of Tokyo—by tradition each emperor is designated by an imperial name and title to which the Japanese calendar is adjusted and referred to as "Heisei 1" or "Showa 63" (the sixty-third year of reign under Hirohito). The other official ceremony, held November 22, 1990, known as the *Daijosai* or "Great Food Offering Ritual," and conducted according to traditional Shinto religion, was controversial in that it revived the Shinto practice of the state religion of prewar Japan, which propagated absolute loyalty to the emperor as the ideological foundation of ultranationalism.

Article 8 of the 1947 constitution states:

> No property can be given to, or received by, the Imperial House, nor can any gift be made therefrom, with the authorization of the Diet.

Despite the ongoing debate among Japanese elites over the constitutional status and role of the emperor in today's Japan, there is still an enormous amount of reverence for and emotional attachment to the emperor as the focal point of all Japanese political institutions.

The new emperor, Akihito, was brought up somewhat differently from his father. He traveled extensively abroad as crown prince. His early schooling with commoners and his marriage to a commoner broke the bounds of imperial tradition.[104] More startling was Akihito's remark in his first official court address that he was in support of the 1947 constitution in the midst of a national debate as to whether the emperor's status and role be strengthened. It is too early to predict what kind of emperor Akihito will turn out to be, but several things seem to be certain about this key Japanese political institution: The role of the emperor will continue to be the symbol of unity of the Japanese people, devoid of actual participation in politics or policymaking, and the institution will not be used again as a "convenient shield" by any political force. There is evidence that the new emperor is aware of his destiny.

The Japanese Parliament: The Diet   The term *Diet* refers to the bicameral national parliament first used in the Meiji constitution of 1889. The American occupation advocated initially a unicameral parliament, for there was no federal system contemplated for postwar Japan to warrant an upper house. The draft that was finally promulgated and accepted by the Japanese was a bicameral national legislature. Article 42 provides that the Diet shall consist of two houses, namely, the upper House of Councillors and the lower House of Representatives. Article 41 states, "The Diet shall be the highest organ of state power, and shall be the sole law-making organ of the State." The term of office for members of the House of Councillors is six years and for the House of Representatives four years. A bill becomes law when it is enacted by both houses. Under Article 59, the lower House may enact a law if it is passed a second time by a two-thirds majority over which the upper House has made a different final decision. All budgetary matters must be submitted to the House of Representatives. In case of disagreement over the budget or a treaty by the two Houses, Articles 60 and 61 grant the lower House the final say after a lapse of thirty days during which the two Houses attempt to iron out the differences in a joint conference committee. A large proportion of the bills introduced to the annual session of the Diet originates from government ministries, which usually engage in extensive discussion and research before the bills are submitted to the Diet if approved by the Cabinet.

A major improvement has been made in the 1947 constitution over a glaring defect of the Meiji constitution: the power of the Diet to control the government budget and finance. Under the Meiji constitution the Diet was powerless to even reduce a budget item without the approval of the Cabinet. If the Diet failed to pass the budget in a particular year, the current or existing budget was automatically in force for another year. Now, under the 1947 constitution, Articles 83–91 provide a remedy to that defect in prewar Japan's governmental operation. First, Article 83 states, "The power to administer national finances shall be exercised as the Diet shall determine." Article 84 prohibits the imposition of new taxes except by law, and Article 85 makes it clear that no money shall be expended except as authorized by the Diet. Under Article 86, the Cabinet must submit the annual state budget for approval by the Diet, thus reinforcing Article 60, which states that the budget must be first submitted to the House of Representatives. Article 90 creates a Board of Audit to make a systematic accounting to the Diet of all expenditures and revenues. Another power entrusted to the Diet by the 1947 constitution is that specified under Article 62 for each chamber to conduct investigations regarding the conduct of government.

The internal organization and operation of the Diet follow closely the workings of most parliamentary practices of the world. The presiding officers, the Speaker and Vice Speaker of the House of Representatives, are chosen from the membership of the majority party. Consideration of bills is made in the committees—there are at present a total of sixteen permanent committees paralleling the organization of the major ministries of the national government. Committee assignments are made by the political parties in the Diet. In other words, the ruling party controls deliberation and passage of measures in the Diet except for occasional use of obstructionist tactics, including filibuster and street demonstrations, by the opposition parties to force the LDP to make concessions or to abandon its desire to enact a controversial measure.

The Diet can hold three types of sessions as provided by the 1950 election law. The regular session is convened once a year beginning in mid-December for a minimum total of 150 days, and usually lasts all year (Article 52). The regular session may be extended by a vote of the Diet. Then there is a special session that can be convened within thirty days following a general election for the purpose of electing a prime minister (Article 54). Extraordinary sessions may be convened by the Cabinet or by a vote of a quarter of the members of either House to consider supplementary budget or other urgent matters (Article 53).

Since the Diet operates on generally accepted practices of a parliamentary system, the lower House can be dissolved. Dissolution of the House of Representatives can come about in two ways. First, under Article 69, dissolution of the House of Representatives occurs when an opposition party's motion of non-confidence vote is carried. Then the government falls and the House of Representatives dissolves until a new election takes place within forty days from the date of dissolution. Under Article 7 the prime minister can go perfunctorily to the emperor and ask for a dissolution of the House of Representatives, to be followed immediately by a new general election. (This occurred twice during a six-month period in 1952–53.) Dissolution of the lower House occurs when the prime minister resigns because of ill health or scandal. During the Recruit stock scandal—the distribution of unlisted stocks to political leaders in the majority LPD at discount rate before the shares were publicly listed on the stock exchange—the opposition Socialist and Communist members of the lower House pushed unsuccessfully for dissolution of the entire Diet.[105]

The Japanese Diet also follows the British parliamentary tradition of interpellation, or time for questions, posed on pending issues by the opposition party members to the Cabinet ministers.

The upper House in the Diet, the House of Councillors, does not dissolve and calls for a recess when the House of Representatives is dissolved. Both Houses resume their normal activities after the general election when there is a new mandate from the people. While the term of office for members of the House of Councillors is six years, Article 46 also requires that half of its members—from a total of 252—must be elected every three years. By the 1950 election law, membership for the House of Councillors is based on a system of 100 at-large seats for the nation as a whole, and 152 seats, including Okinawa, elected by the prefectures.

In its July 23, 1989, election the majority Liberal Democratic party suffered a massive defeat by winning only thirty-six seats as compared to a forty-six-seat majority for the Japan Socialist party (JSP). The defeat was followed by Prime Minister Sousuke Uno's resignation. For the next three years opposition parties controlled the upper House in the Diet. As discussed earlier, a bill becomes law only when it is passed by both chambers (Article 59). In case of a disagreement between the two chambers, the lower House may enact it into law by passing it for a second time by a two-thirds majority vote, or by reaching a compromise in a joint conference committee. This meant the ruling LPD (which went on to lose the election in 1993) had to seek compromises with the opposition parties in the Diet, particularly in the upper House, on crucial pending issues facing the government.

The Leadership: The Prime Minister and the Cabinet   Under Article 67 of the 1947 constitution the chief minister for the government must be designated by a resolution of the Diet. In this case it is the House of Representatives that designates the premiership, after the majority party has agreed to nominate one of its leaders. The House of Councillors may have ten days within which to make a designation, but after the lower House has made its choice, it then becomes the designation of the Diet.

Article 72 defines the main responsibilities of the prime minister as submitting bills, reporting on domestic and foreign affairs to the Diet, and exercising "control and supervision over various branches" of the government. This means that the Prime Minister selects qualified persons to head the various administrative agencies and they collectively constitute the Cabinet, to be discussed later.

Since the postwar constitution came into effect on May 3, 1947, there have been eighteen persons designated and elected as prime minister. With the sole exception of Tetsu Katagama (1947–48), a member of the Japan Socialist party, all Premiers have been leaders of the various factions within the LDP.

The most important staff agency providing needed assistance to the premier is the prime minister's office. In addition to overall supervision of the administrative ministries, the prime minister's office administers the pension system, statistical analysis, Imperial Household, economic planning, defense, and the National Safety Commission. As discussed by Maki, this office is mainly responsible for developing national police policy, coordinating police activities at the prefecture level, providing control of large-scale riots in urban centers and conducting research of criminal activities.[106]

The year 1989 was marked as a politically turbulent year in Japanese politics. During this year a parade of prime ministers came into the scene as a result of the troubled ruling party's (LDP) leadership crisis. First, the forceful Yasuhiro Nakasone vacated the Premiership in the fall of 1987 after three terms in office, from 1982 to 1987. He was a well known figure in the West for his dynamic leadership to enlist Japan as a world partner. (He was on a first-name basis with former president Ronald Reagan.) He ran into trouble with factional leaders within the LDP over the issue of imposing a new sales tax. His popularity sank so rapidly in 1987 that he had to resign from the office. He was succeeded in November 1987 by Takeshita Noburu. Takeshita's stewardship as the prime minister was beset by the Recruit stock trading scandal. In October 1986, this affair involved a sizable number (160 persons in total) of leaders in the LDP, including Takeshita and his aides, business leaders, and media figures who received bargain price shares in a real estate subsidiary (Recruit-Cosmos) of a conglomerate before they were traded publicly in the stock exchange. Recipients of Recruit stock benefited financially, doubling their shares in value as a result. For the politicians the gains augmented their election campaign coffers. Investigation of the stock scandal led to prosecution of businessmen involved in the deal and the resignations of Finance Minister Miyazawa and Justice Minister Hasegawa.[107] After months of incessant media exposure and opposition party pressure in the Diet, Takeshita announced his resignation on April 25, 1989.

He was replaced by Sousuke Uno on June 2. However, on his twenty-seventh day as prime minister, he too was exposed in a scandal for keeping a geisha as his mistress at one time. Under pressure both inside and outside of the ruling LDP, Uno resigned on July 24 and a new prime minister, Toshiki Kaifu, assumed the office on August 9.[108] Ironically, Kaifu, the first Japanese prime minister who grew up during the American occupation when profound changes were taking place, admitted to receiving as much as $100,000 in political contributions from the Recruit real estate company over a five-year period (1984–87). He maintained that the contribution was legal and that it was reported to the tax office.[109] In 1992–93 Prime Minister Kuchi Miyazawa's government was troubled by revelations of illicit ties between politicians and organized crime.

Under Article 65 the executive power is vested in the Cabinet, which consists of the prime minister, who heads it, and about two dozen ministers. The Cabinet is "collectively responsible" to the Diet, since it is "the creature of the Diet."[110] Article 73 lists these as basic functions of the Cabinet:

administering the law faithfully; managing foreign affairs; ratifying treaties; administering the civil service; preparing the budget; making rules and regulations; and making decisions on amnesty, reprieve, and restoration of rights for citizens. Following closely the British parliamentary practice, all, or a majority, of the Cabinet members must be chosen from members of the Diet in accordance with Article 68. In some instances a prominent citizen may be selected as a Cabinet member who, at the time of appointment, may not be a member of the Diet. But that Cabinet member will be persuaded to run for a Diet seat at the next general election. However, one study points out that a Diet member does not become a Cabinet member until he has been elected at least five times.[111] Another tabulation showed that eleven Cabinet members who served under Takeo Miki in 1975 had been elected to the Diet from seven to fourteen times.[112]

As discussed earlier the Cabinet is the creature of the Diet and serves as the "collective executive" branch of the government at the pleasure of the Diet. Thus, when a no-confidence vote is carried in the Diet, the Cabinet must, under Article 69, either resign en masse within ten days or dissolve the House of Representatives and call for a general election. In the latter case, the Cabinet must resign nonetheless after the new Diet convenes, so as to allow a new prime minister to be appointed (Article 70). This has occurred twice—in 1948 and 1953—under Prime Minister Yoshida. Dissolution of the Diet does not occur frequently in Japanese parliamentary politics because of the party discipline exercised by the leaders, or a coalition of leaders, in the ruling LDP. Constitutionally speaking, it provides the Cabinet with a powerful weapon for maintaining party discipline or forcing Diet members to campaign for reelection.

While the appointment to a Cabinet position is considered a recognition and reward for loyal party service,[113] too often it is the result of group association or a process of co-option in making group representation by the principal decision makers in the various factions. Cabinet reorganization or reshuffle by a prime minister after a year in office is intended to redistribute or realign power among the factions.[114] Traditionally, the more powerful factions within the LDP receive more Cabinet appointments. Thus, when Noboru Takeshita reshuffled the Cabinet in December 1988, a little more than a year after he had become prime minister, it was a design to place older leaders—the median age of the fifteen-member Takeshita Cabinet was sixty-nine—who had close ties to the major factions of the ruling LDP and who had held Cabinet positions previously.[115]

However, Toshiki Kaifu, who became the prime minister on August 9, 1989, determined to have a Cabinet untainted by the Recruit stock scandal, even though he admitted in March 1990 that he too had received $300,000 in donations from Recruit. This was in addition to the involvement of at least two of his ministers in foreign and finance affairs in the Recruit scandal. Kaifu's attempt since the February 1990 general election to form a new (his second) Cabinet reflected to a large extent the wishes of the party bosses within the ruling party. However, he was successful in refusing to appoint a few old-time politicians from several factions because of their involvement in the Recruit scandal and the 1974 Lockheed bribery case.[116]

The Japanese Bureaucracy   Major decisions on economic and industrial policies in Japan are made by the elite bureaucracy, the heart of Chalmers Johnson's study of Japan as a "corporate developmental state." The bureaucracy also "drafts virtually all legislation, controls the national budget, and is the source of all major policy innovations in the system."[117] Karl von Wolferen would consider Japan an "authoritarian bureaucratic state."[118]

Despite a provision in Article 15 of the constitution that "all public officials are servants of the whole community and not of any group thereof," there exists in Japan to this day the traditional image of the bureaucracy's infallibility and superior status. A Japanese bureaucrat, not withstanding Article 15, is not a public servant in the Western sense. He is protected and shielded from the consequences of his actions. The Japanese bureaucracy—at both national and local governmental levels—employs over five million with about half of them in the service of the national ministries. Out of this large size only a small number of them, probably not more than six to seven thousand, are really important enough to be considered as higher or top bureaucrats (i.e., those who are in grades 1–3 in an eight-grade classification system). Entrance to higher levels of the bureaucracy is by competitive examination among bright young university graduates, dominated by one or two leading prestigious institutions such as the University of Tokyo (Todai). For the decade 1949–59, 69 percent of the higher bureaucrats and more than 80 percent of those in the vice minister or bureau chief levels were graduates of Todai.[119] The situation had not changed in the 1980s, when 88.6 percent of higher-ranking bureaucrats in the Ministry of Finance and 73.3 percent in the Ministry of Foreign Affairs were graduates of Todai.[120] Thus, there is considerable inbreeding among Japan's top bureaucrats.

Another characteristic of Japanese bureaucracy is the career pattern of top bureaucrats once they reach the retirement age of fifty-five. They tend to move from the bureaucracy into either the business corporations (some three hundred bureaucrats join annually) as executives or as elected LDP dietmen. The result is a sort of iron-triangle of "mutual aid" system. The ruling LDP in the Diet shield and protect the bureaucrats by not interfering or meddling in policies; the bureaucrats formulate and innovate policies and strategies to keep Japan's economy stable and in continuous prosperity; the business corporations funnel political campaign contributions to LDP dietmen and recruit top bureaucrats as executives with higher salaries and better fringe benefits. Then, both LDP and the bureaucrats "keep the businessmen in business by protecting their businesses against foreign competition and underwriting their expansionist programs."[121]

The Judiciary[122]   The Japanese judicial system contains several major features. Some of them were imposed by the American occupation in the 1947 constitution and were designed to correct the abuses and defects of prewar Japan's legal system, and others represent innovations modeled on American practices.

First, Article 76 establishes the Supreme Court as the body in which the entire judicial power is vested. This is intended to prevent the abuses of prewar Japan, where special tribunals were formed at the behest and convenience of the government. Now there is to be one judicial power, which is the Supreme Court. Second, Article 76 also states that all judges must be independent in discharging their responsibilities and are bound only by the constitution and the laws promulgated by the Diet. In other words, courts and judges are not affiliates of the justice ministry. In reality, how independent are the judges in Japan? Some argue that since all judges, except the Chief Judge of the Supreme Court who is constitutionally appointed by the emperor, are appointed by the Cabinet under Article 79, there is therefore the possibility to exercise control by the Cabinet or agencies created by it.

Karel van Wolferen points out that the administrative authority for the courts rests with the General Secretariat of the Supreme Court, a body of bureaucrats who "control appointments, promotions, salaries and dismissals" of judges, performing those tasks that the prewar Ministry of Justice used to administer.[123] It has been argued that it is not the judges, but the judiciary officials or bureaucrats who control and dominate the judicial system. Since the 1970s judges are graded by court administrators using a secret evaluation system that provides points for the number of cases cleared or referred for conciliation, a procedure generally preferred by the judiciary bureaucrats.[124] It is "bureaucratic standards" rather than a judge's own "conscience" that in the end determines judicial behavior in Japan today.[125]

Judicial independence is also hampered by the constitutional requirement (Article 79) that judges' appointments must be reviewed by the people in a form of referendum at the general election following their appointment, and at ten-year intervals thereafter.

A third feature in Japan's judicial system is the constitutional provision under Article 81, which states that the Supreme Court is the court of last resort with power to decide the constitutionality of any law or regulation. This is the familiar American judicial review concept. However, the Japanese Supreme Court has rarely invoked the judicial review provision in the constitution by declaring any laws or activities of government unconstitutional. Generally, the Supreme Court adheres to the principle of the supremacy of the Diet or the Cabinet on issues of political controversy. For instance, in the 1959 Sunakawa case the Tokyo district court ruled that the 1952 security treaty between the United States and Japan was unconstitutional because it violated Article 9 (the renunciation of war provision) of the constitution by permitting the stationing of American forces on Japanese soil. The Supreme Court took the position that the case was a political matter and thus was beyond the Court's jurisdiction, and, at the same time, overruled the lower court that the issue or treaty was not unconstitutional.

Then there was the Naganuma Nike missile case involving a Sapporo district court ruling in 1973 that the building of an antimissile base on a forest reserve in Hokkaido was unconstitutional because both the Self-Defense Force and the missile base violated Article 9 of the constitution. In 1982 the Supreme Court finally ruled that the original petitioner in the Naganuma case could not sue for its lack of standing and said nothing about the constitutionality of the Self-Defense Force and its right to construct anti-missile bases in Japan. It has been pointed out that the lower courts in the Japanese judicial system are more willing to rule on issues of constitutionality than is the highest court.[126] Robert E. Ward attributes the willingness of lower court judges to rule on constitutionality issues as a reflection of differences in age and "professional and political views."[127]

These differences in age and political views between younger lower court judges and the older senior judges are also reflective of the career development for each group. Karel van Wolferen indicates that about two-thirds of the fifteen Supreme Court judges came from other government administrative units as bureaucrats, in contrast to the more liberal lower court judges who most likely were members of the Seihokyo, the young lawyers and legal scholars association formed in 1954.[128] Lawyers in Japan are scarce commodities in many respects. As of 1986, the total number of lawyers in Japan who had been admitted to the bar was 13,161.[129] This means there is one lawyer for every 9,294 persons, as compared with one to every 360 in America.[130] It also is indicative of the cultural aversion to litigation—the preferred method of dispute settlement is by informal arbitration. Group emphasis, rather than individual, as a societal value tends to make the Japanese nonlitigious.

Entry into the legal profession as judges and lawyers is controlled by the Ministry of Justice through the Legal Training and Research Institute. In 1985 it allowed 486, or barely 2 percent of 23,855 candidates who took the bar examination, admission to practice law or to serve as prosecutors. Once admitted through the bar examination, prospective lawyers, prosecutors, and judges must undergo training controlled and eventually screened for political suitability by the Legal Training and Research Institute.

Another feature in the Japanese judicial system is the predominant role of the prosecutor. Following the procuratory practice of the French and German influence, in Japan a prosecutor is both public defender and prosecutor, as is the case in the Chinese legal system. In essence, in the Japanese system he is more than a judge. In the 1920s and 1930s it was the procuracy that exercised social control in "upholding the national essence ideology" and monopolized the work and behavior of prosecutors and judges.[131] It is standard practice for the prosecutor to submit a preliminary report to officials in the Ministry of Justice for instruction or consent on action to be taken against government officials for wrongdoings such as the Lockheed bribery case.[132] After having questioned thirty-eight hundred witnesses and seized thousands of pieces of evidence, only two lesser-known officials were indicted by the prosecutor for the Tokyo district in the Recruit scandal.[133]

Organization of Japan's court system is rather simple. First there is the Supreme Court of fifteen judges for a fifteen-year original appointment. The highest court operates through four benches for division of labor over caseload. Then there are as many as eight high courts throughout the country that act as courts of appeal in criminal and civil cases (including jurisdiction over election disputes). Below the high courts there are fifty district courts located in the prefectures and major cities. These courts handle mainly major crimes such as grand larceny and theft. There are also 570 summary courts in cities and towns, which handle minor offenses and misdemeanors and civil claims. In addition, there are fifty family courts with 235 branches, which handle domestic disputes, inheritance, divorce, and juvenile delinquency and rehabilitation.

THE POLITICAL PROCESS: PARTICIPATION, ELECTIONS, POLITICAL PARTIES, AND GROUP POLITICS

China: Control and Direction by the Party

A unique feature in Chinese political life has been the high degree of mandatory and nonvoluntary participation in a variety of political activities. Few Chinese citizens can escape from participating in these political activities. There is almost no exception to this uniform practice because every Chinese belongs to and is under the control of some sort of organizational unit. It is the responsibility of these organizational units to provide a steady diet of political education to their members. In fact, the Chinese communist movement owes a great deal of its success to its ability to organize the populace. Everyone is expected to take part in a variety of political activities that are invariably designed to help the party execute its policies and programs. The mass participation and mobilization techniques, developed through many years of experience dating back to the guerrilla days of the 1930s, are based on the concept of mass line formulated by Mao Zedong. We may summarize the concept of Mao's mass line as a process by which the leaders (cadres) seek mandatory compliance from the masses. In practice, it is a process of "mutual education of leaders and led," by which unity among the masses is achieved on a given issue, and through which the masses can lend their overwhelming support by participating in the implementation of the decision.[134] Participation in Chinese politics involves three sets of actors—the top leadership at the Politburo level, the cadres in the middle level, and the masses at the bottom—and a host of actions, which include listening, learning, reacting, summing up, interpreting or re-interpreting changing attitudes, and decision making.

Although Mao has been criticized posthumously for his policy mistakes in his later years, his mass line concept has been enshrined in the 1982 constitution, which states:

> All state organs and functionaries must rely on the support of the people, keep close touch with them, heed their opinions and suggestions, accept their supervision and work hard to serve them.[135]

Citizen participation in political activities is always accompanied by political messages formulated by the party for the purpose of mass persuasion and acceptance or political action. The Chinese masses, both rural and urban, are constantly being exposed to the networks of the political communication system: controlled mass media in the form of newspapers, radio broadcasts, and wall posters; the organization units to which the masses in one way or another become attached; and the "small group," or *xiaozu*, into which the masses have been organized and through which mass mobilization efforts are achieved.

The Electoral Process   While voting in elections may be the single most important act of citizen participation in Western democracies, it is only one form of legally approved political action for the people of China. The election process in China differs from that in Japan or Western democracies in several crucial respects.

First, the Chinese communist party manages the electoral process at all levels. Most important is the CCP control of the election committees, which prepare approved slates of candidates for all elective offices, from the national to the basic level. Before 1980, these slates presented only one candidate for each office and thus determined the outcome of the election. Since 1980 more than one candidate may run for a local office. However, in one election provincial party authorities interfered by deleting a candidate from the final list of nominees because he declared openly as a non-believer in Marxism.[136]

Second, local county elections for people's congresses may now permit campaign rallies with speeches by candidates. The new election process among the masses is used as a vehicle to arouse interest and heighten the political consciousness among the people.

Third, in 1979–81 direct elections by secret ballot were held only at the county and township levels. By 1981 it was reported that 95 percent of the 2,756 local governments at the county level and below had elected people's congresses and other local government officials.[137]

Fourth, while the frequency of elections is prescribed by law, the legal schedule has seldom been followed in practice. There have been nine elections since the founding of the People's Republic: 1953–54, 1956–57, 1958, 1961, 1963, 1966, 1979–81, 1986–87, and 1991–92. Accounts published by the Chinese for the 1980 county-level elections indicated that the typical local election process involved the following procedures.[138]

The first step was to establish electoral districts for a county. In the 1979–81 election, districts were designated under the following criteria: communities with populations between 5,000 and 20,000; production brigades with populations between 5,000 and 8,000; industrial units with requisite populations within the county. The local county and township governments determined their own ratios of population per deputy. For example, Tongxiang County in Zheijiang Province established a ratio of one rural county deputy for every 1,600 people and one township deputy for every 400 people.[139]

The second step in the local election process was to publicize the election laws, particularly reforms introduced in 1979: direct election at the county level and below; secret ballot; a requirement of 50 percent majority to win; and the mandate that there must be more candidates than the number of elective offices on the ballot. Publicity about the election laws was carried out by *agitprop* teams dispatched to villages and towns, by radio and wall posters, and by small study groups.

The third step involved the registration of eligible voters. Everyone who was a citizen and at least eighteen years of age had the right to vote or be a candidate for election, except those who were deprived of political rights by law.

The fourth step in the election was the nomination of candidates. The CCP, other minor "democratic parties," and the mass organizations were permitted to nominate candidates for election. A voter or a deputy could nominate candidates if seconded by three other persons. At this stage the list of candidates was announced and circulated publicly, and "consultations" were held among the voters' groups within the electoral districts. The purpose of "consultations" was to allow the various groups, including the CCP, to screen out candidates and narrow the list to manageable proportions so that only the preferred candidates could be presented for final balloting. In one case in the preliminary round of the 1979–81 election in a rural county there were more than 6,000 nominations for 500 deputy seats. The list was finally narrowed to between 750 and 1,000.[140] At this stage a voter could raise objections to anyone on the list. Of course, a large proportion of those on the list were party members.[141]

Next, the actual campaign for votes was initiated by the candidates and the voting groups who nominated them. Information about candidates was printed and distributed among the various voter groups and broadcast over the radio. Posters were hung on public bulletin boards throughout the district. Finally, on election day, balloting was held within the various electoral districts. Election day in China usually has been a festive day accompanied by fireworks and the beating of gongs. After the ballots were counted, the newly elected deputies made speeches at meetings called by the election committee.

Monopoly by the Chinese Communist Party   The Chinese Communist party is the source of all political power and has the exclusive right to legitimatize and control all other political institutions. The CCP alone determines social, economic and political goals for the society. The attainment of these goals is pursued through careful recruitment of its members and their placement into party organs, which supervise and control all other institutions and groups in society.

THE STRUCTURE OF THE CCP   The structure of the Chinese Communist party is typically hierarchical and pyramidal. At the base is the lowest level of party organization known as primary party units or cells. These are the party branches in "factories, shops, schools, city neighborhoods, people's communes, cooperatives, farms, towns, companies of the People's Liberation Army and other basic units." There are more than 2 million party branches or cells at the lowest level. It is at this level that the functions of the party are carried out: membership recruitment, ideological study and training, party discipline inspection, and the maintenance of close ties with the masses.

The second layer of party organs consists of the provincial party congresses and committees. The 1982 party constitution mandates that party congresses from provincial levels and autonomous regions be held once every five years. The provincial party congresses elect provincial party committees, which are responsible for supervision and direction over five basic areas: (1) organization and control of the party in the provinces; (2) economic activities in agriculture, industry, finance and trade; (3) capital construction of heavy industries; (4) mobilization of women and youth; and (5) research for policy development. Since the provincial party committees and their subordinate basic-level party units within the province are responsible for the implementation of party policies, they hold a unique position within the party structure. The first secretary of the provincial party committee wields an enormous amount of power. Provincial party secretaries have on occasion deliberately refused to carry out directives from the party center.[142] During the post-Mao era, provincial party secretaries have been allowed to initiate and experiment with new programs.

At the apex of the pyramidal party structure are the central-level organizations: the National Party Congress, the Central Committee, and finally the Politburo, the apex of the apex. These are the national party organs that provide direction and supervision over the Chinese Communist party as a whole.

THE NATIONAL PARTY CONGRESS   In conformity with the tradition of a Leninist party, on paper the CCP vests its supreme authority in the National Party Congress. Since its founding in 1921, there have been fourteen such congresses; the latest, the Fourteenth Party Congress, was convened in October 1992. By tradition a new National Party Congress must be convened every five years. The party charter adopted by the 1982 Party Congress stipulated that the party congress may be convened if more than one-third of the provincial party organizations request it. Since the party congress generally meets in a perfunctory manner to approve party policies and programs recommended by the Central Committee, its sessions have been short, a week or two in duration. It has a large membership of several thousand. Thus, the Party Congress is not really a deliberating body with actual power. Delegates to the National Party Congress are presumably selected at the provincial levels to reflect the "constellation of power" at the center. It is very possible that the powers at the center, as well as at the provincial level, engage in slatemaking. The process of packing the congress at the various levels of the party organization to represent factionalized leaders has occurred.[143] It was revealed in 1968 that delegates to the Second through the Seventh Party Congress had been appointed.[144]

For the 1982 election, the Central Committee instructed that delegates at every level of the party structure were to be elected "by secret ballot after full consultation at party congresses." For the first time, the instructions stipulated that "the number of candidates shall be greater than the number of delegates to be elected."[145] This was an attempt to democratize the party's election process.

A major task of the National Party Congress is to select the new Central Committee. In the actual process the key leaders in the hierarchy draw up a preliminary list of those to become members of the Central Committee, and then the list is presented to the Party Congress for formal ratification. It was reported that at the 1982 Twelfth Party Congress, delegates were given colored computer cards listing the names of all nominees for the Central Committee; they were permitted to delete names on the list during the balloting. For the first time, delegates also were permitted to write in names not on the nomination list.[146]

Some students of Chinese politics have pointed out that, in addition to the important tasks of ratification of the party constitution and election of the Central Committee, the Party Congress accepts and reviews political reports from party leaders.[147] Reports presented at the National Party Congress have been published, and one can infer policy shifts and program emphasis from them. Since the Central Committee debates are never published except for occasional communiques summarizing policy formulations and personnel changes, reports of the National Party Congress provide a unique source of information about the issues and programs of concern to the party. For example, economic goals or party reforms have been made public in general form.[148]

Finally, there has always been a great deal of fanfare and publicity focused on the Party Congress. It instills in them what Franklin Houn calls the "sense of commitment" to the unity with their leaders and the party.[149]

THE CENTRAL COMMITTEE The party constitution vests in the Central Committee the supreme power to govern party affairs and to enact party policies when the Party Congress is not in session. Although the Central Committee as a collective body rarely initiates party policy, it must approve or endorse policies, programs, and major changes in membership in leading central organs. There are several reasons why the membership of the Central Committee has increased to the present enormous proportions, at least a total of more than 300 members. First, increased membership reflects the phenomenal growth of the party membership as a whole since the Cultural Revolution, from approximately 17 million in 1961 to about 50 million in 1993. Second, membership in the Central Committee has been used as a reward for loyal service to the party and to the government. Preeminent scholars and scientists have been recognized and elevated to Central Committee membership.

With a few exceptions, the Central Committee usually holds enlarged annual plenary sessions, either with its own full and alternate members in attendance, or with non-Central Committee members as well. Chairman Mao frequently called these enlarged sessions to ram through some of his policies that did not really have majority support in the Central Committee. These regularized plenums of the Central Committee are the forums through which party and state policies and programs are discussed and ratified.

THE POLITBURO AND ITS STANDING COMMITTEE The principle of Lenin's democratic centralism calls for decision-making power for the party to be vested in a small number of key leaders who occupy positions at the apex of the power structure, the Political Bureau. The formal language in the party constitution does not reveal the actual power of this top command for the CCP. The party constitutions of 1969, 1973, 1977, and 1982 simply stipulated that the Politburo shall be elected by the Central

Committee in full session and shall act in its behalf when the Central Committee is not in session. Day-to-day work of the Politburo is carried out by its Standing Committee, the apex of the pyramidal structure of the party.[150] In essence, it is the Politburo and its Standing Committee that possess "boundless power" over the general policies of the party and all important matters of the regime that affect the government organs.[151] It is the Politburo that selects top personnel to direct the vast apparatus of the party, the government, and the military.

The Politburo holds frequent meetings; discussion is said to be frank and unrestrained. It has been compared to a corporate board of directors.[152] Decisions of the Politburo are generally reached by the group's consensus after thorough discussion of the available alternatives. The 20-member Politburo elected by the new Central Committee in October 1992 elevated new faces who replaced eight old members.

CENTRAL PARTY SECRETARIAT   The Central Committee and its Politburo are serviced by a host of centralized organs, responsible for executing party policies and managing party affairs. Some of this machinery deals with the routine matters of party organization, propaganda, and united front work. However, the principal central party organ has been the Central Secretariat, the nerve center of the party.

The Central Secretariat, as it existed from 1956 to 1966, was the administrative and staff agency that supervised the party's numerous functional departments, paralleling the functional ministries of the central government. The total number of these central party functional departments may once have reached more than eighteen. Membership of the Central Secretariat was not fixed; it ranged from six to eleven top-ranking Central Committee members.

The reinstitution of a general secretariat and the abolition of the post of party chairman may be viewed as an obvious rejection of Mao's practice of "overconcentration of personal power" in the party. Daily work of the party of the Central Committee is now supervised by the Central Secretariat, headed by a general secretary, who in turn is assisted by eleven other members, four of whom are concurrently members of the Politburo. The 1982 party constitution made it clear that the daily work of the Central Committee would be carried out by the Central Secretariat under the overall direction of the Politburo and its Standing Committee.

The Central Secretariat now consists of seven major departments:[153] organization, propaganda, united front work, liaison office with the fraternal parties abroad, publications, a policy research office, and party schools. Members of the Central Secretariat, elected by the National Party Congress, can initiate and formulate policies on anything they wish. We now know that the Central Secretariat meets twice a week behind the red walls of Zhongnanhai, a part of the former imperial palace, now serving as both party headquarters and seat of the central government, the State Council.

Group Politics and Conflicts   The Chinese social structure is made up of broad occupational groups in society: peasants, industrial workers, party/government bureaucrats, intellectuals, and military personnel. Each of the occupational groups listed here possesses a certain amount of political influence in society and articulates its vested interests. In the following sections we briefly discuss the characteristics of each of the occupational groups and the source of conflict that exists between them.

THE PEASANTS AND INDUSTRIAL WORKERS   Peasants today constitute about 80 percent of China's total population of 1.1 billion. The rural peasants' primary concern is the individual families' ability to cultivate the land under a system of contract with the commune. Their desire to be able to sell their sideline products in the free market is their second most important interest. Basically, they want the continuance of these practices, which have yielded increased income for their families. Also, they would like their children to have access to expanded educational opportunities.

At present, China has 348,000 industrial enterprises employing about 90 million workers. The bulk of these industries is located in urban areas. A main concern of the industrial workers is better wages. In addition to wage increases, a system of bonuses has also been introduced for quality work, as well as for the fulfillment of quotas. The state has also allocated a large sum of funds for price subsidies for daily necessities, housing, and social welfare for workers in the cities. Educational opportunities are made more readily available in urban areas.[154]

Before the 1980s the ratio of urban to rural income on a per capita basis was about 2:1.[155] The lower rural standard of living was obvious to any Western observers who visited China in the 1970s when the doors were opened to the West. Life was hard for a peasant, and earnings for a member of a collective were rather meager. Recent data provided by the State Statistical Bureau has shown no significant change in the rural-urban ratio of income earned—it is still roughly about 2:1.[156]

Recent economic reforms aimed at providing incentives for urban workers and peasants through the introduction of the "responsibility system" will most likely increase the disparities between the sectors. In fact, the peasants' income increased dramatically in the early days of the reform. Peasants receive grain as part of their income. But they pay more for housing and fuel cost, as well as articles for daily use. A compensating factor for the peasants is that they can now keep all income earned from the private plot and sideline production. In addition, the state subsidizes food, clothing, housing, and transportation for urban workers. Industrial workers also receive old-age pensions, labor insurance, and other welfare entitlements. Only in 1982 did some peasants in a few well-off provinces and municipalities begin to receive pensions when they reached age 60 for women and 65 for men.[157]

During the Cultural Revolution, emphasis on medicine was oriented toward the expansion of health care in the rural areas. This led to the rapid development of rural "barefoot" doctors for the peasants and rural cooperative health care programs. Since the post-Mao reform, emphasis has been on medical service development and better hospitals. This policy shift will no doubt benefit more the industrial workers who reside in urban areas, where hospital facilities are available. As David Lampton points out, the result will be more inequality in rural-urban medical care and health services as more trained medical specialists tend to stay in cities, and more trained medical personnel are needed to staff modernized hospitals and clinics in urban areas.[158]

THE INTELLECTUALS   In 1982 there were about twenty million intellectuals in China. By definition, anyone who has had more than a secondary education is an intellectual. Thus, a teacher, a university professor, a technician, an economist, an engineer, and a writer would be called an intellectuals. In most societies this group of people who possess knowledge and skill is generally treated with respect and valued as a precious human resource. This was not the case in China between the years 1957 and 1978. In 1957 Chinese intellectuals were labeled as "rightists" or "counterrevolutionaries," and therefore not to be trusted. Their persecution and vilification lasted through the Cultural Revolution decade (1965–76). They were not considered productive members of the socialist society.

Given that one of the most important assets of intellectuals is the possession of knowledge, information, and skills, efforts have been made since 1977 to correct the "leftist" mistake in their treatment. Better treatment of the intellectuals is also dictated by the hard reality of putting their brain power into service for successful implementation of the modernization programs. The Tiananmen crackdown in 1989 not only silenced the intellectuals, but forced some more prominent ones into exile abroad. Inside China they have been subjected to indoctrination and intimidation by the regime. After investigation, many dissidents have been dismissed or expelled from the party.

THE MASSACRE ON JUNE 4, 1989   By June 2–3, 1989, it was estimated that there were at least 150,000 People's Liberation Army (PLA) soldiers, backed by armored vehicles and tanks, taking positions in various parts of Beijing, waiting to move into the square occupied by the students. The decision to order the PLA into the square was made on the afternoon of June 2 by Deng and Yang Shangkun, members of the Politburo's Standing Committee.

At 6:00 P.M. radio and television broadcast the government's emergency warnings to the residents to stay home. Instead, thousands of them defiantly rushed to the square. Three hours later great numbers of troops moved from the eastern suburbs, a heavily populated district of Beijing, where they encountered blockades erected by the residents. The students on the square were conducting classes beside the temporarily erected Goddess of Democracy statue, now a prominent site on the square. However, to the west of Tiananmen peasant soldiers of the 27th Division from Hepei had opened fire with automatic weapons aimed indiscriminately at buildings and people. The best unofficial estimate of the number of students killed by the troops put the figure between 1,000 and 1,500.

Military Politics Militarism has always played an important, if not decisive, role in Chinese politics. Each dynasty employed military force to attain power. Although a new dynasty was legitimatized under the Confucian precepts, each new ruler would be required to see to it that military power would remain under centralized control—that is, the military must be subject to the control of the central civil bureaucracy. According to Martin Wilbur, the military has consistently served as "the ultimate power" and the "normal arbiter in the distribution of power and in the establishment of policy."[159] Modern Chinese political development has, to a large extent, been influenced by the power of armies, on one hand, and by the technique in the use of armies and military organization, on the other.

For decades prior to the unification effort undertaken by the Chinese Nationalists in 1926, a system of regional military separatism dominated the political scene in China. Under the system, independent military-political groupings, each occupying one or more provinces, functioned as separate political entities and engaged in internecine warfare with each other in order to preserve their own separate regions and to prevent their rivals from establishing a unified and centralized political system. That contemporary China has been plagued by the problem of control of armies is really an understatement. It is largely by military means and through military organization and technique that the Chinese Nationalists tried, and the Chinese communists succeeded, in reestablishing a "unified hierarchical and centralized political system."[160] The military thus constitutes a dominant group in Chinese society, and the military institution has played a dominant role in political development.[161]

The 3.5 million soldiers and officers of the People's Liberation Army always have been considered an influential group in Chinese politics. To a large extent Mao's rise to power was helped by the military organization he developed, dating back to the Jiangxi guerrilla days in the 1930s. On the eve of and during the Cultural Revolution and in its aftermath, the military was not only the most prestigious organizational establishment in China but the most influential politically. Until very recently party leadership has depended upon party members in the military to carry on political work, to restore order, and to use the PLA as a coercive instrument in the contest for political power and succession.

Members of the military establishment have been considered the most prestigious in the Chinese society. Their recruitment and compensation system are the most efficient and most professional in China. In many ways the military personnel in China constitute a distinct class in the social hierarchy. Not only do members of the PLA receive special privileges, but their families and close relatives also receive these same honors, prestige, and privileges. For many poor peasants, entry in the military ranks was once a means of achieving upward social mobility. Since the military as a group has been molded and nurtured by Mao, it is considered the ardent adherent of Mao's revolutionary ideas. The military is by no means united in their views toward the economic reform introduced by Deng Xiaoping. Its officer corps are factionalized. In a power struggle, the military is still a force to be reckoned with.

Japan: Competitive Politics and the "Money Politics" Scandals

While China has yet to devise direct popular elections under which the Chinese Communist party does not exercise direct control, elections in Japan are on the whole partisan and competitive. Not only does Japan have a unique electoral districting system, but the campaigning style is distinctively Japanese, marred frequently by money scandals indulged in by parliamentary political candidates.

The Electoral Process and Campaigning Style in Japan   The basic law that governs elections in Japan is the Public Office Election of 1950, as amended subsequently. The law provides universal adult suffrage for any citizen twenty years old, with a three-month residence requirement in order to vote. There are three types of elections in Japan: the general election for the lower chamber of the Diet, the House of Representatives, held every four years or sooner when dissolved by the Cabinet; the election of the upper chamber, the House of Councillors, held every three years for half of its members; and local elections for prefecture governors, mayors of cities and villages, and their respective assemblies, every four years. All elections are supervised by the Central Election Administrative Committee, but with local election committees at each administrative level. Of these three types of elections, the most important is the general election for the House of Representatives because its decision on the prime minister and the Cabinet is final under the constitution. However, in the July 23, 1989, upper house election a great deal of attention and importance were focused on the House of Councillors. For, as an aftermath to the Recruit scandal, the ruling party, the Liberal Democratic party, lost its majority in that chamber for the first time since its founding in 1955.

Japan has a unique electoral districting system. For the purpose of the lower house election, the nation has been carved into 130 electoral districts—the total number of districts has been increased from 124 in 1976 to the present 130 in 1986 following reapportionment. It is from the 130 election districts or constituencies that a total of the present 512 deputies are elected to the House of Representatives. The electoral districting system is unique in that it is multimember, but each voter in each of the districts can cast only one vote. It is better described as single-nontransferable-vote (SNTV) system in political science literature. Most of the 130 electoral districts have from three to five members to be elected. Thus, in a three-member district, a voter can cast his vote for only one candidate and the three who receive the most votes are declared winners for the three seats to the lower house of the Diet.

The multimember districting and single-nontransferable-vote system for the House of Representatives election has presented problems for political participation in Japan. First, the multimember districting system is still biased toward the rural, but less populated, areas, which tend to be more conservative in social and political orientation. It is not unusual for a rural area to elect a candidate who garnered only one-quarter or one-fifth of the votes in an urban area. (In April 1976 the Supreme Court of Japan, in a rare occurrence, declared the electoral district system for the lower house unconstitutional on the grounds that it lacked equal representation, or the "one-man, one-vote" concept.) The 1986 redistricting system now in effect was an attempt to address the problem by giving more representation to population centers such as Tokyo and Osaka. Rural representation declined somewhat prior to the 1986 election in the Diet as a whole. Kent E. Calder points out that, in the early 1980s, rural representation in the House of Representatives provided as many as forty seats for the ruling LDP that it otherwise would not have had, as well as benefiting the opposition party, the Japan Socialist party.[162]

But the biggest problem created by the unique electoral districting system for the House of Representatives has been the difficult decision for the ruling party, as well as leading opposition parties, to decide how many candidates should be entered in a district. If the party enters too many candidates in a given multimember district with voters casting a single vote, it may cause dispersion of votes, which would result in fewer candidates to be elected and fewer seats for the party. If too few, chances for the opposition parties to win the seats are much greater. For the ruling LDP the system further complicates the problem in that the majority party is revolving around factions that compete within the party for parliamentary seats at election time. Because of this political reality the strength of the majority party can be weakened, with the result that a weaker opposition party can take advantage of the situation by providing support to one or two of its candidates to win a seat or two at the expense of a divided majority party. In other words, it may be a political disaster for a majority party to field five candidates in each of the forty-three electoral districts that elect five members, if it could get only three elected at best. Reischauer points out that the electoral system does provide slow change and is more predictable and stable because a shift in voter preference in a district affects a few seats only.[163]

Nevertheless, on the whole, the system tends to work in favor of the majority party, for it receives more seats in the lower house than the proportion of the votes it receives in a given election.[164] In the July 1986 election the LDP received 300 seats, or 59 percent of the total, to the lower house, which represented about 49.4 percent of votes as a whole, in contrast to the 85 seats, or 16.6 percent of the total in the lower house represented by 17.2 percent of the votes for the opposition Japanese Socialist party.[165] This is the inevitable consequence of the multimember districting system under which a winning candidate may win with less than a majority of the total votes in a district election. Attempts to replace the present electoral system with a single member district system have been unsuccessful, as it would give an enormous advantage to the majority party to the detriment of opposition parties, such as the Japanese Socialist party. In the spring of 1990 an advisory committee appointed by Prime Minister Kaifu recommended that the multiseat district for lower house elections be abolished and replaced by a 301 single-seat district system, supplemented by an additional 200 seats to be awarded on a proportional basis of each party's voting strength at any given election. The recommended change has met resistance from the opposition parties and the LDP's bosses. The issue was the heart of the failed reform attempt in May 1993 that brought in a censure vote on prime minister Miyazawa, who had to dissolve the low house and call for a new election on July 18, 1993.

The results of the general elections for the lower house of the Diet, from 1979 to 1990, are presented in Table 1.2.

Table 1.2   Election of Lower House of the Diet, 1979–1990

Political Party	1990 (Feb. 18)			1986 (July 6)			1983 (Dec. 18)			1980 (June 22)			1979 (Oct. 7)		
	Seats Won	% Seats	% Votes	Seats Won	% Seats	% Votes	Seats Won	% Seats	% Votes	Seats Won	% Seats	% Votes	Seats Won	% Seats	% Votes
Liberal Democratic Party (LDP)	275	53.7	46.1	300	58.6	49.4	250	48.9	45.8	286	56.0	47.9	249	48.5	44.6
Japan Socialist Party (JSP)	136	26.5	24.4	85	16.6	17.2	112	21.9	19.5	107	20.9	19.3	107	20.9	19.7
Komeito (CGP)	45	8.7	7.9	56	10.9	9.4	58	11.4	10.1	33	6.5	9.0	57	11.7	9.8

Table 1.2   (continued)

Japan Communist Party (JCP)	16	3.1	7.9	26	5.1	6.4	26	5.1	9.3	29	5.7	9.8	39	7.6	10.4
Democratic Socialist Party (DSP)	14	2.6	4.8	26	5.1	8.8	38	7.4	7.3	32	6.3	6.6	35	6.9	6.8
New Liberal Club	1	0.1	0.2	6	1.2	1.8	8	1.6	2.4	12	2.4	3.0	4	0.8	3.0
Social Democratic Federation	4	0.7	0.5	4	0.	0.8	3	0.6	0.7	3	0.6	0.7	2	0.4	4.9
Minor Parties and Independents	21	4.0	7.2	—	—	—	—	—	—	—	—	—	—	—	—
TOTAL	512			503			495			502			511		

Source: Figures for 1979 to 1986 are taken from Kent E. Calder, *Crisis and Compensation: Public Policy and Political Stability in Japan, 1949–1986* (Princeton: Princeton University Press, 1988), p. 493. Figures for the 1990 election are taken from *The Japan Times*, February 1990, p. 1.

Prior to 1983 the House of Councillors used the single-nontransferable-vote system for election of the fifty country-at-large district candidates, with each voter casting a vote for only one candidate. Since 1983, in the House of Councillors, an election is called for half of its total 252 seats every three years. The electoral system used is a combination of proportional representation for 100 seats and a districting system for the remaining 152 seats. Thus, at the three-year election interval, fifty seats are determined by proportional representation, which works in the following manner: (1) each political party must present a list of its candidates to the voters; (2) a voter must register preference for the party list; and (3) the number of seats won by each political party is based on the percentage or proportion of votes the party list received. For example, if a party list of candidates receives 20 percent of the votes, the party is entitled to ten of the fifty seats for that particular election. The top ten candidates on that list are the ones to take seats in the upper house.

Under the present system for the House of Councillors election, the party bosses control the list for the proportional representation of the fifty seats up for election every three years. Then for 76, or half of the 152 seats, the districting basis is the forty-seven prefectures each, with a different number of councillors to be elected, usually ranging from one to four. Again, the single-nontransferable-vote is used by each voter—that is, each voter can select only one candidate by designating the party; and the candidates with the most aggregated votes are declared winners. However, twenty-six prefectures are single-member districts, mostly rural Japan. In the July 1989 upper house election, rural districts turned against the majority party, the LDP, because of the imposition of the 3 percent consumption tax, designed to raise funds for increased welfare program costs. It is interesting to note that the July 23, 1989, upper house election attracted candidates from six major political parties and thirty-four single-issue parties on issues ranging from banning nuclear power plants to better tax treatment for employees of business firms. With intense competition among so-called mine parties in the 1989 upper house election, it becomes inevitable to see an increase in campaign spending on advertising for winning voters' preference.

Political structure reform became one of the two main issues in the no-confidence vote that brought down Miyazawa's government in June 1993, which forced him to dissolve the parliament and call for an election on July 18, 1993. The other issue was the rampant political corruption fostered by "money politics" in recent years that has resulted in celebrated scandals. The most recent one involved Shin Kanemaru, a powerful backroom operator within the LDP, who admitted receiving illicit campaign contributions from businessmen who had dealings with organized crime.

Miyazawa pledged to the LDP reformers and the public to enact legislation to resolve these two issues. Regarding the political structure reform, his proposal for single-member districting met considerable opposition from hardliners within his LDP but was supported by the more reform-minded. However, Miyazawa was not skillful enough to work out an acceptable compromise, and the issue was postponed. Then Miyazawa dropped the campaign contribution reform proposal, an action that angered the opposition parties.

Miyazawa could have survived the no-confidence vote, for the LDP had the majority, but it soon became obvious that the LDP was split. Forty-four members formed the New Life Party (Shinseito) under the leadership of two long-time backroom power brokers: Tsetomu Hata, Miyazawa's former finance minister, and Ichiro Ozawa, a former protege of Kanemaru, the disgraced insider of the LDP. The combined forces of the opposition parties, plus the New Life Party and the Japan New Party—another splinter group from the LDP formed after the last lower house election in 1992—constituted a real threat in the July 18 election to the four-decade dominance of the LDP in Japanese politics.

The July 18, 1993 election yielded the following results: the LDP, 223 seats—a reduction of over fifty-two seats from its 1990 total and thirty-three seats short of a simple majority in the 512-seat lower house of the Diet; the traditional opposition parties, the Japan Socialist Party and Komeito, seventy seats and fifty-one seats, respectively; the new parties, Shinsieto, the Japan Party, and Shinto Sakigake, fifty-five seats, thirty-five seats, and thirteen seats, respectively; the independents, thirty seats; and the communists and others, thirty-four seats. Thus, three coalitions emerged from the July 18 election to contend for control of the Diet. The LDP, wounded seriously for the first time since 1958, when it controlled the Diet, had to seek a coalition for the formation of a new government in the selection of a new prime minister. It could count on the votes of the independents who supported the LDP in the past, or the LDP could make a deal with the Japan New Party and the Sakigake, which now have a combined forty-eight seats in the lower house, or the opposition parties and the new parties could form a new united coalition with a combined voting strength of more than 250 seats in the lower house, enough to constitute the simple majority needed to form a new government. The constitution states that a new prime minister must be chosen thirty days after the election by a special session of the Diet. This constitutional provision makes it necessary for the parties to seek a possible coalition to select a new prime minister before the deadline arrives. A seven-party coalition was formed, headed by Morihiro Hosokawa of the Japan New Party. In August Hosokawa was elected to be the new prime minister.

CAMPAIGNING JAPANESE STYLE   In the February 1990 House of Representatives election, some 66 million voters took part in casting their ballots in the general election, representing about 73.3 percent of the 90.6 million eligible voters in Japan. Voter turnout in Japan's general elections has been on the rise from 27.3 percent in 1947 to about 73 percent in 1990.

An election date is usually set for the voters in Japan when a regular election is called for either of the branches of the parliament or when the prime minister dissolves the lower house. The House of Councillors election was set for half of its 252 seats on July 23, 1989, when the Japan Socialist party made a significant gain by taking forty-six seats against the ruling LDP's thirty-six seats. Then the House of Representatives was dissolved for a new election set on February 18, 1990. Under Article 86 of the 1975 Election Control Law, amended January 1976, a definite period for election campaigning is determined, which requires that candidates must register first for the election within four days of the official announcement of the election. Then campaigning is allowed during the brief period between the date for candidate registration and the day preceding the election—generally not more than three to four weeks.

Campaign activities are regulated by the election law, which incorporated many of the electioneering practices of the past. In fact, there are almost minute details consisting of prohibitions on the types of campaign activities to be undertaken by the candidates. These restrictions include no house-to-house canvassing, no publishing of private polls, no serving of free food, no sidewalk speeches after 9:00 P.M., no more than one campaign car and campaign headquarters, and limited quantities of written materials.[166] Moreover, a candidate can speak only at sidewalk ("must be stationary") and private speech meetings.[167] Gerald Curtis indicates that although these restrictions are intended to ensure fair elections for all candidates, they nonetheless produce "undesirable effects" such as bias in favor of the incumbents, hardships on new candidates, and prevention of voter participation in campaigns—reducing elections into "beauty contests."[168]

"MONEY POLITICS"   Similar to election campaigning in the United States, the availability of funds to carry on the permissible election activities is extremely crucial. In the February 1990 lower house election, the LDP was reported to have spent about $40 million to help its candidates win the contest. Each LDP incumbent in the House of Representatives received from $130,000 to $172,000. Just days before the February 18 election, the 270 endorsed candidates went to party headquarters to pick up their brown bags containing cash. Although the 1975 election law restricts the amount each candidate is permitted to collect and spend (about $60,000 to $75,000), there are many loopholes through which a candidate gets around the legal limitation at election time. Generally, it takes at least $300,000 to $500,000 to get elected to the Diet. Usually, campaign money comes from individuals and business concerns and is funneled to the candidates.[169]

The system of campaign contribution provides ample opportunity for corruption and for buying influence from the politicians.[170] The Recruit scandal is one such example. Former prime minister Toshiki Kaifu admitted that he received $96,000 to $100,000 in contributions from the Recruit Company from 1984 to 1987, a matter he revealed in the question period of the Diet, but he denied wrongdoing, as half of the amount was in small amounts which required no public disclosure.[171] Former prime minister Takeshita and his aides received Recruit stocks, donations, and loans totaling $1.5 million.[172] Then there was the contribution, estimated to be at least $1 million, by the crime-infested pinball or pachinko machine parlor operators to key politicians of LDP and its major opposition, the Socialists, for blocking bills intended to regulate the pinball industry. It has been estimated that the ruling LDP raised about $206 million in campaign funds mostly from businesses for the February 1990 House of Representatives general election despite the Recruit scandal.[173]

Another feature in Japanese election campaigning is what Reischauer calls the "strong personal flavor."[174] The multimember districting and single-nontransferable-vote system compels the development of a candidate's own campaign support organization, for there is intense competition by candidates for votes within the party as well as between the parties. These personal support organizations associations are known as the *Koenkai*.[175] *Koenkai* is not a party organization; it is simply an informal voluntary personal campaign organization of supporters and leaders from the local community at the prefecture, city, county, or village level. Gerald Curtis points out that a typical *Koenkai* is made up of a women's group, a young ladies' group, a youth group, or a senior citizen group.[176] In towns and villages candidates tend to be identified with *Koenkai* rather than with parties. While its membership is rather informal with a nominal fee of 100 yen, its size may be enormous. Former prime minister Kakuei Tanaka's support groups had a membership of 92,000 in Niigata Prefecture alone.[177] At election time the nucleus groups could expand horizontally to reach millions of voters. Frequently the branches of the *Koenkai* for a particular politician, usually a dietman, serve as employment agency and marriage counseling center, and arrange trips for senior citizens and settle local disputes. Kent E. Calder indicates that one-third of all LDP voters are associated with such groups.[178] (Curtis estimated the figure for voters of all parties members of *Koenkai* in 1971 at 12 million.)[179] Taken as a whole, these are the personal grassroots campaign organizations—which engage in "routinely fierce grassroot intraparty rivalries"[180]—associated with the candidates who run for Diet elections.

Political Parties   Today Japan has a multiparty system even though one of the political parties has dominated since 1955. In the 1986 and 1990 House of Representatives general elections there were seven political parties—excluding the independents—which had their candidates elected as Diet members.

When war ended and the American occupation of Japan began in 1945, there was a mushrooming of political groups and associations, encouraged by the occupation policy of democratizing the political process. Out of the myriad organizational forms and the seeming chaos they created, there gradually evolved four viable political parties: the Liberal party and the Progressive party; also, there emerged the Socialist party and the Communist party, tracing their origin to 1901 and 1922. Although Japan has a multiparty system, it has been characterized as a "one and a half party system," alluding to the dominance of one political party (Liberal Democratic party) and the only possible threat to that dominance by an opposition party (Japan Socialist party).

A brief sketch of the development and vicissitudes of Japan's seven political parties is provided here as basic to an understanding of political participation and process in Japan.

THE LIBERAL DEMOCRATIC PARTY[181]   The present-day Liberal Democratic party traced its roots to the 1945 Liberal party, whose forerunners were the prewar *Seiyukai*, and the Democratic party, both formed in 1945 by men associated with the prewar *Minseito*. To some the LDP is a forerunner of those who associated with the Imperial Rule Assistance Association, the military-endorsed government party in 1940.[182] In 1955 it became necessary as a tactical move to merge into one Liberal Democratic party in order to respond to the threat posed by a united Japan Socialist party. Since then the LDP has become a large, but loosely knit, political conglomerate of many factions and interests. Somehow the so-called shotgun marriage of 1955 persisted to allow it to become the ruling party of Japan, until the 1993 election for the lower house.

The LDP is basically conservative or status quo oriented, and as such it does not have a well-defined ideology. It is on the right of the socialists and communists, but more moderate than the extreme rightists. Thus, it is essentially centrist on the opinion spectrum. The LDP has been identified with these objectives throughout its more than thirty-five years of dominance in Japanese politics: continued economic growth, expert trade orientation, and a close cooperation with the United States on defense and foreign policies. In addition, the LDP has consistently looked after the interests of the Japanese farmers and thus receives in return the support of the rural constituencies. Because of its conservative outlook and advocacy of continued economic growth, it has the consistent backing of Japan's big business and financial groups known as the *Zaikai*, particularly the powerful *Keidanren*, the federation of major industrial and trading organizations such as iron and steel, automobile, petroleum, chemical associations, and banks.

While the LDP has been able to win general elections since 1955, it is not really a party with a massive membership. In 1975 it had a registered membership of 1.2 million, and by the 1980s its rank-and-file membership stood at about 1.5 million at best. Ward points out that former party membership means little at the local level, and the party's effectiveness lies in its branch offices tied closely to the fortunes of local politicians.[183]

In many respects the LDP revolves around the election of its candidates for the Diet. For as long as its Diet members constitute the majority in the parliament, particularly in the House of Representatives, the party is ensured control of the national government through the majority party's selection of the prime minister. Thus, the inner-party maneuvers in the selection of party president are very important, since the leader so selected becomes the premier-designate when the LDP becomes the majority party in the Diet, particularly in the House of Representatives.

FACTIONALISM   A characteristic of the conservative LDP, and to a lesser extent the opposition parties, is the ubiquitous factional politics within the organization, the *habatsu*. In essence, the LDP is a collection of competing groups, ranging from five to ten in number; each is composed of a boss or faction leader who has a group of followers, elected members of the Diet from the party. Large factions have sub-factions whose leaders make demands on the boss for political favors and financial support. Factions are generally informally organized and are identified by the name of a prominent senior party leader who in many instances has previously served as a prime minister or held a Cabinet position. Thus, in the 1970s and 1980s there were the Ohira faction, the Nakasone faction, the Tanaka faction, and the Miki faction. As shown in Table 1.3 six main factions within the LDP were identified by the *Asahi Shinbun* in July 1989.[184]

Table 1.3   LDP Factionalism within the Diet

LDP Factions	In House of Representatives	In House of Councillors	Total
Takeshita	70	35	105
Nakasone	60	15	75
Miyazawa	60	18	78
Abe	57	23	80
Komoto	23	7	30
Nikaido	11	3	14
No faction	12	8	20
TOTAL	293	109	402

Source: Asahi Shinbun, 25 July 1989.

Kent E. Calder explains that there are four major factors involved in formation of factional rivalries in the LDP.[185] First is the wartime experience and purges during the occupation among those who entered into politics as Diet members. This served as a convenient basis for forming a faction of likeminded within LDP membership. Then, the "shotgun marriage" of the left and right wings of the conservative LDP in 1955 provided the basis for intensified intraparty rivalries as candidates of LDP needed to compete among themselves in the electoral multimember district and single-nontransferable-vote system. Third, the desire to capture a choice Cabinet post with an economic stake in terms of "distributive political resources" compels the leaders in the conservative party to compete more rigorously among themselves. And finally, as one of the inevitable consequences of group politics in Japan, personal rivalries among the party's key leaders are more pronounced and contribute to party disunity and crisis.

Factional leaders within the LDP are expected to perform a number of tasks for their followers, a classical example of patron (*oyabun*) and client (*kukun*) relationship. But the most important function for the faction leader has always been providing the necessary financial support for followers. In Japan this is the essence of *kinken seiji*, or "money-power politics." Since big business, the *zaikai*, played a significant role in the merger formation of the LDP, it thus became the primary source of funding for leaders of the party. Since 1955 corporate money has been channeled through a sort of political action committee, the People's Politics Association, organized by the *Keidanren*, the federation of big business groups. Karel van Wolferen estimates that big business groups supply as much as 90 percent of the LDP's needed funds.[186] Typically, big business representatives would meet with top LDP leaders on New Year's Day, when a target amount would be determined as the former's donation and contribution to LDP's income for the coming year. (In 1986, the Home Ministry reported a total of 167 billion yen for politicians of all political parties.)[187] Additional money amounting to several hundred million could be raised by ticket sales to "encouragement parties" of individual LDP members—tickets usually purchased by big businesses. Money raised by the LDP would be subsequently distributed by party leaders to the factional bosses, who in turn would redistribute the war chest to their followers who are Diet members or candidates for election to the Diet. For the February 1990 House of Representatives general election the LDP was said to have raised a total of 30 billion yen (or about U.S. $206 million at the exchange rate at that time).[188] Through bank loans and donations from the *Zaikai*. In the case of the 1990 general election the LDP secretary-general targeted specific amounts to be contributed by each individual business concern member of the *Keidanren* under the threat that the LDP might revise upward the consumption tax, which would cost more to the auto and electronic industries in particular.[189] Bank loans to the LDP, guaranteed by major auto, electronics, and construction industries, are a device aimed at circumventing the 1975 Election Control Law, which limits business contributions to a maximum of 100 million yen per year. In the 1989 and 1990 elections, guaranteed bank loans to the LDP more than filled the gap left by the reduced amount of money raised by the scandal-ridden faction leaders. The end result has been the ability of LDP candidates to outspend their opposition party opponents, and thus enable the party to emerge as a tarnished political force, but still maintain its majority party status.

THE JAPAN SOCIALIST PARTY   The Japan Socialist party emerged in the 1989–90 Diet elections as the largest opposition party to the ruling LDP. In the July 25, 1989, election of the upper house, when 126 seats, or half the total 252 member seats, were up for contest, the JSP won forty-six seats against the LDP's thirty-six. This provided the LDP with only 109 seats in the upper house, a number far short of majority control. In the general election for the lower house held on February 18, 1990, the JSP captured 136 seats, a gain of 50 seats over the last election in 1986—the only party garnering an increase in seats in the 1990 general election. While the LDP maintained solid control, with a 275-seat majority of a total of 512 in the lower house, its leaders were required to negotiate with the opposition parties, particularly the JSP, on all pending legislation in that body. The JSP captured only 70 seats in the lower house election in 1993, as compared to the 136 seats it won in the 1990 election.

The present JSP is the result of a merger in October of 1955 of the right- and left-wing socialists. The socialist roots date back to the prewar radical Socialist Mass party, which captured thirty-seven seats in the old imperial Diet in 1937.[190] In 1947 the socialists reorganized as a national party and entered the 1947 general election for the lower house by capturing 143 seats, or 31 percent of the total, and 26 percent of the popular votes.[191] Then its popularity declined, primarily because of the left- and right-wing feuding within the socialist movement; by 1955 it had to reorganize by merging the separate divisions. In the 1958 election the JSP, as a united party, captured more than 166 seats, or 35 percent of the total, in the lower house. In the general elections from 1979 to 1990, the JSP has been the strongest opposition party, maintaining approximately 20 percent of the lower house seats. But the JSP's popular appeal declined from a high of 32 percent in 1958 to a low in 1986 of 17 percent. However, in the 1989 and 1990 Diet elections and the Tokyo municipal election on July 2, 1989, the JSP catapulted into the front line as the potential successor to the scandal-riddled factionalized conservative LDP in future electoral contests. Future success at the polls for the JSP depends to a large extent on its ability to sustain the fragile voter dissatisfaction with the LDP, its willingness to modify its ideological rigidity, and the mending of its internal discord.

The JSP's success in the July 1989 upper house election was attributable to the general voter weariness with the ruling LDP's corruption and arrogance. The JSP and other opposition parties were able to capitalize on voter disillusionment by concentrating their attack on the scandals and the unpopular consumption tax.[192] There was the general consensus among Japanese political analysts that the Recruit scandal hurt the LDP at the July upper house election. Related to the Recruit stock scandal was the public's concern over housing space and the high cost of consumer goods. The Tokyo regional election in early July signaled to the LDP the trouble to come later—the JSP increased its representation in the Tokyo municipal assembly from eleven to thirty-six, the highest gain for the JSP since the 1950s. JSP candidates denounced the LDP in both the Tokyo municipal and upper house elections in July with the theme of the LDP's arrogance in pushing for the Diet's enactment of the 3 percent consumption tax. This campaign strategy swayed the women voters against the LDP in both elections. The farmers, traditionally the backbone of LDP support, were antagonized by the government's reduced rice support. And, finally, many Japanese voters, particularly women, were embarrassed by the prime minister's admission of keeping a geisha as his mistress. The JSP's victories at the regional municipal and the House of Councillors elections in 1989 were the result of protest votes against the arrogant and scandal-riddled LDP. The protest was not sufficient to unseat the LDP at the February 1990 lower house election for the simple reason that the voters were not sure about the JSP's ability to govern, a theme propounded repeatedly by the LDP candidates. In other words, the voters were not ready to turn over power to the JSP for fear of political instability and economic change. The general orientation of conservatism of the Japanese voters kept the LDP in power in the lower house, but their unchallenged power is now checked by a coalition of opposition parties, led by the JSP, in the upper house.

Basically, the JSP has been a party that is burdened with ideological rigidity. Now it attempts to modify some of its views. Prior to the July 1989 election for the upper house, the JSP's long-held position was to oppose the U.S.-Japan security treaty, and to keep Japan unarmed. As a way of appealing to the centrist-oriented Japanese voters, the JSP has begun to modify or soften that position by stating that it is no longer advocating the repeal of the U.S.-Japan security treaty. Instead, Takako Doi, the charismatic JSP leader and constitutional lawyer, has advanced the proposal that Japan must now renegotiate or reexamine the defense treaty, in view of the events unfolding in Eastern Europe. (The proposition was made in the February 1990 general election along with the promise, aimed at appealing to the Japanese farmers, the backbone of LDP support, that the JSP would not permit the importation of American rice into the domestic market.) In the past, the JSP was in favor of building closer ties with North Korea. Now it joined the other opposition parties in moving closer to South and North Korea, favoring balanced ties with both.

In the Tokyo municipal election in July 1989 the familiar JSP ideological planks of abrogating the U.S.-Japan security treaty and dismantling the Self-Defense Force were conspicuously muted. But Takako Doi, a former professor of constitutional law, still holds rigidly the position that the existence of Japanese armed forces is a violation of Article 9 of the constitution. She resigned in 1991 and the party selected Takata Tanabe as its new leader.

A basic problem for the JSP in forging a strong coalition of opposition parties to the LDP was its inability to secure agreement from other opposition parties on foreign policy issues. At a special meeting of JSP leaders in September 1989, a policy report was endorsed by the JSP's Central Executive Committee for approval by the Party Congress. In the report it proposed the following key planks as a basis for talks with other opposition parties: continue the U.S.-Japan security treaty for the time being; end joint U.S.-Japan military exercises; reduce and eventually remove U.S. bases in Japan; adopt a nuclear-free Japan; and maintain the 1 percent GNP ceiling for defense spending.[193] The JSP's chances for a coalition government to replace the LDP depended heavily on compromises on these issues between the various opposition parties. The JSP did become a part of the seven-party coalition after the 1993 election.

The JSP must be given credit for energizing participation of women in the 1989 and 1990 elections. Women voters were a pivotal factor in JSP's victory in the Tokyo municipal and upper house elections in July. About one-third of the JSP winning candidates in the Tokyo municipal election were women. Women voters in their thirties and forties, inspired by JSP leader Takako Doi, voted not only for JSP, but became the party's activists. For the 1990 general election, a record of sixty-six women (7 percent), out of a total of 953, filed their candidacy for the lower house. Of those sixty-six women, thirty-seven (about 56 percent) were from the JSP or the Communists, as opposed to none from the LDP. In the July 1989 upper house election women voters supported the JSP candidates and provided a doubling of its popular votes over the 1983 and 1986 elections. Doi's decision to field a large number of unknown and older women candidates in the July 1989 upper house election caused some friction within the JSP, which is by no means immune from inner-party factionalism based on a combination of Left-Right issues and personality differences.[194] The JSP has been dominated for some time by the doctrinaire Left faction, the *Shakaishugi Kyokai*. At one time in the 1970s there were eight factional groups within the JSP.[195] The intense factional feuding within the JSP on Japan's relationship with China in the 1970s caused some respectability for JSP and forced the Chinese to seek cooperation with the LDP instead.[196] Doi, as an independent, has also aroused the concern of the JSP old guards, who traditionally relied on support of the public union federation known as the *Sohyo*. Doi's recruitment of women, housewife organizations, and consumer groups for the JSP may create friction and antagonism from *Sohyo*.

In the final analysis, the future of the JSP depends on its willingness to seek accommodation with other opposition parties on some of the key ideological issues that divide them and the emergence of consensus and unity among its own inner factions.

THE DEMOCRATIC SOCIALIST PARTY   In 1960, a right-wing group, consisting of thirty-five Socialist members of the lower house, broke away from the JSP to form a moderate and centrist Democratic Socialist party (DSP). The focal point of the split was the U.S.-Japan security treaty. At the time, the DSP had the backing of the private sector labor unions confederation, the *Domei*, reorganized in 1987 as *Rengo*, aligned with the big corporations. It is pro-United States and anticommunist. Since its inception in 1960, the DSP has been moving closer to the views of the LDP, particularly on both domestic and foreign policy issues such as defense and relations with the United States. Its electoral support comes mainly from semirural areas. DSP members elected to the Diet are generally seasoned politicians who have served for a long time in the Diet.

As seen from Table 1.2, DSP voting strength has been on the decline. In 1979 it had thirty-five members elected to the lower house and represented about 7 percent of the votes. By 1986 it had only twenty-six elected Diet members, or 5 percent of the total; and the 1990 election resulted in a drop from twenty-six to fourteen (or barely 3 percent of the total) Dietmen elected to the lower house—the lowest in its history.

The DSP is still not able to reconcile its ideological differences with the JSP. After the victory by the JSP at the July 1989 election for the upper house, the DSP refused to cooperate with the JSP in voting for Doi as prime minister. In a runoff vote in the upper house between Doi and the LDP's Kaifu, DSP members left their ballots blank instead of casting their votes for the JSP's Doi. When it comes to the question of coalition government, the DSP's preference is to go with the LDP rather than the JSP, the fellow socialists. The DSP's problem now is to survive while facing the trend of a growing JSP. The DSP's fear is to be swallowed by the JSP, thus depriving it of its centrist choice, halfway between the JSP and LDP. However, DSP positions in the Diet have been undistinguishable from those of the LDP.

THE KOMEITO ("THE CLEAN GOVERNMENT PARTY")   *Komeito*, or, "the Clean Government," is Japan's third-largest political party and made its political debut in local elections in 1955. It is an off-shoot of a postwar religious movement of the Nicheren sect of Buddhism, the *Sokagakkai*, or "the Value Creating Society." As a new religious movement, *Sokagakkai* advocated building a new messianic world in accordance with the millennial teachings of Nichiren Shoshi: The never-ending process of value creation such as beauty, goodness, and eternal world peace can be realized by accepting values that would be of benefit to mankind. In pursuing its religious goal adherents of *Sokagakkai*, who were then mainly urbanites in search of meaning in life in postwar Japan, engaged in proselytizing tactics that were fanatical, militant, and nationalistic. Some *Sokagakkai* members even believed that laws may be violated in order to build a just and happier world. When it entered in the Tokyo municipal election in 1955 militant members of the *Sokagakkai* youth corps employed violence and disregarded election laws. The behavior of the arrested *Sokagakkai* militants aroused fear among the public who viewed the society as "authoritarian" and "militaristic," reminiscent of prewar Japan under military rule.

To allay the public's concern about close identification of religion with politics, a decision was made to separate the political operation from *Sokagakkai* religious teachings. Thus, Komeito, "the Clean Government party" became an independent organization on November 17, 1964. In its declaration for the formation of a separate political party, the aims of the Komeito were to achieve "purification of Japanese politics, the establishment of parliamentary democracy, and the realization of the welfare of the public" in a union of government and Buddhism.[197] *Komeito* entered in the 1967 general election by electing twenty-five members in the lower house and about 5 percent of the total votes. It selected a winning electoral strategy that served as a base for subsequent gains in the general elections to make it a national party (fifty-one seats are needed in the lower house to qualify a party for bill submission): Nominate only young and attractive candidates; enter candidates in large urban areas where there is a large number of *Sokagakkai* members; avoid running candidates who would be competing against each other.[198]

Komeito's electoral record since the 1967 general election has not been stable. Its gain in the 1976 election was impressive when fifty-five of its candidates were elected to the lower house and its voting strength was almost 11 percent of the total. In the 1979 election fifty-seven of its candidates were elected, which accounted for almost 12 percent of the total seats (511) in the lower house. After a setback in the 1980 election, the *Komeito* surged forward as the third-largest political party in the 1983 and 1986 elections with fifty-eight and fifty-six of its candidates elected, respectively. But in the 1990 general election, its share of candidates to the lower house was reduced to 45 against the JSP's gain from 85 to 135 seats. Part of the explanation for this is due to the need to field more *Komeito* candidates who must compete with each other in multimember districts. Another reason for its decline may lie in the lack of rapid growth in *Sokagakkai* membership, which in 1990 stood at the level of 6 million, half of its expected target of 12 to 15 million by 1990—for about 90 percent of *Komeito* support comes from *Sokagakkai*. A third possible explanation may be its confusing positions on issues such as the U.S.-Japan defense treaty, which it opposes while supporting a limited self-defense force. Its centrist position on international neutrality does not represent the mainstream thinking in Japan today. The 1990 general election setback may force the *Komeito* to lean more closely toward the LDP, rather than the JSP, which it now blames for its recent misfortune. So long as the *Komeito* stays away from the JSP the chances for a coalition government to unseat the LDP remain slim indeed.

THE JAPANESE COMMUNIST PARTY   The Japanese Communist party (JCP) is one of the oldest political parties in Japan. It was formed secretly on July 15, 1922, in Tokyo. Its first party platform was considered extremist and radical, for it called on Japan to abolish the emperor system, the Diet, military conscription, and a host of other established institutions.[199] In the 1930s party members were hunted and existed illegally insofar as military authorities were concerned. One of its leaders, Nosaka Sanzo, who later surfaced in Yenan in the 1940s under control of the Chinese communists, was the only evidence then to indicate the continued existence of the JCP—the Chinese communists did not publicly reveal his presence in China until 1943.[200]

Soon after the American occupation forces released all political prisoners in the fall of 1945 (among them surviving leaders of the prewar JCP, in addition to Nosaka, who had then reached Japan from China), the party was legally organized and expanded its membership rapidly so that by the 1950s it totaled more than 150,000. By the time of the 1949 general election, the JCP had thirty-five candidates elected to the lower house representing almost 10 percent of the total votes cast. But it was the last time the JCP had shown any credible electoral strength, for in the subsequent general elections of 1952, 1953, 1955 and 1958 its popularity had sunk so rapidly that it seated only one or two of its candidates, and its popular vote was barely 2 percent of the total. Then it made a comeback in the general election of 1972 by seating thirty-eight candidates with more than 10 percent of the total votes. As seen in Table 1.2, it has been able to maintain its strength by capturing anywhere from thirty-nine to twenty-six for the general elections of 1979, 1980, 1983, and 1986.

In the February 1990 general election its strength fell from 26 to 16 seats, or barely 3 percent of the total 512 lower house seats. A possible explanation for its poor showing in that election is that it was not able to counteract the LDP candidates' claim that a strong JCP would lead Japan to economic ruin. Besides, the Japanese voters are generally suspicious of the JCP and other extreme socialists. Its success in the 1970s may be attributed to its willingness to join the wave for environmental control and protection that was then sweeping the nation.

The JCP has been the leanest political party with a mass base in local elections in urban areas. In the 1989 Tokyo municipal election, the JCP won fourteen seats, down from the previous twenty. Its total registered membership ranges from at least 350,000 to half a million at the most. It can mobilize the youth through the All-Japan Federation of Student Self-Governing Associations, the *Zengakuren*. The JCP also has some influence over the *Sohyo*, the general council of trade unions. For some time, the JCP also exercised considerable influence over the Japan Teachers' Union, the *Nikkyoso*. The JCP is considered to be well endowed financially, for its daily newspaper, the *Akahata* (Red Flag) has a Sunday edition of about 2 million, which provides a lucrative steady income for the party.

As a political party it has a rather limited future at the national level. Its role is also limited for joining with other opposition parties to unseat the LDP, for antagonism toward the JCP by the right-wing JSP and the DSP would make such an event most unlikely. Under these circumstances, the JCP has begun to exert its independence away from doctrinaire Marxism-Leninism by attacking the former Soviet Union for its refusal to return the Kurile Islands and criticizing the Chinese government for its bloody crackdown on student demonstrators at Tiananmen in June 1989. The unfolding events in Eastern Europe and the collapse of the Soviet Union have forced the JCP to rethink its dedication to a socialist revolution. In the meantime, the Japanese voters and other political parties are distrustful of the JCP's commitment to parliamentary democracy.

THE NEW LIBERAL CLUB   It is really questionable whether this new entity on the Japanese political scene is a political party in its own merit or a *habatsu* (faction) of the ruling LDP. It was organized after six LDP Diet members resigned in June 1976 and announced the formation of a new political group, the New Liberal Club (NLC), a conservative party hoping to eventually replace the ruling LDP. Basically, the dissidents' complaint was the lack of party reform within the LDP in the aftermath of the politicians' influence peddling and bribery associated with the Lockheed scandal. The New Liberal Club first entered candidates in the 1976 general election and came away with a creditable win of seventeen candidates elected, representing over 4 percent, or 2.3 million, popular votes. It was also a victory for young politicians within the LDP, which had been increasingly controlled by aging old guards, the factional leaders. Its accent on youth is reflected in the party rules—for instance, there is an age limit of fifty-five for the party head, and for delegates to its national convention. The NLC advocates a high level of moral standards for politicians, the elimination of social inequities, the strengthening of the capitalist system, and closer cooperation with the United States in defense matters. Its electoral appeal has been on the decline since its debut in 1976, and by the 1986 general election it had six candidates seated with not more than 1.8 percent of the popular vote. In the 1990 general election it managed to capture only one seat, with 0.2 percent of the total popular vote.

In practice, however, the NCL has not shown to a great extent its independence from the LDP. Its elected dietmen voted with the LDP on most issues and supported the LDP leadership. The best the NCL could expect, as happened in the 1983 general election when the LDP lost some seats, would be for the LDP once in a while to award the NCL a Cabinet position to give the illusion of a "coalition government."

The July 1993 election for the lower house produced a ruling coalition that included three new parties: the Japan Renewal Party (55 seats), the Japan New Party (35 seats), and the Harbinger Party (13 seats).

Japan's Self-Defense Force   Under the 1947 constitution Japan is to renounce war forever and maintain no armed forces. Article 9 states:

> Aspiring sincerely to an international peace based on justice and order, the Japanese people forever renounce war as a sovereign right of the nation and the threat or use of force as a means of settling international disputes.
>
> In order to accomplish the aim of the preceding paragraph, land, sea, and air forces, as well as other potential, will never be maintained. The right of belligerency of the state will not be recognized.

Notwithstanding the constitutional prohibition of maintaining armed forces, Japan has established a Self-Defense Force (SDF) under the 1954 Self-Defense Forces Law enacted by the Diet. Japan's defense budget for 1990 was about $28 billion, ranked as the world's third largest after the

United States and the former Soviet Union, but more than 50 percent of the defense budget is for personnel and related costs. It is named Self-Defense Force because of the constitutional restriction, now a debatable point by some, of deploying military forces outside the national boundary for offensive purposes and for possessing nuclear capability. The actual strength of the SDF is about 247,000, of which 68 percent are ground forces, 14 percent maritime or coast guard, and 17 percent air force. It is a small armed force in view of Japan's population. But the emphasis is really on quality and sophistication in the weaponry provided for the SDF.

A unique feature of Japan's SDF is its control by civilian authorities. All uniformed SDF are members of the civil service and subject to control by the Defense Agency. Under Article 66 of the constitution the Defense Agency and its director-general must subordinate to the civilian authority. That is, it is an agency of the Office of the Prime Minister and the agency head, the civilian director-general, must be appointed by the prime minister. Military personnel who commit offenses are tried by civilian courts in accordance with civil procedures. On defense matters, the prime minister has an advisory body, the National Defense Council, whose membership is limited to the prime minister, deputy prime minister, foreign affairs minister, the director-general of the Defense Agency, and head of the Economic Planning Agency, for advice and consultation. Below the civilian authorities are the uniformed SDF.

Since 1978 Japan has had a five-year defense plan or estimate. The current one, the third, ending in 1991, sets the government's guidelines on defense policy and goals for defense acquisition.[201] The five-year defense plan has been based on the framework and a set of principles established by the 1976 National Defense Program Outline. The 1976 Defense Outline determined the interim target of force structure to be completed by 1987, to include twelve divisions for the ground forces, including one armored division, sixteen submarines and sixty destroyers, and 250 combat aircraft. The original target has been subsequently revised, often under inconsistent pressure from U.S. defense officials.[202]

DEFENSE SPENDING: THE 1 PERCENT ISSUE   Until 1987, one of the governing principles for the five-year defense plan or estimate had been not to incur more than 1 percent of Japan's GNP for defense spending. There have been debates in Japan and within the National Defense Council over the question of whether to project Japan's total defense spending beyond that limit. A problem inherent in these estimates has been the rate of economic growth for Japan for a given period. For instance, in the second plan, 1983–87, based on the slower growth rate of 2–3 percent, the defense spending projected for the five-year period at $83 billion (240 yen to a dollar) would have pushed the amount beyond the 1 percent ceiling.[203] Thus, the 1987 defense budget was 15 percent of the GNP.[204]

Compounding the problem has been the constant pressure from the United States during the Reagan administration in the 1980s for Japan to modernize its SDF and assume a larger responsibility as the Soviet invasion of Afghanistan became a major concern. These concerns were expressed by the United States at the 1981 Joint Conference in Hawaii. Despite the controversy and pressure from the United States for defense buildup, the 1 percent ceiling has been a symbolic limit. For practical purposes there seems to be no real limit.

The extent of Japan's ability for a defense buildup is restrained by a number of factors. One is the constitutional prohibition for offensive military capability. Another is the antimilitary sentiment embraced by students and intellectuals, now somewhat strengthened by the recent electoral gains made by the opposition parties, particularly the Japanese Socialists. Japan's Asian neighbors also worry about a military buildup, as pressured by the United States, at the annual rate of 6 percent, and the expansion of Japan's sea power capacity to a radius of 1,000 miles from the island of Honshu. Furthermore, there is the need for precisely defining Japan's military role and responsibility in Northeast Asia, leaving aside the dramatic change that has taken place in Eastern Europe and the Soviet preoccupation with domestic unrest and reform.[205] Thus, it is necessary to review briefly the U.S.-Japan mutual security arrangement.

The key to Japan's defense policy has been the United States–Japan Treaty of Mutual Cooperation and Security of 1960, successor to the 1952 Security Treaty drawn up when Japan was still under U.S. occupation (during the Korean War). In addition, the 1954 Mutual Defense Assistance Agreement permitted Japan to purchase defense material from the United States and contract for training in the United States.

The most important part of the treaty is Article VI, which allows the stationing of U.S. forces in Japan and grants the United States the use of its land, air, and naval forces at facilities and areas in Japan. Before the announcement in February 1990 by the then secretary of defense Richard Cheney of intent to withdraw 5,000–6,000 U.S. troops from Japan in the next three years, the total U.S. forces stationed there was about 57,000. Japan has been assured that the cut would not involve U.S. combat troops in Japan. Total annual cost for maintaining American troops in Japan is put at $7 billion, up from $5.4 billion in 1987, adjusted because of a stronger yen. In accordance with the 1960 mutual security treaty, Japan has been contributing $1.7 billion, or 31 percent of the cost, for American miliary bases and for porting the 7th Fleet. In addition, the Japanese pay for the rental of privately owned land, making it free for U.S. military use. Japan also provides funds for family housing construction on military bases and pays the health and medical benefits for Japanese workers hired by the U.S. forces.[206] The United States has demanded that Japan assume a larger share of the burden, including paying for all yen-based costs (amounting to another $600 million) for the U.S. forces, such as workers' pay and utility bills.[207]

THE SDF ROLE ABROAD   In 1992, after several delayed attempts, Japan decided to send a civil administrative unit to a peacekeeping mission abroad in Cambodia. (Japan has been participating in United Nations peacekeeping missions in some trouble spots by dispatching only civilian personnel.) Also in 1992 plutonium from spent fuel for the nuclear power plants was shipped to Great Britain and France for processing and then was shipped back to Japan. With the unpredictable international terrorist activities, there was a fear that plutonium to and from Europe might be subject to hijacking. In order to safeguard the transshipment it was necessary to have Japan's navy component of the SDF provide an armed convoy escort. However, the shipment arrived in Japan at the beginning of 1993 without incident. There is also the fear by Japan's Asian neighbors about its overseas military role and the military buildup as renewed militarism of the pre-war Japan.[208] In a poll conducted in May 1990 by *Asahi Shinbun*, 50 percent of the respondents thought it was not necessary for Japan to commit to a defense buildup, since the Soviet threat had diminished in 1989–90.[209]

POLITICAL PERFORMANCE AND PUBLIC POLICY

China: Economic Reform and Market Socialism

The development of the Chinese economy has not been a smooth operation. On the contrary, it has been erratic and volatile. The Chinese revolutionary leaders experimented with a variety of strategies for the purpose of improving the living standards of the people and the material wealth of the society. Beginning in the 1950s it progressed from the Stalinist model of centralized planning in the form of five-year plans with emphasis on development of heavy industries to the chaotic and disruptive mass mobilization model with intensive use of human labor from 1958 to 1960. After returning to an orderly economic development and a period of recovery, it chose to emphasize local economic self-reliance and self-sufficiency while retaining centralized management of heavy transport industries and banking, only to be disrupted to a large extent by the Cultural Revolution in 1968–78. This was a decade of little growth, replete with disruption. Under the leadership of Deng Xiaoping, who came to power as a pragmatic reformer in 1978–79, the initial economic reform strategy shifted from heavy to light industries in order to increase consumer goods for a rapidly expanding population. More important, it became obvious to Chinese central planners and reformers alike that heavy industries consume an enormous amount of energy resources. Light industries require less energy and provide more jobs, particularly jobs for export trade to earn the much-needed foreign exchange, which in turn would enable China to acquire advanced technology.

The economic reform, which also involved opening China's doors to foreign investment and transfer of technology, prompted intensive political debate among the leaders, who were divided into two opposing camps of conservative hardliners and pragmatic reformers. Under the leadership of Deng Xiaoping, what gradually emerged has been the strategy of a socialist planned commodity (market) economy, or market socialism with Chinese characters. In the fall of 1992, the Chinese Communist Party congress embraced the "tools of capitalism" as "magic weapons" to deepen Deng's economic reform, now termed a revolution, to "liberate the productive forces" of China.[210]

Economic Performance Soon after the June 1989 Tiananmen crackdown on the students and intellectuals who demanded speedier economic reform, despite economic austerity and retrenchment, China's gross domestic growth (minus foreign investment) began to rise from 4 percent in 1989 to 5.2 percent in 1990, 7 percent in 1991, 7.8 percent in 1992. The forecast for 1993 is close to 8 percent.[211] Once again China is expecting a high growth period, as the central planners' control over the economy has been weakened by Deng Xiaoping's determination to accelerate the reform program, as illustrated by the March 1993 NPC endorsement to "preserve the reform." This rate of growth for China compares rather favorably with the fast growing economics of the NICs (new industrialized countries) of Asia for 1992: South Korea, 7.3 percent; Taiwan, 7.5 percent; and Singapore, 6.1 percent respectively.[212] Of course, comparative economic indicators show China lagged far behind the industrial power and wealth of Japan, as seen in Table 1.1. For 1989, the latest figure available shows that Japan's GNP was valued at $1.9 trillion (U.S. dollars) against China's $0.27 trillion. For personal per capita it was Japan's $15,888 against China's $258. Japan produced more than 105 million tons of steel in 1989 as compared to China's 60 million tons.

The Changing Government Role We don't really know how fast and how far the pragmatic reformers are willing to go in dismantling the centralized planned economy. From an ideological point of view, China has not completely discarded the "socialist road" in favor of the "capitalist road." In many ways it is a delicate balancing act on the part of China's elderly leaders in their efforts to maintain ideological purity on the one hand, and to employ to China's advantage the capitalist elements of markets on the other hand. In a February 1992 editorial the party control mouthpiece, the *People's Daily*, boldly called for embracing the elements of capitalism or Western culture for China's use in economic reform.[213] Its rationale was that economically backward nations with long histories of feudalism have correctly used capitalism to the material advancement of the people, implying without clearly identifying the economic and technological modernization process ushered in during the Meiji Restoration by Japan, as an example. While China has boldly and officially embraced capitalist elements in its continued economic reform, the heavy hand of state government interlocked with the party is still omnipresent. One of the most dramatic changes in China's government policy in recent years has been the introduction of agricultural (rural) reform, or the responsibility (incentive) system in 1980–82.

RURAL REFORM   It was a party resolution, after debate and discussion in the inner circle of leaders led by Deng, which called for the reinstitution of private plots and sideline production for the peasants. At the direction of the party's Central Committee, peasants as individuals or households were permitted to enter into contracts with the collective, under the almost defunct commune system, for land for a fixed farm output quota. Under the contract the peasants were to assume all responsibility for work on the land and to bear all responsibility for their own profit and loss. In 1984 the success of the rural incentive system prompted the controlling party leaders to "legitimatize" and "institutionalize" the contract for land and farm production system—dubbed by China observers as the "second land reform" after the forceful confiscation of land ownership in early 1950.

Then, in 1984–85, the party's Politburo embraced the reform concept, applicable instantaneously in all rural regions throughout China, of the specialized household system and rural industries of "a factory in every village"—thus gradually and increasingly lessening direction and control by the collective.

Typically, a specialized household signs a contract with the collective village for a piece of cultivatable land, forest, fruit orchard, fish pond, or grazing pasture. Under the contract, the specialized household is obligated to turn over a part of the income derived from the production to the collective, but is allowed to keep the rest. The specialized household must operate and manage its projects without any help from the township. It is the sole responsibility of the specialized household to make its own arrangements with other economic organizations based on market supply and demand. The state and the township come into the picture only when loans and credit are needed. While peasants engaged in specialized production must assume their own risks, they also keep the profits.

The introduction of specialized households in rural China has provided a distinct shift in China's agriculture from basically subsistence farming—providing enough grain to feed the families—to commercial commodity production.[214] Peasants operating under the specialized household contracts enter into service trades, commodity production, manufacturing, and transportation of locally produced goods to distant locations. Thomas Bernstein sees the new development not only as a major shift to commodity production, but also as a way of "unleashing the entrepreneurial talents of China's peasants."[215] The development of specialized households has enabled the peasants to diversify. Under this arrangement, peasants now grow any type of high-yield commercial commodity crop suitable to the land and able to be produced efficiently—as long as the grain quota imposed by the state is met. Diversification is not limited to farming, but extends to cottage industries as well.[216] The new system also allows more mobility for the peasants. During the off season rather than remaining idle peasants may leave their villages for more lucrative jobs at construction sites in nearby towns or cities.

The need to encourage peasants to specialize and diversify led to another important change in rural China. Land contracted from the collective can now be transferred from one household to another, allowing for the more efficient households to replace the less efficient. Specialized households may also form partnerships and companies, either by themselves or in joint ventures with the state or the marketing cooperatives. They can even hire workers as "helpers" under "labor exchange."

URBAN REFORM Rural reform was followed by urban reform, also mandated by the party reformers in spite of considerable opposition by the conservative hardliners. According to the 1984 party document a priority item for reform was to invigorate the state-owned enterprises (numbering about 400,000 with a total labor force of more than 80 million) by separating the ownership from the operational functions. Instead of exercising "excessive and rigid control," the party document said, a state-owned enterprise "should be truly made a relatively independent economic entity." This meant that such enterprises must operate and manage their own affairs, assume responsibility for their own profits and losses, and develop themselves as "legal persons with certain rights and duties."[217] The party decision called for the factory managers to assume "full responsibility" and the party leaders in factories and service enterprises to "provide active support," without interference, to managers so as to establish unified direction in production and operation.[218] This meant that factory managers must have the right to determine matters such as job description and performance for workers as well as the right to set wages and bonuses. Full responsibility also implied that managers must be responsible for profit and loss. As a departure from previous reforms, the October 1984 urban reform advocated the practice of profit retention. In the past, profits from state-owned enterprises had to be returned to the state treasury. The state, then, reallocated these funds as supplies and resources needed for production according to the state plan.

Closely related to the reform in managerial autonomy was the introduction of the industrial contract responsibility system. Under the factory responsibility system, the workers and the factory director sign a contract with the state obligating them to turn over "a certain amount of taxes and profits to the state" and allowing them to keep for their own use "any or almost any amount above the set quota." However, they must make up any amount below the quota.[219] Between 1985 and 1987, all small-sized state-owned enterprises with fixed assets of less than 1.5 million yuan (about $400,000)—mostly retail service, repair, and catering businesses—were to be leased out under contract to individuals or cooperatives for a period of five years. These arrangements were to be managed independently without state supervision, provided that rent and taxes were paid to the state treasury. According to one estimate, these new arrangements accounted for more than half of the value of total gross industrial output in China in 1985.[220]

Decentralization and decontrol under urban reform did not curb the growth of bureaucratic power and prerogatives. For more than thirty years, China had operated under a rigid system of centralized control. The party cadres, who held the decision power, had become a special privileged class. Reform in the urban areas yielded two conflicting trends. One was cadre resistance, or foot dragging, against introduction of the market mechanism called for by urban reform. Jan Prybyla has pointed out that in fact "marketization" threatened the bureaucracy's role as planners and supervisors.[221] At the same time, bureaucrats in the cadre system were the ultimate survivors. They had access to both information and power. Therefore, they were in a position to exploit the new circumstances to enrich themselves. Soon they had transformed their position and seized the unique opportunities made available to form instant "briefcase" companies. (These were bureaucratic entities organized overnight by the cadres who became the new owners of enterprises.) Many of these bureaucrat-entrepreneurs now behaved "like capitalists" and committed economic crimes, such as black-marketeering, embezzling public funds or resources, and "lining their own pockets."[222]

Large-Scale State-Owned Enterprises: Declining Influence The urban (factory) reform allowed existing large-scale state-owned enterprises not engaged in vital productive activities to become joint stock companies with limited liability.[223] New companies thus formed became shareholding enterprises "with stocks purchased by workers and individuals outside the enterprises."[224] In place of the heavy-handed government-party management style, a board of directors was to assume the overall management policies for the new shareholding enterprises. (The government, however, retained 51 percent of the stock, or the controlling shares, for these large-scale enterprises.) The arrangement also applied to joint ventures with participation from foreign investors. Members of the boards of directors could be shareholding or nonshareholding, the latter elected by and representing the interests of the workers and small individual shareholders.

In effect, urban enterprise reform created a "two-tier ownership" structure: (1) large and key enterprises with their controlled subsidiaries as industrial combines engaged in high-tech development, and (2) massive small enterprises, cooperative and individual enterprises with mixed ownership, but devoted to the processing of farm and sideline production and improvement of services in both urban and rural areas.

Large-scale state-owned enterprises in China are going through a difficult time. Some state-owned firms are in deep financial trouble because they no longer produce goods that people want or "they make too much of what people don't want."[225] Their goods are stockpiled in warehouses, and about 40 percent of these state-owned enterprises are in debt—estimated at (U.S.) $30–50 billion. Many were thinking of selling out to foreign investors.[226]

These enterprises were originally built with Soviet aid in the 1950s, and the machinery has become obsolete. For decades they operated under tight state controls and with government support. As market economy under the reform grew, the state-owned enterprises failed to keep up, and they now face the inevitable outcome of closing down for good.

Education While Japan introduced compulsory education during the Meiji modernization era (1867–1912), it was not until 1986 that the CCP proclaimed nine years of compulsory education for all school-aged children in China. A new national law was enacted by the National People's Congress in 1986 calling for a step-by-step implementation, beginning with urban areas by 1990, most rural areas by 1995, and for all backward areas by the end of this century. Under the law school-aged children in rural areas are guaranteed a nine-year compulsory education by the year 2000. The Seventh Five-Year Plan (1986–90) increased educational outlays by 72 percent to 116.6 billion yuan (about $40 billion). Under the national compulsory educational law local governments are permitted to collect "educational funds." The new law mandates that parents send their children to school and, thus, makes illegal the traditional practice of sending children into the field to work. The law prohibits recruitment of school-aged children for employment. It also prohibits local government officials from engaging in the practice of diverting (or misappropriating) funds earmarked for education, and local government is prohibited from seizing educational buildings for noneducational use.

However, in practice there has been no strict enforcement in rural areas for compulsory attendance by school-aged children. Primary schools in urban areas require five to six years of school. In 1990 over 122 million children were enrolled in primary schools. In 1989 there were about 47 million students enrolled at secondary schools, which provided three years of schooling. A major problem for China's primary and secondary education has been a teacher shortage. Not only has the morale of trained teachers been low, but there has been a widespread practice of recruiting teachers into lucrative employment in noneducational activities. The average monthly wage for a teacher in China has been about 50–60 yuan, the equivalent of U.S. $26, one of the lowest wages paid in China. It is no wonder that many teachers have left the profession.

In higher education, the main problem has been the limited number of students who can be admitted into the universities. In 1985 about 1.7 million secondary school graduates took the grueling three-day nationwide entrance examination in the hot and humid month of July, but only 560,000, about one-third, were admitted to the universities. China expects to increase total university enrollment to 7 million by the year 2000, as compared to 1.7 million in 1985–86 and 1.9 million in 1987. Only a slight yearly increase is expected in the total number of institutions of higher learning, numbered at 1,016 in 1986 and 1,054 in 1987.[227] In 1989 total enrollment in higher education in China was about 2 million students. By the year 2000 only about 8 to 9 percent of those who take the national entrance examinations will be admitted to the universities. This leaves a large number of disappointed, if not psychologically damaged, youth to be absorbed into gainful employment. It also creates the prospect of discontent and unrest among a significant number of talented young people.

A possible solution lies in the expansion of vocational education and training—a neglected area that needs to be emphasized. It is estimated that by the turn of the century China will need as many as 17 million polytechnic school graduates.[228] In fact, the number of junior and middle-level technicians and managers required for 1990 has been put at eight million—an enormous need that can be fulfilled only by expanded vocational education and training. The 1985 party decision on educational reform made it very clear that vocational and technical school graduates must be given preference in job assignments.[229] In 1984 there were only 3.7 million students enrolled in technical vocational schools, compared to over 45.5 million students enrolled in general middle schools.[230] The dire need for skilled technicians in all fields has resulted in an upsurge in part-time education for workers and staff members in state-owned enterprises. Special courses have been designed in areas such as computers, drafting, and accounting. Government departments, factories, and trade union congresses have set up schools to promote vocational education. Special courses are offered over radio and television or through correspondence arrangements. Television and radio universities graduated 160,000 students in 1984. These electronic universities, *Dianda* as they are known in Chinese, now enroll over 1 million students. It seems obvious that only through expanded vocational education funding by the central and local governments can unemployed youths become skilled workers in a rapidly expanding, but increasingly technically oriented economy.

Japan: National Consensus and Economic Miracle

Economic Performance Despite a slump in Japan's economy—corporate earnings plunged and joblessness rose to 2.3 percent in 1993—Japan is a supereconomic power in the world today. Its GNP was $1.9 trillion in 1986, second only to the United States, whose GNP was $4.86 trillion. In terms of personal per capita income, Japan stood at $15,888 against $19,800 for the United States. Japan has also become a financial superpower. According to figures released by Japan's External Trade Organization, in 1989 Japan's direct investment in the world was over $40 billion.[231] The market value of Japan's corporate capital in terms of stocks and bonds was $4 trillion, as compared to $3 trillion for the United States.[232] Nine of the world's ten largest banks are Japanese.[233]

FACTORS CONTRIBUTING TO JAPAN'S ECONOMIC SUCCESS There have been many explanations offered to answer the question: "What made Japan's economy a success?" Some attribute Japan's success to innovative Japanese management theories.[234] Others, led by Chalmers Johnson, argue that it was the unique role of government that formulated and implemented economic and industrial policies.[235] An earlier, but more popular, thesis has been that Japan placed emphasis on education and knowledge, and the dominant role of government for "meritocratic guidance and private initiative."[236]

The Government Role: The Corporate State Thesis It has been fashionable to argue that Japan's economic success is attributable mainly to the full play of capitalism under conditions of democracy in Japan. To use the words of T. J. Pempel, of Japan, Inc., in the mid-1950s there appeared in the outside world the "hoary image" of Japan as a monolith committed collectively to work hard and compete in the world market.[237] The Japanese nation, according to this image, behaved as though it were a corporate board of directors, a unified management with a coordinated set of high economic growth strategies.[238] For more than two decades the world viewed Japan as a success story, the result of capitalism and a free competitive market system.

In 1982 Johnson published his book in which he postulated the thesis that Japan was a "capitalist developmental state." Under this theory powerful national bureaucratic ministries, such as the Ministry of International Trade and Industry (MITI) and the Ministry of Finance, exist and operate in symbiotic relationship with corporate conglomerates in Japan to develop economic strategy and formulate national industrial policies.[239] Johnson argues that there is governmental intervention by all states in their economies in one form or another. In the case of Japan it is "the question of how the government intervenes and for what purposes."[240] The "corporate developmental state" is a system in which the "state intrudes into detailed operations of individual enterprises with measures intended to improve those operations..."[241] In Johnson's model the dominant function of the state, in the case of Japan, is not the setting of rules or regulations, but "the setting of such substantive social and economic goals...."[242]

There have been many explanations of the so-called economic miracle of Japan and proposals for competing with Japan: learning from Japan;[243] the proposition that what Japan has done is invent more efficient capitalism;[244] a call for a new American consensus by developing "a shared vision of our interests, purposes, priorities and values" and by advocating a policy of "managed trade" and the establishment of a new powerful MITI-like Cabinet-level department on trade and industry;[245] the containment of Japan's economic machine.[246] There is considerable support for Johnson's thesis that Japan is a "corporate developmental state" that is best described as a "bureaucratic authoritarianism" containing many undemocratic features that cannot and should not be replicated elsewhere.[247]

The case for developing Japan's superiority in electronics and computers is used here to illustrate the role of government in providing "administrative guidance"—government manipulation of economic activity through issuance of directives or decrees that make cooperation and compliance from business corporations possible—and nurturing the industry in long-range planning. Of the twelve national ministries, MITI is the most important and influential government agency in manipulating industrial policy, economic production, and market strategies. The ministry was the outcome of reorganization of the wartime munitions and commerce industry ministries under the U.S. occupation.[248] In fact, the 1949 Foreign Exchange and Foreign Trade Control Act under the occupation power, SCAP, transferred control over foreign exchange and international trade to the newly formed MITI (subsequently reorganized in 1952 and 1973) in order to reinvest initially foreign exchange funds in industries in order to speed up Japan's economic recovery.[249] Since then MITI has played a decisive role in the rapid development of new technology and market strategies in Japan's industrial development, particularly in the electronics industry. Thus, MITI is more than a think-tank. It is a powerful government agency that controls Japan's industrial policy, encompassing the "protection of domestic industries, development of strategic industries, and adjustment of the economic structure" to meet possible internal and external changes in order to safeguard the "national interest," as understood only by MITI bureaucrats.[250]

Case illustrations of MITI's role can have the following significance: (1) A governmental bureaucracy can help to develop a new technologically oriented industry; (2) with help from a government bureaucracy and cooperation through consensus on the part of private industry, a new market strategy can be developed to meet the high-growth objective; (3) the government bureaucracy can perform the task of "nursing" new industries.[251] MITI also assisted in forming "industrial cartels" with the enactment of appropriate legislation in the Diet, drafted largely by MITI bureaucrats for their former bosses who had become LDP Dietmen. MITI, through its authority in issuing licenses of foreign exchange to private industries, can force declining companies to form mergers in order to enhance production efficiency and competitiveness. Frequently, MITI serves as a forum for corporate executives, scientists, academicians, and politicians to develop consensus and unified strategy for industrial policy. Here MITI's ability to gather information and provide analysis becomes very crucial in persuading all concerned to develop consensus. The ministry can even order production cuts, as in the 1965 case of MITI's order to Sumitomo Metals. Growth industries generally obtain needed capital from banks and insurance companies for expansion once blessings are received from MITI. The ministry also attempts to protect small companies from complete domination by the giant enterprises.[252] MITI always serves as a "referee" in cases of forced sales of technology by foreign companies to Japanese competitors by ensuring that prices, royalty, and expert limits are placed in the contract when Japanese companies are in an unfavorable negotiation position.[253]

There is a caveat to the above discussion about Japan as a "corporate developmental state," or the "Japan, Inc." concept. Recent electoral politics, discussed earlier, indicate clearly declining control by the LDP and the rise of opposition parties in articulating and setting political agenda. As pointed out by some of the current studies, policymaking in Japan has become increasingly complex and less coherent in the 1980s and 1990s, and MITI can no longer force industries to follow the dictates of the bureaucrats.[254] There have been serious challenges to MITI's dominant control, a sign of increasing bureaucratic competition. And there are now many centers of influence and power in the political bargaining process instead of "the exertion of influence by fiat."[255]

The Oligarchical Corporate Groupings   There are the corporate groupings, or conglomerates, that have played an important role in Japan's success as a world economic power. Japanese corporations, large or small, are the key to understanding the Japanese economy. At the outset it must be pointed out that Japan has a dual economy in which 73 percent of the labor force in manufacturing, 87 percent in wholesale and retail distribution, and 69 percent in services are employed by small businesses.[256] The popular image of large-scale and ultramodern business corporations, the *kaisha,* which employ more than one thousand workers, constitutes only 0.2 percent, or more than 2,000, of all Japanese corporations.[257] And, more important, most large Japanese business corporations form even larger "economic groupings," the *keiretsu* or *garupu,* with complex networks in cross-share-holding of hundreds of "interrelated industrial, financial and commercial enterprises."[258] Both van Wolferen and Clyde V. Prestowitz list six such colossal conglomerates that play dominant roles in the Japanese economy and influence industrial policies: Mitsui, Mitsubishi, Sumitomo, Fugo, Sanwa, and Dai Ichi Kangyo Bank.[259] Added to the list of the six colossal "economic groups" are the new groups: Toyota, Hitachi, and Matsushita. Prestowitz points out that the six represent 17 percent of all business sales in Japan and 18 percent of the business profits, excluding the group's banking and insurance companies.[260] Most of the largest manufacturing companies are affiliated with one of the six. For instance, Toyota is associated with the Mitsui group and Nissan with the Fugo group. One colossal, the Sumitomo group, which has total sales of over $200 billion, has three key components in chemical, banking, and metal, which in turn control major subsidiary companies in a variety of businesses that include insurance, electric (the Nippon Electric Company), steel, electronics, oil, cement and glass, and metal.[261]

A major subsidiary company of the group can always count on the group's other affiliates to come to the rescue when in trouble. The case of the rescue of Mazda by the Sumitomo group in the 1970s is illustrative of how financial assistance and other needed help were given by the group and its affiliates to nurse Mazda back to being a healthy auto industry.[262] Members of the group, or *keiretsu,* often meet and exchange trade information regularly. In addition, members of the group deal and trade with each other—Hitachi has been the main supplier of electric goods to Nissan, for both are affiliates of the Fugo group. The six conglomerates as a whole serve as suppliers of raw materials, and sales and export agents in distribution, for the companies affiliated with the groups. They collectively handle half of Japan's nonoil imports.[263] In short, most major corporations in Japan are "linked" and affiliated with one of the colossal "economic groups" in a complex diversified "alliance of companies" in manufacturing, import-export trade, distribution of goods, and services. Of more significance is not only the carving up of the markets by these colossal *keiretsu*, but their incestuous corporate cross-holdings and mutual trading to prevent trade penetration by foreign companies. A recent study by a professor of business administration at Kobe University indicated that 45 percent of capitalization in shares for some of the 180 largest corporations in Japan is controlled by the top twenty shareholders affiliated with the colossal *keiretsu* such as Mitsui, Mitsubishi, and Sumitomo.[264] It is probably not an exaggeration that "the entire structure in each case is tied together by interlocking directorates," and that between 60 to 70 percent of all shares in the Tokyo stock exchange are held by the top corporations and financial institutions.[265]

Thus, the Japanese economy has an oligarchical corporate structure that is best described by the following: "The awesome combination of intertwined hierarchies nourish a myriad of subcontractor firms reaching right down to the small sweatshops, at which level one may still find whole families working a ten-hour day."[266] As pointed out by van Wolferen, it is this part of the Japanese dual economy that can be regarded as capitalism at play.[267]

Education   The key to the development of Japanese technocracy and the elevation of Japan as a world supereconomic power today is its educational system. The system contains a number of unique features that produce students with the highest intelligence in the world today—the mean national IQ score is over 111, as compared to the American norm of 100.[268] Japanese students from first to fifth grade generally score 10 percent higher in mathematics than their American counterparts.[269] The Japanese literacy rate is about 99 percent, the highest of any nation in the world today. Japan is an education-oriented and highly education conscious nation.

Since the introduction of universal compulsory education in Japan during the Meiji period (1867–1912) enrollment in elementary schools today is about 100 percent of school-aged children, or 9.6 million in 24,560 primary schools. In 1989 there were 516 million enrolled in secondary schools in Japan. In higher education Japan in 1989 had about 500 universities and graduate schools with more than 2 million students enrolled, excluding those enrolled in junior and technical colleges.

Even though there are more than 500 colleges and universities, plus numerous junior colleges, in Japan today, a large portion of the more than 40 percent secondary school graduates who enter into higher institutions of learning want to enroll in the prestigious and elite schools such as Tokyo, Kyoto, or Waseda. The entrance examination to top-flight universities usually requires a student's mastery of mathematics and an almost encyclopedic accumulation of facts. It is strictly a competitive merit system and excludes consideration of a student's other attributes, wealth, and social class.

The competitive-elitist admission system to the prestigious universities is related to another unique feature of its technocratic education system: The recruitment of college graduates into government and industry tends to center in one or two top-flight universities. In the early 1980s, Tokyo University graduates accounted for 40 percent of the presidents of Japan's leading companies, and another 40 percent of company presidents came from the other four prestigious universities of Kyoto, Keio, Waseda and Hitotsubashi.[270] A large percentage of government bureaucrats in a number of national ministries recruited graduates of Tokyo University who had high scores on separate examinations administered by the ministries, and so have a majority of Japan's prime ministers and leading politicians who were graduates of prestigious universities, particularly Tokyo University. The dominance of Tokyo University graduates in top governmental positions, business, science, and technology is undeniable. The principle of meritocracy in a technocratic Japanese system encourages ambitious graduates of less academic attainment, measured by competitive examinations, to enter into employment with medium- and small-sized companies by "taking big risks to achieve extraordinary gains" in order to compensate for their lesser academic talents.[271]

Finally, the Japanese education system places emphasis on the attainment of general, but not specialized, education. It should be noted that more than 65 percent of the working force in Japan has at least a high school education. The general education curriculum consists entirely of solid academic subjects: mathematics, biology or general science, foreign languages and world history. There are vocational schools, established since the 1970s, at the high school level, but students prefer to take general education courses as preparation for a college education.

SUGGESTED READINGS

China

Ch'i, Hsi-Sheng. *Politics of Disillusionment: The Chinese Communist Party under Deng Xiaoping, 1978–1989.* Armonk, NY: M.E. Sharpe, 1991.

Gittings, John. *China Changes Face: The Road from Revolution, 1949–1989.* London and New York: Oxford University Press, 1990.

Gu, Zhibin. *China beyond Deng: Reform in the PRC*. New York: McFarland, 1991.

Harding, Harry. *China's Second Revolution: Reform after Mao*. Washington, DC: Brookings Institution, 1988.

Hsu, Immanuel C. Y. *China without Mao: The Search for a New Order*. London and New York: Oxford University Press, 1990.

Mackerras, Colin, and Amanda Yorke. *The Cambridge Handbook of Contemporary China*. London: Cambridge University Press, 1992.

McCormick, Barrett I. *Political Reform in Post-Mao China: Democracy and Bureaucracy in a Leninist State*. Berkeley: University of California Press, 1990.

Nathan, Andrew J. *China's Crisis: Dilemmas of Reform and Prospects for Democracy*. New York: Columbia University Press, 1991.

Ogden, Susanne. *China's Unresolved Issues: Politics, Development, and Culture*, 2nd ed. Englewood Cliffs, NJ: Prentice Hall, 1992.

Rosenbaum, Arthur Lewis. *State and Society in China: The Consequences of Reform, 1992*. Boulder, CO: Westview Press, 1992.

Townsend, James R., and Brantly Womack. *Politics in China*. 3rd ed. New York: HarperCollins, 1992.

Unger, Jonathan, ed. *The Pro-Democracy Protests in China*. Armonk, NY: M.E. Sharpe, 1992.

Wang, James C. F. *Contemporary Chinese Politics, An Introduction*, 4th ed. Englewood Cliffs, NJ: Prentice Hall, 1992.

White, Lynn T. III. *Policies of Chaos: The Organizational Causes of Violence in China's Cultural Revolution*. Princeton: Princeton University Press, 1991.

Japan

Abegglen, James C., and George Stalk, Jr. *Kaisha: The Japanese Corporation*. New York: Basic Books, 1985.

Akita, George. *Foundations of Constitutional Government in Modern Japan*. Cambridge, MA: Harvard University Press, 1967.

Buckley, Roger. *Japan Today*, 2nd ed. New York: Columbia University Press, 1990.

Bunge, Frederica M., and Donald P. Whitaker, eds. *Japan: A Country Study*. Washington, DC: U.S. Government Printing Office, 1983.

Burstein, Daniel. *Yes! Japan's New Financial Empire and Its Threat to America*. New York: Fawcett Columbine, 1990.

Calder, Kent E. *Crisis and Compensation: Public Policy and Political*

Stability in Japan, 1949–1986. Princeton: Princeton University Press, 1988.

Cohen, Theodore. *Remaking Japan: The American Occupation as New Deal*, Herbert Passin, ed. New York: Free Press, 1987.

Curtis, Gerald L. *Election Campaigning Japanese Style*. New York: Columbia University Press, 1971.

————. *The Japanese Way of Politics*. New York: Columbia University Press, 1990.

Kim, C. I. Eugene, and Laurence Ziring. *An Introduction to Asian Politics*. Englewood Cliffs, NJ: Prentice Hall, 1977.

Langdon, Frank. *Politics in Japan*. Boston: Little, Brown, 1967.

Lincoln, Edward J. *Japan: Facing Economic Maturity*. Washington, DC: Brookings Institution, 1988.

Maki, John M. *Government and Politics in Japan: The Road to Democracy*. New York: Praeger, 1962.

Morley, James W., ed. *Security Interdependence in the Asian-Pacific Region*. Lexington, MA: D.C. Heath, 1986.

Okimoto, Daniel I. *Between MITI and the Market: Japanese Industrial Policy for High Technology*. Stanford: Stanford University Press, 1990.

O'Neil, Robert J. *The Samurai Have Landed: Understanding the Global Success of Japan*. New York: Vantage Press, 1989.

Pempel, T. J. *Policy and Politics in Japan: Creative Conservatism*. Philadelphia: Temple University Press, 1982.

Pharr, Susan J. *Political Women in Japan*. Berkeley: University of California Press, 1980.

Prestowitz, Clyde V., Jr. *Trading Places: How We Allowed Japan to Take the Lead*. New York: Basic Books, 1988.

Pye, Lucian W. *Asian Power and Politics: The Cultural Dimensions of Authority*. Cambridge, MA: Belknap Press of Harvard University Press, 1985.

Reischauer, Edwin O. *The Japanese*. Cambridge, MA: Belknap Press of Harvard University Press, 1978.

Richardson, Bradley M., and Scott C. Flanagan. *Politics in Japan*. New York: Harper and Collins, 1990.

Tsurutani, Taketsugu. *Political Change in Japan: Response to Postindustrial Challenge*. New York: David McKay, 1977.

van Wolferen, Karel. *The Enigma of Japanese Power: People and Politics in a Stateless Nation*. New York: Knopf, 1989.

Vogel, Ezra E. *Japan as Number One: Lessons for America.* Cambridge, MA: Harvard University Press, 1979.

Ward, Robert E. *Japan's Political System*, 2nd ed. Englewood Cliffs, NJ: Prentice Hall, 1978.

Welfield, John. *An Empire in Eclipse: Japan in the Postwar American Alliance System.* London: Athlone Press, 1988.

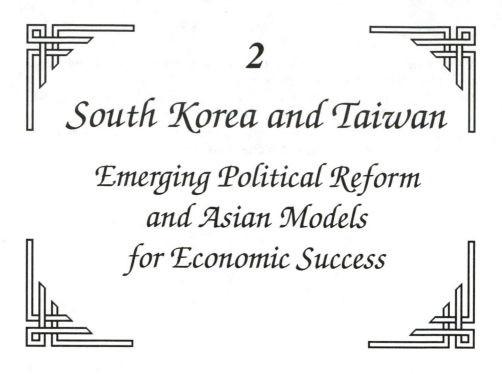

2

South Korea and Taiwan

Emerging Political Reform and Asian Models for Economic Success

In addition to the fact that South Korea and Taiwan were Japanese colonies before World War II, there are a number of developmental experiences that both countries have in common. First, the Chinese Confucian influence dominates people's daily lives, the style of leadership, and the centralized governmental structure. Second, both South Korea and Taiwan have emerged from the dominance of military and one-party control in politics to that of democratic pluralism. Third, both South Korea and Taiwan are experimenting with a presidential form of government. And, finally, at about the same time, both countries have become the East Asian model in economic development by adopting a new strategy—from what has been termed "import-substituting industrialization (ISI)" to "export-oriented industrialization (EOI)".[1] Of course, there have been many important differences as well as the comparable stages of development—all of which are discussed in this chapter.

As an introduction we begin with a brief discussion about South Korea and Taiwan with a description of the land and the people.

THE CASE OF THE KOREAN PENINSULA

The Korean peninsula, bordered by the Yellow Sea on the west and the Sea of Japan on the east, lies strategically in the northeastern corner of Asia sharing boundaries with China's Manchuria to the north and Siberia to the northeast. Then the peninsula extends southwestward to within 195 miles of the southern islands of Honshu, Japan. This strategic location of the Korean peninsula provides a key to understanding Korea's historic development—that is, it has become the object of international rivalry.

Total land area of the Korean peninsula is about 85,000 square miles. However, 80 percent of the peninsula is mountainous and too rugged for agriculture. Only about 20 percent consists of lowlands, coastal plains, and river valleys suitable for cultivation. But another key point is that the Korean peninsula is divided, the result of international rivalry in 1945 at the end of World War II. The 38th parallel served then, as now, as the line of demarcation between North Korea (People's Democratic Republic of Korea) and South Korea (Republic of Korea).

There are six major rivers: the Yalu, Tumen, Taedong, Han, Kum, and Naktong on the Korean peninsula—useful mainly for irrigation and for generating hydroelectric power, as they are swift, short, and unsuitable for navigation. Most of the rivers empty into the Yellow Sea, except the Tumen, which flows for some 300 miles and empties into the Sea of Japan. The Tumen River Area Development Program will involve as many as six regional powers in northeastern Asia: South and North Korea, China, Japan, Russia, and Mongolia. The river valleys are utilized as fertile farm lands.

The Korean peninsula has a coastline of about 5,400 miles. There are fine harbors on the east, west, and south coasts, such as Wosan, Inchon, and Pusan. Coastal plains also contain fertile farmlands. An average yearly rainfall of 30 to 40 inches is generally expected for more than half of the peninsula, mostly in the months from April to September. South Korea's plains are more extensive and the winter climate is milder than North Korea. With a smaller area, South Korea supports twice the population than that of North Korea. Since the agricultural soils for farming are mainly alluvial and are found in river valleys and on coastal plains, they are usually infertile and sandy unless heavily fertilized during cultivation. The Korean peninsula is endowed with coal deposits, iron ore, copper, gold, silver, and tungsten (a hard metallic element that is resistant to corrosion and heat). However, most of the resources—coal deposits, metals, and hydroelectric power—are found in North Korea.

Total population of the Korean peninsula is about 65 million, and is distributed in politically divided Korea as follows: 21.9 million, or 34 percent, in North Korea, and 43.4 million, or 66 percent, in South Korea. The Korean people are ethnically homogeneous, for they all belong to a branch of the Mongoloid ethnic division, originate from the northern part of central Asia, and share a common history, language, and culture. There is a continuing demographic trend toward more urban growth in both North and South Korea. Urban growth reached a rate of 5 percent per year in South Korea—resulting in more than 50 percent living in cities of more than 150,000 inhabitants; this urbanization resulted from rapid industrialization in the 1970s and 1980s. The capital city of Seoul has a population of about 8.4 million, 23 percent of South Korea's population. In short, one can make an overall generalization that, compared with North Korea, there are twice as many people in South Korea, but less land area. And, also, there has been a steady increase in population in the past decades for the Korean peninsula as a whole caused primarily by a relatively high birthrate and a declining death rate.

THE CASE OF TAIWAN

The Republic of China, hereafter referred to as Taiwan, consists not only of the island of Taiwan (or Formosa), but also some sixty-four small islands in the Pescadores, or P'eng-hu group, plus the offshore islands of Chinmen (Quemoy) and Maza (Matsu), just a few miles off the Chinese mainland province of Fujian. The main island of Taiwan measures 250 miles in length and 80 miles in width with a total land area of 13,900 square miles (36,000 square kilometers), about one-third the size of Ohio. It is shaped like a tobacco leaf and lies about 115 miles off the southeast coast of mainland China, the People's Republic of China (PRC). Taiwan (Republic of China) has laid claim to the continental shelf between the Taiwan group of islands and Japan—the overlapping claim centered recently in the dispute over the Diaoyutai (Senkaku) Islands between Japan and Taiwan. Over the protests of the PRC, in 1970 Taiwan and Japan agreed to exploit jointly the oil resources in the overlapped continental shelf.[2]

Roughly half of Taiwan Island is mountainous covered with thick forests. Yu Shan, the Jade Mountain, has an elevation of more than 13,000 feet above sea level. Water for the island's rivers originates in the central mountains. All the rivers have short courses with rapid streams, and they do not create flood problems. While the rivers are not suitable for navigation or transport, they have been used for hydroelectric power-generating projects. The mountains on the eastern coast of Taiwan drop sharply to the sea, and there are mountain slopes on the west and north coasts to provide tidal flats and some of the best harbors, such as Kaohsiung and Keelung.

Most of Taiwan's land is not suitable for cultivation—only about 25 percent is being used for farming along the western alluvial plains and on the terraced hillsides. Rice farmers can expect three plantings each year with high yields. Farms are small, averaging 2 to 3 acres in size.

The total population of Taiwan is about 20 million, with an annual growth rate of 1.2 percent. The projection for the year 2000 would most likely be 22 million.[3] The population density is about 1,424 persons per square mile, thus making Taiwan one of the world's most densely populated nations. About 67 percent of its population are considered urban and the rest rural. It is a rather young population with 56 percent under twenty years of age.[4]

POLITICAL CULTURE AND POLITICAL DEVELOPMENT

South Korea: From Colonial Rule to Independence and War

Historic Legacies Soon after its vassalage under the Chinese Han dynasty (100 B.C.), a unified Korean empire was established, known as the Silla dynasty.

The Silla rule, 668–892 A.D., was characterized by the influence of Chinese culture and system of government administration. A central administrative service, modeled after the Tang dynasty, was installed and recruited by competitive examination (open only to sons of aristocracy), which in turn relied on learning of the Confucian classics. Silla rulers built extravagant palaces and a state capital, a replica of Ch'angan under the Chinese Tang dynasty. The rulers also borrowed from China the systems of local and provincial administrative arrangement and taxation. Buddhism entered the peninsula in the fourth century and flourished, particularly among the aristocracy.

The Silla dynasty declined about 780 A.D., when violent regional rebellions erupted over succession, aggravated by corruption, peasant riots over taxes, and famine. These disturbances paved the way for the rise of provincial lords in a prolonged contest for power. Then came the Mongol invasion, which ravaged the nation until 1258 A.D., when a peace agreement was negotiated with the ruling Mongols, who supervised the government administration and collection of taxes. It was not until the Yi dynasty (1392–1910 A.D.) that the name *Chosen* ("Morning Calm") was adopted for Korea. In recorded history, it was the longest continuous ruling dynasty, with twenty-six monarchs spanning over 500 years, even though its founding had the blessing of the powerful Chinese emperor next door.

Political Belief The Yi dynasty was characterized by a number of significant developments during its long rule in the peninsula. First, its rulers installed Confucianism as the political and moral basis of government. In fact, the precepts of Confucianism had been carried out in extreme forms: a civil service examination system exclusively reserved for the hereditary nobility, debate over the duration of funeral services, child marriage, banning of remarriage by widows, untrained civil officials over the military, replacement of Buddhism by Confucian code ethics, and recruitment of Confucian scholars into important government positions. However, Korea, or Chosen, was mainly a Chinese tributary state.

The traditional social structure was basically Confucian. The Yangban, the elites, at the top of the social structure extolled the Confucian doctrine that the state was ruled by men of virtue and talent who were knowledgeable in the Confucian classics. Human relationship was defined in a code of ethics and all in society were obligated to strive for harmony with nature. The Korean traditional social structure was hierarchical and denied individual rights. All were required to exercise control over one's own emotions and were subservient to social obligations of status and authority. Filial piety and extended families were the basis of social and economic life. Nowadays, in South Korea, it is common for the father in a nuclear family to support sons through thirty or forty years of age until the eldest one is able to look after the aged parents—a built-in social welfare system. Family values stress the work ethic, and workers in factories place a high value on self-sacrifice, hard work, and a sense of pride in achievement.

International Rivalry and Western Impact   After almost two centuries of relative peace, Japan embarked on its invasion of the Korean peninsula in 1592 A.D., when soldiers of Hideyoshi captured Hanyang (Seoul), the capital of the Yi dynasty. The Japanese invasion was repelled by military aid from the Chinese Ming army and navy. In 1597 a second Japanese attempt to invade Chosen soon collapsed after Hidyoshi's death a year later. However, as the Manchus conquered China, it also mounted two successive invasions in Chosen in 1627 and 1636. Wrecked by wars with Japan and China, Korea, under the Yi dynasty, suffered economic destruction so severe that it accepted China's claim to overlordship of the entire peninsula by the mid-seventeenth century. In spite of economic problems facing the Yi regime, factional strife became rampant, followed by purges, administrative paralysis and official corruption. In the early years of the nineteenth century the regime was faced with drought, famine, and peasant rebellions. And, finally, like China and Japan, the Yi dynasty was under Western pressure to open its doors for contact and trade. The introduction of Catholicism into Chosen was permitted in the sixteenth century, but by the mid-nineteenth century Catholic converts were being persecuted. The Yi dynasty finally bowed to pressure by signing treaties with Japan in 1876 and with European powers in 1882. For over a decade, from 1882 to 1894, the Chinese exercised control over the peninsula; the Korean military insurrection in 1882 had provided the Chinese with the pretext for dispatching an expeditionary force to Seoul. Thus, for a quarter century, from 1876 to 1905, Korea was the prize in international rivalry between China, Japan, and Russia.

Russian interest in the Korean peninsula began in the late eighteenth century as Russia expanded into its Far Eastern maritime provinces. Russia, after the Sino-Japanese War of 1894–95, desired to expand its influence southward over the Korean peninsula and Manchuria in northeast China. Russian troops were stationed in Manchuria, presumably to protect the trans-Siberian railroad. Korea became the focal point of the contest between Japan and Russia. Japan demanded troop withdrawal and recognition of Japan's paramount interest in Korea. Result: the Russo-Japanese War.

***Korea under Japan, 1910–1945*[5]**   The Russo-Japanese War, 1904–05, was fought over Russia's refusal to recognize Japan's imperial interest in Korea and Manchuria. When Japanese naval forces attacked Port

Arthur, then a Russian naval base on the Yellow Sea, the Korean government declared its neutrality. Through mediation by President Theodore Roosevelt, the Russo-Japanese War was terminated by the 1905 Treaty of Portsmouth. In effect, the treaty granted Japan "paramount political, military and economic interests in Korea." By a subsequent pact between the United States and Japan, the Taft-Katsura agreement of 1906, the latter gained practical control of the Korean peninsula. By 1910 it had annexed Korea as a Japanese possession.

The thirty-five-year rule of Korea by Japan was best characterized as an imperial rule accompanied by suppression. As a colony, Korea was governed by a high-ranking Japanese military officer, and the colonial administration was staffed by Japanese. Order was maintained by a brutal police force, trained and backed by the Japanese military garrison. The Koreans were not permitted to exercise freedom of the press, speech, or assembly. The Korean language was forbidden in schools, and children were asked to adopt Japanese names and worship at Shinto shrines.

Economic policy under Japanese rule was geared to exploitation of resources in the Korean peninsula for the benefit of the Japanese empire. Development in communication and transportation infrastructures and hydroelectric power was undertaken for the purpose of delivering needed raw materials to industrial plants in Japan. Korea became a market for Japanese goods and investment. There was extensive appropriation of land through a land-claim reporting decree, which deprived Korean farmers of their land ownership. In addition, agricultural activities concentrated on rice production to meet Japan's shortage.

The oppressive Japanese rule brought about a resistance movement in Korea. Motivated to a large part by President Woodrow Wilson's pronouncement in 1919 for self-determination and independence, peaceful rallies were held throughout the peninsula in the spring. On March 1 a rally in Seoul, with participation by students and citizens, called for independence. While about 2 million people took to the streets, leaders of the movement met in a restaurant and issued a Declaration of Independence for Korea. They then notified the Japanese authorities and surrendered. The Japanese response to the independence movement was brutal suppression. Police and armed soldiers arrested more than 40,000 Koreans and killed nearly 20,000 of them. A number of the movement leaders, among them Syngman Rhee, fled to Shanghai, China, and formed a provisional Korean government. This marked the end of the *Samil* ("March 1") independent movement under Japanese rule. The exiled Korean independence movement in China was largely ineffective because of factional bickering among its leaders. When war broke out in China in 1936–37, the exiled movement splintered into two opposing factions: Syngman Rhee's group, which formed a fighting unit as a part of the Chinese Nationalist forces, and a procommunist faction, which operated a guerrilla force, the Northeast Anti-Japanese

United Army, under a Chinese communist commander, in the Korean-Manchurian border area.[6] The provisional government of Korea in wartime China declared war on Japan in 1942, and its small army fought in China until the Japanese surrendered in 1945, ending Japanese rule in Korea.

Liberation and Partition, 1945–1950[7]   The postwar future of Korea as a free and independent nation was determined by three Allied conferences: the 1943 Cairo Conference and the 1945 Yalta and Potsdam conferences. The communique issued in Cairo on December 1, 1943, by the three Allied leaders—Franklin Roosevelt, Winston Churchill, and Chiang Kai-shek—stated that Japan must return all occupied territories after its defeat to China, and declared that Korea must be set free and become independent in due course. At the Yalta Conference in February 1945, the Soviet Union endorsed the Cairo agreement and pledged its war against Japan as soon as Adolf Hitler's Germany could be defeated. At the July 1945 Potsdam Conference the Allied leaders defined the terms of Japan's unconditional surrender and restricted Japan's sovereignty to only its home islands. The Soviet Union declared war on Japan on August 8, 1945, one week before Japan's surrender on August 15. Within a very short period after its declaration of war against Japan, the Soviet forces marched swiftly into Manchuria and entered into the northern tip of the Korean peninsula. By August 15, 1945, the Soviet troops were already in North Korea and moving southward. On September 8 the U.S. forces arrived in South Korea via the sea route and established an occupation government, one month after Soviet entry into the war against Japan. Evidently there was a general agreement, probably reached August 11–13, 1945, between the United States and the Soviet Union that the former would accept Japan's surrender south of the 38th parallel and the Soviet Union north of it.

Who, how, and why the 38th parallel line of occupational division was determined have been a historical mystery to this day. One possible origin of the 38th parallel division could be a simple decision of convenience, a hasty one at that, to permit the two powerful armies of the United States and the Soviet Union to divide the peninsula for the purpose of accepting the Japanese surrender. Or the decision could have been made in Washington to prevent the Soviet armies from overrunning the entire peninsula. Thus, on August 13, 1945, the United States could have proposed the 38th parallel as a division for temporary occupation zones, and the proposal then accepted by the Soviet Union. There might have been some agreement reached at the 1945 Yalta Conference to encourage Soviet entry into the Pacific war by allowing its troops to occupy the latitudes north of the 38th parallel.[8] However, for whatever reason, the partition of Korea by the Allied powers was to be only temporary. Failure to unify a divided Korea and its continuance to this date of the wartime partition are tragic, for once again the people of the Korean peninsula have become victims of power politics.

Within less than a year after the two powerful forces occupied the Korean peninsula, the divided regimes south and north of the 38th parallel became fixed. In the United States occupation zone, the American military commander, Lieutenant General John P. Hodge, attempted to provide an orderly administration and to foster the development of self-government under Korean leadership to be supported by democratic political parties. General Hodge failed to accomplish the latter task as rival political groups formed along conservative (Right) and radical (Left) lines. The recognized Korean independence advocate, Syngman Rhee, returned to Seoul from his exile in Hawaii to lead the Korean Democratic party of conservative landlords and businessmen in a political contest with the Korean provisional government having close ties to the Chinese Nationalist in wartime China. There was also the leftist element, which supported the Korean provisional republic formed by a group of political leaders prior to the arrival of the U.S. army in September 1945. Caught between the rival political forces of the Left and the Right in South Korea, General Hodge was unsuccessful in forging a united political leadership.[9]

Taiwan: Disputed Legal Status

Historic Legacies   Part of the tourist attraction to Taiwan are the exhibits of the aborigines of Taiwan. Most anthropologists adhere to the theory that the original people of Taiwan migrated from Malay tribes to these islands, for there are linguistic similarities between the two cultural groups. Some, however, propose that the aborigines in Taiwan were related to the Miao people from southern China.[10] At any rate, Chinese migration to Taiwan occurred during the Tang dynasty in the seventh and eighth centuries. And the first Chinese settlement did not take place until the fourteenth century under the Yuan, or the Mongol rule. It was during the seventeenth century that Western contact with Taiwan began.

First, around 1517 Portuguese sailors sighted and named the islands *Formosa*, the "beautiful islands." In 1624 the Dutch arrived in southern Taiwan and used it as a base for harassing the Portuguese, and in 1626 the Spanish arrived at the northern portion of the island. In 1642 the Dutch drove out the Spanish, and by 1661 Chinese Ming loyalists under Cheng Chi Lung, a pirate in the Taiwan Strait who married a Japanese or Okinawan, had driven out the Dutch and passed rule over the islands to his legendary son, Koxinga. For years before Koxinga's rule and thereafter he raided the coast of Fujian province on the mainland for the purpose of harassing the Manchu Empire, which had conquered China. The Manchu authorities evacuated the coastal areas in fear of Koxinga's marauding pirates. During this evacuation the Fujian people migrated to the Taiwan islands. In 1663 Manchu troops finally prevailed and the islands became a part of the vast Manchu empire. For the period from 1663 to 1895 Taiwan was administered as a part of the Fujian province. The Manchu empire had no interest in providing effective and efficient rule for the islands, which were beset with uprisings and rebellions to the extent that China was reluctant to even claim its sovereignty over Taiwan. This indicated to the Western powers, including the United States, that China was not really interested in possessing the islands, even though more than 200,000 mainland Chinese had sought refuge there before its war with Japan in 1895.

Japanese Rule, 1895–1945   In 1886 Taiwan became a province of the Chinese empire. Three years later the Sino-Japanese War was fought over the control of Korea. By the Treaty of Shimonoseki, signed on April 17, 1895, China ceded to Japan the island of Taiwan and the Pescadore Islands, in addition to suzerainty over Korea and the Liaodong Peninsula. For the next fifty years, Japan fully exploited Taiwan's agricultural resources in rice and sugar, as well as vegetables, meat and fruit, which were exported to Japan to meet the people's food needs. The Japanese also built roads, railroads, a communication system, modern banking facilities, and hydroelectric projects. There were also improvements in health and education. Taiwan was for all intents and purposes a colony that served the needs of the Japanese nation. The Japanese also established in Taiwan a regimented political control system that divided the population into households with the head of each 100 households responsible for law and order.[11] Political stability, except for occasional aborigine uprisings in the mountainous areas, and economic improvements enabled the doubling of Taiwan's population on the eve of Japan's war in the Pacific. By the 1940s Taiwan had already become a formidable Japanese military base in the Pacific.

Chinese Nationalist Rule, 1947–Present   At the Potsdam Conference held from July 17 to August 1, 1945, the leaders of the Allied powers—Harry Truman, Clement Attlee and Joseph Stalin—dictated the terms of Japanese surrender to include implementation of the Cairo Declaration: Namely, Japan was to be confined to its home islands and Taiwan was to be returned to China. The Japanese forces and the colonial administration departed Taiwan in the fall of 1945. By October Nationalist Chinese authorities had taken military and political control of Taiwan, and Taiwan became a province of China. Chiang Kai Shek appointed General Chen Yi the military governor. Immediately, ill feelings developed under the military government between the Taiwanese and the Nationalists. Some of the ill feelings or distrust exhibited by both were caused by the inability to communicate in their own languages, for the Taiwanese spoke the language akin to the southern Fujian dialect, which was not understood by most of the Mandarin-speaking Nationalists. The Nationalists maintained the feeling that the Taiwanese were collaborators for the Japanese. The Nationalists were preoccupied with civil war on the mainland and paid little attention to Taiwanese problems.[12]

The accumulated ill will and distrust came to a head on February 28, 1947, when an initial disagreement over black marketeering in cigarettes escalated into a full-blown uprising against the Nationalists, who were obsessed by fears of communist infiltration among the Taiwanese. A crackdown on the populace was ordered by the military governor; it resulted in the killing of as many as 28,000—some private estimates placed the slain in the range of 100,000.[13] The 1947 massacre was not openly revealed until 1992, when an official investigation report of twelve volumes was made public by leaders of the ruling Kuomintang (KMT). While there were no official apologies as demanded by some, except expression of regrets by President Lee Teng Hui, there have been discussions about possible compensation for the victims' families and the designation of February 28 as a memorial day.[14]

Taiwan's Legal Status Disputed   As Mao Zedong's forces gained victories on the battlefields in China's raging civil war, preparation was made by the Nationalists to retreat to Taiwan. By late September 1949 some 2 million Nationalist government officials and soldiers, plus their dependents, were evacuated to the island of Taiwan in wholesale retreat from the mainland which Mao proclaimed on October 1, 1949, as the Peoples' Republic of China. In the meantime, the Nationalists under Chiang Kai Shek vowed to reconquer the mainland in the name of the Republic of China, now exiled to Taiwan. A state of civil war continued, but only to be quarantined or restrained by the U.S. 7th Fleet in the Strait of Formosa.

Nationalist security in Taiwan was guaranteed by the 1954 Mutual Security Treaty, signed between the United States and the Nationalist government in Taiwan, which still claimed to be the lawful government of all China. Soon a diplomatic battle began at the United Nations over the question as to which side should lawfully represent the people of China—the Nationalists were seated at the organs of the United Nations as the Chinese representatives. This contest was finally terminated in 1971, when the Nationalist representatives were unseated and replaced by the People's Republic of China as the United States and PRC moved closer to rapprochement. When the United States recognized the PRC as the only legitimate government for China, the 1954 Mutual Security Treaty was also terminated and replaced by the 1979 Taiwan Relations Act, under which the United States maintained economic and cultural contacts with Taiwan.[15] In addition, the Taiwan Relations Act also permitted the United States to provide defensive arms for Taiwan. U.S. Arms sales to Taiwan aroused controversy in U.S.-PRC relations in the 1980s.[16] By 1991 Taiwan's isolation had been eased as more than twenty nations had established diplomatic relations with it, excluding the expanding commercial and trade relations, including that with the Soviet Union before its disintegration.

Unofficial contacts with the PRC began in the mid-1980s with travel permitted to the people of Taiwan to visit relatives on the mainland. There has been a flourishing bilateral trade across the Taiwan Straits. In 1987 the ruling KMT made a significant decision to end the martial law, which had been enforced for almost four decades in Taiwan. As Taiwan became more prosperous economically and old-guard political leaders aged, the desire for democratic political reform was more evident. In the separate sections to follow, these reforms are discussed fully.

LOCUS OF POWER: POLITICAL INSTITUTIONS AND LEADERSHIP

South Korea: From Patriarchal Leader to Military-Bureaucratic Authoritarianism

By the end of the Korean War in 1953, the separate regimes of North and South Korea had been solidified: one a Stalinist-totalitarian superstate and the other a military-bureaucratic authoritarian system struggling and searching for a workable constitutional government.

After months of protests by students for political change and reform, against whom the government's bill for tear gas alone was estimated at $1.5 million per month, the Sixth Republic was inaugurated in February 1988 under newly elected President Roh Tae Woo, a former high-ranking army general. He had been chosen at the December 16, 1987, presidential election. Political changes in South Korea since 1948 had been characterized by the designation of a sequentially recognized republic with a constitution or constitutional amendments (see Table 2.1).

The President   A constant nagging constitutional debate in South Korea has been whether there should be a presidential system of government or parliamentary system. Should the president be elected by direct popular vote, or by a form of electoral college? Related to that fundamental question of governance has been the term or tenure for the president: four years, six years, or life tenure? The first constitution, drafted in 1948, had designed a parliamentary form of government, with the president serving merely as a titular head of state, and the power vested in a premier elected by the National Assembly. The 1952 and 1954 amendments to the 1948 constitution provided the popularly elected Syngman Rhee with an unlimited term. Rhee was forced to resign after the 1960 election due to widespread discontent with his autocratic rule, election fraud, an economic depression, corruption, and student demonstrations.

Table 2.1 Constitutional Changes in South Korea, 1948–1988

Republic	Date	President/Strongman	Remarks
1st	1948–60	Syngman Rhee	First constitution drawn up in a month in July 1948; amended in 1952 and 1954 to provide unlimited terms for Rhee; student protests forced Rhee to resign after 1960 election.
2nd	1960–61	Chang Myon military junta rule	New Constitution for election of president by National Assembly; military coup on May 16, 1960, ended the 2nd republic; military rule by junta, 1961–63.
3rd	1963–72	Park Chung Hee	New constitution drawn up and election of president and National Assembly in November 1963; centralized executive; amended 1969 to allow Park to run again in 1972.
4th	1972–79	Park Chung Hee	New constitution, the *Yushin* "Revitalization" to permit lifetime tenure for Park; approved by national referendum on November 21, 1972; National Conference for Unification headed by Park to elect president; Park assassinated on October 26, 1979.
5th	1981–87	Chun Doo Hwan	Caretaker government by Choi Kyu Hoh, after Park's assassination, December 1979–August 1980; Lt. Gen. Chun Doo Hwan cracked down on student protests in Kwangju in May 1980; military coup by Chun; new constitution was drafted and approved by a national referendum in October 1980.
6th	1988–92	Roh Tae Woo	Popular referendum on December 16, 1987, produced a new president; Roh inaugurated in February 1988 as president for the 6th republic; 1988 constitution originally approved by twelfth National Assembly by a vote of 254–4 on October 12, 1987; subsequently approved by 94 percent of voters on December 16, 1987; popular direct election of president agreed upon by Roh's government and opposition leaders before 1987 December election.

The new constitution for the second republic, 1960–61, changed the presidential selection system from direct popular election to a parliamentary system of election by the National Assembly. Then Park Chung Hee ordered another constitution to be drafted after he consolidated his military rule, limiting the president to two consecutive terms of office. Later, in 1969 and 1972, the constitution was amended again to allow Park a third term and life tenure. The 1972 *Yushin* or "Revitalization" constitution for the fourth republic returned the presidential election system to that of a newly established National Conference for Unification consisting of some 2,000 to 5,000 delegates who in turn had been elected by the voters. The 1980–81 constitution for the fifth republic under Chun Doo Hwan replaced the National Conference for Unification with a presidential electoral college of more than 5,000 members who were supposed to represent and reflect the political views or sentiments of the nation. A presidential candidate was required to be nominated by a political party or recommended by members of the electoral college, which expired once the new president was inaugurated. Then again, after sixteen years, and under unrelenting demands from massive student demonstrations and pressure from abroad, a direct popular election for the president was instituted on December 16, 1987. In a three-way contest, Roh Tae Woo won the race with only 36 percent of the votes to become the new president for the next five years.

Under the 1980 constitution the president has enormous executive powers, including war declaration, treaty making, cabinet appointment, and emergency measures enactment. Unlike the 1972 constitution, the president can suspend habeas corpus only with the approval of the National Assembly and for only a limited duration. Such emergency measures must be withdrawn by the president if so requested by a majority of the members of the National Assembly. Under the 1980 constitution the president cannot disband the National Assembly without the specific consent of the speaker and the cabinet. Nor can the president dissolve the National Assembly within one year of its formation. The president's office, the Blue House, is assisted by a staff and an array of advisory bodies or special agencies on state affairs, a National Security Council, and a Planning Agency for Security (formerly the Korean Central Intelligence Agency). The president appoints a prime minister, the top bureaucrat, to head the State Council, which consists of twenty executive departments from Foreign Affairs to National Unification. Each executive department or ministry has a consulting advisory body of experts or specialists from the academia.

It must be noted that for more than two and one-half decades (1961–87) political power in South Korea was concentrated in the hands of Presidents Park Chung Hee and Chun Doo Hwan, whose regimes were characterized by military authoritarianism. Their rule rested with the careful appointments of trusted classmates of the Korean Military Academy to three strategic positions in the military: the Defense Security Command, the Metropolitan Defense Command, and the Special Forces Command;[17] whereas under Syngman Rhee, governance had been basically a form of personal autocratic rule. Park and Chun ruled as presidents of the third, fourth and fifth republics by the use of the coercive instruments at their command and by controlling and monopolizing the state bureaucratic machinery.

The National Assembly   South Korea has a unicameral representative assembly. Article 76 of the 1980 constitution states that "legislative power shall be vested in the National Assembly." The new 1988 election law provides the National Assembly with 299 seats: 224 seats elected from single-member districts, and 75 at-large seats to be filled by a proportional system based on party lists. Article 99 empowers the National Assembly to pass motions for the removal of the prime minister or a member of the State Council. However, no such motion is permitted within one year of the appointment of the official. Such motions may be introduced by one-third or more of the National Assembly members and must be passed by a majority of the total membership. Article 101 provides the National Assembly with the power to impeach the president, the prime minister, and other heads of the executive branch. For impeachment of the president, a two-thirds vote of the total National Assembly membership is required.

Another aspect of National Assembly deliberation is the evident adoption of the British parliamentary tradition of the question period. Article 98 provides attendance by the prime minister and members of the State Council at meetings of the National Assembly upon request. They must answer questions when attending the meetings.

Stormy and sometimes unruly sessions have occurred with embarrassing frequency at the National Assembly. In December 1989, after twenty months of negotiation between the government and the opposition party, when former president Chung Doo Hwan testified about his brutal crackdown on the Kwangju student demonstrations, the parliamentary proceedings were interrupted by a melee that terminated the awaited Chun's public appearance and testimony amidst shouting, screams, and shoving by members. Chun was escorted out of the parliament under heavy guard after repeated recesses and interruptions on the floor.[18] In the mid-July 1990 session, two members of the thirteenth National Assembly were hospitalized after a raucous debate degenerated into violent physical clashes on the floor.[19] After the ruling party pushed through a cluster of some twenty-five bills, some seventy-five lawmakers from the opposition parties submitted their resignations and demanded a new election.

The State Council   In Article 62 the 1980 constitution provides that the president shall appoint, with approval from the National Assembly, a prime minister whose primary responsibility is to supervise the executive ministries. In practice the prime minister and members of the State Council serve collectively as Cabinet members, chaired by the president. Not more than thirty, but no fewer than fifteen, are appointed by the president upon recommendation by the prime minister. Article 65 outlines the scope and range of matters that can be referred to the State Council for deliberation: declaration of war, foreign policy, constitutional amendments, state budget, martial law, important military affairs, dissolution of the National Assembly, and requests for extraordinary sessions, amnesty, and action for the dissolution of a political party. As of 1990 the State Council consisted of twenty-five ministries: economic planning, foreign affairs, defense, finance, trade and industry, agriculture-forestry-fishery, energy and resources, science and technology, labor, transport, communications, home affairs, justice, health and social affairs, national unification, education, environment, sports, construction, government administration, information, ministers for political affairs, and legislative affairs.

A recurring controversy in South Korean politics has been the question of what is the most suitable form of government: a presidential form, as provided in the 1980 constitution, or a parliamentary cabinet system as exemplified by the Japanese model. There has been some serious discussion in 1990 that a constitutional amendment ought to be initiated to replace the present presidential form of government with a parliamentary cabinet system when President Roh's five-year term ends in February 1993. The key to the proposal was continued domination by the ruling Democratic Liberal party (DLP) if it could continue to win parliamentary elections. The proposal, however, was not revived after the 1992 presidential election. President Roh's decision in February 1990 to merge two opposition parties—Reunification Democratic party and the New Democratic Republic party (see section on political parties)—was intended to be a first step toward the contemplated constitutional change, with possible rotation of the premiership between Roh and Kim Young Sam. A change toward the Japanese model of a parliamentary cabinet system—a system that has been criticized in recent years in Japan (see Chapter 1) as associated with scandals and dominated by deals among factions within the ruling party— would not alter the basic South Korean political culture that is characterized by "highly emotional conflict, charismatic leaders and refusal to compromise."[20] The merger would provide a controlling majority, as many as 200 out of a total of 299 seats in the National Assembly, to the newly constituted Liberal Democratic party. This is envisaged by the advisors to Roh and Kim Young Sam, as an end not only to the U.S. presidential form of government, but more importantly, the end of strident opposition, legislative paralysis, and refusal to compromise.

Reaction from student protesters on the streets, as well as firebomb attacks on Kim Young Sam's office in Pusan in the spring of 1990, forced Roh to put the proposal temporarily on the back burner. The protest, mobilized by 20,000 students and attracting more than 300,000 people in Seoul, was the first large rally against Roh's government since his election in December 1987.

The Judiciary The 1980 constitution stipulates that judicial power for the South Korean Republic shall be vested in the courts composed of judges. Article 104 states that "judges shall rule independently according to their conscience and in conformity with the constitution and law." Under the constitution, the Supreme Court is empowered to make a final review of constitutionality of regulations and decrees. As the highest court, the Supreme Court can hear appeals from lower courts, and its decisions are final and binding. The Chief Justice of the Supreme Court is appointed by the president with the consent of the National Assembly—the appointee must be at least forty years of age with more than twenty years of judicial experience as a lawyer, judge or prosecutor. Associate justices to the Supreme Court are appointed by the president upon the recommendation of the chief justice. The chief justice serves a six-year term and cannot be reappointed. The associate justices of the Supreme Court are appointed for a five-year term and may be reappointed. Judges in the lower courts are appointed by the chief justice for a ten-year term and are subject to reappointment. Judges may be removed or suspended from office by impeachment and by disciplinary action.

On questions of constitutionality of laws enacted by the National Assembly, in accordance with Article 108 of the 1980 constitution, the Supreme Court must request a decision by the Constitution Committee, which is made up of nine members (three selected by the National Assembly, three nominated by the chief justice and three appointed by the president for a six-year term). The Constitution Committee has jurisdiction over impeachment of public officials and dissolution of political parties.

Below the Supreme Court there are three lower courts. The appellate courts—located in Seoul, Taegu, Pusan, and Kwangju—hear appeals originating in lower courts on civil and criminal cases. The appellate courts may also assume original jurisdiction on cases against governmental agencies and/or public officials. Each appellate court has four judges, presided over by a chief judge. The lowest level of courts is the district court, located in Seoul and eleven other key provincial cities throughout South Korea. A single judge generally handles the cases, except when serious cases are involved—death sentence or a civil lawsuit exceeding 1 million won. In those cases the trial is conducted by a three-judge panel.

There is only one family court in South Korea, located in Seoul. It has jurisdiction over cases involving divorce, juvenile, and other domestic disputes. In order to ensure privacy, proceedings in the family court are not open to the public. In places other than Seoul domestic disputes are handled by the district courts.

The Ministry of Justice maintains and controls the prosecutors' offices. Prosecutors are empowered to conduct criminal investigations into law violations and supervise the judicial police officials, who are attached to the Korean National Police and specialize in crimes relating to railroads, narcotics, and customs. The Supreme Prosecutor office is headed by a prosecutor-general appointed by the president for a fifteen-year term. There are four so-called High Public Prosecutor offices located in Seoul, Taegue, Kwangju, and Pusan, and fourteen district prosecutor offices. Prosecutors attend and address court proceedings and can request the courts for application of law on behalf of the public.

Taiwan: A Strong Executive and the Gradual Emergence of a Representative Assembly

The Nationalist government prepared and drafted a constitution for the Republic of China (ROC) in 1936. In December 1946 it adopted a constitution based essentially on the 1936 draft; it was promulgated in January 1947 when full-scale civil war had already begun. Two years later the Nationalists were defeated by Mao's communist troops and fled to Taiwan. It is this 1947 constitution that the Taiwan government has put into operation for more than four decades. While it had been argued that the 1947 constitution for Taiwan is both parliamentary and presidential,[21] Chiang Kai Shek and his son, Chiang Ching Kuo, had exercised enormous presidential power when each was elected indirectly to the position of chief-of-state and when martial law was in effect. At any rate, the 1947 constitution for Taiwan has distributed political power into five chambers or *yuans*: Legislative, Executive, Judicial, Control, and Examination. Superimposed over all of these powers is the president for the republic.

The National Assembly   This legislative body, as originally established by the 1947 constitution, was to serve two major purposes: election of the president and vice president for Taiwan and for amending the constitution. In its former capacity, the National Assembly served as a sort of electoral college by electing the chief of state.

A most controversial, and certainly most undemocratic, state of affairs was that the old 553-member National Assembly, elected before 1949, reigned until the approval of significant political reforms via the acceptance of a constitutional amendment on April 22, 1991. Of a total of 2,841 elected on the mainland, 1,576 came to Taiwan; and as of 1986, a total of 899 were still serving. Of those serving in 1986, more than 76 percent were age seventy or more and the average death rate per year for 1981–86 was 43.6 percent.[22] In April 1991 some 473, out of a total of 693 elderly members of the old National Assembly since 1949, many aged eighty or over, claimed to represent the mainland provinces of which Taiwan was but one such body. (One took part in the Nationalist revolution in the 1920s.)[23] Here was a main legislative body elected before the Nationalists lost the civil war to Mao's armies still remaining as a legislative entity in Taiwan without facing another election for over four decades. Finally, voters of Taiwan elected a new National Assembly on December 21, 1991.

The constitutional amendment approved on April 22, 1991, called for a new National Assembly to have 325 members, 225 of whom would be elected in multimember electoral districts in Taiwan by a plurality vote. The remaining 100 seats must be apportioned as follows: 80 as national representatives or proportional representation by parties, and 20 for overseas Chinese. The results of the December 21, 1991, election for the new National Assembly were as follows: 179 were elected for the ruling Kuomintang, in addition to an assigned 75 seats based on the party's proportional votes, for a total of 254 seats. The strongest opposition, the Democratic Progressive party, received a total of 66 seats.

The newly elected 325-member National Assembly represented the first stage of political reform for Taiwan. Its members serve for a 6-year term and meet on rare occasions to elect a president and a vice-president and to approve constitutional amendments. For much of its spring 1992 session, the new National Assembly, still under control of the ruling KMT's representation of that body and under the influence of the conservative minority, approved a total of eight minor constitutional amendments—all of which were approved in advance by the KMT's central committee.[24] These amendments included extension of the president's appointive power to the Control, Judicial, and Examination Yuans. In March 1992, President Lee's proposal to the KMT central committee for approval of a direct popular election of the president met with opposition by the KMT conservatives.[25]

THE LEGISLATIVE YUAN   The Legislative Yuan enacts laws, approves government budgets, and confirms emergency decrees. It also must approve the appointments of a premier and his deputies. Similar to the old National Assembly before the 1991 reform, the Legislative Yuan was first elected in 1947 to represent the entire Chinese mainland. After the exodus to Taiwan in 1949 it remained unchanged until 1989, except for increased local representation for Taiwan and overseas Chinese by as much as 25 percent and 40 percent respectively.[26] In 1989 there was a total of 213 members among whom 81 elderly were elected in 1947, but now were forced to retire—the elderly ones, with an average age of eighty, were ill and had to be rounded up to attend the sessions. In the December 1989 election in

Taiwan, 101 seats for the Legislative Yuan were up for election and, in addition to the ruling KMT, were contested by three other opposition parties. The KMT won 72 of the total 101. In a continuation of political reform, all 213 members of the Legislative Yuan were elected anew in December 1992.

The Legislative Yuan meets in two annual sessions—one in the spring and one in the fall. It requires a quorum, one-seventh of the 213-member body. In recent sessions a "legislative fracas" occurred as the opposition, the Democratic Progressive party members, pushed for debate over independence and the antisedition provisions in the Criminal Code.[27]

The President   The office of president is a powerful one in that he is not only the commander of the armed forces and nominates or appoints key officers for the government, such as the premiership, but is also endowed with the power to make emergency decrees. The president is elected by the National Assembly for a term of six years and may be reelected for a second term. The powers of the president must also be seen from the perspective of his strong leadership within the ruling political party, the KMT.

There have been two such powerful presidents since 1950. Chiang Kai Shek occupied that position until his death in 1974. He was then serving his fifth term and was succeeded by the vice president until 1978. In March of that year, the National Assembly elected Chiang's son, Chiang Ching Kuo, to the presidency. He was reelected in 1984 for a second six-year term. When Chiang Chin Kuo died in January 1988, a Taiwanese, Lee Teng Hui, became the president and the head of the ruling KMT.

Lee, with a Ph.D. in agricultural economics from Cornell University, developed a strong leadership and embarked on political reform soon after assuming the office. Lee's presidency broke the Chiang family's long time rule over the nation and the ruling KMT in spite of his Taiwan birth and upbringing. During the short period from 1988 to 1990 Lee was able to reconcile demands of the KMT hardliners, or conservatives on the Right, and the public cry for democratic reform for Taiwan. In March 1990, after having served out the remainder of Chiang Ching Kuo's term of presidency, Lee was nominated in his own right after some inner-party (KMT) maneuvering, and went on to be elected by the National Assembly for a six-year term until 1996. Lee's election may be attributed to two factors: the support of the Taiwan people, for by now 85 percent of the 20 million population are native-born Taiwanese, and his accommodation of the KMT diehards.[28]

A dramatic change took place in May 1991, when President Lee declared the end of the so-called Period of Communist Rebellion, or the emergency rule, a Nationalist decree imposed on Taiwan for more than four decades. He pledged not to use force to unite the two Chinas, to regard the PRC merely as "authorities," not as a "rebel organization," and to accept the reality that PRC does control the mainland.[29] This dramatic change was accompanied by the forced retirement of the National Assembly deputies who had represented mainland provinces, and a new election scheduled by December 1991.

Under pressure from the liberal elements of the ruling KMT and the opposition Democratic Progressive party, as well as from international human rights groups, President Lee succeeded in making significant revisions to the sedition law, which he signed on May 16, 1992. The new law does not permit penalties in the Criminal Code for nonviolent acts, and thus mandates the government to release dissidents and opposition activists who demand independence for Taiwan.[30] While there has been some discussion over the proposal for direct popular election of the president, no concrete or serious consideration has been given to it. In fact, the matter has met with opposition by the KMT conservatives. In effect, the proposal has been postponed indefinitely in order to avoid a split within the KMT.

THE EXECUTIVE YUAN   The Executive Yuan is really the administrative branch of the government in Taiwan headed by a nonelective premier nominated by the president. There are as many as thirty ministries and commissions constituting the Executive Yuan, including economic planning, environmental protection, and the chairman for mainland affairs council. Members of the Executive Yuan—ministers and agency heads or departments—not only implement policies, but work closely with the president in formulating policies. Under the Chinese system of checks and balances, the Legislative Yuan may reject or alter the decisions of the Executive Yuan, at least in theory.

In the fall of 1990, President Lee indicated his choice for a top military leader to become the prime minister or head of the Executive Yuan. His selection of Taiwan's only four-star general, former defense minister Hau Pei Tsun, then seventy-one years of age, prompted strong reactions from opposition leaders due to Hau's inflexibility on democratic reform and his hardline stance on PRC. Since taking office as premier, Hau has exhibited decisiveness as a strong man and has devoted his energies to fighting crime, streamlining the administrative machinery of the government, and promoting economic development with the goal of making Taiwan a leading industrial nation by the year 2000. He has weathered student demonstrations over the revision of the sedition law in May 1991. Reports of a power struggle between Hau and President Lee were publicly denied by both.[31] Some criticism has stemmed from Hau's practice of receiving regular briefings from the armed forces chiefs, a tradition said to be reserved only for the president as commander-in-chief.[32] (Hau was forced to resign under pressure in the spring of 1992.)

While admittedly in recent years there has been an emergence of KMT factionalism—in this case Lee's liberal approach in contrast to Hau's hard line, the basic problem may be constitutional. Not only is there an "ambiguous relationship" in terms of responsibilities existing between the president and the head of the cabinet, but also, as asserted by some Taiwanese scholars, there may have been a deliberate design on the part of the original drafters of the constitution to provide checks against the possible rise of an authoritarian leader such as Chiang Kai Shek. In this view, the presidency, as originally designed, was "largely a symbolic office,"[33] and power was to be centered in the hands of the premier. If one follows this interpretation, it seems that the original 1947 constitution was for a parliamentary system; Chiang Kai Shek modified it by developing the system into a presidential one with one exception: When Chiang's son became premier in 1972, the Cabinet system became more powerful.

The Subsidiary Organs   First there is the Control Yuan, which conducts investigations of official wrongdoing. Thus, the Control Yuan can impeach, censure, or audit officials in the Executive Yuan and the ministers under it. It has fifty-two members indirectly elected by provincial assemblies and local councils for a six-year term. At present, Taiwan representation is about 70 percent; it is scheduled for a completely new election in early 1993 for the entire fifty-two members (twenty-five by the Taiwan Provincial Assembly and ten each by the city councils of Taipei and Kaohsiung).

Then there is the Examination Yuan. This is the all-national civil service board that administers examinations and tests for government employment. John Copper writes that four kinds of special examinations are provided for government employee recruitment.[34] Members of the Examination Yuan are presidential appointees.

THE JUDICIAL YUAN   Collectively speaking, this is the highest judicial organ for Taiwan. It consists of two distinct divisions. One is the Council of Grand Justices, whose seventeen members are appointed for six-year terms by the president, but with the consent of the Control Yuan. The council interprets the constitutionality of laws, statutes, and government regulations. The members meet twice weekly and decisions on constitutional interpretation require a three-fourths vote of the council members present. The Council of Grand Justices is generally under the influence of the ruling party, the KMT.

The other division of the Judicial Yuan is the court system, consisting of a Supreme Court, district courts, and administrative courts. As the highest court, the Supreme Court hears appeals, both civil and criminal; to hear cases it is organized into judicial "senates" of five justices each.

Proceedings are "primarily documentary in nature" rather than of the advocacy nature of judicial proceedings in the West.[35]

THE POLITICAL PROCESS: PARTICIPATION, ELECTIONS, POLITICAL PARTIES, AND GROUP POLITICS

South Korea: Democracy and Stability

The Electoral Process   A scholar of Korean politics writes that a basic characteristic of political participation in South Korea is that the governing elites and the counterelites, or the opposition party leaders, are the active participants. These are the groups that work at securing support from the supreme leader or obtaining the "popular mandate and sanction on key policies and political reform."[36] In South Korea, the "politics of plebiscite" is often the result of manipulation of voter sentiment by the governing elites.[37] However, as a result of the impact of modernization and economic progress, political participation in South Korea is increasing. Surveys conducted in South Korea in 1973–74 indicated the urban elite and mass public had become more politically active than the rural populace.[38]

THE DECEMBER 1992 PRESIDENTIAL ELECTION   South Korean voters went to the polls on December 18, 1992, to elect a new president in a democratic and orderly transition of power from more than three decades of military authoritarian leaders to civilian rule. The election was indicative of the South Korean voters' desire for continued political and economic stability. Kim Young Sam, the choice of the ruling Democratic Liberal party, received 9.7 million popular votes, or about 41 percent of the 29.4 million votes cast. In a three-way contest, Kim Young Sam outpolled Democratic party (DP) candidate Kim Dae Jung, who received 7.8 million popular votes, or about 34 percent of the total cast. Chang Ju Yang, of the United People's party (UPP), also founder of the giant Hyundai industrial conglomerate, garnered 3.7 million popular votes, or about 16 percent of the 29.4 million votes cast.

The significance of the December 1992 election lies not only in a peaceful power transfer from military to civilian, but also in a surprisingly clean and smooth election.

THE 1988 AND 1992 PARLIAMENTARY ELECTIONS[39]   The 1988 election of the National Assembly, the thirteenth, was governed by a new electoral system. Under the old electoral system, adopted in 1973, 184 (two-thirds) of the total 276 National Assembly seats were elected from ninety-two two-member districts. The remaining ninety-two seats (one-third) were appointed by the political parties on the basis of their popular votes or on an at-large basis. In practice, two-thirds (about 60) of the ninety-two at-large seats were awarded to the party that won the largest number of district seats, and the remaining one-third were distributed to other political parties on a proportional basis.[40] The old electoral system required that the ruling party must obtain a clear majority of seats in the National Assembly. As pointed out by one analyst, the old system enabled the ruling party candidates to win the second choice in many urban areas where the opposition parties were stronger. Thus, in the twelfth National Assembly election, the ruling Democratic Justice party won 46 percent of the district seats, but obtained a 54 percent majority in the Assembly.[41]

There was considerable criticism by the opposition parties to the old National Assembly electoral system, which finally led to negotiations for a change in the election law in time for the 1988 parliamentary election of the thirteenth National Assembly. The new electoral law now provides for a total of 299 National Assembly seats, of which 224 are to be elected from single-member districts and the remaining seventy-five seats at-large. The at-large seats are to be distributed among the political parties on a proportional basis: the party obtaining the largest number of district seats, but not the absolute majority, receiving thirty-eight of them. The remaining thirty-seven at-large seats would be distributed to those political parties that capture a minimum of five district seats or more in proportion to the party's share of district seats. Under the new electoral rules, the 1988 National Assembly election produced results as given in Table 2.2.

Table 2.2   Results of Thirteenth National Assembly Election, 1988

| Party | % Vote | Number of Seats Won | | |
		District	At-Large	Total
Democratic Justice party	34.0	87	38	125
Party for Peace and Democracy	19.3	54	16	70
Reunification and Democratic party	23.8	46	13	59
New Democratic Republican party	15.6	27	8	35
Minors*	2.5	1	0	1
Independent	4.8	9	0	9
Total	100.0**	224	75	299

* Includes nine major parties
** Total does not correspond to 100 due to rounding errors
Source: Chan Wook Park, "The 1988 National Assembly Election in South Korea: The Ruling Party's Loss of Legislative Mandate," *Journal of Northeast Asian Studies* 7, no. 3 (Fall 1988): 65.

The 1988 National Assembly election results were disappointing to the ruling Democratic Justice party. Of the 224 single-member seats, the ruling party captured only 87 (about 34 percent) of the votes, less than half of the total. While it was the party receiving the largest number of district seats, plus an additional 38 of the 75 at-large seats, the ruling party membership was only 125 of the total 299 seats in the Thirteenth National Assembly. The two leading opposition parties, the party of Peace and Democracy (PDP) and the Reunification and Democratic party (RDP), obtained a combined total of 129 seats, or 43.1 percent of the votes. Clearly, the ruling party has been the largest party in the Thirteenth National Assembly, but it lacks majority control of the parliament. It was this lack of a controlling majority in the National Assembly that motivated, perhaps more than anything else, the February 1990 merger of the ruling Democratic Justice party (DJP) with RDP and the New Democratic Republican party (NDRP) to form the Democratic Liberal party.

In the March 24, 1992, National Assembly election, Roh's Democratic Liberal party suffered a loss by winning 113 seats of the 237 seats contested, or 47 percent of the total. The new Unification National party, headed by Hyundai founder Chang Ju Yang, a novice in national election politics, won a surprising 10 percent of the seats to the National Assembly. This meant that the ruling Democratic Liberal party had to woo the independents in order to maintain legislative control.

Political Parties   In November 1980 a new political party law was enacted as a significant step toward democratization for South Korea as pledged by Chun Doo Hwan. The new law promoted the emergence of a multiparty system: In the March 1981 parliamentary election eight political parties were represented. In the 1988 National Assembly election, there were four major political parties plus nine minor parties.

THE DEMOCRATIC JUSTICE PARTY   Since its inception on November 28, 1980, this had been the ruling political party for South Korea. It was formed to provide Chun Doo Hwan a political vehicle for power, presumably for the purpose of building "a democratic and just welfare society" and "the peaceful unification of the homeland." Incorporated in the party platform were these five basic concepts: national integrity, democracy, justice, welfare and national unification.[42] In the March 1981 election the party won 151 of the 276 seats in the National Assembly. In January 1982, one year after its inception, party membership was said to be 170,000.[43] As explained by Young Whan Kihl: Although the Democratic Justice party received only 35 percent of 16 million votes cast in the 1981 National Assembly election, "the election law enabled the DJP to control 55 percent of the seats."[44] As a ruling party, the DJP had the advantage in fund-raising over all other political parties. In 1981 it raised about U.S.

$8 million, or about 92 percent of the total funds raised by all political parties.[45]

A recurring characteristic of South Korean political parties has been inner-party factionalism. The ruling DJP is beset with factional conflict for control of the party. One strong faction has been the so-called "TK mafia", whose members come from Taegu and the neighboring Kyongsan province. This faction has been unhappy with Roh Tae Woo's fixing of the blame on Chun Doo Hwan for the 1980 Kwangju massacre of student protesters and the proposed constitutional change from a presidential to a cabinet system.[46] Then there is the "KS" faction, composed of members who come from Seoul and the Kyongyi region near the capital. In addition, there is a basic struggle between the party's liberal and authoritarian wings over appeals to woo the middle class who voted the party into power in the 1987 and 1988 elections. In a recent party reshuffle, supporters of Chun Doo Hwan in the TK faction won appointments to key party positions, a move considered to be keyed to the 1992 presidential election.

THE DEMOCRATIC LIBERAL PARTY   In February 1990, the ruling DJP merged with two other conservatively oriented and central political parties—the Reunification Democratic party and the New Democratic Republican party—into a new Democratic Liberal party, modeled after Japan's ruling Liberal Democratic party. In effect, the merger replaced the four-party system with a two-party system that controlled about 221 of the 299 seats in the National Assembly. The merged RDP was primarily rural based and was led by Kim Young Sam, the second largest vote-getter in the December 1987 presidential election. He captured 6.1 million votes (27.4 percent) of the total. Kim Young Sam, together with Roh, led the new coalition, the DLP. It was said that Kim Young Sam was destined to become Roh's successor, and the 1992 December presidential election showed that he was indeed Roh's successor. A small number of the old RDP have refused to follow Kim Young Sam and instead have formed a small Democratic party.

The third group in the merger to form the ruling Democratic Liberal party was the New Democratic Republic party, led by Kim Jong Phil, a former prime minister under President Park. The NDRP was formed to rehabilitate the old Democratic Republican party, which ruled from 1963 through 1979. As a party, the NDRP was the most conservative and smallest in membership. The coalition move with Kim Young Sam's Reunification Democratic party was designed to perpetuate the personal rivalry between Kim Young Sam and Kim Dae Jung, the head of the party for Peace and Democracy, but also to undermine the PDP as the largest opposition party. Aside from these political motives and personal rivalry, these political parties differ little in party ideology or platform.

THE PARTY FOR PEACE AND DEMOCRACY   With the formation of a new coalition under the Democratic Liberal party, the only opposition came from Kim Dae Jung's party for Peace and Democracy, which garnered 5.8 million votes (26.5 percent) in the 1987 presidential election. It is ironic that Kim Dae Jung had joined forces with Kim Young Sam to form the Reunification and Democratic party in their successful opposition to Chun Doo Hwan's military authoritarianism. However, the two Kims failed to agree on one presidential candidate to oppose Roh in the 1987 election, so Kim Dae Jung formed his own party for Peace and Democracy, which drew support from Kwangju and Cholla provinces in the southwest. Kim Dae Jung was once sentenced to death by President Park for sedition and organizing mass rallies. The PDP has the image of being to the left of center, and its leader has been regarded by the conservatives as a radical.

Kim Dae Jung is opposed to a change from a presidential to a cabinet system. He views the cabinet system as a threat to democracy in South Korea, and the change would in effect keep him out of the 1992 presidential contest. He has vowed to take the issue to the streets if necessary. In a rally in a Seoul park on July 21, 1990, Kim Dae Jung announced the formation of an opposition merger of three minor political groups: the dissident Democratic party, the Rev. Suk's nonparliamentary group opposed to Roh, and the banned National Teachers' Union. The opposition merger demands new elections, dissolution of the National Assembly and the defeat of the ruling party, the Democratic Liberal party of Roh and Kim Young Sam. Support for the opposition unit also comes from radical students, workers, and South Korean farmers opposed to relaxation of import restrictions. Supporters for the opposition unit elected under party labels of the PDP and Democratic party have boycotted the parliament by demanding instead new elections. Kim Dae Jung and his party lost out to Kim Young Sam in the December 1992 presidential election, having garnered only 7.8 million popular votes, or barely 34 percent of the total.

Interest Groups   SOCIAL GROUPS AND SOCIAL FORCES   In South Korea there are four social groups or forces that dominate today's society and play a prominent role in political, economic, and social development: the corporate business-administrative technocrats, workers and labor organizations, student-intellectuals, and the military establishment.

The new elite of South Korea today are the managers and technocrats in business enterprises and government service. This group has gained its status and influence as economic development has accelerated and reached the take-off stage and beyond. The group is well educated; the members are graduates of universities of a defined rank order. (A survey showed that 34.6 percent of the high government officials attended the leading Seoul National University.)[47]

The labor force in South Korea has been increasing at the rate of 3 percent to 5 percent per year for the period 1963–80. The total work force in 1990 was about 16.9 million and distributed as follows: 25.5 percent in commercial services, 27.7 percent in manufacturing, 20.7 percent in agriculture and fishing, 6.1 percent in construction, and 19.8 percent in government service.[48] Before 1990 there were some sixteen industrial unions—all of them affiliated with the Korean Federation of Trade Unions. In September 1989 the National Teachers' Union was banned by the government on the grounds that the union was being used by radicals to spread revolutionary and antigovernment ideas among students. The ban triggered demonstrations by teachers, students, and supporters in eight cities.

Labor unrest and strife since 1986 reflect the growing tendency of workers in South Korea to assert their influence and power as an important force in society. The number of labor disputes or strikes has declined in frequency in recent years.[49] However, the duration of strikes has increased somewhat.[50] In the worker strikes at the Hyundai Ulsan shipyards and the 27,000-worker strike at the Hyundai Motor Company in 1990, the government ordered riot police to suppress the union's activities. Issues for striking workers were not limited to wages or working conditions, even though these have been the key concerns. Beginning in 1988 average Korean wage increases outpaced the rate of productivity. The government's policy has been to limit wage increases to below 10 percent per year, while the average was about 20 percent from 1987 to 1990. The labor union position has been that of shorter working hours, about forty-four hours as against fifty-four hours per week. The rationale for higher wages has been to compensate for inflation, estimated at more than 10 percent for the first time in many years, and rampant land or real estate speculation, which has affected housing—the need was to build at least 2 million housing units to ease the shortage.

As of 1989, there were 1.29 million university students in South Korea. They have a tradition of protest for political change, a tradition established in April–May 1960, when the students emerged from their docile and subservient stance to that of harbinger of change through demonstration and protest. Having toppled off the authoritarian regime of Syngman Rhee in May 1960, with the support of the military, university students have become an important force in society and politics. In 1987 university students took to the streets to force Chun Doo Hwan to resign from office. After years of protest and demonstration in the face of tear gas and the brutality of riot police, in December 1987 they demanded a popular election for president, which occurred in the 1992 election.

In addition to the traditional protest theme of opposing military authoritarian rule, student demonstrations in recent years have focused on two other controversial themes. One has been the call for reunification of the two Koreas, and the other denunciation of continued stationing of some

40,000 U.S. troops in Korea. Slogans for violent protests from February to May 1990 were "Yankee Go Home" and "Oust Roh Tae Woo." Protesters consisting of students, farmers, and workers staged huge protest rallies in Seoul and seventeen provincial cities. The anti-American rallies demanded the end of U.S. pressure to open South Korean markets for trade. One of the largest protests was on May Day 1990, when more than 100,000 protesters clashed with the riot police; more than 100 police officers and scores of workers were injured.

Military Politics   Defense expenditure for a modernized South Korean army ranged from 6 percent of its GNP in 1984 to about 4.2 percent, or about $10.1 billion (7 trillion won) in 1990. In terms of the national budget, defense spending still stood at about 31 percent for 1990.[51] South Korea has a growing sophisticated defense industry revolving around some eighty major companies led by seven of their giant conglomerates, or *chaebols*, such as Samsung Aerospace Industries, Daewoo Heavy Industries, and Hyundai Corporation. Roughly 30 percent of South Korea's defense budget is for weapon purchases and investment in the defense industry—the obvious emergence of a military-industrial complex. But the United States still supplies about 80 percent of its military imports.[52]

The South Korean military has played a dominant role in politics from 1961 to the present. Twice the army officers seized power in South Korea: the 1961 coup under Park Chung Hee and the 1980 coup by Chun Doo Hwan. Since the 1987 presidential election the question remains: Will there be another military coup in the foreseeable future? There are a number of factors that serve to explain why military intervention will be less in the future.[53] First, since diplomatic relations have improved with the former Soviet Union and China, it is going to be increasingly difficult for the military officers in South Korea to conjure up anticommunist pretexts for intervention in politics. While there has been no concrete agreement on a formula for reunification, the dialogue has begun between South and North Korea. Second, the South Korean economy has matured to such an extent that it is no longer dependent upon military officers for managerial and professional recruitment. The South Korean economy and private industry rely more today on university graduates, mostly trained in the United States, for managerial skills and know-how. Military officers who entered into politics and industry in the 1960s and 1970s are now professionals and "salaried workers."[54] Third, most of the officer corps have come from a new generation that grew up after the 1961 military coup and who represent "a mood of depoliticization."[55] And the young conscripts in the army, the "perpetual coup makers," in South Korea today probably have no taste for military intervention in politics since they were the street protesters against Chun Doo Hwan's military rule in the late 1980s. Fourth, former President Roh Tae Woo launched a series of military reforms before he vacated office at the end of 1992. One such reform is intended to transform the South Korean armed force from its authoritarian mold into a democratic framework by stressing the values of individualism and professionalism.[56] Then there is the plan to abolish universal conscription in order to release more manpower for private sector needs. Finally, former President Roh attempted to ease out the influence and control of the leading senior army officers' secret society, known as the *Hanahoe* ("One Mind society").[57] Hanahoe, an example of factionalism within the South Korean military establishment, was formed in 1963 among young alumni officer graduates of the Korean Military Academy (Class 11 to Class 20). In 1973 these colonels and generals, numbering 200, led by Chun Doo-Hwan, banded together in secret to promote industrialization and political stability, but against dissent.

In 1990 South Korea agreed formally to a U.S. plan to cut 7,000 of the 43,000 American troops to 36,000 by 1993. The decision to reduce the U.S. forces has been made on the grounds that the South Korean defense is sufficient to deter the perceived threat from North Korea. The cost to the United States has also been a principal reason for gradual reduction and withdrawal of U.S. troops. In recent years South Korea has contributed $340 million annually to support U.S. troops stationed there. However, in terms of contribution in real estate, personnel and other indirect subsidies, the total South Korean contribution has actually been estimated at $1.6 billion per year. President Clinton reaffirmed U.S. stationing of troops in South Korea during his July 1993 visit to Korea.

The military has played a dominant role in South Korean politics, as pointed out earlier. There have been two major military coups d'etat in South Korea. Two thousand army officers led a bloodless coup on May 16, 1961, which ushered in the rule of Major General Park Chung Hee, and established the military as the most powerful group in society. Then there was the December 12, 1979, coup led by younger army generals, products of the South Korean Military Academy. Major General Chun Doo Hwan came into power after the assassination of Park Chung Hee in order to preserve the continuance of the military authoritarian rule; martial law was imposed and demonstrations or protests and all forms of political activities were prohibited. Nevertheless, the military crackdown under Chun Doo Hwan touched off a student demonstration May 18, 1980—the Kwanju massacre or uprising, which resulted in the death of thousands of students. Continued student protests brought about the eventual downfall of Chun's authoritarian regime and his replacement by Roh Tae Woo, another high-ranking military officer. Kim Young Sam, the new president, is moving cautiously toward the military in politics. He has decided not to jail those military personnel who took bribes through the payoff by promotion. He also made oblique references to the May 1980 army massacre of the protesting students at Kwangju and the moving of troops in December 1979 as unconstitutional actions by Chun Doo Hwan and Roh Tae Woo.

Taiwan: The Emergence of Multiparty Democracy

Taiwan's march toward democratic reform is best demonstrated by the two recent elections: one in 1992 and the other in 1991. In many ways these elections served as a test to see whether the ruling party, the KMT, was willing to share power that it had practically monopolized for over forty years.

The Electoral Process   THE 1992 PARLIAMENTARY ELECTION   This was the first full election of the Legislative Yuan, Taiwan's law-making parliament. Three major political parties, plus independents, fielded a total of 348 candidates for 161 seats in parliament. The results of this election showed a dramatic gain for the opposition Democratic Progressive party (DPP), which advocated a referendum on the issue of an independent Taiwan. The power sharing in the Legislative Yuan, produced by the December 1992 election, was as follows: the Nationalists (KMT), 96 seats; the DPP, 50 seats; the Social Democratic party, 1 seat; and the independents, 14 seats. However, the KMT won only 53 percent of the popular vote; for the first time its popular vote appeal fell below the usual level of more than 60 percent. The DPP won about 30 percent of the popular vote. The KMT, which still maintains majority control in the parliament, suffered from voter's anger about corruption and vote buying.[58]

THE 1991 NEW NATIONAL ASSEMBLY ELECTION[59]   On April 22, 1991, the old assembly approved a constitutional amendment to provide for the election of a renewed National Assembly to be held at the end of the year. A total of 325 members were to be chosen with 225 to be elected directly in Taiwan. This election took place on December 21, 1991. This was the first general national election since the Nationalists had arrived in 1949. There was an air of a new Taiwan permeating throughout the election months: Taiwan would be free of the old image and dependence; no longer would it be a part of mainland China. Thus, underlying the December 1991 election was the "pressure for independence," an attitude that neither the Nationalists nor the PRC would want to tolerate.[60] The real significance of the 1991 election certainly was the feeling of trust exhibited by the Nationalists in the Taiwanese people's ability to decide the future of Taiwan. In many ways the 1991 election must also be viewed as an attempt at last to address the serious problem of Taiwan's identity.[61]

Voter turnout was 8.5 million, or 68.3 percent of the eligible voters.[62] Table 2.3 provides the breakdown of election results. The KMT fared very well in the election, for it won a total of 254 seats, a comfortable majority in the new National Assembly. The 1991 election also gave local factions within the ruling KMT more importance in winning elections to the National Assembly. A Taiwanese scholar at Wayne State University made this observation about the emergence of local factions: "These people have no national vision, only local interests. They will be easy to buy off with government patronage."[63]

Table 2.3   Results of the Election for the National Assembly, December 21, 1991

	Seats Won	Percentage of Popular Vote
KMT	254*	71.17
Democratic Progressive party (DPP)	66**	23.94
National Democratic Non-Partisan Alliance	3	2.27
China Socialist Democratic party	0	2.18
Independents	2	0.44
Total	325	100.00

*179 elected seats, plus 75 assigned based on proportion to total party votes.
**41 elected seats, plus 15 assigned based on proportion to total party votes.
Source: Figures are based on *Far Eastern Economic Review*, 9 January 1992, p. 28; Jurgen Domes, "Taiwan in 1991: Searching for Political Consensus," *Asian Survey* 32 (January 1992): 49.

Political Parties   In May 1986 the KMT relaxed its ban and allowed organized groups to participate in elections. There were as many as thirty to forty political parties permitted in the contest for the 1991 election. The following is a brief discussion about the two leading ones: the ruling KMT and the opposition DPP.

THE KMT   The history of the KMT dates back to the 1920s when Sun Yat Sen organized the Nationalists for the revolution. Under the leadership of Chiang Kai Shek the KMT was behind the government recognized during World War II. In the postwar period of civil war, the Nationalists lost to the Chinese communists under Mao and fled in 1949 to Taiwan to continue the struggle against Mao's government, which had effective control over mainland China. Since then, the KMT has dominated, if not monopolized, politics in Taiwan.

In 1984 the ruling KMT became more confident; it relaxed and began to introduce reform. Chiang's son, Chiang Ching Kuo, took over the top party leadership and won the argument for party rejuvenation by permitting the emergence of the opposition *tang wai*, which campaigned for seats to be elected from Taiwan to the old National Assembly and other governing bodies. It also demanded legalizing the formation of political parties other than the KMT. These pressures were symptomatic of changing demographic conditions, for by the mid-1980s more than 80 percent of the Taiwan population were native Taiwanese; even more significant is the fact that more than 70 percent of the KMT's 2 million members were native Taiwanese. While barely 14 percent Taiwanese were on the 1983 KMT Central Committee Standing Committee, the apex of the ruling KMT, in 1988 there were sixteen Taiwanese members in that body, or over 52 percent.[64] The ruling party has become increasingly Taiwanized.

In 1986 the party's Central Committee elected Lee Teng Hui, then a vice president, to a high-ranking position to succeed the already-ailing Chiang Ching Kuo as KMT head. In late 1986, acting as president, Chiang lifted martial law and the ban on formation of political parties, thereby ushering in political reform and democratization in Taiwan.

The ruling KMT not only dominates Taiwan's politics and runs the government, but operates a number of large-scale business enterprises, including cultural and media.

Factionalism has risen within the KMT as power has shifted from the conservatives and second-generation Chinese mainlanders to the Taiwanese. This seems to be evident among the KMT elected members in the Legislative Yuan. For instance, two rival factions contending for power and control have been identified: the Wisdom Coalition of about forty-five native-born Taiwanese members who generally support business interests for Taiwan; and the New KMT Alliance of second-generation mainlanders with ties to the military who strive to protect the mainlanders' interests. Then there is the third factional group, the Parliamentary Reform Association—about fifty members who are more reform minded and support legislation to make the Legislative Yuan more democratic.

THE DEMOCRATIC PROGRESSIVE PARTY   The critics and dissidents against the continuance of martial law and the ban on formation of political parties formed the new Democratic Progressive party in September 1986. It entered in the December 1986 elections and won eleven seats to the old National Assembly and twelve in the Legislative Yuan.

The DPP has stood for the right of self-determination for the people and has advocated Taiwan's independence. For instance, on October 13, 1991, the DPP voted to place in its party charter the call for a plebiscite on the establishment of a "Republic of Taiwan." This action was condemned by the ruling KMT as "irresponsible" and it threatened to dissolve the party under the sedition law. DPP has since made Taiwan independence a major issue. The December 21, 1991, elections demonstrated that the DPP most likely has 23–25 percent of voter support on the independence issue (see Table 2.3).

Membership in the DPP is probably 20,000 to 30,000, as indicated by supporting crowds in party demonstrations in the spring of 1991. The party won a surprising victory in April when the ruling KMT conceded to a proposal for a constitutional amendment putting a time limit, set for 1993, on the continued authorization of the security and intelligence agencies controlled by the ruling KMT.

In recent years, the DPP has become a grass-roots political organization supported by Taiwanese, workers, urbanites, and students. In lending support to workers and the poor, the DPP alienates the business sector in Taiwan. The party's willingness to take issues to the streets has also antagonized those who would prefer a more moderate approach.

Group Conflicts   Ethnically the 20 million population in Taiwan can be categorized into three main groups. The Taiwanese are the descendants of those who migrated in the eighteenth and nineteenth centuries to the island from the southern coast of China, particularly the Fujian coastal province. Today they constitute about 85 percent of the island's total population. Within the category of Taiwanese they identify themselves as Hakka, or descendants of Chinese refugees from Guangdong who came to the island in the nineteenth century, and Fujian or Hokkien (Amoy), descendants of those who migrated to the island as peasants in the eighteenth and nineteenth centuries. Hakka represent the earliest Chinese who migrated to Taiwan and their total population is estimated at about 2 million. These Hakkas are self-reliant and undertake hard work such as road building and farming. In general, the Hakkas see themselves as Taiwanese, not as Chinese. It is often very difficult to identify the Hakkas, for they are usually grouped with the Fujians as Taiwanese. The Republic of China's president Lee Teng-hui is a Hakka, but is often referred to simply as Taiwanese.

The Fujian (Hokkien or Amoy) Taiwanese who constitute the bulk of the Taiwanese population (about 75 percent) are differentiated from the 2 million mainland Chinese who came with the Nationalists in 1949. Their forebears came to the island as farmers, and today the Fujian Taiwanese dominate business and economic activities. They are also increasingly involved in island politics through their activities within the ruling KMT. The Fujian Taiwanese view others as "outsiders" and hold ill feelings toward the 2 million mainlanders. As a group they are resentful of the February 28, 1947, massacre. Fujian Taiwanese regard Taiwan as their original home, and until very recently few even wanted to visit the Fujian Province. They speak the Fujian dialect, and many can also speak Mandarin, the principal languages used in schools, by the government, and by the 2 million mainlanders. Many, particularly the older generation, also speak fluent Japanese, a legacy of the Japanese rule.

The 2 million mainlanders—exiled KMT government workers, soldiers, and their families—are really the ethnic minority who populate the urban areas. Many came to Taiwan in 1947–49 with financial resources and dominated the government and politics for decades thereafter. As Taiwan has gained in prosperity and as Taiwanese acquire wealth and political strength, the mainlanders and their offspring have become inferior in social status. Their hope lies in upgrading their status by education. Some aged mainlanders who came to Taiwan as KMT soldiers have returned to the mainland to be with their families. They can be identified by the language they speak, Mandarin, or by their mainland regional dialects. Among themselves they identify one another by the provincial mainland homes from which they originally hailed.

The last ethnic group is comprised of the 320,000 aborigines of Malay-Polynesian origin who live in the central and eastern upland areas. Anthropological studies designate as many as seven major tribes. They are considered to be the most disadvantaged minority in Taiwan.

Family is still the cornerstone for most of the Taiwanese and mainlanders in Taiwan. Hou Hsiao Hsien's award-winning film *City of Sadness* depicts the upheavals and changes, including the dynamics of the extended family in the lives of three brothers, and gives a vivid view of Taiwan social life in the period immediately after World War II, and the establishment of the Nationalist government in Taiwan. Of course, vast changes have taken place since then. Most families, if not all, have benefited from the economic prosperity. Urban life is more complicated now, as crime, particularly among the juveniles, has been on the increase. However, the traditional family system in Taiwan is still strong despite the pervasive influence of industrialization and Westernization in the daily lives of the island people. These influences also have reduced the need for large extended families.

Military Politics In 1990, Taiwan's armed forces numbered about 425,000, down from a high of over 600,000, augmented by a reserve of 1.5 million. There is a compulsory two-year universal military service requirement for those male citizens eighteen years old and older. While defense expenditures were only 5.2 percent of the gross domestic product, it was 20 percent of Taiwan's total $32 billion budget for 1990.[65] As pointed out by Tien Hung Mao, a China scholar from Wisconsin, for the years 1950–65 only 1.3 percent of the generals and 9.6 percent of the colonels were Taiwanese; by 1978–87 the percentage rose to 15.8 percent and 32.6 percent, respectively.[66] Among rank-and-file soldiers, for 1950–65 about 47 percent were mainlanders as opposed to 52.8 percent

Taiwanese. The figure changed for 1978–87 to only 21 percent mainlanders and 79 percent Taiwanese.[67] While there is no precise figure for the 1990s, there is no doubt that the percentage distribution has risen considerably for the Taiwanese, making their numbers dominant in the armed forces, since the Taiwanese today constitute 85 percent of Taiwan's total 20 million citizens.

While Taiwan's armed forces are considered strong and the morale is high, it is not strong enough when compared with the superior (both in numbers and equipment) PRC armed forces, which possess nuclear weapons. Thus, one of the options left for Taiwan is the purchase of advanced and sophisticated weaponry from abroad in order to bolster its defense and deterrence capability.

For years, armed with a hard currency reserve through trade, Taiwan has embarked on a sustained program of arms purchase, arms development, and weapons research. There has been a continuing arms transfer between the United States and Taiwan under the government-to-government Foreign Military Sales (FMS) program agreements; for the period from 1983 to 1987, a total of $3.1 billion worth of arms transfer has taken place.[68] In short, U.S. technological transfers included "new fighter aircraft, tanks and guided missile frigates" for Taiwan's defense.[69] For the first six months of 1989, the value of U.S. Department of Defense licensed arms exports to Taiwan was $2.1 billion in electronic assemblies and $1.1 billion in computer equipment.[70] For developing air superiority, Taiwan's defense industries have undertaken research and development projects on new fighters, missiles, and main battle tanks with American technological transfers. The crucial aspect of Taiwan's development in fighter planes is that air capability is the key to its defense against a PRC attack or invasion.[71]

Since the end of the Gulf War, Taiwan has been an ideal market for military arms contractors; they offer for sale a whole range of advanced weaponry and electronic warfare equipment.[72] However, the United States has a policy, enforced since 1980, not to sell F-16 fighter jets to Taiwan due to concern and criticism by the PRC. Now Taiwan wants to revive the issue of F-16 fighter jet sales based on the argument that the PRC may obtain advanced weapons from the demised Soviet Union.

For some time there has been concern both inside and outside over Taiwan about President Lee Teng Hui's ability to control the military and its conservative supporters within the KMT. This concern was indicative of the protests over the selection of mainland-born General Hau Pei-ts'un as prime minister in the spring of 1990. (He resigned in February 1992 under pressure.) Admittedly, Hau's elevation to the premiership was a concession to the hardliners in the ruling KMT. However, events since then have indicated Lee's continued support within KMT to such extent that he has been able to introduce further political reforms for Taiwan. Besides, the military has increasingly been undergoing "Taiwanization," the process of domination by native-born Taiwanese. President Lee traces his roots to and identifies with this group. So does the new premier, Lien Chan, the former provincial governor who succeeded General Hau. Lee was reelected by the KMT party congress in August 1993 for a second four-year term as the party head.

POLITICAL PERFORMANCE AND PUBLIC POLICY

South Korea: A Clone of Japan

Economic Performance In 1965 South Korea emerged from status as an underdeveloped Third World nation to become one of the leading new industrialized countries (NICs) of Asia. During the period 1965–81, South Korea's gross national product multiplied twenty times from U.S. $3 billion to U.S. $ 63 billion. For the same period, its per capita GNP increased about sixteen times from U.S. $105 to U.S. $1,628. South Korea's GNP for 1988 was U.S. $ 230 billion, or over U.S. $4,040 per capita. Beginning in the 1960s South Korea's economic base has shifted from a basically agrarian one to that of manufacturing and construction—contributing to 49.1 percent of its economy by 1986. In 1990 South Korea's GNP grew by about 8 percent; its first-quarter GNP for 1991 increased as much as 8.9 percent, considered to be the strongest and fastest increase in Asia—after having made a swift recovery from a 1989 slowdown.[73]

There was a sustained economic growth in 1990, even though it was down from its double-digit growth for 1987 and 1988. Per capita gross domestic product was hovering around $5,000, still an impressive accomplishment.[74] The South Korean economy made a speedy recovery largely through a shift in the government's overall economic policy from "stabilization-oriented" to "growth-oriented."[75] The new growth-oriented economic policy also focused on curtailment in the importation of luxury goods from abroad, under the so-called anti-consumption campaign.[76] The surge for public and private consumption goods and the good life accelerated in the 1989–90 period from 10 percent in 1988 to 11.7 percent in 1989. Accompanying the annual increase in consumption was the inflation rate, which rose from 3.7 percent in 1987 to 7.1 percent in 1989 and 8.2 percent in 1990—which in turn has been caused largely by wage increases, particularly in the manufacturing sector: 12 percent for 1987, 20 percent for 1988, and 17.3 percent for 1989.[77]

As a whole, the South Korean economy remains strong despite some long-term problems such as inflation and wage explosion. Throughout the 1980s its economy grew at an average rate of 8.2 percent.

Government Intervention: Planning and Leadership   The South Korean economy is a mixed system of public ownership and private enterprise. The size of the public sector in the economy is considerable. For instance, one study showed that in 1972 public enterprises in South Korea produced two-thirds of the nation's electric, gas, and water supplies; 30 percent of transport and communication facilities and services; 15 percent of manufacturing; 30 percent of mining; and 80-90 percent of banking services.[78] Many of these public sector enterprises were originally established by the Japanese and "inherited" by the South Korean government at the end of World War II in 1945. However, private enterprises exert more influence over productivity, since three-fourths of the national output and expenditure come from that sector.[79] It is an unusual system in that the government plays an influential role in an otherwise free enterprise economy.

The Economic Planning Board (EPB) was established in 1961; it has been a key instrument in the government's role in South Korea's economic development. It is responsible for preparing the integrated government budget and the five-year plans. The EPB is comparable in many respects to Japan's Ministry of International Trade and Industry. The planning board is staffed with Western-trained technocrats who make strategic decisions about what is to be produced, what industry is to be targeted for development and growth, which favored industry is to get what government credit and/or favorable tax treatment. For the past decade, the overall objective of the South Korean EPB has been growth. It makes recommendations to the central-government-controlled banking system relative to the allocation of credit and control of foreign exchange access. The EPB has mapped out a series of economic strategies designed to achieve that objective. Under military strongman Park Chung Hee's personal attention and the government's willingness to intervene, the overall strategy began with rapid development of South Korea's infrastructure of railroads, roads, harbors, and electrification under the first five-year plan (1962–66). Simultaneously, it adopted a basic, but persistent, export-growth strategy by taking into account South Korea's comparative advantage of skilled labor and low-wage structure. Through a series of such five-year plans, the South Korean export-based economy progressed from labor-intensive toy and textile industries to steel making to shipbuilding and car manufacturing to sophisticated high-tech (but high-priced) electronic products.

Emulating its counterpart in Japan, the MITI, the Economic Planning Board has been able to shift its development strategy to meet changing world market conditions. There have been a number of reasons that serve to explain why the South Korean government has been able to direct, influence, and intervene in its economy. First, it may be argued that the long period of stability under the "military-bureaucratic-authoritarian" regime of Park Chung Hee had been the condition under which economic success took place, even though some scholars indicated a lack of such correlation.[80] However, Kuznets offered the argument that it is the "hierarchical and authoritarian Confucian tradition of family and political relationships" that provided support for the regime's policies as a sort of "Mandate of Heaven" permitting government "activism" in the economy.[81]

Then, two factors served to enable South Korea's economic miracle: effective administration under a highly centralized government with little or no regional or local autonomy, enabling the government to "transmit and enforce" its policies; plus total dedication of the regime and its populace to economic goals. In the final analysis, it was "the combination of planning and effective policy implementation" that provided the answers to the success.[82]

The Dominance of Chaebol, Family-Owned Conglomerates   The success of the South Korean economy is partly attributable to the development, at the government's encouragement and nurturing, of family-owned and operated manufacturing and trading conglomerates known as the *chaebol*.[83] They are comparable to the formation of Japan's oligarchical companies, or monopolies, in the nineteenth century. For decades they became the authoritarian regime's convenient instruments for economic development.

There are literally thousands of family-owned enterprises in South Korea. But only about 100 of these are chaebols. The top ten chaebols are really giant multinationals. The top four chaebols—Samsung, Hyundai, Lucky-Goldstar, and Daewoo—had total sales in 1988 of more than $105 billion, or about half of South Korea's GNP of over $200 billion for the same year. The top seven chaebols and their trading companies controlled about 40 percent of South Korea's exports.

Most of these giant conglomerates had their debut in the early 1960s with rather humble assets and talents. The founder of the Hyundai Group was a bricklayer who ruled the company for over twenty years. Hyundai grew and developed in accordance with government demands, first as an engineering and construction firm. It was then chosen by Park Chung Hee's planners as one of the capable potential entrepreneurs and was assigned tasks for economic development; the government saw to it that Hyundai and the other chosen chaebols were provided with easy credit and necessary financing at low interest rates. The government also suspended income taxes on profits and reduced or waived tariffs on imported raw material. From construction, Hyundai grew and expanded to steelmaking and then on to shipbuilding and car manufacturing. By the mid-1980s, the Hyundai Group and its subsidiaries amassed assets valued at $8.2 billion in U.S. dollars and sales of $14 billion while employing 150,000 people. In 1984 its overseas construction contracts, mostly in the Mid-East countries, reached more than $3.5 billion.

Small and medium-sized concerns have been highly critical of the chaebol's economic power, which has stifled the growth of small entrepreneurship and competition. The chaebols controlled not only major businesses such as steel and auto manufacturing, but also "local markets for squid and kim chi pickles".[84] In 1987 the government of former President Roh imposed restrictions on extending low-interest credit and loans to chaebols, a preferential measure long enjoyed by the oligarchy, and prohibition of shareholdings among the giants and their subsidiaries. These government measures were intended to enable small entrepreneurs a chance to grow.[85]

After introducing these anti-chaebol measures in 1988–89, the government then abandoned these actions as the South Korean economy experienced a slowdown, and as it realized that these giant conglomerates were needed for the new emphasis on investment in new technology industries to compete successfully in the world market. A new coalition emerged between the conservative Roh regime and the chaebols under which their new target of attack has been the trade unions.[86] Large amounts of funds were amassed to elect the Democratic Liberal party under former President Roh.[87] The chaebols have cooperated with the Roh regime by allowing public listing on the stock market and by forcing them to sell chaebol land holdings. (By 1989 there were a total of 626 companies listed publicly.)[88] The chaebols have also become more autonomous and have been investing heavily abroad in order to meet stiff international competition with domestic labor costs rising significantly in recent years.

Education in South Korea   South Korea's economic success is attributable fundamentally to its education system. In 1945 about 50 percent of the population was illiterate. By 1986 the literacy rate in South Korea was more than 98 percent. It is obvious that their economic success would not have been possible without an educated and skilled work force.

As in Japan, South Korea also places enormous importance on education; educational attainment has been a top priority in South Korea's Confucian-oriented society. The student population has grown more than 10 percent since 1965. By 1988 there were 104 institutions of higher learning with a university student enrollment of over 1 million, not including 75,117 graduate students in 251 graduate schools. Graduate students from South Korea enrolling in American universities have been on the increase. (The generation of chief executives in the chaebols are graduates of American universities.) The talents and knowledge of university graduates have been recognized by the government, which recruits them into well-funded think-tanks, or places them in decision-making positions in various government bureaus. As a consequence, scholars and academia have been influential in public life.

In South Korea, as in Japan, all secondary school graduates wish to be admitted into the universities, and nationally administered university entrance examinations are extremely competitive. The "examination hell" places an enormous amount of pressure on high school students the very minute they enter into secondary school, for the total number of high school graduates has been on the rise steadily while only one-third of the graduates in a given year can be admitted into the universities.[89] Entrance to colleges and universities is based on three sets of records: a student's scores on the national entrance examination, high school test scores, and a combination of an essay and interview by the university of the student's choice. Tests or exams are basically multiple choice, modeled on American standardized tests. In the winter of 1989, 900,190 students took the seven-hour national entrance examination; only one in five expected to pass. As a consequence the educational objective in South Korea, as in Japan, has been to pass the university entrance examinations. Reform in the entrance examination system is long overdue.

As of 1988 there were over 1 million students enrolled in colleges and universities. Rising university enrollment also has increased problems of academic quality. The end result has been large classes and overemphasis on grades and memorization in lieu of learning. Until 1985, as in Japan, academic demands at institutions of higher learning were modest. Before 1985 the government imposed the unpopular requirement that there must be a failure rate of 30 percent before graduation.

Taiwan: Economic Well-Being as a Contributing Factor to Political Reform

Economic Performance   Taiwan has enjoyed a miraculous economic performance since the 1960s and 1970s that continues today. A World Bank report provided its 1970–81 average annual growth rates as 9.3 percent, next only to Hong Kong, which was 9.9 percent.[90] In recent years Taiwan's GNP has been as follows: 1991, 7.1 percent; 1990, 5.3 percent; 1989, 7.3 percent; 1988, 7 percent; 1987, 11.4 percent; and 1986, 13 percent. In 1990 Taiwan's per capita income was $8,000, one of the highest in Asia, trailing slightly behind that of Singapore and Hong Kong, which had per capita incomes of over $10,000 for the same period.

Factors Contributing to Taiwan's Economic Miracle   There is no question that the security and political stability provided under the 1954 Mutual Security Act by the U.S. military presence in East Asia in general and Taiwan in particular, in addition to U.S. aid for Taiwan, have shielded Taiwan from the mainland China communist threat. This arrangement has allowed the ruling KMT to devote its time and energy to economic development. Yuan-li Wu, an economic authority on Chinese economic development, has listed four principal factors that played an important role during the first crucial decade from 1949 to 1960: the successful completion of land reform in 1953, the control of inflation, the restoration of Taiwan's infrastructure, and the "harnessing of the country's external resources."[91] Of these factors, perhaps land reform was the most important in Taiwan's initial stages of economic development.

LAND REFORM   One of the most remarkable socio-economic changes that took place in Asia in the 1950s was Taiwan's successful implementation of land reform. Taiwan's land reform must be viewed in contrast to the ruthless forcible land reform in mainland China for the same period. Taiwan's land reform was an endeavor of the Joint Commission on Rural Reconstruction (JCRR) by two American aid specialists and three Taiwan agrarian technical experts, including Lee Teng Hui, Taiwan's president. The key feature of the land reform was the role played by the government in the sale of public land to tenant farmers at favorable credit terms or 2.5 times the value of one year's crop; a total of 96,000 hectares were sold to 156,000 tenant farm households.[92] Then the landlords were asked to sell to the government their surplus land, which they did not need. Here was the most significant aspect of the socioeconomic transformation for Taiwan: the landlords then were compensated with shares of stock in publicly owned industrial enterprises or with government bonds that could be redeemed for cash. In Taiwan's case two goals were accomplished with one stroke: creation of a new urban entrepreneurial class of landlords, all of them Taiwanese, and ownership of land by eight of ten farm households.[93] Native Taiwan landlords used their government bonds as capital for Taiwan's first stage of economic development that paved the way for the subsequent "Taiwan economic miracle."[94] Lucian Pye points out that this transformation enabled "a strange inversion of economic and political power" to take place in Taiwan: The politically elite, the 2 million mainlanders, had a lower living standard than the native-born Taiwanese.[95]

This 1949–53 land reform was accompanied by expansion of infrastructure of roads, availability of fertilizer, and credits for the farmers who worked on the land. Then in the mid-1970s and early 1980s the reform was followed by consolidation of irrigated farm land and mechanized farming with advanced techniques and funds to enlarge the farmers' operations. As a result, agricultural production increased dramatically: for the period 1952 to 1980 net agricultural growth rose by 15.4 percent a year.[96] Now, as urban industries grow, only 80,000 farm families remain to produce enough to meet the agricultural needs of Taiwan.

LIBERALIZED TRADE AND INDUSTRIAL EXPANSION   Another example of the government's role in fostering economic development lies in a deliberate policy toward liberalized trade by removing import controls as early as 1958. The government also encouraged domestic industries to produce exportable items to meet world market demands, particularly in the U.S. consumer market. In order to stimulate investment in export industries, a foreign export processing zone in the southern port city of Kaohsiung was established in 1966. Manufacturing grew at an annual rate of 17 percent from 1961 to 1973. Foreign investment grew as Taiwan's export trade expanded from 1965 to 1975. Confronted with a worldwide oil price rise in 1975, the Taiwan government stepped in and provided tax rebates to selected industries to reduce their cost of production and enable them to compete favorably in the world markets. For more than twenty years, from 1965 to 1985, Taiwan's leading export industry was in textiles and clothing manufacturing; by the mid-1980s textiles represented about 14 percent of all of Taiwan's industrial production.[97]

In the 1980s the government began to place increased emphasis in these areas: expansion of investment in high-technology oriented products; diversification of exports to markets other than the United States with increased investment overseas; and further liberalization of imports to tie Taiwan closer to a world of free trade.[98] It has been pointed out by Yuan-li Wu that from the 1980s greater emphasis was also placed on research and development (R & D).[99] In 1990 the cabinet earmarked $436 million for investment in high technology.

The overall result has been Taiwan's ability to accumulate an export surplus with the United States estimated at $12 billion in 1989, declining to about $9 billion for 1990. Export to the United States constituted 32 percent of Taiwan's total export trade, followed by Japan at 14 percent and Hong Kong at 13 percent. By October 1991 Taiwan's exports totaled $70.4 billion and imports $58 billion.[100] Taiwan's foreign reserve has been estimated at more than $70 billion for 1990. Taiwan's overseas investment in Thailand, Malaysia, Indonesia, and the Philippines was close to $2 billion for 1989; total Taiwan business investments for Southeast Asia has been $12 billion in 1992.[101] Trade with and investment in mainland China has also multiplied by leaps and bounds. In short, a large part of Taiwan's prosperity was centered in foreign trade.

State Enterprises and Privatization   Until 1985, as much as 85 to 90 percent of Taiwan's industrial production has been in private hands. This was due to a government policy introduced in the 1960s to ensure that most industries would be operated by the private sector, except for those under government control due to size and national security or defense. However, the government manages and monopolizes the remaining 10 percent of industries. The Commission of National Corporations oversees 10 of the largest state-owned enterprises in steel, petroleum, shipping, iron works, and banks.

As the result of concern in the mid-1980s by bureaucrats and economic planners, a new effort was made in 1991 to embark on a privatization program with the goal of raising as much as $40 billion by the sale of state-owned enterprises. The amount thus raised would be channeled toward a national economic development plan. The program utilized a gradual approach of perhaps relinquishing government ownership and control of about half of the state-owned (mostly by the provincial government) companies at the initial stage, with complete privatization by the year 2000.[102] Scheduled for complete privatization by 1992 were two banks, a shipping concern, and an iron works. Already listed for privatization were China Steel (88 percent government ownership), China Petroleum Development Company (79 percent government owned), and the First Commercial Bank (72 percent government owned).[103] There was opposition from labor unions and criticism of the lack of a "clear legal framework," so much so that in June 1991 the Legislative Yuan enacted a law requiring establishment of a compensation fund for state employees who lose their jobs.[104] Some of these state-owned enterprises were not able to successfully vie with private competitors. While the privatization program would ultimately result in a reduction in government revenue from surplus profits, estimated at 10 percent of the total government income, the strongest argument for privatization has been the creation of more gainful employment opportunities culminating in faster growth.[105]

For future economic development, the government has approved a massive long-range plan for 1991–96, which would incur an outlay of $303 billion to upgrade transportation, environment, energy, social welfare, education, urban housing, and technology so that by 1996 Taiwan's per capita income would rise to about $14,000.

Education   Taiwan's economic miracle would not have been possible had there not existed an industriousness within its people strengthened by their technical skills through education. Out of Taiwan's 1990 government budget of about $32 billion, close to 22 percent was allocated for education. In 1990–91 about 26 percent of the total population of 20 million were attending schools from primary to higher education, as compared to only 14.6 percent in 1952.[106] In 1990–91 there were 2.4 million primary school students, or about 99 percent of school-aged children, 1.8 million secondary and vocational students, and over one-half million students in institutions of higher education, about 13 percent of the total population. Taiwan students constitute consistently the largest group enrolled in graduate work in United States universities—more than 20,000 each year. There is no longer a "brain drain" problem with Taiwan students studying abroad, as there had been in the 1950s and 1960s—now they all return to Taiwan to contribute to the making of the Taiwan miracle.

***Reunification or Independence?*[107]**   An extremely sensitive policy question concerning Taiwan's future is whether to aim for reunification with mainland China or independence for a separate Taiwan. In 1978–79 at the time of U.S. negotiations for the PRC recognition, Beijing had suggested that as a start there should be an exchange of mail, trade, and air/shipping services between Taiwan and mainland China. Taiwan's response was the official formula of "no talks, no compromise and no contacts." In 1984 when Beijing and the United Kingdom signed their agreement to return Hong Kong to China by 1997, it was suggested by the PRC that Taiwan could also accept a similar arrangement under which there would be "one country, but two systems," for Britain had obtained assurance from Deng Xiaoping that there would be no change for fifty years after Hong Kong's reversion. In 1987 the PRC even intimated that if the Taiwan reunification question is not resolved soon, Beijing might have to resort to force to have it settled—reflecting perhaps Deng's dilemma over the deadlock.[108]

However, influenced by several recent developments, since then Taiwan's attitude toward the reunification problem has been modified. First, indirect trade between Taiwan and the mainland has expanded to reach close to the $1 billion mark. Official contact had in fact taken place in May 1986 in Hong Kong over negotiation for the transfer of a Taiwan China Airline cargo jet from Guangzhou after the pilot defected—an indication of Taiwan's flexible policy change. A more dramatic Taiwan policy change was the October 1987 repeal of an almost forty-year ban on visits of relatives by those mainlanders in Taiwan who fled without their families in 1949. For a period of time, from 1987 to 1990, the so-called *dalu re* (mainland heatwave) prevailed, so that by October 1990 a total of 1.8 million Taiwanese visited the China mainland.[109]

President Lee Teng Hui and former prime minister Hau Pei Tsun adopted a cautious attitude toward the Taiwan reunification issue. However, despite the note of caution, in the summer of 1991 the Cabinet issued a set of "guidelines" with respect to contacts with Beijing. As reported, the first stage would allow informal contacts based on "the principle of reciprocity and parity between the two sides." Attached to the proviso is the demand made by Taiwan that Beijing must carry out economic reform and political democratization, which would include freedom of expression. Beijing must also "renounce the use of force" against Taiwan and "accept Taiwan's presence in the international community."[110] The second stage would open up official communication, direct trade, and official visits on the basis of equality. The final stage would involve "consultation and discussion on reunification" in accordance with the will of the people in both the mainland and Taiwan areas.[111] President Lee lectured to KMT cadres in June 1991 that there was no timetable and that it might require decades to reach goals set in the Cabinet's guidelines. As reported by the *Far Eastern Economic Review*, liberal KMT lawmakers and the opposition DPP took the position that the guidelines represented no consensus of public endorsement, but merely a "hypothetical progression open to interpretation."[112] In the meantime cultural and academic contacts are ongoing under the auspices of the Straits Exchange Foundation, which also undertakes dispute settlements on indirect trade.

A complicating factor in the cautious move toward a possible solution to the Taiwan reunification problem is the movement for Taiwan independence, which is opposed by both the KMT and PRC. As discussed earlier, in the 1989 and 1991 elections the opposition party, DPP, supported and campaigned for Taiwan independence. The point that needs to be made here is that not only did the 1991 election serve as a strong signal to the DPP that an independent Taiwan is not acceptable to the voters, many of them native-born Taiwanese, but as Taiwan becomes more democraticized and as more political reforms take place, the rationale for an independent Taiwan may be hard to justify.

To conclude this discussion of the reunification problem, it must be pointed out that increased contact between Beijing and Taiwan has yielded beneficial economic gains—transit trade across the strait had reached over $5.8 billion in 1991, and Taiwan's business investment in China's Fujian Province was $1.5 billion.[113]

SUGGESTED READINGS

South Korea

Bunge, Frederica M. *South Korea: A Country Study*. Washington, DC: U.S. Department of the Army, 1982.

————. *North Korea: A Country Study*. Washington, DC: U.S. Department of the Army, 1981.

Clough, Ralph N. *Embattled Korea: The Rivalry for International Support*. Boulder, CO, and London: Westview Press, 1987.

Gregor, A. James. *Land of the Morning Calm: Korea and American Security*. Lanham, MD: University Press of America, 1990.

Haas, Michael, ed. *Korean Reunification: Alternative Pathway*. New York: Praeger, 1989.

Hinton, Harold C. *Korea under New Leadership: The Fifth Republic*. New York: Praeger, 1983.

Kaufman, Burton I. *The Korean War: Challenges in Crisis, Credibility and Command*. Philadelphia: Temple University Press, 1986.

Kihl, Young Whan. *Politics and Policies in Divided Korea: Regimes in Contest*. Boulder, CO, and London: Westview Press, 1984.

Kim, Ilpyong J. and Young Whan Kihl. *Political Change in Korea*. New York: Korean PWPA, 1988.

Lee, Manwoo. *The Odyssey of Korean Democracy: Korean Politics, 1987–1990*. New York: Praeger, 1990.

Park, Chi Young. *Political Opposition in Korea, 1945–1960*. Seoul: National University Press, 1980.

Sanford, Dan C. *South Korea and the Socialist Countries: The Politics of Trade*. New York: St. Martin's Press, 1991.

Sohn, Hak-kyu. *Authoritarianism and Opposition in South Korea*. New York: Routledge, 1990.

Suh, Dai-Sook. *Kim Il Sung: The North Korean Leader*. New York: Columbia University Press, 1988.

Taylor, William J., Jr., Cha Young-Koo, and John Q. Blodgett. *The Korean Peninsula: Prospects for Arms Reduction under Global Detente*. Boulder, CO: Westview Press, 1990.

Taiwan

Chiu, Hungdah, ed. *China and the Taiwan Issue*. New York: Praeger, 1979.

Copper, John F. Taiwan: *Nation-State or Province?* Boulder, CO, San Francisco, and London: Westview Press, 1990.

Feldman, Harvey, Michael Y. M. Kau, and Ilpyong J. Kim, eds. *Taiwan in a Time of Transition*. New York: Paragon House, 1988.

Lasater, Martin L. *A Step toward Democracy: The December 1989 Elections in Taiwan, Republic of China*. Washington, DC: University Press of America, 1990.

Lee Lai To. *The Unification of China: PRC-Taiwan Relations in Flux*. New York: Praeger, 1991.

Long, Simon. *China's Last Frontier*. New York: St. Martin's Press, 1991.

Nathan, Andrew J. *China's Crisis: Dilemma of Reform and Prospect for Democracy*. New York: Columbia University Press, 1990.

Simon, Dennis Fred, ed. *Taiwan: Beyond the Economic Miracle*. White Plains, NY: M. E. Sharp, Inc., 1992.

Winckler, Edwin A. *Contemporary Approaches to the Political Economy of Taiwan*. White Plains, NY: M. E. Sharp, 1988.

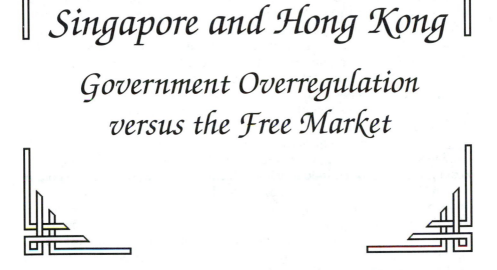

3

Singapore and Hong Kong

Government Overregulation versus the Free Market

Singapore and Hong Kong both have been British crown colonies. Singapore, however, has been independent and sovereign since 1965, when it broke away from its merger with Malaysia. Hong Kong will remain a crown colony until its reversion to China in 1997.

In both Singapore and Hong Kong the ethnic Chinese dominate the population and constitute an overwhelming majority demographically, even though the total population for both is small.

Singapore has had ten parliamentary elections, the last held on August 30, 1991. In the case of Hong Kong the main concern of the people has been economic prosperity, not political participation. The voter turnout for the August 1991 election to the colony's Legislative Council (an advisory body to the governor, who is an appointee from London) was not more than 39 percent of the 1.9 million registered, of 3.8 million eligible. With respect to economic development, Hong Kong has been a model of free-market economy with little government interference—except that there has been a long-time "coalition" between the island's banks and trading companies with those "lifetime expatriates" who run the government,[1] while Singapore has been a government-regulated society under the paternalistic leadership of Lee Kuan Yew for about four decades. To some critics Singapore is the epitome of an overregulated centralized political and economic system. While Singapore has been struggling with its multilingual and multicultural identity, Hong Kong's social and cultural makeup has been essentially Chinese.

THE CASE OF SINGAPORE

Today, Singapore, or Singupura (a Sanskrit word meaning "Lion City"), is a city-state comprised of the main granitic Singapore Island plus about fifty other mostly uninhabited smaller islands. Singapore Island is approximately 238 square miles, accounting for 93 percent of the total land area. The city-state of Singapore lies on the southern tip of the Malay peninsula, which separates the Indian Ocean from the South China Sea. Singapore Island itself is separated from the Malay peninsula by the Strait of Johore—a causeway less than a mile long linking Singapore with the Malay mainland.

Due to its geographic vantage point, in terms of commerce and trade Singapore has been in a position to dominate the Strait of Malacca and the sealanes leading to the Indonesian archipelago. In many ways Singapore is the crossroads serving as a trading center for the Malay peninsula and the Indonesian archipelago, where there is an abundance of natural resources. Today the wide, deep, and well-protected port of Singapore is the fourth largest in the world and a major transportation nucleus. Dating back to the thirteenth century A.D., Singapore, then known as Temasek, was already a trading center under the Sumatran empire, the Srivijaya. In the fourteenth century the city was destroyed as the rival Indonesian empires fought against one another. It remained a deserted outpost for more than 400 years thereafter, until Sir Thomas Stamford Raffles of the British East India company arrived in 1819 and transformed the island into a major commercial port that dominated Southeast Asia.

The city of Singapore is a modern metropolis of glass and concrete buildings; to some it has lost its charm and character as an oriental city. As a modern city it is the cleanest anywhere in the world. The regulations against spitting and littering are enforced vigorously by the authorities. Once covered by dense jungle and swamp, Singapore has no natural resources. Its land is primarily flat with soil generally low in fertility. Yet since its independence in 1965 Singapore has been a success story in terms of economic development; it is a city-state oriented toward the future by relying on the development of human resources. The leaders of Singapore are determined to build a postindustrial society that will be based on the development of "sunrise industries," stressing the importance of information and knowledge acquisition.

Singapore as a city-state is highly urbanized. It is also a multiethnic and multicultural society populated by Chinese, Malays, and Indians. The 1990 census for Singapore revealed a total population of 3 million, an increase of about 2.2 percent over the 1980s.[2] The ethnic composition of Singapore's population is as follows: Chinese, 2.3 million (77.7 percent); Malays, 420,000 (14.1 percent); and Indian, 210,000 (7.1 percent). On the whole, the ethnic distribution of Singapore's population did not change significantly in the decade of 1980–90. The Chinese percentage declined slightly from 78 percent in 1980 to 77.7 percent in 1990; and the Malay percentage declined from 14.4 to 14.1 percent. The only ethnic group making a slight gain was the Indian population: from 6.3 to 7.1 percent.[3] Two other demographic features need to be mentioned. One is the youthful composition of the Malay population: 29 percent of its total of 420,000 are below the age of fifteen. This compares significantly to 22 percent for the Chinese population and 23.7 percent for the Indian population. The other is the number (now estimated at over 42 percent) of Chinese women of marriageable age, twenty-five to thirty-nine, who prefer either late marriage or no marriage at all. For some time this phenomenon has been the focus of government officials, notably former prime minister Lee Kuan Yew. Their aim has been to devise methods for encouraging Chinese women, particularly the educated, to marry and have more children in order to maintain a Chinese numerical strength in electoral terms, and to fulfill the need for superior quality of human development as Singapore enters into the postindustrial age.

THE CASE OF HONG KONG

Hong Kong, as it is now administered by Great Britain as a crown colony, consists of three parts: (1) Hong Kong Island, a rock of about thirty square miles; (2) Kowloon peninsula, 3.5 square miles, the southern extension of the Chinese mainland below the hills of the so-called nine peaks; and (3) the New Territories, 377 square miles that extend into the Guangdong Province. These land areas, plus some 235 outlying islands, add up to the present crown colony total land area of 415 square miles. Hong Kong Island was ceded in perpetuity to Great Britain by the 1842 Treaty of Nanking at the end of the Opium War; the Kowloon Peninsula was ceded to Great Britain under the 1860 Treaty of Peking; but the New Territories were leased by China to Great Britain for ninety-nine years beginning in 1898.

There is some uncertainty with respect to Hong Kong's exact boundary once the colony reverts to China in 1997 as the Hong Kong Special Administrative Region (SAR) under the Basic Law of Hong Kong, the post-1997 constitution for the territory. Paragraph 2 of the formal statement, issued by China's seventh National People's Congress (NPC), Third Session, on April 4, 1990, in establishing the Hong Kong SAR, states:

> The area of the Hong Kong Special Administrative Region covers the Hong Kong Island, the Kowloon Peninsula and the islands and adjacent waters under its jurisdiction.[4]

While the official statement also indicates a map for the Hong Kong SAR will be published by the Chinese government on the boundaries of these administrative divisions, some questions have been raised that will need further clarification. One, nowhere in the official statement is reference made to the leased New Territories, a term the Chinese do not use because of its "colonial connotation."[5] One local Hong Kong delegate revealed that the term *Kowloon Peninsula* refers to the New Territories.[6] There have been jurisdictional disputes over the maritime boundaries; these were brought on by efforts made by the Hong Kong police to suppress smuggling. So long as the ambiguous Basic Law provisions on what exactly constitutes the Hong Kong SAR is not clarified, even more disturbing will be the talk about the possibility of the future Hong Kong SAR to include the current Chinese Shenzhen Special Economic zone next door. Some have contended this may possibly be the reason for the deliberate ambiguity in the Basic Law, which does not describe the exact boundary of the Hong Kong SAR; prior to 1842 the Chinese Xin An County included Hong Kong Island, Kowloon, and the New Territories, as well as the present Shenzhen Special Economic Zone.

At dispute from time to time is the Walled City, a slum area, populated by no less than 33,000 people, located close to the airport in the middle of the Kowloon district. Because of an ambiguity in the 1898 Peking Convention provisions, the Chinese claimed jurisdiction over the Walled City, an abandoned fort and seat of the local magistrate. They were expelled and denied the claim by the British in 1899—a unilateral action never acceded to by the Chinese under the Manchu dynasty. The People's Republic of China reasserted its claim in 1948 and in 1962. Before 1960 the practice had been to deport criminals caught in the Walled City to China instead of prosecuting them in Hong Kong.[7] The Chinese raised objections on legal grounds at any British attempt to clear the slum conditions in the Walled City. However, only recently have the Chinese and British agreed to tear down and clear the slums in the Old Walled City of Kowloon.

The total population of Hong Kong in 1991–92 was about 5.8 million, excluding illegal immigrants. Taking Hong Kong as a whole, it is one of the most densely populated areas in the world with an average density of more than 5,000 persons per square mile; on Hong Kong Island it has been over 1,500 per square mile. About 98 percent of the 5.8 million total population are Chinese by ethnic origin; they speak the southern dialect, Cantonese. Since 1984 a movement has been launched to encourage Hong Kong people to learn to speak Chinese Mandarin, or the *putonghua*. However, there are two official languages for Hong Kong: English and Chinese.

POLITICAL CULTURE AND POLITICAL DEVELOPMENT

Singapore: From Entrepot to "Singapore Identity"

Historic Legacy For 400 years, from 1400 to 1826, Singapore was deserted and abandoned as a seaport and trading center in the Malay peninsula. Later, commerce and trade shifted to the Malacca and Sunda straits, which had become major links between Europe and the Far East. Singapore then became a fishing village and the home of a few Malay tribes, whose chiefs used the island as a burial ground.[8] By the seventeenth century, trade in the Indonesian archipelago was dominated by the Dutch, who fortified Batavia (Jakarta) on Java and Malacca. Singapore was entirely ignored and bypassed in the Dutch's main concern for colonizing the rich Indonesian archipelago.

By the mid-nineteenth century trade between India and China had flourished under the British East India Company. In their contest with the Dutch, who controlled commerce in the Malay peninsula and the Indonesian archipelago, the British needed bases of operation along the trade routes between India and China. In 1819 Sir Thomas Stamford Raffles, an employee of the British East India Company, obtained permission from the Malay chiefs who governed Singapore Island and the long-deserted port to use it for a foothold as a trading post on the Singapore River. In 1824, on behalf of the company, through monetary rewards and promises of lucrative pensions for the Malay chiefs, Raffles was able to entice them into ceding Singapore Island to the British East India company in perpetuity. It was primarily at Raffles' insistence that Singapore was maintained as "the principal entrepot," a strategically located free port, since "all vessels to and from China via Malacca" must pass the station.[9] The British East India Company administered Singapore from Calcutta with insufficient funds and inadequate personnel.

In 1826 the British East India Company merged Singapore with Penang and Malacca on the Malay peninsula into a single unit known as the Straits Settlement Presidency. For several reasons this arrangement did not really work.[10] Since the administration of the Straits Settlement must still be supervised by the British East India Company headquarters from India, it suffered monetarily due to financial crises faced by India in 1830. In fact, the Settlement was reduced to a lower status as a Residency under supervision from the company's Bengal presidency.[11]

In 1867 the Straits Settlement became a separate crown colony. As a crown colony under direct British control, the Straits Settlement was ruled by a governor appointed by London. In turn, the governor appointed councillors to a legislative body and an executive council to assist him in administering the colony's affairs. With the opening of the Suez Canal in 1869, the port of Singapore and the Strait of Malacca became a pivotal trade center between Europe and Asia.

Soon Singapore developed into the political and economic center for the Southeast Asian region. The free port of Singapore was the magnet that attracted traders and immigrants from China, India, and Java, for, dating back to the days of Raffles, there had been no restriction until 1929 on human migration. Flourishing tin and rubber plantations in the hinterland of the Malay peninsula made Singapore the commercial and financial center as well. For sixty years, from 1869 to 1929, Singapore and the Malay peninsula enjoyed long-term stability and economic expansion under British rule.

SINGAPORE UNDER JAPANESE OCCUPATION AND POSTWAR UNREST   On February 15, 1942, the British surrendered to the Japanese, who came by land instead of by sea. While the British had control of the air and sea, the invading troops moved swiftly, some on bicycles, marching south at an average of ten miles per day through the northeastern part of the Malay peninsula to Singapore Island, for the British were not prepared to defend against a land attack. Japanese occupation of British Singapore was harsh and repressive. The occupation force engaged in torture of interned Europeans and the civilian population.[12]

Political Belief   Sociologists in Singapore have been engaged in the study of what constitutes the "Singaporean identity."[13] The term refers to multiracialism, multilingualism, multiculturalism, and multireligiosity.[14] In short, the "Singaporean identity" is reflected in the population makeup, the language diversity, and the religious harmony that describe Singapore as a nation. With the exception of well-educated Singaporeans such as Lee Kuan Yew, whose education and political thinking have been basically British and who frequently espoused the virtues of Confucian precepts, Singaporeans are influenced by ethnic upbringing and religious influences, which in turn influence their political beliefs.

Malays who came to Singapore from the mainland, Malacca and Sumatra constituted a cohesive group because of their religion (Muslim), culture, and language. By 1840 they were the third-largest ethnic group, after the Chinese and the Indians. By 1990 they constituted 14.1 percent of Singapore's 3 million total population. However, viewed from a larger perspective, Singapore Malays are a part of the majority Malays in the peninsula. In Singapore their language is considered only one of the three officially recognized, but not a major one, except within the Malay community. As a multiethnic society, since independence the emphasis in Singapore has been generally on merit, not race or national origin. As Malays lagged behind the Chinese and the Indians in social and economic advancement, the government attempted somewhat to provide "self-help" for the Malays in education and business. These efforts at "self-help" have not produced the desirable results in elevating their social and economic standing in Singapore's multiethnic makeup.

Increasingly, young Malays have sought the Islamic religion "as a source of inspiration" to upgrade their status.[15] In the midst of a worldwide Islamic upsurge as a dynamic political and religious force, Singapore's leaders have frequently raised questions as to where Singapore's Malay loyalty would lie in time of crisis.[16] In 1987 Singapore restricted recruitment of Malayans into the armed services; the relaxation of that policy would ultimately be dependent upon national integration of Malayans into the society that has national identity.[17]

In 1990 the Indian component of Singapore's multiethnic society occupied the third-largest position, with 7.1 percent of Singapore's total population. It is the only group that has made gains in the 1980–90 decade. Indians came to Singapore originally as laborers and traders. The early arrivals were single males; a majority of them speak Tamil, a major language group in southern India and Ceylon (now Sri Lanka). The Indian community is divided by those who have command of the English language and those who do not, in addition to the linguistic diversity within the Indian community in Singapore. Within the Indian community there is also diversity in religious preferences between Hindu and Buddhist.

In the 1980s the government launched the Moral Education Program as a means of promoting the study of and education about other religions. Christianity and Christian influence have been predominant in education as they are closely associated with spread of the English language as an essential tool for business, government, and career development.[18] Thus, a revival of non-Christian religions became the policy in order to "redress the imbalance in the extent of Christian influence in the educational system."[19] Secondary school students were to receive instruction in other religions and alternative moral education, including Confucian ethics for the majority of Singapore's people whose ancestry was molded by that Chinese tradition. Confucian scholars were invited from the United States and Taiwan for consultation. In the end Confucian ethics was one of the six options made available to secondary school students for choosing as part of their moral or religious studies.

As argued by Confucian scholars brought to Singapore for consultation, Confucianism is not a religion but a "universal system of ethics" that had permeated other Asian societies such as Japan and Korea.[20] However, one invited Confucian scholar pointed out that, if promoted by the government as a moral education policy, Confucianism "may be used by the government to displace other religions."[21]

Union with Malaya and Independence   British military administration of Singapore ended in April 1946. Singapore maintained its status as a

crown colony under a governor-general who was accountable to the colonial office in London. In the British government proposal, other units of the
prewar Straits Settlement were to be constituted as a new Malayan Union.
The British government intended a "fusion" of Singapore and the Malayan
Union into a wider federation.

The proposal to include Singapore in a Malayan Union generated
opposition among the Malayans, who feared domination by the numerically
stronger Chinese. This opposition also received support from the Malayan
Communist party, as well as the United Malays National Organization
(UMNO) in the peninsula. After flourishing briefly, the movement fell
apart as the Malayan Communist party withdrew its support. However, it
still controlled the Singapore Trade Union. There were repeated failures at
organizing general strikes in Singapore in 1947–48 as an overall strategy to
foment urban revolution. British authorities in Singapore enacted emergency regulations prohibiting meetings and placing in detention those suspected of fomenting unrest. Communist leaders in the labor unions finally
left Singapore in the spring of 1948 for mainland Malay. Singapore was
then provided a period of relative peace, a period during which constitutional reform took place and paved the way for eventual self-government
and independence.

In 1953, with the fever for Singapore's elected self-government running high, Sir George Rendel was appointed to study possible constitutional changes. The Rendel commission recommended a legislative assembly
of thirty-two members with twenty-five (78 percent) to be elected.The
commission proposed a cabinet of nine—six of whom would be recommended by the political party with a majority of seats in the legislative
assembly—to assist the governor in the administration of Singapore, except
in the area of foreign affairs. Upon acceptance by London, an election was
set for April 1955. In the election contest two radically oriented parties
formed an alliance to defeat the more conservative Progressive party, which
was dominated by Chinese businessmen. These were the Labor Front, led
by David Marshall; and the People's Action party, led by Lee Kuan Yew,
but supported by the leftist trade unions and the English-speaking educated
Chinese. They won eighteen out of a total of thirty-two seats (56 percent)
in the legislative assembly. However, the alliance was a shaky one, for the
leaders elected to the legislative body were a collection of socialists, liberals, and independents. It was not until the 1959 election that one party, Lee
Kuan Yew's People's Action Party (PAP), won a comfortable majority,
forty-three of the fifty-one legislative seats, to become the majority party in
Singapore until the present.

UNION WITH MALAY   In the pre-1955 election rallies, the PAP campaigned on the theme of merger with the Malayan Federation as the only
appropriate strategy for Singapore's independence. In the midst of Malay's

own struggle to rid itself of communist insurgency in the peninsula, Malay leaders such as Tunku Abdul Rahman discarded their long held fear of Chinese domination under a merger of a wider Malayan federation. They advocated a new proposal that would provide a union with Singapore by also bringing in Sarawak and Sabah (North Borneo) to neutralize the numerical strength of the Singapore Chinese population in a larger federation. Under Lee Kuan Yew's leadership the PAP was eager to endorse the idea of a wider Malayan Union to include Singapore, but was troubled by its more radical trade-union-dominated elements within the party. In a stormy discussion and debate in the legislative assembly over the issue, the radical elements of the PAP seceded from the party to form a dissident Socialist Front.

In 1962 a public referendum was held in Singapore that approved Singapore's joining the Malayan Federation. In July 1963 the Malaysia Agreement was signed and the Federation of Malaysia—Malaya, Singapore, Sarawak, and Sabah—was officially established on September 16, 1963. Singapore then unilaterally declared its own independence and the end of colonial rule.

Singapore's association with the Malayan Federation was anything but smooth. For one thing, Malay leaders, conservative and anticommunist, felt uneasy when the PAP fielded as many as nine successful candidates in the 1964 peninsula-wide election. Mainland Malayans were concerned and alarmed by racial riots in June and September 1964 in Singapore. There was fear that Indonesian saboteurs had infiltrated into Singapore in its "confrontation" with Malaysia. Then Lee Kuan Yew's exhibition of personal aggressive behavior annoyed the more docile nonconfrontational mainland Malayans. Lee was critical of special rights accorded to the Malayans. Singapore-Malay relations within the union were strained from the outset and became increasingly intractable, reaching a crisis situation. After a series of talks between Prime Ministers Lee Kuan Yew and Tunku Abdul Rahman had failed to produce any accord, the federal government in Kuala Lumpur demanded Singapore's withdrawal from the Federation of Malaysia. Singapore agreed and pulled out of Malaysia on August 9, 1965.

After having won a decisive victory in the 1968 election, under the PAP, Singapore began to implement a multifaceted program to enable it to survive as a nation. While the British did not completely withdraw their military presence in Singapore until well into the 1970s, the Singapore parliament enacted legislation providing for compulsory military service for all eighteen-year-old male adults. Singapore's armed force became a small, but professionally trained one (with aid from Israel). The government embarked on a program designed to develop full employment by encouragement of foreign investment and export-oriented industrialization. Publicly subsidized social programs for housing and education were implemented.

Political development in Singapore since 1965 had been monopolized by the PAP under the continuous paternalistic leadership of Lee Kuan Yew. In 1990 Lee retired from government service as the prime minister but retained his advisory status in the PAP.

Hong Kong: From "Dying City" to Crown Colony

Historic Legacy   At the very beginning when the rock on which the island of Hong Kong rested was taken over by the British in 1842, it was basically considered a barren piece of real estate, periodically subject to typhoons and epidemics of disease. For the British the island was the place for supervising trade with the newly opened treaty ports from south to east China. Then it became obvious, in the vision of some of the early governors of the Crown Colony, like Palmeston and Aberdeen, that Hong Kong could be developed as the military and commercial center for the Far East as it was the only British possession east of Singapore.[22] British commercial firms were persuaded to begin operating in Hong Kong by 1844. Hong Kong as a new trade center was then dominated by the British pattern in India and under the influence of the British East India Company—Jan Morris points out that the three Crown Colony governors were of Anglo-Indian background. With the trading firms there came European merchants, shopkeepers, and physicians. Trading companies were dominated by Jardine and Matheson.[23]

The colonial administration for the Crown Colony was best characterized as "minimal"[24] in that it was the London-designated governor who ran the affairs of the colony with an assist from his appointed counselors. Administrative concerns were largely those of land reclamation and management, law and order, the development of reservoirs, and improvement in sanitary conditions and public works. For the first decade, taxes collected were not sufficient to do anything beyond paying government employees. In matters of budget and finance the merchants had a more influential voice with the governor. Hong Kong's economy prior to the end of World War II was based on entrepot trade consisting of shipping, marine insurance, banking, and warehouse facilities and services. Manufacturing was rather underdeveloped and insignificant.

After the Japanese surrendered and the war ended, with the return of the British administration and garrison command, Hong Kong struggled to survive and support the feeding of a population of 600,000. It recovered quickly, but remained as an entrepot and export center for primary commodities of bristles, feathers, goat skins, tea seed oil, and knitted fabrics. For most of the 1950s Hong Kong was not by any means considered an industrial city.

As the People's Republic of China was established in October 1949, refugees flooded to Hong Kong and boosted its population to 2.4 million in

1950. Then the Korean War broke out in June 1950, and the United Nations imposed an embargo on China. Hong Kong soon went into a serious economic depression—unemployment was at a 30 percent high and the colony lacked capital for economic development. Hong Kong was "a dying city," for trade with China was at a low ebb and the entrepot trade as a whole was not sufficient to enable the colony to survive economically. In addition, Hong Kong's future was politically uncertain in the light of a war in the Far East involving the major powers.

A shift of strategy then took place with hardly any input from the colonial government—from the old pattern of an entrepot to that of an export-oriented manufacturing base. By then refugee entrepreneurs, the Shanghai owners of industries, particularly the textile complex, brought to Hong Kong capital, know-how, and hardworking labor—factors needed for the development of light industries geared to export to the U.S. markets. As indicated by the Hong Kong government's 1966 annual report, by the 1960s textiles constituted 52 percent of Hong Kong's export trade, employing 41 percent of the colony's industrial force. By then Hong Kong was well on its way to sustained economic growth.

From the end of the Korean War in 1953 to 1982 Hong Kong was caught in a rapid whirl of economic growth (to be discussed shortly). Politically, it was a period of relative calm and apathy on the part of the population. The calm was interrupted briefly by riots: one caused by a rise in the ferry boat fares across the harbor from Kowloon to Hong Kong Island in 1956, and another, communist-instigated demonstrations in 1967 inspired by the Cultural Revolution upheaval in China.

Political Belief One could be cynical and say that Hong Kong Chinese have no real interest in any political belief except one that promotes moneymaking. However, this cynical view has been demolished whenever an occasion has arisen when Hong Kong people are called upon to take a stand. The 1989 Tiananmen demonstration is a good case in point. The Hong Kong populace demonstrated daily in support of the students in China. Hong Kong was the focal point for rallying overseas Chinese for political reform and democracy inside China. The Hong Kong based Democracy for China Alliance raised money from the colony's general population to finance the overseas Chinese dissident movement.

On the whole, Hong Kong's population is said to be deferential to authority. That is, there is a general acceptance of actions by the colonial government. Few in Hong Kong challenge the right of government to make and enforce laws. This political docility is explainable by the long period of colonial rule and a large influx of refugee population, reinforced by the Chinese Confucian tradition of accepting, instead of challenging, authority. In one sense it is the general populace's ready acceptance of authority that makes the Hong Kong colonial administration one of the most stable and easiest to operate.

In contrast with Singapore, another aspect of the political culture in Hong Kong is the atmosphere of a free press. The Hong Kong colonial government has rarely exhibited paranoid tendencies toward the free-wheeling press. The government's hands-off attitude in its press relations and its less-regulated stance toward business and commerce have contributed to Hong Kong's political stability, an ideal environment for economic development.

The 1984 Sino-British Joint Declaration on Hong Kong   As the ninety-nine-year New Territories (across from the Hong Kong island) lease is to expire in 1997, Prime Minister Margaret Thatcher's September 1982 visit to China ushered in a series of negotiations between the People's Republic of China and Great Britain over the future status of Hong Kong. In December 1982 China's National People's Congress promulgated a new constitution, drafted under the direction of Deng Xiaoping, in which Article 31 provides a legal device to allow Taiwan or Hong Kong to be reunited with China as a Special Administrative Region.[25] The idea that Hong Kong, if reverted to China, could have its own constitution and administration as a special region was conveyed repeatedly to visiting Hong Kong delegations by Chinese officials.

The two years of negotiation produced the 1984 Joint Declaration of Britain and the PRC on Hong Kong, which was signed by British prime minister Thatcher and Chinese premier Zhao Ziyang on December 19, 1984. Key provisions of the joint agreement contained the following:[26]

> 1. China is to resume its sovereignty over Hong Kong effective July 1, 1997.
> 2. In accordance with Article 31 of the PRC constitution, Hong Kong will become a special administrative region under the authority of the PRC central government, but enjoy a high degree of autonomy except in areas of foreign affairs and defense.
> 3. Laws in force in Hong Kong will remain unchanged.
> 4. Current social and economic systems, as well as life style, in Hong Kong will also remain unchanged.
> 5. As an SAR Hong Kong may establish its own economic and cultural relations and conclude agreements with other nations, regions, or relevant international organizations.

While the Joint Declaration does not provide a time limit for Hong Kong's autonomy as an SAR, China's paramount leader, Deng Xiaoping, has stated repeatedly that the social and economic systems would not change for as long as fifty years operating under Deng's concept of "one country, two systems." Thus, until Hong Kong is reverted to China in 1997, the Joint Declaration also entrusted Great Britain to continue administering Hong Kong. The implementation of the agreement and the actual transfer of sovereignty are to be consulted upon by a Joint Liaison Group of PRC and British representatives during the interim.

By decree on April 4, 1990, the PRC president promulgated the Basic Law of Hong Kong Special Administrative Region as the post-1997 constitution for Hong Kong, prepared for approval by the Chinese National People's Congress by a fifteen-member Drafting Committee for the Basic Law. The draft was the result of four and one-half years of work. Details on political structure, future Hong Kong government, and its power as an SAR under China are discussed in the pertinent parts to follow.

LOCUS OF POWER: POLITICAL INSTITUTIONS AND LEADERSHIP

Singapore: The Long Reign of Paternalism

One of the first acts undertaken after separation from Malaysia was to revoke the requirement for a two-thirds majority vote in Parliament for amending the constitution—a process needed at the time when Singapore must have flexibility to reestablish its independent government structure. The requirement was reinvoked in 1979 through Article 5, which now stipulates that the constitution can be amended only by a two-thirds majority in Parliament. The constitution provides for the following political institutions: the presidency, the Parliament, the prime minister and Cabinet, and the judiciary.

The President as Head of State   Article 17 of the Singapore constitution provides for the role of head of state in the office of the president, elected by the Parliament. The president's power includes appointment of the Cabinet and designation of the prime minister. These powers are generally ceremonial in nature, for under the parliamentary form of government it is the majority party that determines the ministers for the Cabinet. Thus, the president must act with the consent of the Cabinet as provided in Article 21(1). However, under Article 25 the president may use his own discretion on matters such as the appointment of a prime minister or on a request for dissolving the Parliament. In the final analysis, the president must consult with and be accountable to the Parliament. It is in this respect that the office is considered ceremonial and the person who occupies the office is considered a figurehead.

In 1990 a bill was proposed in the Singapore Parliament to change the office to an elected position instead of appointment by the Parliament. The bill was enacted into law in January 1991 for a more powerful elective presidential post. Election of the president was to take effect in 1993 when the four-year term of the present incumbent Wee Kim Wee expired. In August 1993 a presidential election was held in which Ong Teng Cheng became Singapore's first president elected for a six-year term.

The constitutional amendment providing for an elected president seems to lead to the end of the British parliamentary system, opening the way for inauguration of a presidential form of government.[27] A new set of powers is entrusted to the elected president. First is the presidential veto power over budgetary matters. A presidential veto over the budget would ensure responsible and prudent management of Singapore's reserves, which in 1990 were estimated to be more than U.S. $23 billion. The government-controlled forced saving system under the Central Provident Fund, which reaches to more than U.S. $20 billion, would also be responsibly administered.[28] Also, the elected president, if supported on budget matters by a majority of his appointed council, can veto the budget; and the veto shall be final. The only recourse the Parliament and/or the Cabinet would have is to amend the constitution by removing the presidential power. However, for ratification, such exercise would require a two-thirds majority vote to be followed by a popular referendum.[29]

Also, presidential consent must be obtained when a minister enforces a prohibition order on "mixing religion with politics" or "causing ill-feeling between religions."[30] The elected president has a decisive say on key appointments in the government, including state-owned enterprises, boards, police, judiciary, and armed forces. Finally, the elected president can order investigations into accusations of corruption by high-level government officials even if that investigation has been blocked by the prime minister.

The Parliament   The Singapore Legislature is unicameral and at present has a total membership of eighty-one. Until the 1988 election members of Parliament were chosen by single-member constituencies for a four-year term if there were no dissolution of Parliament during the period. In 1987 the ruling party (PAP) introduced the Parliament Elections Act, which provides for the Group Representative Constituency (GRC), or the "Team MPs System."[31] In plain language, the GRC system permits combining of three single-member constituencies into one group or voting block. A political party must now offer four candidates, or a team, if contesting a GRC, one of whom must be from an ethnic minority (a Malay or an Indian). Voters would then have a choice of voting for the entire slate presented by a party. Whichever party team or slate received the largest number of votes would be declared as winner of the contest, and all three candidates on the slate would become elected members of the Parliament.

The underlying purpose of the GRC was to devise a voting system for Singapore's minorities—the Malays in particular—to have a better chance for election to Parliament. Under the single-constituency system a candidate from a minority group (Malay or Indian) would have difficulty in getting elected from predominantly Chinese communities.[32] Another consideration for establishing the GRC system was to make elected members of Parliament serve concurrently with mayors or leaders of the town councils of their respective constituencies for dealing with local affairs such as public housing and sewage disposal.[33] (Singapore had abolished local government in 1959). Another possible reason might be to provide a better chance for the PAP's minority candidates—non-Chinese—to get elected on the coattails of stronger candidates (the PAP's minority candidates made a poor showing in the 1984 election).[34]

The PAP-dominated Parliament has been criticized by back-bench members for spending time on ceremonial duties and for the lack of staff and research assistance in the performance of their legislative duties.[35] More significant has been the criticism by Malays that PAP Malay members of Parliament were not truly representing the Malay community, since they must abide by the PAP's wishes.[36] However, criticism from its own back-benchers is not generally tolerated by PAP leadership. In one case a veteran PAP member of Parliament and a former Cabinet member, Jek Yuen Thong, was silenced by the party leadership for his outspoken criticism of the PAP's unwillingness to entertain new ideas and engage in open debate on issues, and for fostering an "elitist and arrogant attitude."[37]

Even more intolerance is directed toward criticism offered by opposition members of Parliament. An example is the celebrated case of Joshua Jeyaretnam, a one-time elected member of Parliament from the Workers' party, which consumed media and public attention from 1985 to 1987. Jeyaretnam, elected in the 1981 by-election, advocated a citizen's right to "challenge arbitrary government decisions" and freedom for trade unions to protect workers' rights.[38] Jeyaretnam made a charge in Parliament that there was some tampering by the executive branch with the independence of the Judiciary. A parliamentary investigation committee researched the charges and found that there was no basis for the accusation and that Jeyaretnam had abused his parliamentary privileges.[39]

Jeyaretnam lost his seat in Parliament after being convicted as the result of a 1972 lawsuit filed by the Workers' party against a PAP member of Parliament for alleged defamation at an election rally. The Workers' party lost the case in court and lost again on appeal. In 1982 the PAP member of Parliament demanded payment for costs from the Workers' party. When the Workers' party went into bankruptcy receivership, Jeyaretnam, as the party's secretary-general, then voluntarily declared the party's assets as "fair and true" value. He was charged with making a false statement and with illegally transferring party funds to avoid creditors. After much legal maneuvering a High Court justice in November 1986 rendered the final verdict by upholding the previous court ruling against Jeyaretnam with a sentence and fine. Singapore's constitution provides that a member convict-

ed on a criminal charge be removed from Parliament. The Parliament subsequently enacted a constitutional amendment that strips a member of his
privileges and immunities from legal action in the event of statements made
or behavior judged to be improper from a "cultural" perspective.

The Prime Minister and the Cabinet   Fashioned after the British
parliamentary system, Singapore's office of the prime minister is indeed the
most powerful. Although in Article II the constitution stipulates that it is
the president of the Singapore republic who appoints the prime minister
and the Cabinet, it is also the standard practice in the parliamentary system
to automatically assign the leader of the majority party to the prime minister position. In the case of Singapore, the PAP has been the majority party
and Lee Kuan Yew, until he resigned the premiership on November 18,
1990, has been the founding leader of the party since 1959, when the
British granted limited sovereignty for Singapore. Thus, Singapore's premiership has been in the hands of one leader for thirty-one years, one of the
longest ruling leaders in Asia.

Lee's ascendancy to power provided Singapore with over three
decades of political stability and economic growth. Lee's style of leadership has been paternalistic, authoritarian, and even arrogant according to
most of his critics. Lee was an outspoken opponent of communism and an
advocate of capitalism in conjunction with close government control and
interference. His political ideology has been that of building a stable
political base, or efficient government institutions, as a foundation for
Singapore's economic achievement. He has been a forceful leader, but by
no means omnipotent. He is said to have been one strong voice in the
"dynamics of leadership within the team" or "concentric circles" orbiting
around "the hub," which is Lee Kuan Yew.[40] As the prime minister, Lee
often engaged in debate over policy issues with his close colleagues, and
during these occasions he won most, but lost some.[41] According to
Robert Tilman, as a leader Lee has tried to build consensus in the inner
circle of government and party on major issues with members of the
Parliament prior to a debate by that body.[42] In other words, prior to the
1970s Lee operated as a party leader and the prime minister within a team
of close advisors rather than in the general public image of an all-power-
consuming authoritarian. Under the framework of team-style leadership,
differences or disputes were given opportunity to surface, but only within
the inner circle of the team, which met frequently in the prime minister's
office to air the members' views on issues before the Parliament.[43] Lee
made contacts with leaders outside of the inner circle to seek additional
information. In 1981 Lee proceeded deliberately to build a cadre of new
talents as potential leaders for the PAP and candidates for Parliament—
the coming of the political scene of a "second generation" of leaders that
included Goh Chok Tong, who succeeded Lee as prime minister in 1990,

and Lee's son Lee Hsien Loong, the minister for trade and industry in the Cabinet.[44]

Leadership Style and Succession   In the past, Lee Kuan Yew had been known as an outspoken leader on a variety of subjects and issues. For instance, he was once quoted as stating that failure of democracy in Pakistan or Burma might be attributed to the Western concept of "one-man-one-vote."[45] He preferred "wise paternalism" rather than leaving political power in the hands of the uneducated or the semi-illiterates.[46] His war waged against the foreign press left him with the widely accepted image of a leader who does not tolerate dissenting views or criticism.[47]

His retirement or resignation as the prime minister in 1990 does not mean he has given up influence in Singapore's politics. He has retained the position of secretary–general for the PAP, a post of considerable power. In his farewell speech to Parliament, Lee held firmly to his vision for Singapore's future as he argued his case on some contentious issues. First, he still felt strongly that Singapore's women university graduates must marry in larger percentage (now 50.3 percent as against 37.6 percent in 1983) to ensure a society of talent and skill for the twenty-first century.[48] He still had reservations about Western values or culture being appropriate for Singapore. Instead he asked for "cultural bearings,"[49] for he has long advocated the need to bring back Confucian influence to check the spread of "cultural imperialism" in Singapore.

GOH CHOK TONG: THE NEW PRIME MINISTER FROM THE SECOND GENERATION OF LEADERS[50]   The long-awaited uncertainty surrounding the succession or power transfer for Singapore was settled in the fall of 1990. Lee Kuan Yew decided to step down as the prime minister to be succeeded by a man he had groomed for years as his deputy. Goh Chok Tong became the first deputy prime minister from the second generation of leaders.

Goh was not Lee Kuan Yew's first choice. However, Goh was the Cabinet's choice to succeed Lee, particularly among the younger members. At the time of his selection in the fall of 1990 Goh was only forty-nine years of age. Like many Singapore leaders, he attended the Raffles Institute. He enrolled at the University of Singapore and received his M.A. degree in development economics at Williams College in Williamstown, Massachusetts. Upon his return from the United States he joined the finance ministry. Goh made his mark as a capable administrator when he bailed out the financially troubled government-owned shipping line, the Neptune Orient. Thereafter, Goh became a prominent technocrat, holding key ministry posts in finance, trade, health, and defense. In 1976 he was selected as the PAP candidate for Parliament and won. He became the assistant secretary-general for the PAP and took part in the party's strategy development for the 1980 election. As Lee Kuan Yew laid out his plan for building a cadre of younger ministers as a second generation of Singapore leaders, Goh was endorsed unanimously by six of his younger colleagues in the Cabinet, and received approval from Lee as the deputy prime minister in 1985. He was subsequently elevated to the position of first deputy prime minister in line of succession.

Goh's personality and style are in contrast with those of Lee Kuan Yew. Goh is more cheerful and somewhat more humble, even though his six-foot frame may intimidate people.[51] Goh is quite a reserved person and awkward at public speaking, but he has a reputation for listening to what the people have to say.[52] He has relaxed Singapore's standards in censoring films considered offensive by the older generation. (R-rated films are now permitted in Singapore.) He also has lifted restrictions on foreign media, the latest move involving permission for the Cable News Network (CNN) to expand its transmission in Singapore. With a slight upset in the August 1991 election, Goh has decided to slow down the pace of reform by focusing on the problems of low-income people.[53] Goh will be judged by what political, economic and social changes he can bring to Singapore in the years to come. In turn, these will depend on Goh's continued support from his younger colleagues in the Cabinet and his control over the PAP.

The Judicial System   The legacy of the British legal system for Singapore has been rather persistent and lasting, dating back to at least 1826, when Singapore was a crown colony. The British legal system which prevailed in the Crown Colony of Singapore was in the main statutes and common law, or English law, principles.[54] (Until January 1991 Singapore Supreme Court judges wore the traditional white wigs while sitting in sessions, and referred to one another in the British usage of "your lordship.")

The judicial structure for Singapore is based on the British system in that the Supreme Court of Judicature Act, as amended subsequently by the Legislature, provides for a Supreme Court to consist of three components: the High Court, the Court of Appeals, and the Court of Criminal Appeal. The High Court has the original jurisdiction over civil, as well as criminal, cases. In addition, it serves as the appellate court. However, until recently, appeals on civil matters could be heard by the Privy Council in London. In 1988–89 Parliament amended the constitution to prohibit the right of appeal to the Privy Council. The amendment was enacted as a reaction to the Jeyaretnam case when the appeals court in Singapore in 1986 sentenced and fined him for misusing Workers' party funds (as discussed earlier) and disbarred him from law practice. Jeyaretnam took his case to the Privy Council, which in 1988 overturned the Singapore court of appeals ruling.

Also, in the initial handling of the Jeyaretnam case the question of judicial independence had been raised. In the 1984 trial of Jeyaretnam's case for misuse of Workers' party funds, the appeals court judge acquitted Jeyaretnam on several counts and imposed a light fine—not enough to qualify him for dismissal from Parliament. The judge was transferred to the attorney general's office some months later. Jeyaretnam charged that the prime minister had interfered with the judicial independence of the courts, as guaranteed by Article 93 of the constitution.[55]

To ensure judicial independence Article 98 of the constitution provides that judges once appointed to the courts cannot be removed except through a special impeachment process. All judicial appointments are made by the Legal Service Commission, a nonpolitical and independent body established for the purpose of making appointments to the courts.

Hong Kong: A Chinese "Special Administrative Region" after 1997

Discussion of Hong Kong's political institutions will be divided into two segments—first, the pre-1997 political system, followed by an analysis of the post-1997 political system and structure as provided in the Basic Law of Hong Kong as a special Administrative Region of the PRC.

The Existing Political System for Hong Kong: Pre-1997   The most important political institution of a crown colony is the office of the governor, who is directly responsible to the British government in London. There have been twenty-nine governors appointed to Hong Kong, including the outgoing David C. Wilson and the incoming, probably the last governor, Christopher Patten. With a few exceptions most governors have been career officers in the colonial service. The appointments of Edward Youde in 1982 and David Wilson departed from the old pattern, for they had been career foreign service diplomats specializing in Chinese affairs. Christopher Patten, appointed in 1992, has been the key campaign strategist for the Conservative party for the 1992 parliamentary election, and he is not a career government official. Patten has irked the Chinese with his blueprint for voters election of 1995, two years prior to reversion, for a majority of the members of the Legislative Council. There have been many rounds of Sino-British negotiations on this controversial issue in 1993. The governor of Hong Kong has enormous power in the administration of the colony's affairs, subject indirectly to supervision from London. Governors in the olden days were "aloof, remote, almost vice-regal figures."[56] One of the most respected modern governors has been Murray MacLehose, who was visible and who maintained constant contact with the local Chinese. The governor and his government are served by 17,000 civil servants, 98 percent of them Chinese. It is one of the most efficient civil services in Asia.

The governor has an eleven-member Executive Council, known as ExCo; the bulk of them are nominated by the governor as unofficial members to represent the elites (business tycoons or prominent lawyers) in society. In 1926 a Chinese was made a member of the ExCo for the first time.

Today the ExCo membership is dominated by prominent Chinese elites, men and women of outstanding achievement and ability.

Then there is the sixty-member Legislative Council, known as LegCo. Only eighteen of the group are elected directly at-large from nine multi-member districts. Also elected are twenty-one members from the so-called functional constituencies representing interest groups aligned occupationally and professionally. The remaining twenty-one are appointed by the governor as unofficial members. Thus, the elected thirty-nine constitute the legislative majority. Sessions of the LegCo, a sort of Hong Kong legislative assembly, are presided over in person by the governor. He can intervene in the deliberation if he so wishes, but mostly he serves the function as speaker of assembled delegates.

The judicial system for Hong Kong is British and operates in accordance with British jurisprudence. The system of courts in Hong Kong is as follows: the Supreme, Court, which consists of a Court of Appeals and a High Court, and the District Court or magistrate courts. The Supreme Court is presided over by the chief justice. The High Court has unlimited jurisdiction in civil and criminal cases and has sixteen to seventeen judges. The Court of Appeals, presided over by the chief justice, considers appeals from magistrate courts. Cases are tried in English. A typical magistrate court proceeding involves lawyers trained in British law and judicial practice, aided by interpreters familiar with the Chinese language.

A controversy has been smoldering over the status of the ultimate court of appeal, which at present, or before the 1997 turnover to the Chinese, is the Judicial Committee of the Privy Council in London. The Privy Council hears appeals from all remaining British overseas possessions, which have drastically shrunk in number since the end of World War II.

Magistrate courts in Hong Kong handle a large volume of administrative cases dealing with immigration, vending, gambling, and business licensing. Thus, the magistrates are really government administrative officials whose decisions are subject to "political whims" rather than "due process."[57]

***Hong Kong under Basic Law from 1997 On*[58]**   The future political structure for Hong Kong as provided by the Basic Law of the Hong Kong Special Administrative Region (hereafter referred to as Basic Law) approved by China's seventh National People's Congress on April 4, 1990, consists of four institutions: the chief executive, the legislature, the judiciary, and the district organizations.[59]

THE CHIEF EXECUTIVE   The chief executive for Hong Kong SAR is accountable to the Chinese central government and the Hong Kong SAR under Article 43 of the Basic Law. The central government here refers to the State Council, headed by a premier who is appointed by the PRC president, based on prior arrangement by the Chinese Communist party (CCP) Politburo, of which the premier and the PRC president are members. The reading of Article 43 leaves no doubt that the Hong Kong SAR has the same status as any other Chinese province or autonomous region. If there is any difference, the Basic Law has not defined it clearly or singled out a differentiation.

Under Article 48, the powers and authorities of the chief executive include the following: to lead the government and to implement laws applicable to the Hong Kong SAR, to sign and promulgate laws enacted by the Legislative Council, to approve budgets and decide on policies, to implement directives issued by the Chinese central government, to conduct external relations on behalf of Hong Kong as authorized by the Chinese government, and, finally, to appoint and remove judges and other public office holders. The text of the Basic Law provisions on the powers of the chief executive for the Hong Kong SAR leaves no doubt that he is designed to be a strong and powerful executive with a rather vague restraint that he is accountable to the Chinese central government and the Hong Kong SAR.

The qualifications, term of office, and method of selecting the chief executive are laid down in Articles 44 and 45 and Annex I, 46 and 47. He or she is to be a Chinese citizen, not less than forty years of age, and a permanent resident, with no right of abode in any other country; he or she must have resided continuously in Hong Kong for at least twenty years, and must be a person of integrity, dedicated to his or her duties. The term of office (Article 46) provides for a five-year term, but limited to not more than two consecutive terms.

While Article 45 states that the chief executive will be ultimately selected by universal suffrage upon nomination by a broadly representative nomination committee, meantime the selection of the first chief executive is governed by Annex I to the Basic Law.[60] Annex I provides for an Election Committee, a sort of electoral college, of 800 members to represent basically the "functional constituencies" of occupational and professional groups, distributed as follows: 200 for industrial, commercial, and financial sectors; 200 for the professions; 200 for labor, social services, and religious groups; and 200 for members of the Legislative Council and district-based organizations plus representatives from Hong Kong to the National People's Congress and to the Chinese People's Political Consultative Conference (a CCP-manipulated and controlled rubber-stamp body for the Chinese NPC). This 800-member Election Committee shall serve for a five-year term and vote by secret ballot in their individual capacities. However, the most important aspect of the selection process is the veto power that may be exercised by the Chinese central government over the appointment, in this case the State Council. For Article 45 states clearly that "the chief executive shall be selected by election or through consultations held locally and be appointed by the Central Government."[61] As indicated by a Chinese official, the appointment to be approved by the Chinese central government is not "a mere formality" but a rather "substantial one."[62] As argued by a Hong Kong scholar, there would be "a constitutional crisis" that would affect Hong Kong's "stability and prosperity" if an impasse develops in the future when selection by universal suffrage is not accepted by the Chinese central government.[63]

There is also to be established under Article 54 of the Basic Law an Executive Council to assist the chief executive in policymaking. Under Article 55, the chief executive appoints an unspecified number of persons to the Executive Council, which functions in much the same manner as the pre-1997 Executive Council, except that the Basic Law now stipulates that members must be Chinese citizens.

THE LEGISLATURE   Legislative powers rest with the Legislative Council of sixty members, as stipulated in Annex II on the method for formation of the body for the Hong Kong SAR. Under Article 67 membership is divided into two categories: Chinese citizens with permanent residence, but with no right of abode in any foreign country; and non-Chinese permanent residents who have the right of abode in foreign countries—the total for this category must not exceed 20 percent of the total Legislative Council membership. Members are to serve for a term of four years, except those elected for the first term, which is limited to two years.

In accordance with Annex II and the decision by the Chinese National People's Congress on the first term of the first Legislative Council, there shall be a sixty-member Legislative Council distributed as follows: twenty members by geographic constituencies through direct election, ten by an Election Committee, and thirty by functional constituencies (occupational and professional groups). For the second term, membership composition for the Legislative Council will be as follows: thirty by functional constituencies, six by the Election Committee, twenty-four by geographic constituencies through direct election. For the third term: thirty by functional constituencies and thirty by geographic constituencies through direct election.

As provided by Article 73, powers and functions of the Legislative Council include the following: to enact laws; to approve budgets and public expenditures; to debate on public issues and to raise questions on the work of the government; to appoint or remove judges on the Court of Final Appeal and the chief judge for the High Court. A bill so enacted by the Legislative Council cannot take effect unless it is signed and promulgated by the chief executive (Article 76).

Another form of checks-and-balances is provided under Article 73(9), which grants the Legislative Council the power of impeachment of the chief executive on a motion passed by a two-thirds majority vote, or forty of the entire membership. However, impeachment of the chief executive must be based on an investigation by an independent committee headed by the chief justice of the Court of Final Appeal. This impeachment provision may be interpreted as a needed safeguard to protect Hong Kong against a chief executive who is too subservient to the officials of the central government in opposition to the expressed wishes of the people of Hong Kong. Or this impeachment provision is a mere facade in view of the overall power of the Chinese central government, for the action—that is the impeachment—must be reported to the Chinese State Council for a final decision.

Executive-legislative relations for the Hong Kong SAR are governed by Articles 49–52 in the Basic Law. If the Legislative Council passes a law that in the view of the chief executive is not compatible with Hong Kong interests, he or she must return it to the Legislative Council for reconsideration within three months. If the original bill is passed for the second time by a two-thirds majority vote, the chief executive must sign and promulgate it within a month. If he or she refuses to sign it, then Article 50 comes into play: The Legislative Council is to be dissolved by the chief executive after consultation with the Executive Council. The Legislative Council can also be dissolved if it refuses to enact a budget or any other important bill introduced by the government. However, the chief executive may dissolve the Legislative Council only once in each term of his or her office.

As a means of resolving a possible legislative impasse or refusal to act over the budget, Article 51 allows the chief executive to apply to the Legislative Council for provisional appropriation. If such appropriation is not possible because the Legislative Council is already dissolved, then prior to the election of the new Legislative Council, the chief executive merely approves on his or her own the provisional short-term appropriation at the previous year's level.

Article 52 also states that the chief executive must resign if, after having dissolved the old Legislative Council, the new Legislative Council again passes by a two-thirds majority vote the disputed original budget bill, but which has still been refused by the chief executive. Or the chief executive must resign if the new Legislative Council still refuses to enact the original bill in dispute.

According to one Hong Kong scholar, the above procedural provisions to resolve executive-legislative conflict over the budget or any other key bills may not even be necessary, for the chief executive "controls" the budget submission process in the first place. He or she can alter the bill to meet any objections from the Legislative Council, so as to ensure final passage and thus make it unnecessary to be forced to resign.[64] Or after a Legislative Council has been dissolved and a new one formed, the chief executive makes concessions or seeks compromises on the disputed bill to such an extent that it is ensured of passage, and thus avoids the necessity for resigning the office.[65]

THE JUDICIARY   Under Articles 8 and 18 of the Basic Law for the Hong Kong SAR, the laws previously in force in Hong Kong and the laws that may be enacted by the Legislative Council shall be applicable. Article 8 specifies the previous laws enforceable for the Hong Kong SAR as follows: the common law, rules of equity, ordinances, subordinate legislation, and customary law, except those that may contradict the Basic Law.

Under Article 81, the court structure consists of the Court of Final Appeal, the High Court (Court of Appeals and the Court of First Instance), district courts, and magistrate courts. Article 85 states that the courts must exercise independent judicial power and must be free from any interference. The principle of jury trial shall be maintained and the principles previously applied to Hong Kong and the rights previously enjoyed by parties to criminal and civil proceedings shall also remain intact under the provision in Article 86.

Judges are appointed by the chief executive for the Hong Kong SAR based on recommendations of an independent commission made up of local judges, the legal profession and other eminent persons. They can be removed only for inability to discharge their duties; dismissal is by the chief executive upon recommendation from a tribunal of at least three local judges appointed by the chief justice of the Court of Final Appeals (Article 89). All judges must be Chinese citizens who are permanent residents with no right of abode in any foreign country (Article 90).

A most controversial aspect in the Basic Law on the judicial system for the Hong Kong SAR has been the changes made dealing with the Final Court of Appeal. As stated in Article 82, the final adjudication power rests with the Final Court of Appeal composed of five judges with some of them being invited judges from other common law jurisdictions. This final appeal court will replace the old system of appeal to the British Privy Council sitting in London. A point of dispute or controversy has been that perhaps two out of the five sitting judges for the Final Court of Appeal should be invited judges from other common law jurisdictions. But, in the September 1991 London meeting of the Chinese-British Joint Liaison Group for Hong Kong, agreement was reached to establish such a final court for appeal in 1993 to be composed of the chief justice, three Hong Kong local judges, and a fifth invited member from two alternate panels: Panel A from retired Hong Kong judges, and Panel B from retired judges from other common law jurisdictions, to ensure the presence of a foreign judge for only half of its sessions.[66] However, the presently constituted Hong Kong Legislative Council by a vote of 34–11 rejected the agreement reached as described above, but the rejection was ignored by both the British and Chinese authorities.[67]

THE POLITICAL PROCESS: PARTICIPATION, ELECTIONS, AND POLITICAL PARTIES

Singapore: The One-Party State

The Electoral Process   There have been ten general elections in Singapore since 1955. The first election was held when Singapore was not independent, but was given the chance for self-government by Great Britain. The most recent election was held August 30, 1991. Table 3.1 provides a summary of these elections.

Table 3.1   Singapore's Elections, 1955–1991

Date Held	Total No. of Seats	No. of Parties	Majority Party	No. of Seats Won by Majority Party	% of Votes Won by Majority Party
April 2, 1955*	25	5	Labor Front	10	26.7
May 30, 1959	51	10	PAP	43	53.4
September 21, 1963	51	8	PAP	37	46.4
April 13, 1968**	58	5	PAP	58	84.4
September 2, 1972	57	6	PAP	65	69.02
December 23, 1976	54	7	PAP	69	72.4
December 23, 1980	75	8	PAP	75	77.7
December 2, 1984	79	9	PAP	77	64.8
September 3, 1988	81	7	PAP	80	63.1
August 30, 1991	81	6	PAP	77	61.0

*Elections from 1955 to 1963 were for the Legislative Assembly.
**Elections from 1968 to 1991 were for the Singapore Parliament.
Sources: See *New York Times*, 2 September 1991, p. A-3; *Far Eastern Economic Review*, 12 September 1991, p. 11; Thomas J. Bellows, "Singapore in 1988: The Transition Moves Forward," *Asian Survey* 2 (February 1989): 145; Jon S.T. Quah, "Singapore in 1984: Leadership Transition in the Election Year," *Asian Survey* 25, 1 (February 1985): 227.

About 1.4 million voters, including over 200,000 new registrants, took part in the 1984 election.[68] In the 1991 election the total number of voters reached over 1.7 million from a total population of 3.0 million.

The campaign period for elections is limited to not more than ten days. Campaigning in Singapore is a clean and noiseless occasion; there is a law prohibiting the use of trucks with music blaring, as found in many other Asian nations where elections take place. In Singapore televised political advertisement is not permitted. Those who want to advertise their candidacy may be allowed to post bills with strings, but not paste, on walls or buildings so that they can be removed easily and quickly. The commonly employed campaign style has been door-to-door canvassing by candidates and daily rallies in housing and ethnic neighborhoods in the evenings. Media coverage of election is generally ample to expose voters to the views of the PAP and opposition candidates for election. Voting is compulsory in Singapore.

Political Parties   In the August 31, 1991, parliamentary election there were candidates from six political parties, plus those who were independent with no partisan affiliation. Table 3.1 is a comparative summary of the contesting political parties' "scoreboard" for the 1988 and 1991 elections and their share of the total vote cast for the 1980, 1984, 1988, and 1991 elections.

While Singapore's elections are based on a multiparty system, they are primarily single-party dominated. As seen in Table 3.1 the Singapore Parliament has been ruled by one political party, the People's Action Party, since 1959. In the 1991 parliamentary election, the five opposition parties pulled an aggregate of 37 percent of the votes against the PAP's 61 percent, the lowest since 1963. Despite the larger percentage of votes obtained at the 1991 election, opposition parties won only a total of four seats to Parliament against seventy-seven seats for the PAP. One explanation is that it was difficult for the opposition parties to find a Malay or Indian to run as a minority candidate in the slate system known as Group Representative Constituency (discussed in the section "The Locus of Power").[69] This difficulty was created by the government's move to place percentage limits or quotas on the number of minority people living in housing complexes.Thus, the GRC system of slatemaking worked against opposition minority parties. The merging of parliamentary districts into GRCs caused the disappearance of opposition strongholds. As a result, the opposition parties chose to contest only in five of the fifteen GRCs under which only the party with the slate that receives the largest number of votes can be declared as a winner. In this case, none of the opposition parties' slates were successful in the five contested GRCs. However, the opposition parties—the Workers' party and the Singapore Democratic party—fared better in the single-member districts by capturing a total of four seats.[70]

People's Action Party[71]   The party was formed in November 1954 to be a "political party for the people." In the beginning the PAP was dominated by the leftist trade unionists. In the early days the party split into two groups: the leftists, and the moderates led by Lee Kuan Yew. The early alliance of the two groups was motivated by the goal for independence and end of British colonial rule. Lee's group made contacts not only with the left-wing socialists and communists by "riding the tiger," but also made appeals for support from Chinese cultural associations and Chinese middle schools, particularly the cadre of student leaders in these schools. The educated Chinese in Singapore who expressed admiration for Chinese communism also supported him.

In the 1955 election rallies, PAP supporters came from the rank and file of trade union groups and Chinese school students who went door to door canvassing for PAP candidates. Results of the 1955 election showed three of its candidates elected to the twenty-five-member Legislative Assembly dominated by the Labor Front. However, the three PAP winning candidates pooled impressive plurality votes.

Then came the 1959 election for the fifty-one-seat Legislative Assembly. By this time the PAP had become a better-organized political party. In 1958 PAP membership was under 5,000; but by 1959 it had risen to over 17,000. In 1957 the moderate faction led by Lee Kuan Yew had broken away from the procommunist group in an internal fight over the control of the party's twelve-member Central Executive Committee.

The PAP came to power in the 1959 election after the Legislative Assembly was dissolved over the issue of a financial "gift" from the United States to the newly formed Alliance party. The PAP contested the entire fifty-one seats or constituencies and won forty-three of them with over 53 percent of votes cast. The PAP organized weekly mass rallies at which PAP candidates presented the party's election platform and policies on education, health, and the economy. The party's policy was to achieve a merger with the Federation of Malaya.

For the next eight elections, from 1963 to 1991, the PAP had been the exclusive majority party in Singapore with Lee Kuan Yew as its leader and prime minister until 1990. While the PAP is still the ruling party in Singapore, a number of problems and concerns have emerged to trouble the PAP in Singapore politics since the 1991 election. First, the 1991 election result gave the PAP 61 percent of the votes cast, a reduction of 2 to 3 percent over the 1988 election. In addition, the PAP won seventy-seven out of a total of eighty-one parliamentary seats, a point that made Lee Kuan Yew unhappy, for he still was the head of the PAP. Prime Minister Goh has been somewhat more candid in that he has admitted the party's failure to provide answers to the concerns of low-income and Chinese-speaking members of the society.[72] Goh's own analysis was that the party has lost the support of its traditional support base, the less affluent workers.[73] The fact that voters preferred Chinese candidates from the opposition parties was a clear signal to the PAP that it had neglected speakers of the Chinese dialects and had maintained a long-time bias toward English-speaking Chinese.

There has been some criticism from outside observers that the PAP is not really a democratic institution.[74] The party is known to conduct most of its business in secrecy.[75] Lee Kuan Yew is known for building a highly secretive party-cadre system of several hundred whose membership is perhaps known to only one person—Lee, the party's general secretary. He has been quoted as saying that the cadre appointed by Lee selected the twelve-member Central Executive Committee, which in turn elects Lee as its leader. The system is analogous, according to one critic, to the pope's position in the Roman Catholic Church: He appoints the cardinals, who in turn elect the pope.[76] However, it must be pointed out that all opposition parties employ the organizational technique of using the selective, but secret, party cadre system.[77] As is usually the case, the PAP's central executive committee members are also cabinet ministers who run the Singapore government. Thus, the PAP is the government of Singapore.

OPPOSITION PARTIES   The strongest opposition party to the ruling PAP is the Singapore Democratic party (SDP) whose leader, Chiam See Tong, won a seat in Parliament three times. In the 1991 election, SDP captured three seats and a total of 12 percent of the votes cast. Chiam See Tong is one of the two opposition candidates elected in 1991 who are Mandarin speaking and graduates of the Chinese language Nanyang University. This was the basis of Goh Chok Tong's and Lee Kuan Yew's assertion that the PAP needs to pay more attention to the Mandarin-dialect-speaking Chinese electorate. In the 1991 election the SDP contested in nine constituencies and won 48.6 percent of its votes.

The Workers' party is the result of a merger for the 1984 and 1988 elections of the Barisan Sosialis and the Singapore United Front, two socialist-oriented political parties. It seeks to establish a democratic socialist government for Singapore to provide basic civil liberties for all. One of the components of the present Workers' party is the Barisan Sosialis, which advocated the abolition of military service for Singapore, free medical service, and tax reduction. In the 1991 election, the Workers' party fielded thirteen candidates who pooled a combined total of 41 percent of the votes in its contested constituencies. One of its candidates, businessman Low Thia Khiang, won election to Parliament.

The Role of the Military   A basic mission of the Singapore Armed Forces (SAF) has been its responsibility to defend the city-state of 2.7 million against external threat, presumably from Malaysia or Indonesia. The Singapore government has a "total defense" strategy aimed at making Singapore as strong militarily as Switzerland.[78]

As a consequence of the "total defense" strategy, throughout the past three decades Singapore has developed a highly sophisticated armed force capable of conducting a formidable offensive against its presumed external threats. As of 1991 the SAF has a total strength of 310,000 in five divisions, and an additional 250,000 reservists. Singapore has a compulsory national service (current strength is about 35,000), which requires two and one-half years in the military for the young. This requirement creates a constant irritation between the government and youth due to the traditional cultural disdain for soldiering. The SAF has 350 AMX-13SMI light tanks, one of the largest armored forces in Southeast Asia, second only to Thailand.[79] The SAF's offensive strength lies in its advanced air force of 150 combat aircraft (about six F-16s and fifty Northrop F5Es) equipped with air-to-surface missiles, as well as laser-guided bombs. Singapore plans to acquire as many as sixteen additional F-16s for 1991–93. By that time Singapore would be in a very strong offensive position to protect its strategic sealanes extending from the Malacca Strait to the waters of Singapore.

CIVIL-MILITARY RELATIONS: THE MILITARIZATION OF SINGAPORE'S POLITICS In 1971 the Singapore government established an academic overseas scholarship program for six or eight military officers in the SAF to study in top foreign universities. Now this small number of about 148 men-only recipients of the scholarship program occupies the leadership positions in the civilian-military hierarchy. Currently the first deputy prime minister, Brigadier General Lee Hsien Loong (son of Lee Kuan Yew) and Cabinet ministers for national development, information, home affairs, the economic development board, and the private secretary to Lee Kuan Yew (the secretary general for the PAP) are all recipients of the overseas scholarship program. One observer points out that there is "the close and growing nexus between the civil and military leadership of the country."[80] Once these scholar-soldiers have graduated from overseas universities, they are obligated to serve for eight years in the SAF and receive speedy promotion until they reach the senior rank in their mid-thirties.[81] Then, while maintaining their rank in the reserve, a number of them have been appointed under Lee Kuan Yew to top government positions. While the military in Singapore is under civilian control, it is this "growing nexus" between the government policymakers and the military command structure that has caused concern for some. They feel that the relationship tends to "undermine" the separation of civilian-military relations in Singapore.[82]

There are also "presidential scholars" funded by the state to recruit the brightest students for both the SAF and government services. These "presidential scholars" (including Lee Kuan Yew's second son, who now directs the SAF's operations and planning) serve as middle-level command officers in the military.[83] A majority of scholar-soldiers have been recruited from the Chinese ethnic group.

As a consequence of the selective scholar recruitment for military civilian officers, a friction has developed between the elites and those career SAF officers known as "farmers."[84] However, the career officers have rarely been selected to receive the prestigious scholarships, and as such face a slower promotion process. As a means of boosting the morale of career officers, a few have recently been promoted ahead of the scholars to the senior rank of brigadier-general.

A related problem has been that the scholar-soldiers devote their energy and skill to management rather than to combat preparedness or readiness.[85] A much greater concern seems to be the increasing influence of the military in civilian bureaucratic affairs. This phenomenon may serve to explain why Singapore's defense spending budget is one of the highest in Asia.[86]

Hong Kong: Free Democratic Reform before Reversion to China

The most significant election so far that has occurred before Hong Kong's scheduled reversion to China was that for the Legislative Council held on September 15, 1991. It was significant for a number of reasons. First, this was the first time in 150 years of Hong Kong's history that a direct election for legislative seats by the eligible voters had taken place. Second, the direct election took place two years after the Chinese military crackdown at Tiananmen, which had suppressed demonstrations by students for democracy and political reform for China. Third, this was the election in which organized liberal groups participated; one leading group that supported a speedy democratic reform for Hong Kong and China won a stunning victory at the polls, a feat that embarrassed the Chinese government during the countdown toward its takeover of Hong Kong in 1997.

At stake for the September 1991 election were eighteen seats from nine multimember districts on the sixty-member Legislative Council for the crown colony to be chosen by direct popular vote. There was a total of fifty-four candidates competing for the eighteen seats. While local issues of traffic and crime were debated by candidates, the subjects of China's control of Hong Kong affairs and the Tiananmen crackdown as a violation of human rights were some of the more emotional topics raised in the debates; two of the candidates had been labeled by Beijing as "subversive."[87] Other candidates were supportive of China or pro-Beijing.

The Hong Kong government tightly regulated the campaigning for this direct election. There was a stipulation that equal time must be made available to all candidates on radio and television, with the result that there were no election reports on evening news programs. Political advertising was strictly prohibited on radio and television. Candidates relied on posters and leaflets and door-to-door canvassing.

There were 1.9 million registered voters out of a total of 3.8 million eligible. The turnout by registered voters was a low 39.2 percent, or fewer than 800,000 who cast their ballots.[88] This was an indication that the main concern of the people of Hong Kong was still economic prosperity rather than political participation. In a public poll taken by a Chinese daily newspaper in August 1991, more than 41 percent of those polled indicated economic development as their primary concern, whereas only 11.4 percent viewed political development as more important.[89]

A 1988 study made by Lo Shiu Hing, a doctoral candidate at the University of Toronto, points out that from 1982 to 1986 there were four local district board elections in which a high 38 percent participated; the 1986 urban council election drew a low 22 percent.[90] The 1985 limited election for the Legislative Council drew a respectable 57.6 percent—it was limited only to less than 1 percent of the population eligible to vote.[91] Hong Kong citizens tend not to have political awareness; under the British there seems to be a pattern of "depoliticization," which causes them to be inactive political participants.[92] At any rate, the liberal prodemocracy groups won a total of sixteen out of the eighteen directly elected seats for the Legislative Council. And fourteen of the sixteen elected seats were captured by the United Democratics of Hong Kong in the 1991 election.

Political Parties and Groups   Prior to 1982 organized groups such as the Professional Teachers' Union, the Federation of Civil Service Unions, the Workers' League, or others affiliated with the Chinese Communist party organization exerted their influence and pressure on government policies in Hong Kong through protests, demonstrations, and petitions.[93] From 1982 to 1984 there appeared a number of political groups organized to lobby for Hong Kong's future in view of the British-Chinese Joint Declaration to revert Hong Kong to China. Among those were the Reform Club and Civic Association, an alliance that at first advocated moderate constitutional changes and then in 1982 lobbied in London for Hong Kong's future. After 1984 new political interest groups grew, including the Meeting Point of 350 members, who not only supported reversion of Hong Kong's sovereignty to China, but also advocated democracy and nationalism. Basically it is considered a liberal group. There was also the Hong Kong Affairs Society of thirty-some members who engaged themselves in the study of government policy. In addition, there was the New Hong Kong Society, a study group concerned with influencing government policies on education and housing.

The only declared political party in Hong Kong has been the United Democrats of Hong Kong (UDHK), formed in 1990 and led by Martin Lee, a barrister, and Szets Wah, a school principal. It is a formal political party of six liberal groups. It is generally considered liberal/reform-minded, but anti-Beijing. Lee and Wah were elected to the Legislative Council in 1985 through the functional constituency system of occupational and professional groups. Once elected to the LegCo they became outspoken on issues. In June 1989 they joined other liberals in the Hong Kong Alliance in Support of Democratic Movement in China, the civic group that raised money, among its other activities, for the exiled Chinese dissenters after the June 1989 Tienanmen crackdown.

In opposition to the UDHK is the Liberal Democratic Federation (LDF) formed in November 1990, a conservative elite group of businessmen and professionals who wanted less democratic reform, but are pro-Beijing. One of the leaders of the LDF hailed from a well-known family that owned Wing On Bank, a leading financial institution in Hong Kong. The LDF's position with respect to relations with Beijing has been one of caution and moderation.

FUNCTIONAL CONSTITUENCY   A word must be said about the functional constituency of occupational and professional groups, an electoral college system introduced by the British in Hong Kong in 1985, which has been incorporated into the Basic Law for Hong Kong to constitute half of the Legislative Council in post-1997 Hong Kong. It is a system of limited representation for professional and business groups that elect twenty-one of the sixty-member LegCo. For instance, only two representatives are allocated for the 2.8 million workers in Hong Kong. A British reform group describes the functional system as: "flawed in principle and unfair in practice."[94] For the September 1991 election, Table 3.2 shows how the various functional groups participated.

Table 3.2   Hong Kong's Functional Constituencies

Constituency	Eligible Voters	Number Registered	Percent Registered	Candidates
Commercial (HKGCC)	2,380	1,609	67.6	2
Commercial (CGCC)	5,658	2,348	41.5	1
Industrial (HKFI)	744	460	61.8	1
Industrial (CMA)	2,090	1,366	65.4	2
Finance (banking)	398	234	59.1	1
Financial services	1,200	694	57.8	6
Labour (2 reps)	455	378	83.1	2
Social services	207	181	87.4	1
Tourism	1,204	847	70.4	3
Real estate and construction	579	373	64.4	1
Medical	6,518	4,031	61.8	1
Health care	17,073	10,636	62.3	1
Teaching	53,243	38,678	72.6	3
Legal	2,544	1,240	48.7	2
Engineering	3,205	2,848	88.9	2
Architectural, surveying, and planning	2,238	1,438	64.3	4
Accountancy	4,660	2,276	48.8	1
Urban council	40	40	100.00	4
Regional council	36	36	100.0	4
Rural	139	112	80.6	1
Total	104,609	69,825	66.8	40

Source: *Far Eastern Economic Review*, 29 August 1991, p. 17. By permission of the publisher.

It will be recalled from the discussion of the post-1997 legislature for Hong Kong that, as stipulated by the Basic Law, for both the first and second terms, half of its membership of sixty will be composed of functional constituencies whose representatives on the whole have not been really interested in political issues. For most of them, as *Far Eastern Economic Review* points out, "the main attraction of standing for a functional constituency is to gain both prestige and business contacts rather than answering the needs of constituents."[95] Collectively, these functional constituencies are oriented toward the status quo and there have been "abuses and drawbacks" in the system's selection process of candidates for election.[96]

Military Status after 1997   At present or until the reversion occurs on July 1, 1997, there are about 8,000 Gurkha forces in Hong Kong as an integral part of the British forces stationed in Hong Kong. The Gurkhas are known for their bravery in combat dating back to the two world wars, or even the Boxer Rebellion in 1900 in China. They are recruited from villages in Nepal and trained by the British as soldiers.

Since 1945 Gurkhas have been guarding the nineteen-mile border between China and Hong Kong, engaging in prevention and arrest of illegal immigrants from the Chinese side. In July 1991 the British announced a reduction in size of the three Gurkha battalions stationed in Hong Kong from 8,000 to 2,500. The remaining 2,500 will have to be withdrawn as the Union Jack is lowered on July 1, 1997.

There is no reference in the Basic Law for Hong Kong to indicate clearly the stationing of People's Liberation Army (PLA) components in Hong Kong. However, with China repossessing Hong Kong sovereignty, there is no hindrance to prevent China from doing exactly that by posting units of the PLA in Hong Kong. Lieutenant General Xu Huizi, Deputy Chief of Staff of the People's Liberation Army, announced on July 17, 1993, that China plans to station troops in the heart of Hong Kong after the 1997 reversion. Presumably the people of Hong Kong will have to get used to the presence of Chinese military in the Hong Kong territory even if it is only a token demonstration of China's sovereignty.

POLITICAL PERFORMANCE AND PUBLIC POLICY

Singapore: Overregulated Economy

Economic Performance   As a city-state Singapore has no natural resources except land, the people who populate it, and a deepwater harbor. Despite its lack of natural resources, Singapore has one of Asia's most dynamic economies. Its growth rate in terms of its gross domestic product for 1987–91 serves as an indication of Singapore's state of economy: 1987,

6.5 percent; 1988, 8.0 percent; 1989, 9.2 percent; 1990, 8.3 percent; and 1991, 6.5–7.5 percent.[97] Thus, Singapore's economy reached its peak in 1989 and 1990 with GDP growth rates of 8.3 to 9.2 percent, respectively, and a slower expansion for 1991; its GDP for 1990 has been estimated at $25 billion in U.S. dollars. Its 1989–90 economic performance surpassed most fast-growing Asian nations in the region except Thailand. Measured by Clark Kerr's so-called physical life quality, an index of life expectancy, literacy, and infant mortality, Singapore is rated second only to Sweden on top of the scale.[98] Singapore's per capita income in 1990 was about $8,000.

Singapore then served as a great transit point in Far Eastern trade and as a "trading exporium."[99] Raw material, such as spices, rubber, tin, and timber, from the Malay hinterland and Southeast Asia were shipped to the port of Singapore for processing and transshipment to the manufacturing centers of the world. Industrial products were transported to Singapore for redistribution to parts of Southeast Asia. In the process of serving as an entrepot center, Singapore developed as a shipping and banking center for Southeast Asia, in addition to its harbor facilities.

It was not until Singapore was forced to withdraw its affiliation with Malaysia in 1965 that a new strategy was formulated with emphasis on promotion of exports. This strategy was greatly enhanced by escalation of the Vietnam War.[100] It was the Vietnam conflict in Southeast Asia that boosted trade for oil and refinery development in Singapore. This new development also stimulated the shipping industry and shipping services. By then Japan had become Singapore's largest trade partner and Singapore's trade with mainland China also flourished.[101] In promoting export strategy, Singapore dispatched official trade missions to Japan, Southeast Asia, and the United States. The government enacted laws to provide export incentives through tax reduction. While Singapore and Malaysia carried on their bilateral trade by feeding each other's markets, the bulk of Singapore's trade was with Japan and the United States. With the advantages of a well-educated and skilled populace and the development of the city-state as a trading center, bolstered by political stability under Lee Kuan Yew's PAP rule, Singapore embarked on an ambitious Economic Expansion Incentive Act in 1967–68 to provide motivation for development of new industries.

At first, Singapore developed consumer-oriented light industries that were basically labor intensive: shoes, textiles, plywood and hand assembly machines. To provide the needed infrastructure, the government drained the swamps to create thousands of acres of land for roads, buildings, and a modernized port to handle the products for export. In the 1970s new industries developed and included chemicals, petroleum products, metals (iron and steel), and industrial machinery. By the 1960s multinational corporations had invested more than $6 billion in Singapore, and by 1985 investment from the United States alone stood at more than $5.3 billion.[102] Between 1960 and 1980 Singapore's industrial products increased over twenty-one fold.[103] By the mid-1980s Singapore had become a major oil refinery center to meet increased demands from Japan and the new industrialized countries.

As more Asian competitors (Hong Kong, South Korea, and Taiwan) entered into the export-oriented trade strategy in the 1970s and 1980s, Singapore began planning for a future strategy in development: a postindustrial economy that is based on "sunrise industries" or "information industries" for the twenty-first century.[104] This strategy draws on Singapore's assets of highly educated, skilled, and hard-working citizens. It is also vested in the basic assumption that "knowledge is wealth" and "information is power" in the futurist society for Singapore.[105] It was this overriding concern for knowledge and information as a new strategy for future development for Singapore that prompted Lee Kuan Yew in 1984 to propose a new genetic policy for promoting educated women, mainly Chinese, to procreate presumably intelligent offspring.

By the 1980s Singapore had become the world's third-largest refinery center, next only to Rotterdam and Houston, and the industry was producing at two-thirds capacity. Singapore's traditional role as an entrepot was declining as Indonesia and Malaysia expanded their trading role in the region. Singapore planners then decided to diversify their economy by going all out in the rapidly growing high-technology industry, such as "computers, robotics, bio-technology and other research- and information-oriented industries of the future."[106] By that time Japanese and Western multinational electronic companies had already established facilities and subsidiaries in Singapore to take advantage of Singapore's educated and skilled labor, plus the incentives provided by the government to encourage development of high technology as the growth industry. Now Singapore's high-technology industry was tied in closely with the export trade of microprocessors for computers and electronic components geared to meet the demand abroad, particularly in the United States or for American computer firms. In 1984 sales for these electronic components declined in the United States, on top of stiff competition with exporters from Taiwan, Hong Kong, and South Korea. For 1985–86 Singapore's economy went into a slump as manufacturing output—petroleum refining, shipbuilding, ship repair, and the electronic industries—declined by almost 6 percent.[107]

The Role of Government   Singapore has been a government-regulated society since the PAP came into power in 1959 under Lee Kuan Yew. In many respects it has been under the rule of a paternalistic leader; it has been an overregulated and mostly centralized political and economic system. For some time it has been characterized as preferring "a corporate state over individual entrepreneurship, and public over private capital."[108] However, Singapore may also best be described as a "highly disciplined society—a bewildering blend of one-party state socialism with free voting and vigorously competitive capitalism."[109] One observer of Asian affairs writes that Lee Kuan Yew has been quoted as saying that "his model is Confucian society," which is "tolerant" and "paternalistic," and that "members of the society accept and respect superiors and authority."[110] Or, as simply put by Lucian Pye, in Singapore it is the "Confucian authoritarian approach" that has prevailed.[111]

Up to 1987, under criticism because of the 1985–86 economic recession and the need for policy review intended to introduce market forces and decentralization, as a "corporate state" the government owned more than 400 business firms with a total capitalization of $2 billion. The government then decided to sell off most of its state-owned enterprises, except utilities and defense industries. Established in 1961, the Economic Development Board (EDB) had been exercising the ownership of state enterprises. Vast development of public housing in large estates, such as Jurong, was done in the manner of a government corporation selling land at a reasonable price and providing the needed roads and related infrastructures.

There is also the National Wage Council (NWC), which regulates wage structures in an orderly manner for Singapore's workers. Upon instruction from the prime minister and Parliament, the National Wage Council can raise or lower wages in accordance with Singapore's economic ups and downs. There have been periods of high wage increase in good economic times, and there have been periods when wages were frozen—as in the 1985–86 recession, when wages were frozen at the $2.37 per hour rate in order to make Singapore's exports more competitive in the world market. It is expected that through the NWC the government must intervene in raising or lowering industrial wages.

Singapore is considered to be one of the thriftiest nations in the world, saving about 40 percent of income. In the mid-1980s each Singaporean had an average of about $6,000 in his or her bank account. This is possible primarily because the government has a compulsory saving and pension system known as the Central Provident Fund (CPF). Every employee in Singapore is required to contribute by payroll deduction at the current rate of 23 percent; this is matched by a 15 percent employer contribution. In the mid-1980s the employee CPF contribution rate was a mandatory 24 percent, with eventual 20 percent from both sectors. The huge reservoir of forced savings, currently estimated to be about $15.5 billion in U.S. dollars, has been diverted by the government as a major source for investment in industry. In fact, the CPF has been the major source of Singapore's development fund, an indispensable financial tool in the country's economic development plan for creating jobs and providing the necessary infrastructure to attract foreign investment. The fund is also used to support public housing for some 80 percent of the people, the airport, and port facilities.

It was estimated in the mid-1980s that the compulsory contribution to CPF by employers accounted for 40 percent of Singapore's labor costs.[112] The 1985–86 recession was attributed partly to this government "tax" that in essence "stifles" investment.[113] The concept of forced saving through the government's CPF is also indicative of the leaders' paternalistic approach in public policy. The fund also became a formidable fiscal instrument to be wielded by the government: In order to stimulate the sluggish economy in the 1985–86 recession the government reduced the employer contribution rate to 15 percent (from 25 percent) for a two-year period, which meant a wage cost reduction of about $1.5 billion that could be used for investment.[114] When this fiscal policy was accompanied by a wage freeze mandated by the National Wage Council, these actions made a powerful impact on the economy, which needed relief at the time. In recent years the government has permitted members of the CPF to buy shares in government-owned enterprises, or a second apartment, or to use the entitlement for medical expenses.

Education for a "Knowledge Society"   As far back as 1956 Singapore's Legislative Assembly adopted, as a reflection of the multilingual and multicultural nature of the populace, an educational policy that called for a bilingual (Chinese and English) education in the primary schools and trilingual education in secondary schools.[115] However, in the years immediately following Singapore's separation from the Malay Federation in 1965, the English language became institutionalized as the language of public life, as well as of international business in Singapore's struggle for economic certainty and survival. At the same time, in order to ensure economic success for a city-state without natural resources, the government under Lee's PAP was striving for educational emphasis on meritocracy, based on "hard work and self-reliance," rather than ethnicity.[116] The educational policy also gave emphasis to "learning of the cultural language" and learning of moral-ethical values as an integral component of education.[117] Thus, by 1969 Singapore's official policy included bilingual education, coupled with the learning of "the cultural language," known as language-exposure-time in primary schools. In other words, a student must learn to speak English and to speak his or her own ethnic or cultural language equally well. Pupils in selected Chinese-medium schools were required to develop competence in both English and Chinese. At the same time, university admission required demonstration of competence in the cultural language.

By the late 1970s and 1980, when Singapore had achieved economic success and had moved away from a labor-intensive manufacturing economy into a high-technology, service-oriented economic base, modifications had to be made to ensure a pool of talented and intelligent human resources to compete with other nations in world markets, and, at the same time, to serve as a basis for Singapore's entry into the "knowledge society." The bilingual education policy included a gifted education program in primary schools. In 1985 the university admission prerequisite of demonstrable proficiency and competence in English and the cultural language was changed to allow students with a good academic record, but who failed to obtain a passing grade on cultural language, to be enrolled in the university. Thus, English is now Singapore's first language; a Singaporean must be proficient in English in order to make a living.

Primary school in Singapore is a six-year cycle for those children aged six to twelve. Upon completing the cycle, a student receives the primary school leaving certificate. As in the case of Japan or South Korea, enrollment to a particular primary school is of extreme importance. There is pressure for parents to enroll their five-year-olds to prestigious primary schools in order to ensure entrance to better secondary schools later on. Better schools are usually private—Raffles Institution, St. Andrew's, Victoria Institution, and so on—and receive government financial assistance. Government-run or public schools are generally considered inferior in that these schools produce poor students.

Since 1984 priority for entrance to better primary schools is given to children of university-educated mothers. This scheme is based on the controversial concept advanced by Lee Kuan Yew that Singapore's future rests in brain power as a "knowledge society" with high-tech or "sunrise industries." He believes that the development of such a "knowledge society" is in turn dependent on assumption of the continued procreation of better genetic quality of its people, particularly the 75 percent of Singapore's ethnic majority, the Chinese.

Secondary schooling is a four-year cycle beginning at age twelve. Upon successful completion by passing the examination, secondary students receive the general certificate of education (GCE). There is a two-year preuniversity education before enrollment at a university or junior college. For most of the 1980s, university enrollment in Singapore was at the level of from 35,000 to 40,000. Academic demand at the university level is rigorous and highly competitive.

In an effort to render needed assistance to families with school-aged children, in January 1991 the new prime minister Goh Chok Tong launched the Edusave Program. Through this program a school-aged child, regardless of family income or wealth, would be receiving a grant of $100 (U.S. $57) toward his or her education. This government assistance would help to defray part of the rising education costs, since subsidies to educational institutions have been discontinued.[118] According to the plan, the government will eventually outlay about $2 billion toward support of the program, providing a limit of not more than $7,000 per family as a means of "the state declaring a dividend for its citizens."[119]

Hong Kong: Economic Prosperity on Borrowed Time

Economic Performance Hong Kong is one of Asia's newly industrialized countries with a record creditable rate of economic growth. Its
gross domestic product ranged from 6 to 8 percent in the 1950s. Then the
GDP soared to 9 to 10 percent in the 1960s as Hong Kong shifted from
entrepot to manufacturing exports. From 1950 to 1984 the average annual
GDP was about 8.3 percent, followed by a rate of record growth in 1987,
which chalked up almost 14 percent, and in 1988, which recorded a 7.9
percent rate. However, by 1989 and 1990 Hong Kong's growth rate was 2.3
and 2.4 percent, respectively. Its GDP for 1991 was estimated at 3.5 percent. A number of reasons serve to explain the rather modest economic performance beginning in 1989. First, the double-digit growth for 1986–88
had created "the capacity and the manpower constraints" as the labor force
became static and aged.[120] Then the Tiananmen massacre in June 1989
generated fear and uncertainty for Hong Kong's future. And a worldwide
slowdown in developing nations has had some bearing on Hong Kong's
economic performance. But despite the modern growth rate, Hong Kong's
per capita income is still one of the highest in Asia: For 1990 it was over
$10,000, next only to Singapore and Japan.

Hong Kong economist Y. C. Yao has attributed Hong Kong's "economic miracle" to at least three major factors.[121] First, Hong Kong has
enjoyed political stability under British colonial rule for the past four
decades. There has been a high degree of "rule by consent" practiced by "a
paternalistic and enlightened colonial civil service."[122] Second, while there
has been frequent reference to Hong Kong as a model of Adam Smith's
laissez-faire economy or free capitalism at its best, Hong Kong does enjoy
economic freedom to a considerable extent. However, the government does
play a leading role in public housing, the bus and mass transit system
(including ferry services), rent control, social welfare and labor legislation,
and inflation control in recent years when the rate reached almost 14 percent in the spring of 1991.

Third, under British colonial rule Hong Kong has a well-established
legal system that protects individual rights as well as property and contract
rights. Yao points out that it has been the enjoyment of these economic
freedoms and rights—for instance, the guaranteed "flow of funds across
national boundaries in the Asian-Pacific area"—that has enabled the development of Hong Kong as a financial center for the region.[123] The political
stability, economic freedom, and enjoyment of individual and property
rights have created an atmosphere conducive to doing business and for
investment opportunity.

One other factor needs to be added to the list: the industrious character of the people, a large percentage of them refugees from the PRC. To a
large measure it has been the willingness of the Hong Kong people to work

hard, to develop the necessary skills to do the job, and the desire to take risks if given the opportunities that has made Hong Kong what it is today.

Thus, with the combination of the above characteristics of Hong Kong, added to the infrastructure conscientiously developed through the years—the world's busiest free container port, airport (a new one is to be developed beyond 1997), and the automated mass transit system—therein lies their economic success.

The Trade Pattern   Roughly 90 percent of Hong Kong's industries are geared for an export trade that is dominated by textiles and footwear, watches and electronics. Hong Kong's major trade partners in 1990 were the United States (35 percent), China (21 percent), Japan (5 percent). Most of the export industries in Hong Kong are skill-intensive light-manufacturing industries, or so-called small manufacturing establishments (SMEs) with fewer than fifty employees.[124] In the past decade Hong Kong has reemerged as an important re-exporter, particularly in trade with China in the areas of processing and packaging. In 1990 the value of re-exports reached more than $52 billion (27 percent went to China and 58 percent imported from China) in textiles, clothing, and electronics.[125]

It must also be pointed out that 70 percent of China's $12 billion export to the United States in 1989 passed through Hong Kong—a point that the Bush administration emphasized to show that Hong Kong would actually be hurt more if the United States revoked the most-favored-nation status with China.[126]

Education   Compulsory and free primary education for six years was first introduced in 1971, and compulsory free secondary education for the first three years was introduced in 1978 by Governor MacLehose. In 1990 total enrollment in primary schools was over 526,000 and secondary schools more than 455,000. A few of the primary schools are subsidized by the government and a majority are privately operated, but under indirect government subsidy. Then there are wholly privately owned and independently operated schools.

Secondary schools are of three types: grammar, technical, and vocational. After having enrolled for five years in secondary schools, students may be allowed to take the certificate of education examinations. In order to take the advanced-level examination, students must have taken courses for two more years beyond the original five-year secondary school.

Similar to many schools in core cities in the United States, Hong Kong schools are overcrowded and must operate in shifts with inadequate facilities to accommodate all of the enrolled students. The quality of education in nonprivate independently run schools is being questioned by Hong Kong residents. One of the problems with education in Hong Kong, as has been the case in Singapore, is the choice the students must make between English and Chinese with recent emphasis on the latter.

As of 1991 there are seven government supported institutions of higher learning. Two are comprehensive universities: the University of Hong Kong and the Chinese University of Hong Kong. Three are polytechnic institutions and the other two (Hong Kong Baptist College and Lingnan College) had their origins as missionary schools. In 1990 the total enrollment in the polytechnics and Baptist College was about 20,300 full-time students. The universities, including Lingnan College, had a full-time enrollment of more than 14,300 students. The Hong Kong government provides grants and loans to qualified needy students. It is not easy to obtain admission to the two comprehensive universities—Hong Kong University and the Chinese University of Hong Kong—for there are usually ten applicants for every available incoming freshman position. This explains why as many as 30,000–40,000 Hong Kong students each year have gone overseas for their higher education.

Articles 136–137 of the Basic Law for post-1997 education in Hong Kong permit the Hong Kong SAR autonomy in formulating policies for the development and improvement of education, including the language of instruction, funds allocation, and the examination system. Existing educational institutions will maintain not only their own autonomy, but are to enjoy academic freedom, including courses in religion (Article 137). Teachers may use teaching materials from outside Hong Kong. Prior to the reversion in 1997, in preparation for the turnover, the Hong Kong government is struggling to devise a curriculum in secondary schools that will expose students to courses on modern China and the communist revolution—previously unpopular subject matters with teachers and students.[127]

Citizenship, Right of Abode, and the Nationality Issue   In dispute is the fact that about 2.25 million of Hong Kong's total 5.8 million population are holders of special British passports, but without the right of abode—the right to reside permanently in the British Isles. While under Article 24 of the Basic Law they are legally entitled to permanent residence in the Hong Kong SAR after 1997, they literally cannot migrate to Great Britain if they do not wish to remain in Hong Kong. Since the signing of the 1984 Joint Sino-British Declaration, the right of abode for British passport holders in Hong Kong has become an emotional and moral issue. In other words, how can Great Britain deny these British passport holders the right of abode in Great Britain if they choose to leave Hong Kong some time after the 1997 reversion takes place? The dispute reached its height after the June 1989 Tienanmen massacre, when Hong Kong Chinese exited at the rate of 1,200 per week to settle in other countries. After heated debate in the London House of Commons, and some strong opposition to offering British passport holders the right of abode, a bill was enacted to grant a maximum of 50,000 heads of households from Hong Kong full British citizenship. These 50,000 heads of households refer to those who work in key businesses or professions.[128] The first offering in 1991 was made to 87 percent of the 50,000, or about 43,500; the second offering will be made to the remainder in 1993.

SUGGESTED READINGS

Singapore

Choo, Carolyn. *Singapore: The PAP and the Problem of Political Succession*. Singapore: Asiapac Books/Pelanduk, 1985.

Drysdale, John. *Singapore: The Struggle for Success*. Singapore: Times Books International, 1984.

Esterline, John H. and Mae H. *How the Dominoes Fell: Southeast Asia in Perspective*. Boston: Hamilton Press, 1986.

Josey, Alex. *Lee Kuan Yew*. Singapore: Asia Pacific Press, 1968.

Lim, Chong Yah. *Economic Development in Singapore*. Singapore: Federal Publications, 1980.

Milne, R. S., and Diane K. Mauzy. *Singapore: The Legacy of Lee Kuan Yew*. Boulder, CO: Westview Press, 1990.

Minchin, James. *No Man Is an Island*. New York: Unwin Hyman, 1987.

Pang, Cheng Lian. *Singapore's People's Action Party: Its History, Organization and Leadership*. Singapore: Oxford University Press, 1971.

Rolan, Gary. *The Political Economy of Singapore's Industrialization: National State and International Capital*. London: Macmillan, 1989.

Sandhu, Kernial Singh, and Paul Wheatley. *Management of Success: The Moulding of Modern Singapore*. Boulder, CO: Westview Press, 1990.

Steinberg, David Joel, ed. *In Search of Southeast Asia*. rev. ed. Honolulu: University of Hawaii Press, 1987.

Turnbull, C. Mary. *A History of Singapore, 1819–1975*. London and New York: Oxford University Press, 1977.

Hong Kong

Cheng, Joseph Y. S. *Hong Kong: In Search of a Future*. Hong Kong and Oxford: Oxford University Press, 1984.

Ching, Frank. *Hong Kong and China: For Better and for Worst*. New York: Asia Society and Foreign Policy Association, 1988.

Davis, Leonard. *Hong Kong and the Asylum-Seekers from Vietnam*. New York: St. Martin's Press, 1991.

Davis, Michael. *Constitutional Confrontation in Hong Kong: Issues and*

Implications of the Basic Law. New York: St. Martin's Press, 1990.

Domes, Jurgen, and Yu-Ming Shaw. Hong Kong: *A Chinese and International Concern*. Boulder, CO and London: Westview Press, 1988.

Hicks, George L. *Hong Kong Countdown*. Detroit: The Cellar Book Shop, 1989.

Minas, Norman. *The Government and Politics of Hong Kong*. Hong Kong and Oxford: Oxford University Press, 1986.

Morris, Jan. *Hong Kong*. New York: Random House, 1988.

Mushkat, Miron. *The Economic Future of Hong Kong*. New York: Lynne Rienner, 1990.

Rafferty, Kevin. *City on the Rocks: Hong Kong's Uncertain Future*. New York: Viking Press, 1989.

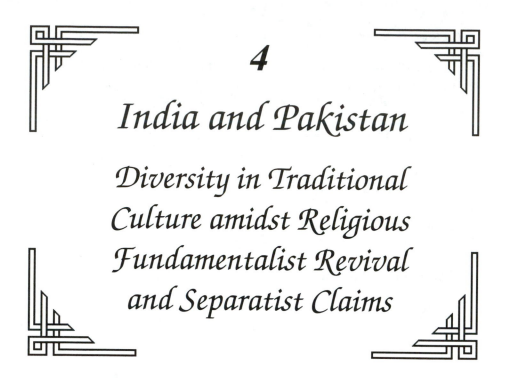

4

India and Pakistan

Diversity in Traditional Culture amidst Religious Fundamentalist Revival and Separatist Claims

India and Pakistan have shared one common developmental experience: They both were administered and ruled by the British as one colonial empire. While they shared the same British tutelage, there have been different paths in political development since independence in 1947. India, whose agrarian society has been characterized by chronic poverty, low educational levels, and low life expectancy, has made parliamentary democracy workable and long-lasting among all of the developing Third World nations. Pakistan, on the other hand, lacking a mass-based political party and institutional and administrative strength since partition, has experimented and endured for long periods under military authoritarianism.

In terms of leadership style, India tends to be in favor of charismatic leaders—Mahatma Gandhi, Jawaharlal Nehru, Indira and Rejiv Gandhi—in contrast to Pakistan's preference for strong military personages such as Ayub Khan, Yahya Khan and Zia Al-Haq. Both India and Pakistan are constantly beset by ethnic strife and religious fundamentalist revivals. Both nations face dichotomous demands for modernization/democracy and for the preservation of religious traditions and sectional separatist claims.

THE CASE OF INDIA

With a land area of 1.27 million square miles, the Republic of India, in South Asia, is the seventh largest nation in the world. Physical features of India are quite distinct and can be divided into four recognizable regions.

The mountainous region is dominated by the great Himalaya range in the north. Lying at the foot of the Himalaya range are the great northern Indian plains, which are irrigated by the Indus, Ganges, and Brahamputra rivers, stretching from the Arabian Sea to the Bay of Bengal. Unlike the barren Indus valley, the eastern plains of the Ganges are the most fertile due to abundant rainfall and rich alluvial soil—it is the heavily populated and most productive area of India. This is the heart of the Hindustan culture. The southern region is known as the Deccan tableland, or plateau of crystalline rocks. The walls of the Deccan plateau fall sharply to sea level; between the walls, or Ghats, and the sea is the coastal plain. The topography of India contains a variety of features including a desert, jungles, broad plains and mighty rivers, and the tallest mountain ranges in the world.

Agricultural life in India depends on the rainfall brought in by the southwest monsoon, which is rather hard to predict, both in terms of its exact arrival time and its duration or intensity. Late or nonarrival of the monsoon inevitably results in drought and hardship for hundreds of millions of people in rural India. In 1987 failure of the southwest monsoon to arrive produced one of the worst droughts in recent years.

The total population of India today is 835 million. The average annual birthrate for 1981–88 was 2.2 percent. At that rate of growth, India most likely will have a total population of over 1 billion by the year 2000. Next to China, India is the second most populous nation in the world. The Indian national government has taken steps to promote birth control by providing contraceptive devices and sterilization for men. Before 1977, during the administration of prime minister Indira Gandhi, the Indian Congress party introduced a compulsory sterilization program for families with more than two or three children—7 million men were sterilized in 1976. This Draconian measure met with hostility and constituted one of the reasons for the rise to power of the Janata party to replace Indira Gandhi.

The Indian population is the most diverse in terms of ethnicity, culture, and language, complicated further by the caste system. In many ways, India is "the greatest ethnographic museum" of the world.

THE CASE OF PAKISTAN

Pakistan today comprises about 310,000 square miles in south Asia. It is officially an Islamic republic. Originally, at the time of partition in 1947, it was divided into East and West Pakistan, separated by over 1,000 miles of Indian territory. At the end of the 1971 war with India, East Pakistan, or eastern Bengal, seceded with the support of India, becoming Bangladesh as an independent country.[1] Thus, the Pakistan of today is basically the West Pakistan of Punjab, Sind, Baluchistan, and the Northwest Frontier.

Pakistan is bordered by China to the northeast, India on the east and southeast, Iran on the southwest, Afghanistan to the northwest, and the Arabian Sea on the south. Because of its geographic location, Pakistan is considered a strategic nation in south Asia as demonstrated during the 1979 Soviet invasion of Afghanistan when Pakistan served as the staging point for aid to the Afghan freedom fighters, the *mujahiddins*.

From the geographic and topographic viewpoint, there are three distinct regions of Pakistan. First is the fertile Indus River plain, which encompasses the province of Punjab and part of the Sind Province. Punjab is irrigated by the waters of the Indus River and its four tributaries: Thelun, Chenab, Ravi, and Sutlej. It is the most densely populated area and the "breadbasket" of Pakistan.

Then there are the northern highlands—the most rugged mountain region of Pakistan. Here one finds the towering snow-capped mountain peaks of the western Himalayas, which include the Hindu Kush, Pamir, and Karakoran ranges with elevations ranging from 20,000 to over 25,000 feet above sea level. K-2, or the Godwin Austen, is 8,611 meters (28,251 feet). Beyond the Karakoran range is China's Xinjiang (Sinkiang) autonomous region. The Karakoran Highway through the world's most rugged passes opened in 1978 and linked Gilgit in the Northwest Frontier Province of Pakistan with China's Kashgar and Urumqi on the ancient Silk Road in the Xinjiang region.

The third geographic region of Pakistan is the Baluchistan, dominated by the Sindhi Desert in the southwest, with arid landscape and sparsely populated towns. In fact, two-thirds of Pakistan is arid or semiarid.

The total population of Pakistan is about 110.4 million, with an annual growth rate in the 1980s of 2.9. Based on that rate, Pakistan is expected to have a population of 145 million by the year 2000. Of the total population, about 72 percent live in rural areas and about 28 percent in urban cities. Pakistan's population is the result of centuries of migration and invasion into this part of the Indian subcontinent and is a complex mixture of many races and ethnic origins: Afghans, Arabs, Aryans, Greeks, Mongols, Pathans, Persians, and Turks. However, about 97 percent of Pakistan's population are Muslims (Sunni). In terms of linguistic and cultural/regional difference, Pakistan's population may be divided into four major groupings:[2] Punjabis, Sindhis, Pakhtuns, and Baluch.

The people who inhabit the province or region of Punjab, the most populated agricultural sector of Pakistan, are the Punjabis. They constitute more than 60 percent of the nation's total population. Historically, the people in Punjab were loyal to the British during and after the 1857 Indian mutiny. As reward for their loyalty, the British protected the peasants in Punjab with the 1901 Punjab Alienation of Land Act, which prohibited money lenders from foreclosing their mortgage debts.[3] In central and western Punjab there were and are still today large land holdings or estates that encompass hundreds of villages. It has been said that the so-called Green

Revolution of the 1960s, the intensive application of improved hybrid seeds, fertilizer, pesticides, and tube wells, has been of more benefit to the middle and large landlords than the Punjabi peasants and laborers[4] (this will be discussed in a later section). A large proportion of Pakistani in Punjab are Urdu speaking, the *lingua franca*, and have dominated the political scene in Pakistan since the 1947 independence. Also, they have dominated the civil and military services of Pakistan. Generally speaking, as a group, leaving aside the various "agricultural tribes" or castes and the landowning Rajputs and the Jats—both have contributed to the recruitment of Pakistan armed services—Punjabis are better educated and more "chauvinistic" in their attitude toward other groups who are not Urdu speaking.

The Sindhis are those people who live in the province of Sind and speak the Sindhi language. Sind is basically a rural area and is dominated by a few families of large landowners. For instance, the family of Zulfikar Ali Bhutto and his daughter, Benazir Bhutto, were members of the landowning upper class in Sind who owned land not in terms of acres, but of square miles.[5] Those who work on the land are poor tenants who support the wealthy landlords. They constitute less than 20 percent of Pakistan's population (about 18–19 million). Karachi, Pakistan's largest city, is located in this province.

Some 12 million Pakhtuns, who speak the Pushtu language, live in the Northwest Frontier province (NWFP). While their share of Pakistan's total population is only 13 percent, they contribute more than 15 percent to the nation's armed forces. The NWFP lies along the Karakoran Hindu Kush mountain range, with passages such as the Khyber Pass and Karakoran Pass in the strategic position bordering China and Afghanistan. The Pakhtuns are considered to be one of the world's "largest tribal groups," with "shifting alliances and enmity." They trace their origin to an early convert by the Prophet in the seventh century.[6] The Pakhtuns are devout Muslims intolerant of those who do not submit themselves to the religion. They follow the Pakhtun code of egalitarian behavior and "glorify the martial virtues."[7] Most important of all, they are fiercely independent, opposing the Mughl (Mongol) and British conquests.

The people who live in the Baluchistan province are the Baluchs; their ancestors migrated from the southern shores of the Caspian Sea about the sixth century A.D. The Baluchi language is a mixture of Persian, Sindhi, and Arabic. The region of Baluchistan is a wasteland, rather inhospitable for living. It is also a region through which Persian and Arab invaders came to conquer the land. Baluchs prefer "indirect rule" ; their social organization is basically tribal and "feudal militarism" with chosen leaders who make shifting alliances. There have been attempts to form separatist movements against the central government rule; these insurgencies have been met with brutal military suppression by Pakistan.

POLITICAL CULTURE AND POLITICAL DEVELOPMENT

India: From Traditional Society to Parliamentary Democracy

Historic Legacy   Before the arrival of Arab Muslims in 711 A.D., India was mostly disunited, except during the periods of the Maurya dynasty, particularly the imperial rule of Asoka in 273 B.C., and the Gupta dynasty from 320 to 413 A.D., which saw the growth of literature, science, mathematics (including the concept of zero), and the development of fabric dyeing. This period represented the golden age of India.

THE MOGUL EMPIRE, 1524–1858   Muslim Arabs came to the Indian subcontinent in 711 A.D. in the form of marauders invading the Indus Valley. By the ninth and tenth centuries Arab traders had achieved control over many port cities along the southwest coast. While the Arabs were primarily interested in trade and conversion, they were not the real conquerors. Muslim conquerors of India were those Islamic converts from central Asia: the Turks, Afghans, Persians, and Mongols. The founder of the Mogul Empire in India was Babur from Samarkand, who was related to Genghis Khan and Tamerlane. In 1524 Babur invaded India by way of Kabul, Afghanistan, with only a small force of no more than 12,000 men. He ruled northern India as the founder of the Mogul, or Mongol, Empire from 1529 to 1707. His grandson, Akbar, expanded and consolidated the empire, and by 1576 he was the undisputed ruler for all of northern India. Akbar was tolerant in accepting Hindus for government employment, and he developed an efficient civil administration. His grandson, Shah Jahan, built the marble tomb Taj Mahal in memory of his wife. However, he was religiously intolerant toward the Hindus, levying heavy taxes on them and embarking on a scheme to destroy all Hindu temples. His son, Aurangzeb, ruled the Mogul Empire from 1659 to 1707 and crushed all opposition by conquering central and south India under his rule by 1690. Then rebellion broke loose in many parts of the subcontinent in opposition to Mogul rule.

Political Belief   Hinduism is the dominant way of life for a vast majority of people in India,[8] about 83 percent of the 800 million total population. The focal point of the belief system is that of Karma:[9] The souls of all living things must pass through a circle of rebirth in accordance with previous deeds. It is a belief that rebirth in a different form after death as another human being, an animal, or a deity can be sustained endlessly. Hinduism is preoccupied with mysteries of life, and the ultimate in the belief is to achieve salvation; or "release of the soul from all bodily restrictions is the ultimate quest, and it is achieved by the final passage of the soul from its earthbound conditions to its cosmological resting place."[10] It is not really a belief with precise texts or church. Hindu temples are sacred places where the deities of Hindu cosmology are venerated. However, Hindus observe their moral duties, *dharma*, wherever they are.

To this day Hinduism maintains a highly hierarchically arranged social structure, known as the caste system, for at least 800 million people in India.[11] It establishes a rigid social order marking clearly the social level to which individual Hindus belong and boundaries within which they must observe the ancient Hindu code or rules in daily life. Caste is determined by birth; it determines where one lives, from which wells to draw water, where and how to eat one's meals inside and outside the home, which temple to enter for worship, and which occupation one is permitted to pursue for life. India's caste system is the most restrictive and rigid social order anywhere in the world.

It is said that when the Indo-Aryans invaded the India subcontinent, they devised the caste system in order to preserve racial purity as they began to make contacts with the Dravidians. But caste refers to more than just racial differences; it applies to differences in occupation, languages, tribal origin, and regional location. The ancient Veda provides the four basic *varnas* (color) to Hindu society: the Brahmans, or the priests at the top; the Kahtriyas, or the warriors; the Vaishyas, or the landowners, traders, and merchants; and the Sudras, or dirty farmers or those who serve as lowly laborers to the other three upon the social scale of hierarchy. Then there is the category of outcasts, or those who were born of *intervarna* marriages across the castes. These—whose numbers are over 100 million—are the "untouchables", the lowest social order of all in India. Gandhi called them Harijans or "the children of God"; they were born into the out-caste and are considered to be the most impure of all human beings, for they must perform the dirtiest jobs in their highly stratified society. Caste ranking is based on relative *varna* purity, or pollution through contact with the impure substances. Taking the population as a whole, not more than 10 percent of India's population belong to the top three caste categories as rulers who wield power in society, for they command more than 50 percent of all government jobs. In addition, there are as many as 3,000 subcastes, called *jotis*, which divide and segregate the Hindu society. The status and functions of the subcastes vary from region to region and some can be found only in a particular locality or village.[12] While India inherited the British legacies of law and respect for established authority, religious values too often override these basic political beliefs.

Western Impact: The British Rule, 1858–1947 Through its trading activities, the British East India Company secured a foothold in India in 1639. Then, this private enterprise, backed by its own naval and military forces, expanded its political control over the Ganges Valley after a decisive military victory against the French at the Battle of Plassey in 1757, as the Mogul Empire was in the process of disintegration being torn apart by tribal and religious wars. With the consent of the British Parliament, the East India Company obtained the right to collect taxes and wage wars against those Indian princes who refused to submit their allegiance to the company rule.

The East India Company's rule ended in 1857 when northern Indians revolted, led by Indian soldiers on the company's payroll known as "sepoys," who refused to bite cartridges greased with animal fat. The Sepoy Mutiny was put down, but the British Parliament in London took over direct rule of India from the East India Company in 1859. Queen Victoria became empress of India in 1876.

British direct rule over India was in the hands of a viceroy appointed by the crown. Land formerly owned by the East India Company was placed under the administration of the viceroy on behalf of the crown and Parliament. This was British India, consisting of eleven provinces. Then there were the Indian princely states of local princes, 562 of them, who supported the company during the Sepoy Mutiny. They were permitted to enter into treaty arrangements with London, but only under indirect rule of the viceroy. At the close of 1945 the largest 24 of the 562 princely states— Hyderabad, Mysore, and Kashmir—comprised almost half of the 715,000 square miles inhabited by 90 to 100 million people.[13] Each of the eleven provinces in British India was in turn ruled by a governor, appointed by the crown, who was responsible to the viceroy. T. Walter Wallbank points out that the vast administrative machinery of British India was in the hands of not more than 4,000 British personnel, augmented by about half a million Indian subordinates, backed by the British forces in India.[14] The ruling elite for governing British India was the Indian Civil Service (ICS), one of the oldest civil services in the world. The civilian service was originally formed by the East India Company as early as 1765. In 1853 it was opened to public competition, presumably to permit recruitment of Indians, through a vigorous examination system. As a civil service, the ICS maintained a good salary and pension scheme with opportunities for advancement in order to attract the most capable young Britains to overseas service.

Prior to the outbreak of World War II, a turning point in the British rule of India was the demand for constitutional reform for India. Under pressure from Gandhi's civil disobedience and increased communal disturbances between the Muslims and Hindus, a series of roundtable conferences was held in London to address these problems. The final outcome was passage of the Government of India Act of 1935. The constitutional reform provided for a federal structure of government with emphasis on provincial autonomy.

Indian Independence and Partition, 1947   The Indian National Congress was formed in 1885 by an Indian Civil Service retiree named

Allan O. Hume and a group of Indian leaders from Bengal. At the beginning it was a debating society participated in by the educated Indian elite. It was not until the 1920s that the Indian National Congress had a mass base, after the 1919 Amritsar massacre, supported by prominent Indian leaders, such as Mahatma Gandhi, who had by then established his reputation as a leader for mass civil and nonviolent disobedience. It was Gandhi who made it possible for the Indian National Congress party to become a mass movement. By the 1930s there was a movement led by the Muslim League for a separate Muslim state from the predominant Hindu Indian National Congress. In 1942 the British agreed to provide India with independent dominion status in the British commonwealth. The plan was not acceptable to either of the major political parties; the Indian National Congress demanded immediate independence, and the Muslim League was determined to have a separate divided India. The wartime viceroy, Viscount Wavell, strived vainly to obtain agreement among the feuding political forces for an independent India. On August 16, 1946, the Muslim League declared for a separate Muslim state of Pakistan, igniting widespread bloody riots between Hindus and Muslims all over India for much of 1946 and 1947. Although opposed by Gandhi, the Indian National Congress reached agreement with the British for a partition of India as the only alternative. On August 15, 1947, India became independent; Pakistan, a day before on August 14. In the months to follow, one of the bloodiest massacres in world history occurred, resulting in half a million deaths and displacement of 12 million refugees as Muslims and Hindus fled from their ancestral homes and moved en masse to their newly declared independent states. They were ambushed on their way to and from their homes, with resulting massive slaughter. Independence of India and Pakistan did not bring joy. Instead, it brought on unprecedented human tragedy.

The Nehru Dynasty A number of significant developments followed the independence of the new Indian state. First, the government was in the hands of leaders for the Congress party, dominated by charismatic Jawaharlal Nehru, a Westernized nationalist. He was aided by a corps of experienced Congress leaders who had acquired considerable parliamentary skills during the colonial days since the 1935 Government of India Act. Second, Nehru and his Congress leaders operated under the basic framework of the new constitution, which basically maintained the features of the Government Act of 1935. There were more than forty amendments to the constitution up to 1977. There was never a moment of doubt about the continuance of a parliamentary form of government for India. During the long period of Congress rule under Nehru's dominant leadership, the country was struggling with Nehru's vague mission of a socialist India by providing simultaneous development of nationalized heavy industries and social welfare services for the impoverished millions. Nehru launched less rigid five-year plans in succession without seeing the fruition of an "economic revolution." His vision began to fade as he was increasingly surrounded by men of less capability. There soon developed a heavy reliance on Nehru to make decisions and to superintend the operation of the Indian government. Nehru became more paternalistic, bordering on authoritarianism, and less patient. After he died in May 1964, there emerged a collapse of control by Congress leaders in the central government and a rapid deterioration of the Congress as a parliamentary party. There followed a brief reign by a more conservative leader, Lal Bahadur Shatri, who died in office in January 1966.

Succession to leadership to Nehru's Congress party fell on the widowed Indira Gandhi, daughter of Nehru, who was chosen by the party bosses to lead the troubled parliamentary majority. Indira Gandhi set out to reorganize the party and took over the post of prime minister with a new vigor by building a personal following. In 1969 she embarked on socialist schemes of nationalizing major banks, land reform, control of large industries, and ceilings on urban income and property. All these measures generated divisiveness and opposition to her leadership within the declining Congress party majority in the parliament.

Indira Gandhi's popularity rose by the time of the 1971 general election when her Congress party won an overwhelming majority of parliamentary seats. Now she was in complete control of the party and demanded personal loyalty of all to her leadership. For three years after the 1971 election victory, the economic situation in India worsened in the midst of rising inflation, food shortages, poor monsoon rains in the countryside, and riots and strikes by railworkers and students. In June 1975 Indira Gandhi requested and obtained a decree from the president of the union to place the country under emergency rule, which included the arrest of opposition leaders and censure of the press. Soon Indira Gandhi expanded the emergency powers to transfer India into an authoritarian state.

In a sudden move, Indira Gandhi announced a March 1977 general election and at the same time a relaxation of her emergency rule. The 1977 election brought down Gandhi's rule as opposition parties formed the Janata coalition to deny her Congress party the parliamentary majority. But the new government of Maranji Desai soon disintegrated amidst widespread discontent and the inability to govern effectively. In July 1979 the Desai coalition government fell apart and resigned. In January 1980 a new general election was called and Indira Gandhi returned to power until she was assassinated by Sikh militants in 1984.

The 1984 parliamentary election produced massive support for Indira Gandhi's son, Rajiv, who was reluctantly drafted as successor to his mother's reign. It was a new beginning in Indian politics when Rajiv became the prime minister. He brought younger, but more technologically oriented, politicians into the party and government. For the second time a Nehru descendant emerged to carry on the dynasty. Tragically, Rajiv, too, was gunned down by assassins—this time the Tamil Tigers—in the midst of the 1991 parliamentary election.

Pakistan: From Military Authoritarianism to Civil War to Islamization to the Return of Zia's Men

Historic Legacy   In its historic legacy Pakistan shared with India the British colonial rule and independence after the war. The immediate years after the 1947 partition were a difficult period of adjustment and organization for the new state of Pakistan. Problems included boundary drawing, division of armed forces, and bureaucracies left by the departing British rule. The creation of an East and West Pakistan, separated by over 1,000 miles of India, made it difficult to establish a unified central government. Internal disagreement emerged between East and West Pakistan focusing on a debate over drafting of a new constitution for Pakistan through a constitutional assembly elected by the provincial assemblies. There was unrest in the provinces, exacerbated by riots, food shortages, and charges of official corruption.

By the time the second constitutional assembly was convened in July 1955, the Muslim League's dominance was challenged by five other political parties and factions that squabbled between and among themselves. On March 23, 1956, a new constitution, the first for Pakistan, was proclaimed, but by then the Muslim League as a political force had reached a state of disintegration.

Disagreement and dissension between the various political parties in East and West Pakistan raged on so that the 1956 constitution became inoperable. In October 1958 martial law was declared by the president of the republic. The emergency decree placed the country under the direction of a martial law administrator, the ranking army general Ayub Khan. On October 7, 1958, General Ayub Khan seized control of the government and abrogated the 1956 constitution. This marked the first collapse of the parliamentary government.

Political Belief   In the spring of 1979, with the backing of the military junta and the fundamental Muslim religious elements, President and general Zia enacted the so-called Hudood Ordinance in order to revamp Pakistan's criminal system and citizen's social behavior bringing them more into alignment with Islamic precepts as defined in the Koran on matters of theft and sex offenses.[15] He banned drinking and gambling and ordered that no tea be served in business and government offices. He ruled that government letters must invoke the name of Allah. Also, in 1961, by introducing an interest-free banking system, he launched the Islamization of financial institutions in accordance with Islamic law.[16] He ordered the formation and development of the Zakat Fund—public monies from local, provincial, and central sources were collected to provide welfare and development at the community level from villages on up.[17] Thus, in addition to the basic framework of government, the values of Muslim religion play an important role in political belief in Pakistan. Zia's Hudood Ordinance was one such illustration. The first attempt in articulating a set of political beliefs was made by Ayub Khan.

Military Rule and "Basic Democracies" General Ayub Khan came from a humble family background of the Pathan tribes. Trained as a dashing military officer by the British, he showed military competence and professionalism. While holding the posts of the army's commanding officer and the defense minister, he was considered to have no political entanglement with the various power forces in Pakistan. Soon it became evident that Ayub Khan and his fellow officers were contemptuous of the inefficiency and corruption of the civil government. When he seized control of the constitutional government, he employed an emergency power under martial law to investigate the civil officials for many "antisocial" behaviors such as hoarding, smuggling, and black-marketeering. He also ordered the arrest and purge or demotion of officials charged with corruption. Between 1958 and 1962 he instituted land reforms by limiting the holdings of the landed aristocracy with the intent of breaking its political influence and power in predominately rural East and West Pakistan. He successfully sought agricultural loans from the United States and encouraged foreign capital investment. For a while there was stability and some signs of economic progress.

As a soldier Ayub Khan tended to view complex political and social problems with simplistic solutions. He somehow disliked the inefficiencies and delays in the parliamentary system. With a largely illiterate populace, he argued against the basically Western-oriented parliamentary system as being unsuitable: He introduced the concept of "basic democracies" as prerequisites for success of democracy in Pakistan. It was simple to understand: A vote is called for only when a voter is knowledgeable, there is effective citizen participation, and there is a stable and strong government. Each village with a population of 10,000 had a union council of ten elected and five appointed members who were responsible for law and order in the village, for rural community development projects, and for levying local taxes. Above these village councils were district and divisional councils responsible for education, sanitation, welfare, and coordination of government activities. However, the main emphasis of the "basic democracies" was on rural economic development and social welfare. The president was supported by some 80,000 electoral constituencies, or the union council, each with 10,000 population. Ayub Khan's distrust of parliamentary democracy and popular election seemed to have been adhered to by the succeeding military strongmen who ruled Pakistan until 1988.

Civil War in Pakistan (1969–1971) and the Return to Military Rule

Ayub Khan resigned the presidency and was succeeded by the martial law administrator, General Yahya Khan. Yahya Khan lacked the political skills needed to patch together the disparate elements in East and West Pakistan for a united government that would command respect and allegiance from the provinces. He even had problems controlling his own close advisors: two high-ranking generals feuding and competing for power and influence. On December 7, 1970, he fulfilled his pledge made earlier to return to constitutional government by calling for a general election on the basis of one-man-one-vote for the National Assembly, which would then draft a new constitution.

Now a new constitutional government rested on the willingness to reach an agreement between three powerful political groups: Mujibur Rahman's Awami League in the East, Bhutto's Pakistan People's party in the West, and Yahya's military regime. The military strongman, Yahya Khan, held talks with both Rahman and Bhutto, but failed to produce any agreement for an outline of a new united constitutional government because the majority parties from the East and West each insisted on their own sole right to form a government and draft a constitution.

As civil war between East and West Pakistan broke out, India lent its support to the demands of the Bengalis for a separate sovereignty, the People's Republic of Bangladesh. Yahya's forces moved in to put down the "armed rebellion" and to ban the Awami League as the majority party in East Pakistan. Full-scale civil war broke out in March 1971. At first, India aided the Bangladesh guerrilla forces in their effort to fight off the regular army from West Pakistan. By early December the Indian army had attacked by land and sea against the Pakistan army and recognized the Provisional Government of Bangladesh. In less than two weeks of fighting, 70,000 of the Pakistan forces surrendered and a cease fire was declared on December 17, 1971. The defeat of the Pakistan forces brought on riots in West Pakistan against the military government of Yahya Khan and finally forced the military dictator to resign.

There was a short civilian rule under Bhutto, who pushed for the adoption of a new constitution in 1973, the third one since 1947 independence. While recognizing powers of the provinces, the 1973 constitution clearly stressed a strong central government—a factor of continuing debate and dispute in the provinces. He employed threats and inducements to seek the needed cooperation from Baluchistan and the NWFP, where there had been a strong movement against central government control.

Zia's Rule: Islamization, Legitimacy, and Political Stability, 1977–1988[18]   General Zia Ul-Haq's military regime was the longest in Pakistan's history, from July 5, 1977, to August 18, 1990, a total of eleven years. He was killed in a plane explosion while returning from an inspection trip, shortly after take-off from a military base. When Zia seized power as the chief martial law administrator by overthrowing the Bhutto government, he suspended the 1973 constitution, banned and dissolved activities of political parties, and curtailed the judiciary's power to review the constitution and basic rights. Zia ruled on behalf of a formidable military junta consisting of top ranking military officers.[19] He and his officers orchestrated former president Bhutto's arrest, trial for masterminding political murder, and the latter's execution by hanging. Under martial rule, Zia embarked on a series of religious, social, and economic reforms in order to consolidate and legitimize the military regime.

Benazir Bhutto: "Politics of Vindictiveness," 1988–1990   Zia was killed in a C-130 transport explosion while returning from an inspection trip at a military base on August 18, 1988. Also perishing in the crash were several high-ranking Pakistan military officers and the American ambassador. Zia's death released the pent-up energy of the fragmented political parties which then participated actively in the democratic process: the November 1988 election—the first free election in eleven years. Groundwork for the 1988 election was put into motion prior to Zia's death when he dissolved the National Assembly on May 29, dismissed his prime minister, and called for an election. The election results swept Benazir Bhutto's Pakistan People's party (PPP) to victory in the National Assembly with 92 seats against the opposition's 8-party coalition of 54 seats out of a total of 237 seats. The PPP also won a simple majority in most provincial assemblies. Benazir Bhutto became prime minister after years of imprisonment and detention.

Benazir Bhutto was the first young woman (aged thirty-five) elected to high office in a male-dominated Muslim Pakistan. Her background was of a wealthy, aristocratic, land-owning family from the province of Sind. Following in her father's footsteps she received her education abroad, at Radcliffe-Harvard as an undergraduate and at Oxford for graduate work. She was articulate, sincere, and modern in her outlook. She learned politics at an early age through a close relationship with her father. After her father's death, Benazir and her mother assumed leadership of the PPP. In a sense, her party's victory at the polls was a vindication of what her father stood for in his years in politics, and thus inflicted vengeance on the deceased Zia and his followers who were responsible for her father's death in 1977.

After years of authoritarianism and oppression under martial law rule and the ever-present old-fashioned political infighting, she brought youth and a fresh outlook to the new Pakistan government. She was said to represent "a symbol of a new democratic Pakistan." [20] However, one year after her assumption of office, the assessment of her management of government affairs was not praiseworthy.[21] She survived the no-confidence motions raised by the opposition in the National Assembly despite the often repeated prediction that her government would collapse within a year. She was constantly troubled by demands for autonomy from Pakistan's provinces, by ethnic violence in major cities such as Karachi, and by corruption in high places.

Rule by the "Troika": The Sacking of Bhutto and the Return of Zia's Men, August 6, 1990 On August 6, 1990, Pakistan president Ghulam I. Khan, invoking Article 58 of the 1973 constitution, issued an order for the dismissal of Prime Minister Benazir Bhutto and dissolution of the National Assembly. He also called for a general election within ninety days, or in October. Twice before—in 1984 and in 1988—prime ministers had been dismissed by the head of the state. An interim premier was appointed until the election. These moves by President Ghulam Khan were undertaken with the cooperation of the military, even though the latter publicly announced that the army was not involved in the political move.[22]

In the October election, the Islamic Democratic Alliance (IDA) defeated Benazir Bhutto's PPP by winning 105 seats in the National Assembly against the latter's 45. Punjab's chief minister, Nawaz Sharif, who led the IDA, became the new prime minister. Sharif's administration has been dependent upon the continued support of President Ghulam Khan and the army's chief of staff, General Mirza Beg. Sharif, like Benazir Bhutto, has been troubled by unrest and violence in the provinces. He has made plans to amend the 1973 constitution, which provides him with emergency power over parts or all of Pakistan and a special ordinance for police to open fire without first seeking a court order.[23]

For most of the summer of 1991, the government faced waves of violence in the provinces. Sharif has resorted to drastic measures, such as mandatory surrender of unlicensed weapons and public hanging of terrorists.[24] Sharif's regime is facing unrest caused by rising prices and the unsolved Kashmir border problem. Sharif's regime has been threatened by the alleged co-op scandal in Punjab involving millions of depositors. Benazir Bhutto has taken advantage of the scandal to mount an offensive on Sharif's administration and by drawing sizable crowds in rallies organized by the PPP.[25]

LOCUS OF POWER: POLITICAL INSTITUTIONS, LEADERSHIP, AND BUREAUCRACY

India: Central or Federal Government?

The 1949 Indian constitution, a lengthy document with 395 articles, provides for a federal union under a parliamentary form of government. Specifically, the constitution established these main political institutions: the presidency for the federal union, a bicameral national legislature, a prime minister, state governments, and a court system. As pointed out by several scholars, the Indian constitution drew from or has been benefited by the political experiences of the British, American, Irish, and Western Europeans, as well as its own experience based on the 1935 Government Act of India.[26]

The President of the Union   The executive officer for the Indian union is the president, the head of state. However, the presidency under the Indian constitution is not merely a figurehead position, for a number of powers are provided for the president to perform if he or she chooses to do so. In addition to the appointment of the prime minister and the council of ministers, the president appoints the attorney general, justices of the Supreme Court of all India, and the governors of the states. Under Article 123 of the constitution, when the Parliament is not in session, the president is empowered to issue ordinances that have the force of law. The president can dissolve the Parliament.

Emergency powers are the most important powers granted the president for the Indian union. There are three major emergency powers the president can exercise in order to preserve the union and the republic as a whole against the ever-present centrifugal forces at play in Indian politics.[27] One such emergency power for the president is under Article 352 of the constitution: to declare a national emergency in case of war or widespread internal disturbance. (On June 25, 1975, Prime Minister Indira Gandhi was able to persuade the president, a compliant Muslim politician, to issue an emergency proclamation that enabled her to arrest opposition leaders, to impose censorship of the press, and to place state governments under central government rule.)

Another emergency power given to the president is specified in Article 356, under which the union president can place a state under national government control upon the advice of the state governor, but subject to parliamentary approval. This is sometimes known as placing a state under "presidential rule."[28] A state may be placed under federal rule for a period from six months to three years. For the period 1950–66, "presidential rule" was utilized eight times, but under Indira Gandhi's prime ministership, from 1966 to 1977, it was utilized thirty-nine times.[29] However, the forty-fourth amendment to the constitution, passed as a reaction to the 1975 emergency, restricted the declaration of a national emergency only to occasions when the nation is under armed rebellion; it must be approved by a two-thirds majority of the Parliament for one month and renewed for not more than six months by a second two-thirds majority vote. The third type is defined in Article 360, under which the president can declare a state of emergency for the nation or a state when there is financial disaster. This has not yet been utilized. Taken as a whole, the use of these presidential emergency powers have affected the federal relationship with the states—a concept that will be discussed shortly.

The president is elected by a special electoral group that consists of members of the Parliament and members of the legislative assemblies of the states in the Indian union. The role of the states in the election of the union president is to emphasize that whoever is so chosen represents national consensus and unity.

The Parliament   The model for the Indian parliament is the British bicameral system. The lower house, the *Lok Sabha* (House of the People) is comparable to the House of Commons; the upper house, *Rajya Sabha* (Council of States) serves similar functions as those of the House of Lords. As in the case of the British lower house, Lok Sabha has most of the legislative power. All bills on finance must originate in Lok Sabha.

Lok Sabha has 542 members elected from single-member constituencies in the states and union territories based on population. The 542 members or seats were fixed in 1971 and will continue until 2001. A certain number of seats in the Lok Sabha are specifically reserved for the untouchables (seventy-nine), backward tribes (forty), and the Anglo-Indian community (two); the latter are appointed by the president if it is without representation.[30]

The Lok Sabha operates much the same way as the British House of Commons. Its meetings are presided over by a speaker. The party with the majority of seats acts as the majority party, which controls the deliberation and proceedings. The opposition leaders, any party with a minimum of fifty seats, are recognized and given the privilege to act as such. Most members of the Lok Sabha speak either English or Hindi while addressing the floor. In accordance with British tradition, the first hour of its daily session is known as the "question period," when the government ministers from the majority party must answer members' questions on matters affecting administration policy. The British practice of calling for a vote of no confidence has also been followed in the Indian parliament to challenge or bring down the prime minister on any given issue. Such challenges or votes of no confidence must be sustained by the majority vote. If not, the government then falls, or a new election may be called if no other opposition party leader can form a new government. One study revealed that between 1962 and 1982, twenty-one no-confidence motions were made against various prime ministers.[31] But more than half of these no-confidence motions occurred during the first thirteen-year reign of Indira Gandhi—almost one for every year of her office. The coalition government under Prime Minister V. P. Singh was brought down by a vote of no confidence on November 7, 1990, over the controversial issues of the Ayodhya Shrine and job quotas for the untouchables. Singh failed to muster the necessary majority vote when the right-wing Hindu nationalist Bharatiya Janata party (BJP) withdrew its support.

The upper house, Rajya Sabha, is the Assembly of State. It is a small house with 250 members. The constitution stipulates that 238 seats in Rajya Sabha be elected by the twenty-two state assemblies in accordance with their population size, with due consideration for those states that have small populations. As with the House of Lords in the British Parliament, the president of the Indian union appoints outstanding citizens in arts, literature, sciences, and social services to the remaining twelve seats. The term for members of Rajya Sabha is six years, but one-third of them must retire every two years. It is a body that is in continuous session and cannot be dissolved. As an assembly of the states, Rajya Sabha must safeguard the interests of the states by revising bills enacted by the Lok Sabha or simply delaying final passage. It is on an equal basis for amending the constitution, since ratification requires a simple majority of both houses, plus a majority of Indian states and the union president's assent. Rajya Sabha has no power to pass motions of no confidence.

The legislative process for the Indian parliament progresses through three stages. First, a non–money bill may be proposed by both houses. In each house a bill must go through three separate readings to be considered for passage. Second, the bill is then transmitted to the other house after the third reading in the house from which it originated. The second house then can accept, reject or amend the bill. If amended by the second house, the bill is returned to the house of origin. Third, in case the bill is rejected or the houses fail to agree (within 6 months), the union president intervenes by calling a joint session of both houses to debate and vote on the bill; it must be passed by a majority of the members of both houses in joint session. One needs to bear in mind that in such a joint setting the numerically strong Lok Sabha would generally have its desires prevail. A bill so voted must have the union president's assent to become law. Under the constitution, the president can refuse assent by sending it back to the parliament for reconsideration. But if it is passed by both houses for the second time, then the president must sign it in order for it to become law.

On money bills, the final authority for passage rests with Lok Sabha, the initiating house. When there is a dispute it is the speaker of the Lok

Sabha who decides. If it is passed by Lok Sabha it is then referred to the Rajya Sabha for consideration and action within fourteen days. If it is amended or rejected by the upper house, the Lok Sabha has the final authority to pass it for the second time and send it on to the president, who has no alternative but to assent.

The Indian Parliament has been criticized, particularly during the year when the National Congress party was in the majority, and when Nehru and his daughter, Indira Gandhi, who succeeded him as prime minister, exercised control of the national agenda.[32] The Cabinet seemed to be in the driver's seat in initiating the legislative agenda. As high as 68 percent of legislative time had been devoted to financial and procedural matters.[33] During the emergency years, 1977–79, Parliament merely served as a "rubber stamp" for the administration of prime minister Indira Gandhi.[34]

The Prime Minister and the Cabinet   India's British parliamentary model calls for the prime minister, the national chief executive, to be chosen from the political party that has the majority in Parliament. Since 1947 to the May–June 1991 elections, India has had nine prime ministers, the most recent being P. V. Narasimha Rao following the assassination of former prime minister Rajiv Gandhi in May 1991. However, since independence in 1947, the Nehru family held the office of prime minister for forty of those years: Nehru (eighteen years, from 1947 to 1964), his daughter, Indira Gandhi (eighteen years, from 1966 to 1977 and 1980 to 1984), and her son, Rajiv Gandhi (five years, from 1984 to 1989). In other words, the national chief executive position of India has been, for most of the time, in the hands of powerful, strong-willed, and charismatic members of the elite Nehru family that dominated the Indian National Congress party. Nehru provided the leadership and consensus. He was the undisputed leader and was rarely challenged. During his long tenure as India's prime minister, Nehru was able to rely on the elites, who for the most part were exposed to the tradition of parliamentary order.

By the time his daughter, Indira Gandhi, succeeded him as prime minister in the mid-1960s, new groups and classes—rich farmers, the regional separatist movement, and the politicized undercastes and untouchables—had entered into the political scene. There was a threat to the national union; social conflict, disorder, and violence were on the rise. Indira Gandhi was faced with the problem of a need for increased centralization of government and for providing direction on national policies from a strong national leadership. The Congress party reduced its strength in the 1967 general election, and the old guards within the party wanted to preserve the status quo, retaining their positions as bosses, or "the Syndicate." Backed by her inner circle of advisors—technocrats and national integrationists—Indira Gandhi moved to challenge the party old guard and, bypassing the Parliament, took her issues and agenda directly to the voters.

In the 1971 election, after having instituted drastic moves by nationalizing India's banks and installing her candidate for the union presidency, she led the Congress to a decisive victory at the polls by appealing to the poor, the Harijans (untouchables), scheduled or backward tribes, and Muslims. Indira Gandhi's enormous prestige and power at the national level did not prevent the entrenched old guards from maintaining their hold at the state level, which became increasingly volatile and unstable. In June 1975 she declared a national emergency by arresting old political opponents and detaining thousands of individuals in the name of law, order, and stability. In the 1977 election for Lok Sabha, she failed to win majority support and was out of office.

Indira Gandhi returned to office in the 1979 parliamentary election when her youthful new Congress (I) won the majority of the parliamentary seats. Her second term as the prime minister was marred by communal riots and caste disputes. To compound the internal crisis, there were continuous militant separatist demands on the basis of regional and religious differences in Assam, West Bengal, and Punjab. It was the secessionist movement pitting moderates against militant Sikhs that led to the Indian army's Golden Temple attack that eventually paved the way for Indira's assassination in October 1984.

Indira Gandhi's premiership was characterized by her desire for a strong centralized national government and personal power. In the process, for the duration of the emergency she dismantled some of India's democratic institutions. However, Myron Weiner has pointed out that Indira Gandhi also established new institutions to enhance the central government's capacity to make decisions.[35] She strengthened the prime minister's secretariat, a body of about 200 senior technocrats and political advisors, for policymaking. Weiner also has called attention to the formation of centralized intelligence organizations, under the authority of the prime minister's secretariat, for obtaining information on opponents, or critics within the Congress party, and on others.[36] These new institutions more or less replaced the role of the Cabinet. Weiner states that during her tenure, power in India became more authoritarian, and it gravitated away from elected officials into the hands of government bureaucrats.[37]

Rajiv Gandhi was reluctant to assume succession to his mother's role as prime minister. His tenure was marked initially by conciliation through seeking consultation with opponents. He brought in new, but younger technocrats after his struggle with the older generation of politicians. He appeased the Sikhs in Punjab by agreeing to free elections and meeting demands from the moderate elements. In spite of these conciliatory moves, Rajiv Gandhi was constantly troubled by regional separatist movements in Assam, West Bengal and Punjab. By mid-1988 the Congress (I) had suffered serious defeats in state assembly elections. By November 1989 Congress (I) was unable to win a majority of seats in the general election.

Rajiv Gandhi resigned his position as prime minister on November 29, 1989, thus ending more than four decades of Indian National Congress party rule.[38] The parliament was dissolved and a five-party coalition of the National Front (Indian Communists and Hindu right-wing groups), with a combined total of 289 seats, emerged and designated V. P. Singh, a one-time close aide of Rajiv, as the new prime minister.[39]

Singh's reign as prime minister was shaky at the start. As a coalition leader of disparate opposition parties, he was required to find ways to hold together the Indian Communist party and the increasingly nationalistic Hindu right-wing parties such as the BJP. In addition to maintaining support of the fundamentalist Hindu rising wave, Singh's coalition government had to deal with the economic problems of inflation, a budget deficit, and government corruption brought on by the Bofors arms deals. It was over the dispute regarding the Hindu-Muslim Ayodhya Mosque that his government lost to a motion of no confidence by a vote of 346 to 142 in Lok Sabha.[40] Ironically, Singh had embarked on action designed to change two primary issues in the Indian society that brought down his short reign as prime minister: to dampen the rising wave of Hindu fundamentalism in a secular society, and to provide more equitable treatment for the oppressed lower castes and backward tribes.

The brief tenure of the new prime minister Chandra Shekhar, from November 1990 to June 1991, could be best described as transitional. His party, the Janata Dal-Socialist, filled only 60 seats in the 525-seat Lok Sabha. He was able to assume the premiership simply because Rajiv Gandhi and his Congress party, with 195 seats, supported him.[41] Chandra Shekhar's rule was marked by confusion and his reliance on the Left to counter the weight of the more conservative parties. He marked time until the 1991 general election, which replaced him with a new leader.

The Judiciary System   The judiciary system for India has been modeled on the British tradition. It is structured along three levels of hierarchical courts. At the top is the Supreme Court of India, whose primary responsibility, at least under the constitution, is to interpret the constitution and laws. It has the original jurisdiction on disputes between the union and the states or between states. The highest court in India also has the appellate jurisdiction in civil and criminal cases. It may consider special appeals on any matter from the lower courts except those cases involving the armed services. The union president can request an advisory opinion on questions of law from the Supreme Court of India. It is also responsible for the general administration of high courts in the states.

At the intermediate level is the system of eighteen high courts for the twenty-two states and union territories, with some of them covering more than one state. The union president also seeks consultation with the chief justice of the Supreme Court of India and the governor of the state prior to appointing a judge to the high court of a state. These courts have the original and appellate jurisdiction in these states and union territories. All criminal cases at this level must have a jury trial.

The lower courts serve as the various judicial districts within a state. Judges for the district courts are appointed by the state governor under consultation with the high court for the state and whatever district courts are administratively responsible.

There are seventeen justices on the Supreme Court of India presided over by the chief justice, who is appointed by the union president. All other justices on the Supreme Court are also appointed by the union president with consent of the chief justice. None of these appointments is subject to parliamentary approval.

Constitutionally speaking, the judiciary system for India must maintain its judicial independence without undue interference from the executive; it is above politics in accordance with the British tradition. For instance, there is a tough requirement on removal of the justices appointed by the union president to protect the judicial integrity. They can be dismissed only after both houses of the Parliament have made such a recommendation. The vote for removal of a justice must be made by a majority of the total number of each house, plus a two-thirds majority vote of those present and voting. Prior to a vote on removal of a justice the speaker of Lok Sabha must appoint a committee, which must include a Supreme Court justice and a high court chief justice, to investigate the charges for removal.

Judicial independence suffered its most serious blow prior to and during Indira Gandhi's emergency rule declared on June 26, 1975. On June 12, 1975, a lower court, the high court of Allahabad, ruled that the 1971 parliamentary election through which Indira Gandhi had won a seat in Parliament was invalid because of illegal campaign practices engaged in by her campaign workers.[42] The high court ordered her to resign, but she refused, and the case went to the Supreme Court of India for a hearing, which did not take place until August 25. At the urging of the prime minister, on June 26 the president had promulgated an emergency in order to quell civil disobedience campaigns waged by the opposition leaders to force her to resign.[43]

Then the parliament, controlled by Congress (I), enacted Constitutional Amendment 39, prohibiting the Supreme Court's review of actions in the election of the president of the union, the prime minister, and the Speaker of the Lok Sabha. The amendment was intended to protect Indira Gandhi against the Allahabad high court ruling regarding the 1971 election violations, thereby enabling her to retain her parliamentary seat. The Supreme Court failed in this particular case to challenge the amendment. Nor did the Supreme Court challenge the forty-second Amendment, which, among other things, barred the Court from declaring laws to prevent "antinational activities" unconstitutional.[44] There were many instances thereafter to indicate that the judiciary had succumbed to Indira Gandhi's political pressure. By the time the forty-fourth Amendment had been pushed through Parliament, there was little judiciary independence remaining, for that extraordinary constitutional amendment had terminated once and for all judicial review of constitutional provisions and granted Parliament the ultimate power to change the constitution at will.[45]

Pakistan: The Unstable Political Institutions

Unlike India, Pakistan's political institutions have been unstable and are subject to constant changes by the military authoritarian rulers. There is the unresolved constitutional question: "What really should be the form of government: a presidential form or parliamentary form that places the executive power in the prime minister as supreme?"

Since independence in 1947 Pakistan has had four constitutions, excluding the temporary application of the 1935 Government of India Act and the 1947 Independence Act as modified: 1956, 1962, 1972, 1973 (as amended). At various times Pakistan has been governed without a constitution, or the adopted constitution has been suspended or modified: 1958–62, 1969–71, 1977–85.

The 1973 constitution was drafted and adopted under the administration of Zulfikar Ali Bhutto, who assumed power in the aftermath of the civil war between East and West Pakistan and the war with India, which Pakistan lost. Under the modified 1973 constitution, the government structure made up of a president, prime minister, the national assembly and the senate, and the judicial system.

The President The concept of a president, both as head of state and government was introduced in the 1962 constitution and retained in the 1972 (interim) constitution. In both instances the president made all the decisions. In fact, under the 1972 interim constitution, President Bhutto possessed the power usually granted to the British viceroy, including the exclusive authority to appoint provincial governors. When the new constitution was adopted in April 1973, the presidential form of government was replaced by the parliamentary system under which the prime minister served as the head of government and the president the head of state. In short, under the 1973 constitution the president of Pakistan was an office on the surface with little real power.

In March 1985 Zia promulgated a modification of that office. Under the Rival of the Constitution of 1973 Order, the president was given the power to appoint and dismiss the prime minister and the provincial governors. In addition, under the 1973 order of modification, the president had the authority to dissolve both the National Assembly and the provincial assemblies. In May 1988 Zia dismissed Prime Minister Mohammed Khan Junejo, whom he had appointed, and replaced him with an interim prime minister by invoking Article 58 of the modified constitution.

Then, on August 6, 1990, at the urging of the military, president Ghulam Khan dismissed the elected Prime Minister Benazir Bhutto on the grounds that the government was ineffective in quelling the crimes of corruption and nepotism in rural and urban Pakistan. The presidential decree then also dissolved the National Assembly and set a new election for October 24, or within ninety days of the dissolution of Parliament.

The Prime Minister: The Constitutional Struggle for Power   Although the 1973 constitution favored a parliamentary form of government, there always has been the desire of the military strongman in Pakistan to ensure that the president is endowed with the special constitutional power to remove or dismiss a prime minister chosen by the majority party of the National Assembly. Before his death in August 1988, Zia had laid the groundwork for the action taken by President Ghulam Khan on August 6, 1990, to dismiss Benazir Bhutto, who had been the prime minister for twenty months since the November 1988 election. Zia's constitutional amendment, known as Article 58, provided the president with two special powers for his challenge to the prime minister who derives power from the National Assembly: (1) The president has absolute discretionary power to appoint anyone prime minister from among the elected members of the National Assembly regardless of who is chosen by the majority party; (2) the prime minister must convey to the president every decision made, and the president has the discretionary power to "place before the cabinet any decision taken by the prime minister alone." [46]

In short, the original intent of the 1973 constitution providing for parliamentary supremacy had been eroded by subsequent constitutional amendments under Zia's rule. Instead, the president, elected by the National Assembly, was given the necessary discretionary power to remove or dismiss not only the prime minister, but to dissolve the national assembly as well.

The National Assembly and the Senate[47]   Under the 1973 constitution the Pakistan parliament was to be bicameral: a National Assembly and a Senate. The National Assembly originally consisted of 200 members elected by universal adult suffrage, plus ten women members chosen by a special electoral college of assembly members. In the 1977 general election, Bhutto's Pakistan People's party won 155 seats against the opposition coalition party's 36. However, from that time on until 1981 there were no legislative institutions because Zia, who governed by decree under martial law, had suspended the 1973 constitution. In 1981 Zia replaced the national assembly by a "federal council" (the Majlis-i-Shura), an advisory body to the chief martial law administrator—himself. It was formally proclaimed in December 1981 with a membership of 350, but later scaled down to 287, appointed by president Zia to reflect the composition of the society.

On March 17, 1985, Zia finally proclaimed the "Revival of the Constitution of 1973 Order (Presidential Order No. 14 of 1985)."[48] The Parliament consisted of the National Assembly of 237 members (207 Muslims, 10 non-Muslims, and 20 women), and a Senate of 87 members (14 selected from each of the four provinces, a total of 56; 8 selected from the tribal areas; 3 from the federal capital; 5 from each of the provincial assemblies, a total of 20 representing technocrats, professionals and *ulema*, or Islamic theologians).[49]

There were a number of significant features in the 1985 constitutional modification order issued by Zia. First, an election for the National Assembly took place February 25 prior to a constitutional modification order issued March 17. However, Zia also issued special restrictive rules for the election, which included a ban on political meetings and political processions, as well as guidelines relating to the election, such as "partyless" or on a nonparty basis and a separate electorate for Muslims and non-Muslims.[50] Second, considered to be the most significant constitutional change under the order, the president was given the power to appoint and dismiss the prime minister, who merely served as an advisor to the president. However, the original 1973 constitution had established a parliamentary form of government under which the leader of the majority party in the National Assembly would become the prime minister. Then the president was given the authority to dissolve the national and provincial assemblies. (On December 19, 1984, Zia had been elected president by a national referendum with a vote of 34 million in favor and only 316,000 opposed—a 97.7 percent affirmative vote.)[51] Moreover, the president was endowed with the power to appoint and dismiss the provincial governors and chief ministers. In effect, the 1985 Revival of the Constitution of 1973 Order created a strong presidential form of government. In addition, in November 1985 the National Assembly enacted the Eighth Amendment, which for all intents and purposes legitimatized all presidential orders and martial law decrees that had been issued from July 1977 to November 1985—not to be questioned by the court on any ground whatsoever.[52]

The Judicial System   The 1973 constitution established the Supreme Court of Pakistan to have the original, appellate, and advisory jurisdictions, which remain basically unaltered today. It can render opinions on disputes between the central government and the provincial governments. It can make advisory opinions on any legal matters referred to it by the president.

It has the appellate jurisdiction over civil and criminal cases referred by the lower courts.

The president appoints the chief justice for the Supreme Court, as well as the other justices after consultation with the chief justice.

Then, for each of the four provinces there is a high court, which serves as the appellate court for the lower or district courts in civil and criminal cases. Below the high court are the district and sessions court, which serve as trial courts in civil and criminal cases. In case of a death sentence the high court must give approval to the decision of a sessions judge prior to execution. Only the sessions judges can try cases of serious crime, such as murder, as well as cases under the Islamic penal codes or the Hudood Code discussed earlier. The district and sessions courts also serve as appeals courts, except in cases dealing with the Hudood Code for the magistrate courts at the lowest level. At the rural or village level disputes or cases are usually settled informally by the so-called conciliation courts. In Sind province minor civil and criminal cases have been traditionally settled by the landlord without formal procedure.

There are also numerous special courts or tribunals for dealing with cases involving banking, customs, traffic, anticorruption, and drugs. In 1980 in his attempt to enact Islamization of Pakistan, president Zia established the Shariah Court as a novel addition to the 1973 constitution.[53] Judges of the Shariah Court, which enforces Hudood codes or laws, are Muslims and *ulema* (religious leaders) who are familiar with Islamic law. The recent sentencing of two American brothers of Muslim faith by the Shariah Court in Peshawa in accordance with Islamic law—the amputation of the right hand and left foot for bank robbery—attracted world attention to the workings of these Islamic, or Shariah, courts.[54]

Scholars on Pakistan's judicial system offer different views on political independence in its turbulent politics. Golan W. Choudbury stated in his book in 1988 that under Zia's military rule judicial independence had been preserved, as the highest court in Pakistan maintained the final say; nor had Islamization affected the judicial system, as the "rule of law" had prevailed.[55] However, Asaf Hussain argues in his work on elite politics in Pakistan that the judiciary "had never taken a strong stand on issues in Pakistan politics" and that most judges were not "free from political pressure."[56] He maintains that the judges are political elites who are not only "loyal to their political benefactors," but want to "legitimatize the actions of the governing elites."[57] The Shariah courts under Islamization are merely used to "suit the political ends of the governing elites."[58]

The most vocal critic of the lack of judicial independence in Pakistan has been Benazir Bhutto, the former deposed prime minister. In her autobiography she condemned the usurpation of the civil courts by the military courts.[59] She points out that the Provisional Constitution Order issued by Zia purged almost 25 percent of the judges on the civil courts.[60]

As a result of president Ghulam Khan's August 6, 1990, dismissal of the National Assembly and Prime Minister Benazir Bhutto, the question of judicial integrity and independence resurfaced. The Northwest Frontier Province High Court declared the dissolution of its provincial assembly to be illegal and unconstitutional, thereby challenging the constitutionality of Zia's unilateral modification and amendments to the 1973 constitution.[61] One of the judges on the NWFP High Court lost his position for dissenting from the majority. The struggle for judicial integrity and independence in Pakistan continues.

Pakistan's supreme court had the rare opportunity to exercise its judicial integrity when President Ghulam Ishaq Khan dismissed prime minister Nawaz Sharif from office in April 1993 by invoking the infamous constitutional amendment that empowered the state chief executive to take such action. The prime minister then filed a protest to the supreme court for a redress on the ground that the head of state had no power to dismiss at will an elected head of the government, the prime minister. On May 27 the supreme court, by a majority vote of ten to one, overturned the president's dismissal of prime minister Nawaz Sharif from office and ruled that the latter was not subordinate to the head of the state on governmental policies. The court asserted in its ruling that the president must abide by the advice of the prime minister and the cabinet. Thus, for the first time in Pakistan history, the judiciary took a stand against a powerful president.

The constitutional crisis came to a halt on July 18, 1993, when, under pressure from the military and the Bhutto opposition, both the prime minister and the president resigned and the parliament dissolved. A new election for Pakistan was set for October 1993, and it was during this election that Benazir Bhutto's PPP was restored to power.

THE POLITICAL PROCESS: PARTICIPATION, ELECTIONS, POLITICAL PARTIES, AND GROUP POLITICS

India: The World's Most Populous Democracy

The Electoral Process   India has been the most populous democracy in the world with 514 million eligible voters. About 60 to 70 percent have gone to the polls at the national parliamentary elections in recent years, a total of ten such elections since independence. In the 1989 parliamentary election the voting age was lowered from twenty-one to eighteen, thus enfranchising about 35 million new young voters.

Election time in India is colorful as well as violent at times.[62] Because a large segment of the voting population is illiterate, an interesting system of balloting has been designed to enable all, including the illiterate millions, to participate at the polls. Each voter is given a rubber stamp at thousands of polling stations. Each political party is designated by an easily recognizable symbol. In the 1989 parliamentary election, a hand denoted the Congress party of Rajiv Gandhi; a wheel, the Janata Dal; a lotus, the fundamentalist Hindu BJP; a hammer and sickle, the Indian Communist Party-Marxist, and so on. A voter uses the stamp by making a mark on the contested candidate's party symbol, which is imprinted on the paper ballot. There are the familiar campaign rallies, speeches by the candidates, and handshaking among the crowd.

Election days in India are often marked by violence. In the May 1991 general election in the Meerut, a district not far from New Delhi, a few days prior to balloting at least seventeen people were killed when street fights broke out after a Muslim candidate was attacked by a Hindu rival. Gangs were organized to hijack ballot boxes for a fee. The most tragic event took place on May 22, 1991, when Prime Minister Rajiv Gandhi was assassinated while campaigning in Tamil Nadu.

Political Parties and Groups   India has a multiparty system; the presence of a large number of competing parties has been a unique feature in Indian politics. However, the Indian National Congress party has been the ruling party except after the three general elections of 1977, 1989, and 1991. The multiparty system in India has produced a unique phenomenon in the 1989 and 1991 elections in that no single party received a working majority in the Lok Sabha. The party structure of India's political parties has been fragmented and is beset with factions. Under these circumstances, more pronounced since the 1989 election, primary concern for the parties has been over what Myron Weiner has described as building "political coalitions capable of winning elections and forming governments."[63] Weiner's thesis regarding Indian political parties after the 1980 election is still valid following the 1991 election in that "the political necessity of coalition building often transcends programs, ideologies and class interests."[64]

THE CONGRESS (I) PARTY   The Congress (I) party is successor to the Indian National Congress, which provided the organizational framework for independence under the leadership of Mahatma Gandhi and Jawaharlal Nehru. The Indian National Congress dominated Indian national politics during the Nehru era from independence to his death in 1964. The National Congress under Nehru was a broadly based political movement that attracted divergent groups and factions of Indian society to provide a semblance of consensus.

The death of Nehru ushered in a period of acute polarization and factional dispute within the National Congress party, such that by 1969 there emerged two powerful forces within the party contending for influence and control: the so-called parliamentary wing led by Nehru's daughter Indira Gandhi, who was now the prime minister, and Kamaraj Nadar's organizational faction of old guards and party bosses, or the "syndicate." In a showdown over the election of a president for the republic, Indira Gandhi won over the party bosses by selecting V. V. Giri as her choice for presidency. The victory also split the party and eventually placed Indira Gandhi in a dominant position after the 1971 parliamentary election, which swept in new recruits in the Parliament. This marked the birth of Congress (I), the party for Indira Gandhi. As some observers put it, "the central leadership became highly oligarchic and autocratic."[65]

Congress (I) returned to power by winning the 1980 parliamentary election, capturing 67 percent of the seats in the Lok Sabha, and almost 43 percent of the popular vote. Congress (I) was able to win the 1980 election because of the support of a combination of social forces: the rich and the very poor on the economic scale, the Brahmins and the untouchables on the extremes of the social structure, the minority religious groups of Muslims, Sikhs, and Christians, and government bureaucrats.

The assassination of Indira Gandhi by the Sikh militants produced massive support in the 1984 parliamentary election for her son, Rajiv Gandhi (see Table 4.1). Congress (I) captured a record of more than 48 percent of the popular vote and about 80 percent (415 seats) in the 545-member Lok Sabha. Rajiv Gandhi's party produced a landslide victory, partly the result of a sympathetic vote and partly because of his youthful image and clean, yet sincere stance as a new politician. The Indian voters in 1984 might have been tired of old politicians and their antics, wanting new leadership. Despite Indira Gandhi's autocratic and centrist tendencies, the Indian voters looked toward Congress (I) as a party of national unity, the central issue of the 1984 election.

Table 4.1   Elections in India, 1984, 1989, and 1991

	% of Popular Vote			Seats Won in Lok Sabha		
	1984	1989	1991	1984	1989	1991
Congress (I)	48.1	38.5	36.7	415	196	217
Regional parties & independents	23.8	22.4	21.1	87	77	33*
Bharatiya Janata party	7.4	11.2	20.3	2	85	102
Janata Dal	12.3	17.2	11.6	13	142	46
Communist parties	8.4	8.9	9.0	28	45	45**

*All-India Anna Dravida Munnetra Kazhangam from Tamil Nadu (11 seats) and Telugu Desam from Andhra Pradesh (12 seats).
**Communist Party-Marxist (34 seats) and Communist Party India (CPI) (11 seats).

Two events served as harbingers of the impending doom of Congress (I). One was India's decision in 1987 to mediate insurrection waged by the Tamil Tigers against the Sinhalese-dominated government of Sri Lanka and to authorize the presence of the Indian troops for peace-keeping. This action merely aggravated the central government in New Delhi and the Indian state of Tamil Nadu, which had been providing substantial assistance to guerrilla forces of the Tamil Tigers. By agreement with Sri Lanka, Indian troops, which had waged war against the Tamil Tigers, were withdrawn in 1989–90 and a cease fire prevailed thereafter.

The other event had caused considerable damage to Rajiv Gandhi's image as a leader of a government free of corruption. This was the "Bofors affairs," in which consistent allegations were made that some officials in the Rajiv Gandhi administration had received payments for the sale of munitions to India from a Swedish arms manufacturer. Rajiv reacted to these allegations by promoting some of the questionable state ministers into his central administration and by reasserting a centralized presidential role in January 1988 in order to eliminate control by the regional party in Tamil Nadu.

The 1989 general election proved to be disastrous for Congress (I); it captured only 38.5 percent of the popular votes and 196 of a total of 505 contested seats in Lok Sabha. In other words, it won only one-half the number of the seats it had obtained in the 1984 landslide. Although Congress (I) was still the largest political party under the 1989 parliamentary election, it was not large enough to form a majority government, and Rajiv Gandhi chose not to form a coalition government with the opposition parties. Janata Dal, with support of the parties from the Right and the Left, selected V. P. Singh, at one time Rajiv's finance minister, to form the new government, which was eventually brought down by persistent religious and ethnic rivalries.

The tragic 1991 parliamentary election, interrupted briefly by the May 22 Tamil Tigers terrorist assassination of Rajiv Gandhi, produced 217 seats for Congress (I)—not enough to give it a clear mandate to rule. This time, Congress (I) decided to form a coalition government with the support of the opposition parties.

JANATA DAL[66]   Janata Dal is a hastily formed coalition that has been an umbrella organization for the Congress party dissenters and leaders who disassociated themselves from the parent Nehru party under Indira Gandhi. The political movement was born in May 1977 as a challenge to Indira Gandhi's autocratic and personal rule. The movement also includes elements of socialist groups. Indian socialists are divided between two major groups: the leftist Socialist party of India, made up mostly of railway workers in India, and the socialist dissenters who were members of the Nehru

National Congress party. These socialist groups joined the Junata movement in 1977–78 with one goal in mind: the defeat of the Congress party under Indira Gandhi.

The issues that catapulted the Janata coalition into power in 1977 were the restoration of constitutional government and the rejection of Indira Gandhi's authoritarian rule.[67] The Janata coalition was beset with personal rivalry and animosity between the leaders of the disparate groups under its umbrella. By January 1979 the coalition functioned ineffectively as a political force and simply fell apart. In the 1980 parliamentary election Indira Gandhi's Congress (I) made a stunning comeback by capturing almost 43 percent of the popular vote and 351 seats (67 percent) of the total seats contested in the Lok Sabha. Using Weiner's term, once again Congress (I) established "the national trend,"[68] and captured the assembly elections in all major states except West Bengal and Tamil Nadu.

In the 1984 parliamentary election in which Rajiv Gandhi rode to a landslide victory after the Sikh militant assassination of his mother, the Janata coalition continued to decline in political influence on the national scene. By that time several parties had disassociated themselves and entered separately into the parliamentary contest on their own. As a result, Janata could attract only 12.3 percent of the popular vote and captured no more than 13 seats in the Lok Sabha against a massive total of 415 seats for Congress (I) under Rajiv Gandhi. It was indeed a humiliating defeat as compared to its emergence in 1977 as a national political force in Indian politics.

However, the Janata coalition made a significant gain in the 1989 parliamentary election by capturing a total of 142 seats in the Lok Sabha against 196 for Congress (I), thus denying Rajiv Gandhi a clear mandate to form the government. Instead, Congress (I) became the opposition party sitting on the sidelines. The Janata Dal party, campaigning under the banner of the National Front in 1989, relied on the support of regional parties: the Hindu nationalistic Bharatiya Janata party and the two major communist parties of India.[69] It campaigned on the issue of anticorruption in government. Its strength came primarily from the Hindu belt, where it garnered two-thirds of its 142 seats in the Lok Sabha.[70] At the time of the 1989 election Janata Dal was basically a coalition of factions and groups opposed to the domination of Congress (I) under Rajiv Gandhi. In the end, the coalition's leader and India's prime minister after the 1989 election, V. P. Singh, was not able to hold together the coalition on the issue of quotas for government jobs for the oppressed castes. As pressure mounted in the tide of Hindu nationalism or rivalism, the coalition government under the Janata Dal's National Front faltered and its associated parties split. The 1991 election saw Janata Dal become barely visible, for it captured only forty-six seats in the Lok Sabha. In 1991

Janata Dal had deteriorated into merely an alliance of old-time socialists and secularists; it no longer had the support of the extreme Right or the radical Left—they competed on their own. In desperation, leaders of the divided Janata Dal mapped a strategy opting for the lesser of two evils by giving support to Congress (I) candidates rather than to the Hindu rivalist Bharatiya Janata party. In the end the Jana Dal coalition achieved a "significant presence" in only three states: Bihar, Orissa, and Uttar Pradesh.[71]

BHARATIYA JANATA PARTY: THE INDIAN PEOPLE'S PARTY[72]   The Bharatiya Janata party (the Indian People's party) is the reincarnation of several militant fundamentalist Hindu organizations whose history dates back to preindependence days: the Jana Sangh movement, the extremist ultraconservative Hindu organization, and the R.S.S. (Rashtriya Swayamseval Sang), or the National Volunteer Organization. The latter was implicated in the assassination of Mahatma Gandhi in 1948. The Jana Sangh movement advocated supremacy of the Hindu culture and opposed Gandhi's and Nehru's religious tolerance and secularism for a pluralistic Indian society.

Under the atmosphere of Hindu revitalization in the past decade the militant BJP has grown in strength and influence. As pointed out by Indian scholars, Y. K. Malik and D. K. Vajpeyi, Hindu nationalism has manifested itself in Indian society in a number of ways, including the cry for revival of Hinduism, rising attendance at Hindu temples, popularity of R.S.S. activities among the young in the Hindi speaking belt of north India, and the consequent increase in communal tensions as the BJP directed its attack on the Muslims and the other minority groups.[73] In the 1984 parliamentary election the BJP captured about 7.4 percent of the popular vote and gained only two seats in the Lok Sabha (see Table 4.1). But in the 1989 election its voting strength increased to over 11 percent, and its gain in the Lok Sabha jumped to 85 seats. In the 1991 election, it captured 23 percent of the popular vote, and its share of parliamentary seats in the Lok Sabha increased to an all-time high of 102; it seized control of the Uttar Pradesh assembly. Its advocacy of Hindu revival and opposition to a secular India brought down the coalition government of V. P. Singh over two issues: erecting the ancient Hindu temple of Ram, the Ayodhya temple, on the site of a mosque, and its campaign against the quota system for government jobs and university admissions for the backward scheduled castes and Muslims. The BJP draws its main support from the upper castes, the Hindu urban middle class of shopkeepers and small business owners, and unemployed professionals.[74] It is a disciplined and well-organized political party—the National Volunteer Organization (R.S.S.) has over 35,000 branches throughout India and can mobilize as many as 100,000 to 300,000 devotees. Next to the faction-ridden Congress (I), the BJP is the party on the rise in the changing Indian political scene.

COMMUNIST PARTIES   There have been three communist parties in India. The oldest, and thus the parent of Indian communist parties, is the Communist party of India (CPI), founded in the 1920s as a part of the Communist Third Internationale (Comintern) effort to organize revolutionary parties in the so-called backward areas of the world. Its greatest growth was during World War II; it supported a partitioned separate India and Pakistan. After India's independence the party was banned in 1948 when it engaged in a campaign of violence and subversion with local communist groups seizing land and the local government in Hyderabad. Nehru's government released the Communist party members in 1951 on the eve of the first national election in response to the pledge by the leaders of the CPI that they would behave as a legal opposition party. The party then gradually gained respectability as it supported Nehru's foreign policy and refrained from insurrection. In the 1957 election, the CPI gained almost 10 percent of the popular vote and became the majority party in the Kerala state assembly. Kerala then was the poorest state in India, with the highest rates of unemployment and illiteracy. In a special election in Kerala in 1960, the CPI was defeated by Nehru's Congress party.

The 1962 Indo-Chinese border war was the cause of a split within the CPI as an opposition party to Nehru's Congress party. The split produced the Communist party-Marxist (CPM), which was pro-Chinese; the CPI was endorsing Nehru's stand against the Chinese military incursion on the Sino-Indian border. The CPM's strategy was to play down the possible Chinese military threat to India, while stressing its opposition to the Congress party, particularly its efforts in defeating communist control in Kerala. The CPM's strong base of support has been in the states of West Bengal and Tripura, drawing allegiance from landless poor, students, industrial workers, and intellectuals. It made a significant gain in the 1980 election by capturing over 6 percent of the popular vote against the CPI's 2.6 percent. While its popular appeal slipped to less than 6 percent in the 1984 election, the CPM captured twenty-two seats in the Lok Sabha, in spite of Rajiv Gandhi's landslide.

There is also the revolutionary radical factional group of the Indian communist movement, the Communist party of India-Marxist-Leninist (CPML). It surfaced in 1969 in West Bengal, led by dissident young communists who were in favor of a Maoist strategy of armed rebellion in the countryside. In fact, in 1976 in West Bengal's Naxalbari, it instigated an armed peasant uprising that spread to the neighboring states of Behar and Andhara Pradesh. This uprising was finally suppressed by the Indian army. Survivors of the group, known as Naxaltes, subsequently either joined the

CPM or formed splinter factions and participated in electoral politics. Its demise as a group dedicated to armed uprisings may also be attributed to improved Sino-Indian relations in the 1980s under China's Deng Xiaoping's reform and rapprochement policies.

Campaigning separately in India's electoral parties, both the CPI and the CPM command some support among the voters. In the 1989 election, the CPM won thirty-three seats and the CPI twelve seats to the Lok Sabha, with a combined 8.9 percent share of the total votes cast.[75] Both communist parties joined with V. P. Singh's Janata Dal National Front coalition movement in the 1989 election to deny Congress (I) the power to form the new government. In a series of pacts agreed to by the parties in V. P. Singh's National Front, parliamentary seats were adjusted after the 1989 election, allocating the communists a total of seventy-five seats in the Lok Sabha.[76] Their main strength and voter support came from West Bengal and Kerala, along with some support for the CPI in the northern Hindu-speaking states of Bihar and Uttar Pradesh. The combined strength of the CPI and the CPM remained roughly unchanged in the 1991 election, when the CPM won thirty-four seats and the CPI eleven seats, for a total of forty-five in the Lok Sabha.[77]

REGIONAL PARTIES   In her study of cultural nationalism in south Indian politics, Marguerite R. Barnett points to the close relationship between the desire for revival of Dravidian culture and the formation of a political movement to achieve that nationalist goal.[78] The emergence of the Dravida Munnetra Kazhangam (DMK) in the 1960s in the then Madras state was the case in point. The Tamils in Madras and other parts of south India had been agitating for recognition of the historic and cultural distinction of the Dravidians, who are Tamil speaking, as opposed to the dominance of the Hindi-speaking Indians in the north. The separatist state rights movement for the Dravidians in the south gained momentum in 1964 when the central government attempted to make Hindi the national official language; and this controversy precipitate riots in southern India. The movement made political history when the DMK ousted the Congress party in the 1967 election and became the ruling party in Madras. In accordance with its avowed goal of an autonomous and even separate state based on culture and language, the DMK changed the name of Madras to Tamil Nadu, or "the land of Tamils."[79]

While the DMK has consistently advocated a separatist movement for Dravidians in south India, the movement in the form of a political party engaged in the electoral process has been beset with factional rifts.

Another regional party surfaced in 1982–83 in the Andhra Pradesh state in central India, the Telegu Desam party. The founder of this political party was N. T. Rama Rao, a popular Indian movie idol who became highly critical of Indira Gandhi's exercise of a personal centralized government in New Delhi, and aroused regional sentiments for more autonomy over local affairs. In the 1983 state election, Rama Rao's Telegu Desam party defeated Congress (I) by capturing 200 of the total 295 assembly seats in Andhra Pradesh. Indira Gandhi employed her power to harass the popularity of Rama Rao. She undermined the latter's control of the state's politics, culminating in his removal as the state chief minister in conjunction with the shootout incident by Indian troops at the Golden Temple in the summer of 1984. However, the 1984 general or parliamentary election saw the spread of the Telegu Desam party's appeal for regional and state autonomy; it won twenty-eight seats in the Lok Sabha. This was followed up with another victory in the 1985 state election by the capture of a majority of state assembly seats. In the 1989 parliamentary election, the Telegu Desam party won only two seats in the Lok Sabha, but increased its share to twelve in the 1991 parliamentary election (see Table 4.1).

From the foregoing summary of the Indian political parties, it seems clear that the political system as a whole is still undergoing significant changes. First, for more than two and one-half decades, since independence in 1947, there had been the "dominant party system" in which Nehru's National Congress party had controlled the majority in the national parliament and in the state assemblies by way of an open competitive electoral process. The dominant Congress party was "a party of consensus" and the opposition parties were "parties of pressure."[80] The aftermath of the 1977 emergency produced a keen awareness among Indian voters regarding "the logic of electoral politics" and "the notion that parties and leaders should respond to those whom they represent."[81] The consequence was the emergence of a more assertive and competitive voting public that tended to vote against the Congress party at the national and state levels.[82]

The Military Role in Indian Politics: "Power Amid Poverty"[83]   The total manpower for India's active armed forces is about 1.4 million strong; it is the fourth-largest military force in the world. During World War II the Indian army grew rapidly under the British and Allied commands, so that by the end of the war over 1 million troops of the British Indian Army were dispatched outside of the country, fighting against the Axis powers in Africa, Italy, the Middle East, Burma, and Southeast Asia.[84] The partition in 1947, a pre-condition for independence, disrupted the armed forces by transferring two-thirds of the manpower and equipment to India and the rest to Pakistan, after initially allocating the Muslim units to it.

THE DEFENSE BUDGET AND ARMS BUILDUP   While India faces an enormous problem of fighting a war on mass poverty, in recent years it has increased its arms buildup, presumably to counteract threats from neighboring China and Pakistan. Its 1990–91 defense allocation is about $9.2 billion, an approximately 10 percent increase over the last budget allotment, or an official estimate of 3.6 percent of the gross national product. However, the actual defense budget for 1990–91 was closer to 5.2 percent of the GNP,[85] since allocations in the government's budget for paramilitary forces, such as the Border Security Force (90,000), Assam Rifles (40,000), and Indo-Tibetan Force (14,000) are allocated under the Home Ministry.[86]

THE COSTLY DEFENSE INDUSTRY   India's maintenance of a highly sophisticated defense industry, including nuclear capacity and the Agni nuclear missiles, has made it a regional military superpower. A series of articles in the *Far Eastern Economic Review* provide a good picture of India's sophisticated defense projects, research, and the "bureaucratic maze" of arms suppliers.[87] First, there are government-owned and controlled public sector defense grant units or corporations, such as Hindustan Aeronautics, which produce fighter aircraft, navigational systems, a host of factories for ordnance making, and army-owned special defense farms with a total employed force of more than 120,000.[88] Defense research in missiles and nuclear weapons is not part of the defense budget—for 1990–91 it alone has been allocated $128 million. In addition, research and development in the defense industries assisted universities in producing technicians and experts so that India today has the world's third-largest "pool of technical personnel."[89] There are a total of 1,700 research "establishments" in India that rely on direct government funding and support.[90] Major criticism of India's expanding and sophisticated defense industry seems to focus on its lack of relationship with domestic economic development, for its export sales of weapons and equipment is practically nonexistent.[91] Little of the Indian expertise has "spilled over into Indian export competitiveness."[92] Growth in arms research and development has also caused India to be more dependent on foreign technology. Defense purchases from abroad became a political issue that contributed to Rajiv Gandhi's Congress (I) defeat in the 1989 parliamentary election.

THE INDIAN MILITARY ROLE: CIVILIAN AND BUREAUCRATIC CONTROL   In his analysis of the Indian military role in policymaking, Steven Cohen points out that the Indian armed forces have played a very small role, or none at all, in defense or other policy matters. Policy matters on defense have generally been made by the Political Affairs Committee of the Cabinet, aided by the professional military's Chief of Staff

Committee.[93] The Ministry of Defense and its top civilian cadres dominate not only defense policies, but matters of "recruitment, training and promotion practices."[94]

While civilian control of the Indian armed forces is a long-established tradition, some scholars argue that it would be unwise to rule out the possibility of military intervention in politics if there is continued and prolonged erosion of "the legitimacy, integrity and competence of the central political system" such as the decline of the Congress party or the inability of the opposition party to rule.[95] However, the decline of Congress (I) in 1989 and the assassination of Rajiv Gandhi in 1991 demonstrated remarkable adherence to the tradition of nonmilitary intervention and restraint exercised by India's military establishment. In the final analysis the Indian military seems to be the "exception" in an Asia where military coups are a common occurrence.[96] In India military officers are bound by the military tradition, a legacy of British training, and stay out of politics. This is in stark contrast to what has happened to Pakistan since the 1960s, to be discussed in the next section.

Pakistan: Parliamentary Democracy Struggles on under the Shadow of Military Intervention

The Electoral System   In its forty-four years of history since the 1947 independence, Pakistan has had only five general elections: 1970, 1977, 1988, 1990, and 1993. For much of this period, 1977–85, Pakistan was ruled by General Zia under martial law.

Pakistan's election law defines an eligible voter as one who is eighteen years of age and enrolled in the electoral list of the person's residence. For the November 1988 general election about 48 million (44.8 percent) of the total population of 107 million were eligible to vote. Of the eligible voters, 43 percent actually went to the polls and cast their votes. Previous general election turnouts were as follows: 1970, 67 percent, and 1977, 55 percent.

Voting is by secret ballot, but with separate voting booths for men and women. As in the case of India, the illiterates vote by party symbols for candidate choices. For the October 1990 general election, an arrow was designated as the PPP symbol and a bicycle for the Islamic Democratic Alliance (the coalition of more than a dozen opposition parties). This election was monitored by a team of forty observers from the National Democratic Institute for International Affairs based in Washington, D.C. Results of general elections for the National Assembly in 1988 and 1990 can be seen in Table 4.2.

Table 4.2   General Elections for Pakistan's National Assembly, 1988 and 1990

	1988 Seats Won (207)[a]	% of Total	% of Popular Vote	1990 Seats Won (207)[a]	% of Total
Pakistan People's Party	94	45.4	38.7	45	20.7
Islamic Democratic Alliance[b]	55	26.5	30.2	105	48.3
People's Democratic Alliance[c]	—	—	—	0	0
Other minor parties[d]	57	27.5	—	50	23.0

[a]There were 207 contested seats for the National Assembly, distributed as follows: Punjab, 115; Sind, 46; NWFP, 26; Baluchistan, 11; federal district Islambad, 1; and tribal areas, 8. The total number of seats for the National Assembly is 237: the 207 contested seats, plus 10 reserved for the religious minorities and 20 reserved for women (chosen by proportional representation after the election).
[b]A nine-party conservative coalition in the October 1990 election; also known as Islamic Jamhooru Ittehad (IJI).
[c]The People's Democratic Alliance organized for the 1990 election in alliance with Bhutto's PPP, the dominant group in the alliance.
[d]In the 1988 election, 30 political parties fielded candidates. In the 1990 election, 16 minor parties aligned with IDA (IJI) to win 50 seats.
Source: *Far Eastern Economic Review*, 18 October 1990, p. 26; and *New York Times*, 24 October 1990, p. A-3, and 27 October 1990, p. A-3.

Political Parties and Groups   THE PAKISTAN PEOPLE'S PARTY   The PPP was born in 1967 after a failed attempt to seal the breach between East and West Pakistan at the February 1966 Lahore conference. Zulfikar Bhutto, who broke away from Ayub Khan as the latter's foreign minister, formed a new political party, the PPP, to represent all social groups regardless of ethnicity and religious affiliation. The PPP's slogan was "*Roti, Kapra, Makan*" (Bread, Clothing, Shelter); it was designed to win over the votes of the poor.[97] Bhutto attempted to create a populist movement based on the theme of "Islamic Socialism."[98] The proving ground for testing PPP's strength was Pakistan's first National Assembly general election in December 1970 decreed by Yahya Khan, who abrogated the 1962 constitution. The result was that the PPP captured 82 (59.4 percent) of the total 138 allotted seats for West Pakistan, particularly in Punjab and Sind. In East Pakistan the Awami League, led by Sheikh Mujibar Rahman, won every available allotted seat, reinforcing and solidifying East Pakistan's demand for secession as a separate entity.

The March 1977 election gave Bhutto and his PPP a larger victory than in 1970. In the contest between the PPP and the Pakistan National Alliance (PNA) coalition of at least eight opposition parties, the PPP won 155 seats in the National Assembly—mostly from Punjab and Sind provinces—out of a total of 200.[99] But the PNA immediately challenged the election outcome as rigged, fraudulent, and manipulated by the PPP and Bhutto; thus, they called for the latter's resignation. Bhutto was unyielding and ordered a crackdown in the provinces and cities as violence and disorder erupted. He even called upon the military to suppress the disturbances. However, on July 5, 1977, the military intervened and Bhutto was arrested by his appointed martial law administrator, General Zia. A military dragnet was cast for the arrest and detention of government and PPP officials. Thereafter and until 1985, party activities were banned and restricted under Zia's martial law. Bhutto was placed on trial for murder; he was sentenced by the military court and hanged in April 1979.

The PPP struggled to exist from 1979 to 1988 under the trying leadership of Bhutto's widow and his daughter. When martial law was lifted and a new general election was called for in 1988, the PPP sprang to life primarily due to the strength and persistent efforts of Bhutto's wife and daughter, who themselves had been in and out of detention and jail.[100] Their motive was to effect a comeback and a vindication of the PPP's founder, the late Zulfikar Bhutto.

Unlike the previous general elections, the November 1988 National Assembly election was marked by spirited competition with minimum violence among the opposing parties. There were none of the usual charges of electoral irregularities, rigging, and fraudulent practices. However, the PPP did complain about the last-minute Supreme Court decision upholding an order that required eligible voters, 48 million in all, to show an identification card before casting a ballot. The PPP claimed that the party's major supporters were rural peasants, rural laborers, and women, all of whom did not possess the ID cards.[101] Nonetheless, PPP won 94 (45.4 percent) of 207 National Assembly seats; it received the support of almost 39 percent of the not quite 50 percent of eligible voters who cast their ballots. The PPP had strong support from the rural poor, the restless youth, and women. Its campaign promises included building half a million homes, providing free schooling for children, and developing fertilizer plants, pipelines, and dams. Benazir Bhutto campaigned to restore the 1973 constitution as it was originally written under her father's reign in 1973, the constitution that called for a parliamentary form of government with power in the hands of the prime minister. She also appealed for selection of the president by the National Assembly together with the Senate and the provincial assemblies.

Under the modified or amended 1973 constitution, the president could designate any elected member of the National Assembly as the prime minister; his designation of Benazir Bhutto was a gesture of good will. But the euphoria soon evaporated as she and her PPP faced major tests of no-confidence votes in the National Assembly. In the first year after the 1988 election, the prime minister and her party were attacked in the National

Assembly by the Right and the Left. Benazir Bhutto developed basic differences over the appointment of higher government officials, particularly Supreme Court judges.

Her PPP was under constant attack by opposition parties for corruption, nepotism, and failure to maintain law and order in the provinces, where there was rampant ethnic violence and gun and drug running. The opposition parties then formed an alliance, the Islami Jamhoori Ittehad (IJI), and in November 1989 challenged the PPP in the National Assembly with a motion for no confidence. Bhutto's PPP was able to fight off the challenge, but not for long. On August 6, 1990, President Ghulam Khan, with tacit support of the military,[102] began to stir uneasily, aided by the Persian Gulf crisis and by the mounting Indian military pressure in Kashmir. The president, the opposition parties, and the military all seized the opportunity of the West's preoccupation (particularly that of the United States, which was more supportive of Bhutto's regime) with the Iraqi invasion of Kuwait to make a crucial move and tacitly allowed President Khan to invoke Article 58 of the modified 1973 constitution removing Benazir Bhutto from the premiership and dissolving the National Assembly and the provincial assemblies. While sensing the general worldwide and Pakistani negative reaction toward military seizure of power once again, the president set a general election for October 24, 1990.

The results of the 1990 election were a disaster for the PPP. Its 1988 strength in the National Assembly was reduced by almost one-half—to 45 seats (20.7 percent) of the total 207 contested seats. The opposition alliance won 105 (48.3 percent) of the seats. There were several reasons why the PPP lost the 1990 election. First, the PPP regained power in 1988 on the strength of its antimilitary rule. In the 1990 election the military was silent, cautious, and almost invisible. Second, the various charges—there were six court cases—of corruption and nepotism against Bhutto and the PPP hurt their image and helped to build up resentment against the party. Third, and perhaps most important, was the opposition coalition of nine parties that campaigned as one group with the tacit blessing of the army and the bureaucracy. In 1988 these minor parties ran independently. The coalition won not only the urban votes, but in the rural areas as well, by capturing a majority of the contested seats in the provinces, including Bhutto's own Sind. In the crucial province of Punjab, which holds 60 percent of the total National Assembly seats, Bhutto's PPP ran against the military-supported Nawaz Sharif. He was the province's chief minister, who had built a powerful political machine ready to oust Bhutto and the PPP, and openly admitted his support of Zia.

THE ISLAMIC DEMOCRATIC ALLIANCE   The nine-party alliance, known as the Islami Jamhoori Ittehad, is led by Nawaz Sharif of Punjab. The conservative coalition includes the Pakistan Muslim League (a revival of the old Ali Jinnah's party), the Jamaat Islami party (an ally of the PPP), plus an independent political group. The IDA is promilitary and fundamentalist in religious orientation—it declares the supremacy of the Koran in all aspects. It singles out Benazir Bhutto and the PPP as too modern for Pakistan and as being antimilitary. The IDA not only has the tacit support of the military, but the industrial-financial power in Pakistan as well; it depicts the PPP as a Bhutto-family-based political party that draws its support from feudal landlords in the provinces. It portrays Bhutto as pro-American; that image hurts the PPP since the United States had suspended its $500 million aid to Pakistan because of former president Bush's insistence that Pakistan must assure the world that it was not building a nuclear bomb.

The strongest group in the IDA is the Pakistan Muslim League, the party that has been dominated by Muhammed Khan Juneto, the prime minister appointed by Zia in 1985. It does not have a coherent ideology, except for its advocacy of national unity. Then there is the Jamaat Islami (Association of Islam) group, which promotes fundamentalist views on Islamic practices in public policies. It generally opposes modernization and is against bank interests and population control programs; therefore, it supports Shariah laws. It is a well-organized political party with operating cells among the educated middle class. It benefited by Zia's Islamization programs and played an active role in the 1985 referendum election for President Zia. It is not really surprising that upon winning the 1990 election, new prime minister Nawaz Sharif, the head of IDA, pushed for speedy enactment in the new National Assembly to make Koran the supreme law of Pakistan, one of his campaign pledges.[103]

THE PEOPLE'S DEMOCRATIC ALLIANCE   During the 1990 election, the Bhutto forces organized a coalition to oppose the IDA. In essence, the PDA has been dominated by, if not entirely composed of, the PPP. The coalition's old appeals to voters on such constitutional issues as central versus provincial authority were no longer attractive, because the electorate were demanding improvements in electric power, sanitation, and education.[104] In the by-elections in the provinces the PDA suffered further setbacks, since its voting appeal declined among the rural voters who were reluctant to turn out to vote.[105]

The Military Role in Politics   Pakistan's military embraces the basic concept that the rationale for its existence is to serve as the "defender of the faith," Islam, and the state, a Muslim Pakistan.[106] From this point of view the military is an integral part of Pakistan's political system; too often in Pakistan's history since independence it has been the final arbiter in political crises. The military has dominated Pakistan politics either directly or indirectly for much of the past forty or so years. In fact, for a considerable time the military regime has been the system of government in operation: 1958–71 (thirteen years) and 1977–88 (eleven years). For the remainder of the state's existence the military has been the force behind the scenes.

As a powerful elite group, the military officer corps is not entirely united in its continued political involvement. There is an evolving dissension on the issue between the military-professional oriented group and the more politically inclined group within the officer corps.[107] The following is a brief discussion of military intervention in Pakistan politics, focusing on the Ayub military rule (1958–69) and the Zia military regime (1977–88). We will conclude by reviewing indirect military influence under Benazir Bhutto and her removal from office in August 1990.

MILITARY INTERVENTIONS FROM AYUB TO ZIA   The military takeover by Marshal Ayub Khan in 1958 was a classical example of the thesis that the military is the agent for modernization.[108] Underlying the thesis has been the contention that the military, as modernizing agent, possesses organization and discipline, two prerequisites for nation building. There is the contention that the military as a coercive force is the only institution in society that can bring out order and stability; and that more importantly military takeover is necessary due to the civilian authority's failure to effectively manage the government. One of the first acts of Ayub's military rule was to purge the "bureaucratic elite" from government for their corruptive practices.[109] Only after establishing military supremacy did Ayub begin to form alliances with the civil bureaucracy, and the industrial and the landed elites in order to secure their support for the 1965 presidential election in which Ayub received more than 63 percent of the popular vote.[110] Ayub Khan then began to place reliance on his newly formed political party by separating his rule from the military, a move that subjected him to constant attack from other groups. Eventually, by 1969, he was forced to return to the military officer corps for help; they did not respond to his request, thereby putting an end to his rule.

Ayub's successor was General Yahya Khan, the martial law administrator. Yahya ran the government from the military high command headquarters. He finally called for a national election in 1970, the first in Pakistan contested by political parties from East and West Pakistan that resulted in civil war and war with India in 1971. With the loss of East Pakistan, which became Bangladesh, Ali Bhutto became the civilian leader. He tried to consolidate his rule by constitutionally placing the military (which had suffered a humiliating defeat by India) under the purview of the prime minister and promoting to positions of power those military officers who had remained loyal to him. But in the end, Ali Bhutto was not able to control the military in a period of intensified ethnic disturbance from the provinces of Baluchistan and Sind. Nor were the military officers content with policing urban riots. Finally, in July 1977, a military coup took place and General Zia-ul-Haq, Ali Bhutto's martial law administrator, seized the power.

Zia's military rule was considered not only "conservative," but ideological. He was more sensitive to ethnic unrest in the provinces. He set out initially to "defuse" the discontent by releasing imprisoned dissidents. Zia also moved toward Islamization to please the religious groups. In addition, he tried to secure the military rule of the country by forming alliances with other powerful elite groups in society:[111] the bureaucratic-civilian administrators, the landlords in the provinces, and the industrial elites with economic power.

It has been said that Zia's plane crash in 1988 was planned by dissidents within the military who preferred a less politicized, but more professional orientation.[112]

THE MILITARY AS BEHIND-THE-SCENES POWER   Benazir Bhutto's election to head a civilian government after more than eleven years of Zia's military rule was made possible presumably by reaching an agreement with the military, which now preferred to be an invisible behind-the-scenes power. Although she denied it, among others, there were three key accepted understandings: the choice of Ishaq Khan, a close supporter of Zia, as president by Bhutto's PPP in control of the National Assembly; noninterference by Bhutto in military affairs; and no effort being made to punish the military for persecuting members of her family.[113] Her fragile twenty-month rule as the elected prime minister was tolerated and acquiesced by the military, which, traditionally from the time of Ayub Khan's first coup, has not trusted the civilians unless they are under its control.

The Pakistan military contended that the prime minister had tried to extend her authority over the military, in addition to creating the uncomfortable situation for the military to accept orders from a woman. This provoked the final removal of Benazir Bhutto as the elected premier when the president invoked the special constitutional amendment, Article 58, in August 1990.[114] Bhutto charged that the action was a "quasi-military intervention organized by the army headquarters."[115] The army chief of staff declared that the military was not involved in politics.[116]

After a long period of direct military rule under Ayub, Yahya, and Zia, the military in Pakistan has now taken a modified stance: that of behind-the-scenes power in the nation's politics. The result is still the same—that is, to make the military the final arbiter and the ultimate power in the turbulent politics of Pakistan.

POLITICAL PERFORMANCE AND PUBLIC POLICY

India: Socialist Planning, Nationalization, and Privatization

Economic Performance   There should be no debate regarding the economic progress India has made in the past four decades since independence in 1947. In 1950–51, India was producing about fifty-three metric tons of grain. It increased to more than 92 million in the 1960s, 120 million in the 1970s, and more than 160 million metric tons in 1988–89. Using steel production as an indicator of industrial progress, India produced only 1–9 million tons in 1950, but the figure jumped to over 11 million in 1988–89. Total industrial expansion probably increased at least six times over that of 1950. However, there is also the general agreement that India is still a poor Third World nation sporting a shining space center in Bengalore alongside of widespread rural poverty in most parts of India.

The long-term problem for the Indian economy is how to expand economic production in order to provide a better life for its people, particularly the impoverished rural villages—about 55 percent of the total population earned less than $30 per month in 1990–91. One needs to bear in mind that 74 percent of the Indian population lives in some 600,000 villages.[117] In the mid-1980s the Indian Planning Commission estimated that 40 percent of the rural and 28 percent of the urban population were considered to be living in poverty, defined as having a monthly income of 50 rupees (equivalent to $2 at the current exchange rate) and a daily calorie intake of 2,400 per person.[118]

For comparison purposes, it will be noted that the growth rate of per capita income in India has been estimated at 1.3 percent per year, as compared with China's per capita growth rate of about 5 percent per year for the period from 1968 to 1982.[119] Raj Krishna argues that it most likely would require an annual growth rate to the 4.5 percent level in per capita income to result in any significant impact on India's poverty.[120]

India's new prime minister P. V. Narasimha Rao, a Congress party loyalist who emerged as the party's leader after Rajiv Gandhi's assassination in May 1991, faced an unprecedented economic crisis. The economic crisis was partly attributable to political instability in the previous two years, 1989–91, when there had been four prime ministers and four finance ministers. At the top of the economic crisis list was the foreign debt, which had reached $72 billion, and thus made India, as of mid-1991, the world's third-largest debtor nation, next to Mexico and Brazil. The huge foreign debt had drained India's hard currency reserve to the point that essential imports were rather drastically curtailed. This forced India to go before the International Monetary Fund (IMF) for loans and credit totaling $2 billion. The IMF recommended that India must reduce its budget deficit as a condition for loan approval.[121] Due to expanded expenditures, particularly in government subsidies and defense outlays, in 1991 India's budget deficit stood at about $17 billion.[122] India has maintained an elaborate system of food subsidies in the form of ration cards and food credits for the rural, as well as the urban, poor. Indian farmers needed government subsidies because fertilizer prices had increased in 1991 by as much as 40 percent.[123] The deficit also caused prices to rise, for the inflation rate reached approximately 8.5 to 9.0 percent in 1990–91.[124]

The Government Role Soon after independence the Nehru government nationalized industries, such as railroads, arms manufacturing, shipping and telecommunications, that were considered to be of national importance. Privately owned industries, such as the Tata steel near Calcutta, were allowed to continue their operations. Soon government ownership was expanded to include all capital goods industries and major service industries, such as insurance and financial. In addition, the union government also formed exclusively state-owned entities and agencies for the control and operation of trade, utilities, and transportation. The Indian parliament enacted legislation authorizing the union government to control prices for cement, coal, drugs, fertilizer, food, grains, metals, steel, and textiles.[125]

In 1950 a National Planning Commission was formed, chaired by prime minister Nehru, but with flexible membership, for the purpose of drafting a comprehensive plan for economic growth and for solving the problem of mass poverty. There have been eight such Five-Year Plans (FYP):[126] first FYP (1951–55), second FYP (1956–60), third FYP (1961–65), fourth FYP (1969–73), fifth FYP (1974–78), sixth FYP (1980–84), seventh FYP (1985–90), and eighth FYP (1990–95). There has been some criticism of India's planned economy. In 1979 John W. Mellor argued that India seemed to have fared favorably when compared with China's economic development and growth in terms of grain production and industrial output for the same period. India's food grain production increase was 30 percent greater than China's, and they were about even—about 6 percent—in industrial growth.[127] (However, for 1990 China's grain production reached 422 million metric tons as compared with India's 160 million metric tons.) Questions have also been raised as to whether planned development "could be relied on as the major instrument for growth in the long run."[128]

Reform in Government-Directed Planned Economy Inevitably, government intervention and control became the consequences of planned economic development. Leaders of India, like Nehru and Patel, embraced British socialism, which advocated government intervention to guide the economy. The following is a brief summary of some of the reform measures introduced in recent years by prime ministers Rajiv Gandhi, V. P. Singh, and Narasimha Rao in attempts to correct the flaws in India's planned economy.

Since 1956 India's industrial policy has called for public ownership of key industries mentioned earlier in our discussion. By 1982 public ownership of key industries included twenty banks, seven insurance firms, the railroad system, and some 200 enterprises, the bulk of them engaged in manufacturing.[129] In addition, states within the Indian federation also established public sector ownership of industries. Both the central government at New Delhi and the states made substantial investment in the public sector. Some of these state-owned and managed enterprises have been profitable, while a majority of them have been considered wasteful and inefficient. One of the problems, a legacy of more than forty years of government-directed economy, has been the inability and unwillingness, for fear of unemployment and layoffs, to close those public sector industries that have been inefficiently and bureaucratically managed.

In recent years there has been discussion about privatizing the state-owned industries to make them competitive and efficient. Neither Rajiv Gandhi, who prepared a detailed plan for privatization in 1984, nor V. P. Singh continued beyond their expressed intention of making drastic changes in public sector management of key industries. This had occurred originally in order to divert scarce capital to meet the planned economic and social welfare objectives of fighting against massive poverty, even though state-owned and managed industries "have been marked by waste, obsolescence and the diversion of resources towards consumption by the well-connected."[130] As recommended by the World Bank and International Monetary Fund, prior to the 1991 election, under the brief reign of Chandra Shekhar, New Delhi took the important step of selling "20 percent of the equity of selected public sector firms" in order to raise U.S. $1.36 billion. These two agencies would be responsible for providing loans and credits for India.[131] The selected list of thirty-seven profitable companies partially privatized included huge companies in petrochemicals, computer maintenance, India air lines, India oil, and one auto manufacturing concern.[132] It would take a great deal of political maneuvering and finesse to counteract the Parliament's traditional opposition to sell key public sector industries to the private sector and to decentralize.

One of the more serious obstacles to India's march for further dynamic economic growth and industrial expansion has been its reluctance to encourage direct foreign investment. Prime Minister Rao seems to have taken a "proinvestment" stance when he remarked recently that he would be in favor of a drastic increase in direct foreign investment to help India "accelerate the tempo of development, upgrade our technologies and to improve our exports."[133]

Educational Progress One measurement of India's educational progress is the enrollment of school-aged children in primary and secondary schools. As of 1989–90, there were 107 million children enrolled in primary schools and 35 million in secondary schools.[134]

Even though the Indian educational system is controlled by both the central and state governments, there is really no uniform educational system as such. In fact, there are as many educational systems in India as there are geographic (coastal versus inland regions), cultural and linguistic differences, as well as variations in British colonization times for the regions. On paper, elementary education (primary and middle schools) is to be free and compulsory for children between ages six and fourteen. In practice it has been largely determined by rural economic conditions, the children's gender and family situation. There are several types of secondary schools with some curricula devoted to university preparation. Because of the existence of so many languages, the language of instruction is determined by that used in the region as well as the school children's mother tongue. Many school children attend only the first four grades to be classified as literate—only 36 percent of the entire population could be classified as such. Secondary education has been reserved generally for children of middle and upper castes who aspire eventually to white-collar jobs in business and/or the government bureaucracy. The wealthy and upper castes send their offspring to private schools in urban centers and in the hill stations such as Darjeeling, Dehra Dun, and Muree.

India today has about 4 million students enrolled at some 150 colleges and universities. Higher education is elitist oriented, and the graduates serve as the main source of candidates for government employment. While the entrance examination for university admission is not as hellish as in Japan or South Korea, it is still a very important part of secondary education. Examinations become even more important when graduates in colleges and universities must be awarded with a degree by obtaining a "pass" in the examinations. A common practice on university campuses has been leaking examination questions to students. Failure to obtain "pass" on the examinations means joblessness and psychological disgrace; the pass rate is estimated at 25 percent. The unemployed youth often becomes a source of discontent in society.

One immediate consequence of India's advancement in technical training has been the "brain drain" abroad. One estimate indicates that "25–30 percent of graduates from India's institutes of technology...find their way overseas within several years of graduation."[135]

Pakistan: Denationalization, Privatization, and Foreign Investment

Economic Performance South Korea's economic miracle is Prime Minister Nawaz Sharif's dream for Pakistan. Development history shows that in the 1960s Pakistan was performing better than South Korea and was a model for the developing nations. Since then, Pakistan's economy has been burdened by government regulation and rules, bogged down by bureaucratic mismanagement and beset with graft and corruption. In the 1960s Pakistan had a market economy and was undergoing rapid industrialization. Then came the period of a state-controlled economy in the 1970s and 1980s. Since the days of Benazir Bhutto, who began to denationalize, Nawaz Sharif has wanted to move with deliberate speed in the 1990s toward the privatization and decontrol of Pakistan's economy.

Under Zia's military rule, 1977–87, Pakistan's economic policy operated on two tracks: some relaxation in government ownership and regulation and introduction of a market orientation. While the strategy provided Pakistan with a steady average annual growth rate of about 5 percent, economic progress was to a large extent bolstered by an annual average remittance of $3 billion from Pakistani workers employed in the rich Middle East countries such as Saudi Arabia, Kuwait, and Iraq, plus economic aid from the United States as the former Soviet Union invaded Afghanistan. By the time Zia died in a plane crash on August 17, 1988, Pakistan's economy was burdened by the mismanagement of public ownership of industries; the budget deficit was $3.2 billion, some of it caused by 3 million Afghan refugees, plus a foreign debt caused by the fact that 60 percent of its development fund was provided by foreign sources. In 1989 debt payment consumed 43 percent of revenue amidst a population explosion at an annual rate of 3.1 percent.

Under Benazir Bhutto, elected prime minister as leader of the PPP in the November 1988 election, the government was required to operate under the guidelines of the International Monetary Fund in order to trim the budget deficit to $2 billion. When this is viewed against Pakistan's need to control drug and gun running, rising violence in rural and urban areas, and a defense threat from India in Kashmir, it would be indeed a miracle if she could provide real answers to Pakistan's economic troubles.

The Role of Government: Nationalization, Denationalization, and Privatization   At the time of partition public ownership was deemed necessary for those industries that were essential and required large capitalization: in defense, railroads, hydroelectric power, and telecommunications. Other industries were in private ownership; however, the government exercised control over industrial investment and trade. In the public sector industries were managed by civil bureaucracies. In urban centers such as Karachi or Lahore the private sector was controlled and managed by a small group of urbanized *muhajirs* (Muslim immigrants from India at the time of partition) and Punjabis constituting the powerful industrial family elites of big business. As pointed out by Asaf Hussain, some forty-three industrial-family-groups controlled 27 percent of cotton textiles, 15 percent of jute, 12 percent of chemicals, and 11 percent of sugar.[136] These industrial family groups saw to it that their management came from within their own ethnic groups of Memon, Sheikh, and Bohra.[137] Even more significant was the revelation by the state planning commission that in 1968 twenty industrial families controlled 66 percent of Pakistan's industrial assets and 80 percent of banking and insurance.[138] Benefits of expanded economic activities and industrialization had accrued to a few industrial elites and their families.

Zulfikar Bhutto came into power on the PPP's slogan of "socialism and Islam"; one of his many reforms was the nationalization in 1972 of thirty-two large manufacturing plants in ten major industries, including iron and steel, metals, auto and tractor manufacturing, petrochemicals, cement, and public utilities.[139] He later expanded nationalization to banking, insurance, shipping, textile mills, and vegetable-oil processing. The government also formed public corporations for cotton and rice export. Private investment in large-scale manufacturing concerns dropped by as much as 50 percent.[140] Bhutto's economic reforms considerably slowed Pakistan's growth for the general population as a whole. For much of the 1970s the annual growth rate was only 3.7 percent.

Zia's eleven-year rule from 1977 to 1988 was marked by his attempt to reduce government's role in economic and industrial development. Some nationalized industries were returned to the private sector, but nationalization was not completely eliminated, so that by the early 1980s the public sector had enlarged somewhat with more focus on improving managerial efficiency. Government manipulation of primary commodity prices and government subsidies were very much the central emphasis, as well as control over investment.[141]

During the twenty months of Benazir Bhutto's administration under the PPP's election slogan of "Socialism is our economy," there was some relaxation of government control over private sector industries, for the prime minister realized the importance of the private sector's role in economic development. However, Pakistan's economy was still bogged down by public monopolies and a rule-infested bureaucracy. However, some economic progress had been made under Benazir Bhutto during her first year as prime minister: Some nationalized industries—Pakistan Steel, Karachi Shipyard and Mechanical Complex—showed profits.[142] Bhutto made a concerted effort to promote private and foreign joint ventures with Australia, Britain, Canada, Japan, and the United States.[143] As a new policy to encourage growth, industrial expansion by existing private industries required no government approval.[144]

Sharif's Economic Reform: Privatization and Foreign Investment   Prime Minister Nawaz Sharif, whose family owned the giant Ittefaq Group in sugar, cement, steel, and textiles, pledged the economic 3-D reform program: disinvestment, deregulation, and denationalization. Since his election victory in October 1990 the focus of his economic reform has been a program for denationalizing 115 state-owned enterprises as quickly as possible by putting them up for sale to private investors under the Privatization Commission. These state-owned industries include automobile and steel making, chemicals, domestic appliances, edible or vegetable oils, farm machinery, heavy engineering, fertilizers, pharmaceuticals, sugar, cotton ginning, and banks. In June 1990 they commanded a total revenue of U.S. $6.5 billion and an employee work force of over 100,000.[145] So far the sale of these state-owned enterprises has not attracted wide interest among Pakistan's industrialists or foreign investors.[146] Recently the government launched a special advertising campaign in the world's leading news outlets in order to attract attention to opportunities for investment in Pakistan. As of this writing, privatization or sale of state-owned enterprises has involved only 30 out of a total of 150 targeted.[147] Major sales have included the Muslim Commercial Bank, the fourth largest in Pakistan, which has been sold to a consortium of twelve private entrepreneurs, and the Allied Bank to its employees.[148] Another major state-owned monopoly, the Pakistan National Shipping Corporation, faces competition from twenty-two private shipping firms that have been granted operating licenses.

On November 18–20, 1991, with the help of the World Bank, the government sponsored a conference in Islamabad for bringing together domestic and foreign investors to explore methods for joint ventures or 100 percent equity projects. In addition, the government enacted new regulations to permit remittance of dividends and profits to be repatriated without central bank permission, foreign exchange convertibility, negotiation for foreign loans by investors without government permission, and full guarantee by Parliament to protect foreign investment. In short, as a strategy for economic growth, there is a new climate in Pakistan for reducing government control, promoting privatization, and encouraging foreign investment. Much of the reform is dependent upon the bureaucracy, which is best characterized as inept and in need of reform.[149]

SUGGESTED READINGS

India

Akbar, M. J. *Nehru: The Making of India.* New York: Viking Press, 1988.

Baxter, Craig, Yogendra K. Malik, Charles H. Kennedy, and Robert C. Oberst. *Government and Politics in South Asia.* Boulder, CO: Westview Press, 1987.

Brass, Paul R. *The Politics of India Since Independence.* New York: Cambridge University Press, 1989.

Chen, Kuan-I, and Jogindar S. Uppal. *Comparative Development of India and China*. New York: Free Press, 1971.

Graham, Bruce. *Hindu Nationalism and Indian Politics*. New York: Cambridge University Press, 1990.

Hay, Stephen, ed. *Source of Indian Tradition: Vol. 2. Modern India and Pakistan*. New York: Columbia University Press, 1988.

Heesterman, J. C. *The Inner Conflict of Tradition: Essays in Indian Ritual, Kinship and Society*. Chicago and London: University of Chicago Press, 1985.

Kohli, Atul. *India's Growing Crisis of Governability*. Princeton: Princeton University Press, 1990.

Kothari, Rajni. *Politics and the People: In Search of a Humane India*, 2 vols. New York: New Horizons Press, 1989.

Limage, Madhu. *Contemporary Indian Politics*. New York: Radiant, 1989.

Naipard, V. S. *India: A Million Mutinies Now*. New York: Viking Press, 1990.

O'Harlon, Rosalind. *Caste, Conflict and Ideology*. New York: Cambridge University Press, 1985.

Roach, James R., ed. *India 2000: The Next Fifteen Years*. Riverdale, MD: Riverdale Company, 1986.

Sen Gupta, Ghabani. *Rajiv Gandhi: A Political Study*. New York: Konark, 1990.

Wolpert, Stanley. *India*. Berkeley: University of California Press, 1991.

Pakistan

Baxter, Craig, ed. *Zia's Pakistan: Politics and Stability in a Frontline State*. Boulder, CO: Westview Press, 1985.

Baxter, Craig, Yogendra K. Malik, Charles H. Kennedy, and Robert C. Oberst. *Government and Politics in South Asia*. Boulder, CO: Westview Press, 1987.

Bhutto, Benazir. *Daughter of Destiny*. New York: Simon & Schuster, 1989.

Choudbury, Golam W. Pakistan: *Transition from Military to Civilian Rule*. Essex, UK: Scorpion Publishing, 1988.

Gauber, Altaf. *Ayub Khan and Military Rule in Pakistan, 1958–1969*. New York: St. Martin's Press, 1991.

Hussain, Asaf. *Elite Politics in an Ideological State: The Case of Pakistan*. London: W. and J. Mackery, Cathan, 1979.

Jalal, Ayesha. *The State of Martial Rule: The Origins of Pakistan's Political Economy of Defense*. New York: Cambridge University Press, 1990.

La Porte, Robert, Jr. *Power and Privilege: Influence and Decision Making in Pakistan.* Berkeley: University of California Press, 1975.

Nyrod, Richard F., ed. *Pakistan: A Country Study.* Washington, DC: U.S. Department of the Army, 1984.

Syed, Anwar H. *The Discourse and Politics of Zulfikar Ali Bhutto.* New York: St. Martin's Press, 1991.

Sayeed, Khalid B. *Politics in Pakistan: The Nature and Direction of Change.* New York: Praeger, 1980.

Wirsing, Robert G. *Pakistan's Security under Zia, 1977–1988.* New York: St. Martin's Press, 1991.

Ziring, Laurence, Ralph Braibanti, and W. Howard Wriggins, eds. *Pakistan: The Long View.* Durham, NC: Duke University Press, 1977.

5

Indonesia and the Philippines

The Archipelagic States

Both Indonesia and the Philippines are the largest archipelagic states in the world. The term *archipelagic state* refers to those island states constituted wholly of one or more archipelagoes, or a group of islands including parts of islands, "interconnecting waters and other natural features which are closely interrelated that such islands, water and other natural features form an intrinsic geographical, economic and political entity or which historically have been regarded as such."[1] Thus, Indonesia is comprised of 13,677 islands—6,000 of which are inhabited—a land area totaling 741,000 square miles. The distance between the outermost points from east to west is over 3,000 miles and more than 1,000 miles from north to south. Similarly, the Philippine archipelago consists of more than 7,000 islands, of which only 900 are inhabited. The total land area of the Philippine archipelago is about 166,000 square miles, the size of Italy or the state of Arizona. These Philippine islands are bordered by the Philippine Sea and the Pacific Ocean on the east, the Sulu Sea on the southwest, and the China Sea on the west.

Over 90 percent of the 179 million Indonesian population are Malay in origin and Muslim by faith—a greater number than in the entire Middle East. While people of the Philippines have the same ethnic origin as those from Indonesia, about 90 percent of the 65 million Philippine population are Christians dominated by Roman Catholicism. The Philippines is the only Asian nation that is dominated by the Christian religion, a legacy of Spanish colonization. The Muslims, the Moros, are the minority religion in the Philippines; they reside mainly in the islands of Mindanao, the Sulu archipelago, and the Moro Gulf.

Indonesia and the Philippines share one cultural makeup: the presence of many ethnic groupings. There are in fact more than 300 ethnic groups and 200 languages and dialects in Indonesia, making it one of the most diverse multicultural nations in the world. In addition, there is a significant Chinese minority in both countries. There are as many as forty primitive Negrito groups inhabiting the mountain areas of Luzon, Palawan, Mindoro, and Mindanao of the Philippines. Both Indonesia and the Philippines face the problem of regional/ethnic rebellions: the Sumatran-Acehnese uprising in Indonesia and the Muslim rebellion led by the Moro National Front in the Philippines.

As a component in the overall comparison between the two archipelagic states, it must be pointed out that Indonesian politics has been influenced to a large extent by the military since the 1960s. Under the control of military strongman Suharto, the Indonesian military now emphasizes its role as one of providing political stability and serving as an instrument for economic development. In the Philippines the dissatisfied junior officers, Reform the Armed Forces Movement, has been a political force since 1986 when it participated in the anti-Marcos "People's Revolution," which deposed the dictator. Under Corazon Aquino the young rebel officers have engineered no less than seven coup attempts to topple the Aquino government.

The 1986 and 1992 elections in the Philippines have removed the uncertainty in political succession. In Indonesia the question of succession is still a matter of concern; Suharto and his well-organized political-military machine, the Golkar, are uncertain to continue in office after the 1993 election. By then Suharto will have been the strongman in control for almost three decades since the fall of Sukarno in 1964–65.

POLITICAL CULTURE AND POLITICAL DEVELOPMENT

Indonesia: From "Guided Democracy" to Suharto's "New Order"

Historic Legacies   By the first century A.D. the major islands of Java and Sumatra had come under Indian influence. Local rulers became converts to Buddhism and Hinduism and proceeded to establish their own kingdoms after having subdued and absorbed the Malays through intermarriage. By the seventh century a powerful Buddhist-Hindu kingdom known as the Srivijaya (700–1200) was established in Sumatra. It exercised control of the pivotal Strait of Malacca, which links the South China Sea and the Malay Peninsula with Sumatra, Java, and the Java Sea. The last of these Hindu-Buddhist kingdoms was that of Majapahit (1300–1520) on Java and

Bali at the time of Marco Polo's visit to the islands. Bali and Borobudur are the only places where the legacy of the Hindu-Buddhist culture has remained.

From about 1602 to 1798 the Dutch ruled the archipelago indirectly through the Dutch East Indies Company, a monopolistic trading operation for the Spice Islands in the archipelago. In 1799, because of corruption and for intensive exploitation of resources, particularly primary commodities such as rice, sugar, coffee, tobacco, tea, and spices, the Dutch decided to provide direct rule of the islands by replacing the already-troubled Dutch East Indies Company. In 1830 the Dutch government introduced the much-criticized exploitation system known as the "Culture System" or the "Cultivation System." Briefly, this plantation system called for setting aside one-fifth of the land for the government on which peasants were forced to work one-fifth of their time without any form of compensation. The government then designated only certain crops permitted to be grown on the land: namely, sugar, coffee, tea or cinnamon.[2] It was a system of forced labor that the natives resisted, but it was supported by the Javanese aristocracy. A direct consequence of the Culture System was that not only were the peasants required to devote half of their irrigated land to control, but became themselves the indentured laborers of the Dutch government. By 1870 the system was abandoned and replaced by a free-enterprise system as the government adopted a more liberal or "ethical" policy. By then resource exploitation, now including mining of rich minerals, which required extensive capital investment by more enterprising Europeans, had extended to other islands beyond Sumatra and Java.

Political Culture: Pancasila Democracy   When Sukarno announced the five principles, known as *pancasila*, to be enshrined in the 1945 constitution preamble (belief in God, humanitarianism, democracy through deliberation or consultation, national unity, and social justice), his basic purpose was to provide an ideology that all Indonesians could accept and depend upon to cultivate consensus and harmony. Under Suharto's "New Order" the emphasis remained on national unity, harmony, and stability. The New Order has not discarded the five principles under *pancasila*. In fact, through the years of Suharto's rule *pancasila* has become the national ideology and political platform for just about everything, from opposition to communism to village democracy to defense of a "responsible" (not necessarily free) press. It is the Suharto government that defines and interprets the proper meaning and application of *pancasila*. Government employees must attend special sessions on *pancasila*, and no Indonesian government official or businessman may receive a passport to travel abroad unless he can produce a *pancasila* certificate to prove he has completed the course. However, not all Indonesians have accepted the government-dictated acceptance of pancasila as cardinal principles for their daily lives. In 1980 there was the

"Petition of 50" endorsed by leading citizens, including retired general Abdul Harris Nasution, former government officials, and intellectuals, protesting the imposition of *pancasila*. The dissenters were silenced and ostracized by the government. Then in 1985 the Suharto government enacted legislation requiring all social organizations, which must register with and be approved by the government, to adopt *pancasila* as the paramount national ideology. While there is really no objection to the general and vague concepts contained in *pancasila*, it was the government enforcement and unilateral interpretation that prompted protests by religious groups and intellectuals.

The Arrival of Islam and Western Impact   Islam has been found to have existed in Sumatra as early as the thirteenth century. The religion, brought over by Arab traders and missionaries, spread and expanded throughout the archipelago during the sixteenth and seventeenth centuries. It was during the same time that the Dutch and the Portuguese arrived in search of trade. The Portuguese came to the archipelago in 1509 in search of spices and other treasures. They also imported Christianity. In 1511 the Portuguese then seized the Strait of Malacca to use as a key trading base. The Dutch came to the archipelago in 1594 by entering into a treaty arrangement with the Javanese states for the purpose of exploring the rich resources of the islands.

In a worldwide contest between the Portuguese and the Spanish seapowers for the control of the oceans and overseas possessions, the Dutch, with the help of the British, seized the Strait of Malacca from the Portuguese in 1640 and established themselves as the unchallenged European power in the archipelago for the next 300 years until the invasion and occupation by Japan (1942–45).

The Japanese Occupation, 1942–1945   The impetus for Indonesian national independence from Dutch colonialism was provided by the Japanese occupation during World War II. Japanese motives were not really pure, for their principal desire was to secure the loyalty of the Indonesian people to freely exploit the rich resources of the islands. Then in 1945 Japanese occupation authorities called upon Sukarno, an officer of Peta, the indigenous Indonesian army organized by the Japanese, to lead an assembly of various religious and ethnic groups in the society to prepare for Indonesian national independence. In August 1945 an eighteen-member All-Indonesian Preparatory Committee (eleven from Java, two each from Sumatra and Celebes, and one for other lesser islands plus the Chinese), with Sukarno as chairman, was formed to provide transfer of civil administration and power to the Indonesians under the Japanese. For the purpose of providing a national consensus and unity, Sukarno pronounced his famous *pancasila* as the ideological and philosophical foundation to unite the various religious, regional, and ethnic groups for an Indonesian national revolution. By then Japan had surrendered, and Sukarno seized the occasion by declaring Indonesian independence on August 17, 1945. Six weeks later British troops landed and restored the colonial rule to the Dutch.

Independence and the Failure of Parliamentary Democracy, 1949–1956
When the Dutch returned to the Indonesian archipelago at the end of World War II, they had to contend with a rising national independence movement, organized, armed, and already battle-tested against the Japanese occupation forces.[3] The Dutch devised a two-pronged strategy: decisively defeat the revolutionary army; and weaken the nationalists based on Java and Sumatra by calling for a political federation in which the Dutch-backed lesser islands would "smother" or "outvote" Sukarno's nationalists.[4] This was the essence of the Linggajati agreement signed in November, 1946. In July 1947 fighting broke out as the Dutch launched an attack on the nationalists. Under pressure from the United States and the United Nations, the Dutch agreed to sign the Renville agreement on January 29, 1948, calling for a cease fire and followed by a plebiscite to determine who should rule the archipelago. The Dutch had no intention of implementing these provisions, so fighting continued until the spring of 1949. It was under the twin pressures of world public opinion and liberal elements and business in Dutch domestic politics that the Round Table Conference was convened at the Hague in November 1949, at which time full independence for Indonesia was granted in return for a guarantee of the preservation of Dutch economic interests in Indonesia. A condition of the 1949 Hague Round Table Conference was that the Dutch must transfer their power to a United States of Indonesia, a federation of sixteen separate entities utilizing a democratic form of government.[5]

The concept and operation of a federated political system (December 1949–July 1950) was soon discarded in favor of a unitary form of government with political power concentrated in Java, as demanded by Indonesian leaders such as Sukarno. As a concession to the wishes of the lesser islands, the 1950 constitution vested political authority in the Parliament, not in the president whose position and power were rather vaguely defined in the provisional constitution. However, in practice and in the absence of an often postponed popular election (one finally held in 1955), national leaders obtained or allocated themselves seats in the 200-member unicameral legislature and permitted Sukarno, the most popular leader, to make arbitrary decisions in the midst of jealousy and competition for power between himself and his vice president from Sumatra, Mohammed Hatta.

The "Guided Democracy" (1957–1965) and the Fall of Sukarno
The introduction of a Guided Democracy, which emphasized authoritarian rule by a strong executive leader who would provide direction

for the nation and who would create harmony and unity, was more than a mere reaction to the ineffective, inefficient, and fragmented parliamentary-cabinet system experienced by Indonesia from 1950 to 1957. Sukarno was in favor of a strong presidential form of government; this was evidenced by the 1945 constitution, which called for a strong presidential system. Sukarno's frequent references to the traditional Indonesian village decision-making process of free discussion or deliberation to allow the emergence of consensus seems to have served as a model for his Guided Democracy.[6]

The showdown for power between the military (army) and the Indonesian Communist party (PKI) came in the fall of 1965. The country was already in a state of uncertainty. On the eve of the October 1 coup, the PKI was the best-organized and most militant political force in Indonesia. It had a mass base of support and extended its influence directly to Sukarno. At the same time, in a view shared by other noncommunist elements in Indonesia, the army, nominally in support of Sukarno and the Guided Democracy, was fearful of the political ascendancy of the PKI. It merely awaited an appropriate moment to strike against the communist left. The moment arrived on the eve of October 1, 1965, when a young army commander, Lt. Col. Untung, then serving on the presidential bodyguard force, rebelled against the military high command for plotting to overthrow Sukarno. A small unit of troops under Untung kidnapped six generals, including the army's chief of staff, General Yami, and killed them by throwing them in a well near the airfield. The surviving military leaders blamed the PKI and other radicals for the initial coup. In their countercoup they unleashed an avalanche of hate and recrimination against the communists. They placed Sukarno under house arrest. With the active support of the various Muslim groups, the military mobilized the youth in an unprecedented blood bath of communists and in the end eliminated the PKI as a political party. By some estimates, there were more than half a million PKI members killed and 116,000 suspects imprisoned (some 25,000 still languish in jails).

At any rate, the Indonesian army's countercoup produced the following results: First, it brought about the demise of the PKI as mentioned earlier. Second, as of today there are still as many as 25,000 confined to jail. Third, a purge was undertaken within the military to rid it of Sukarno supporters. Fourth, Sukarno was finally forced to resign and was exiled to a remote village in Java. General Suharto emerged as acting president on March 12, 1967.

Suharto has been Indonesia's president since March 1968 when the People's Consultative Assembly (MPR) appointed him to the position for a five-year term. Since 1973 he has been reelected by the MPR for four additional five-year terms. His fifth term expired in 1993, and he decided to stay on for the sixth term until 1998. By that time he will have served as Indonesia's president for thirty years.

The Philippines: Democracy under Stress

Historic Legacies   For a long period little was known about the islands of the Philippines until Ferdinand Magellan arrived in 1521 during his first circumnavigation from Spain. This marked the beginning of contact with the West. In 1543 the islands were named the Philippines in honor of the Spanish crown prince, Philip II. Subsequent expeditions were made to the Philippine Islands in 1526, 1527, and 1542 to establish a permanent colony. By then Spanish rulers could see the possibilities for a lucrative triangular trade between its possession in Mexico, which produced the silver needed to trade for Chinese silk to sell in Europe, and utilizing the Philippines as a center of transshipment.

In the meantime, Catholic missionaries made inroads into the lives of native Filipinos; it was successful in gaining a massive number of converts. The church entrusted its task to five religious orders, which also became the largest landowners. At the same time, the clergy acquired political power as well—often the church administrative system became more powerful and important than the colonial government. Catholic missionaries contributed significantly to educational development by training teachers needed in the Latin schools. The Dominicans were responsible for founding the University of Santo Tomas in 1611, and the Jesuits for the Ateneo de Manila in 1859—the two oldest and leading higher institutions of learning in the Philippines.

The colonial rule of Spain continued in the Philippines with little disturbance until the mid-1840s. Stability was maintained primarily by the support received from the rural aristocracy and the "royal fief" system of holding large land estates, supplemented by assistance from the clerical or religious authorities, the friars in the provinces.

In 1841 the first unrest occurred when indigenous clergymen founded their own religious orders in defiance of the control exercised by their European counterparts in denying their acceptance into the regular orders. These clerical revolts paved the way for an awakening of Philippine nationalism which culminated in the rise of Jose Rizal as the nationalist hero who helped to organize the Katipunan Society for the overthrow of Spanish rule in the 1890s. Rizal was arrested and executed for treason in 1896 after an insurrection attempt. Rizal's cause was carried on by other Filipino leaders such as Emilio Aguinaldo, who formed a revolutionary government in the mountain provinces of Cavite and Bulucan.

Political Culture   After a short period of military government for the Philippines, the U.S. Congress enacted the 1902 Organic Act outlining a civil government administration with self-government as the ultimate aim, although annexation of the Philippines was motivated by "duty, dollars and destiny."[7] Beginning with the arrival of William Howard Taft as the first governor-general of the Philippines, the American annexation left a lasting imprint on the Philippines. First, a public education system was established, initially staffed by the "Thomasites," teachers recruited in the United States and brought to the Philippines by the ship *Thomas*; they introduced the English language as the medium of instruction. As a result, more than 80 percent of the people in the Philippines today use English as a major means of communication, and the illiteracy rate was reduced to 51 percent from 85 percent. Public education also was responsible, to a large extent, for the inculcation of American democratic values.

Second, American annexation introduced to the Philippines the system of government that began with elective municipal and provincial governments.[8] Thus, when war broke out in 1941, the Philippines had embraced the spectrum of American political values of representative democracy, a strong presidential or executive form of government, and a general acceptance and respect for rule of law. By the 1940s, as aptly summarized by Theodore Friend, "The Philippine population in general was swayed, even captivated, by American culture."[9]

National Independence and Turbulent Politics   During the Japanese occupation a puppet government of Philippine collaborators was installed while the Japanese forces battled with the Hukbalahap (Huk), the People's Army to Fight the Japanese, a communist-inspired guerrilla operation in central Luzon. The new Philippine government of Manuel Roxas (who defeated Osmena in the April 1946 election but died of a heart attack in April 1948) and Elpidio Quirino (who succeeded Roxas in the 1949 election) was preoccupied with suppression of the Huk rebellion and problems of economic recovery. By this time the Huks had grown in power and changed their name to People's Liberation Army, emulating China's Mao as its model.[10] Quirino's government was faltering and unable to provide solutions to postwar problems. More significantly, the Philippine regular army was ineffective in combating growth of the Huks in the countryside, which by then was threatening Manila's security.

Desperately struggling to prevent the collapse of his government in the face of mounting problems, President Quirino made a wise choice by naming Ramon Magsaysay, a former anti-Japanese guerrilla fighter, as his defense secretary. Magsaysay remolded the military into an effective fighting force by personally leading them into the *barrios* in campaigns against the Huks, who were defeated following capture of their entire leadership in the fall of 1950. He also was aware of the need to provide property for the landless peasants by using army equipment to reclaim land. He prevented corruption in local elections in the provinces. By 1953 Magsaysay's popularity had grown so much that he was chosen by the Nacionalista Party to stand for presidential election and won handsomely over his former boss, Quirino. Magsaysay died in a plane crash in March 1957. The brief period of his presidency represented a period of high hope and expectation for change.

Magsaysay's successors, Carlos Garcia and Diosdado Macapagal, who won the 1961 election against Garcia, both came from the same "old order" of wealthy elites. They were men of limited vision and limited power to carry on with Magsaysay's reforms. Then there emerged Ferdinand Marcos, Senate president, a lawyer, and politician of middle-class background. In 1965 Marcos defeated Macapagal to become the president. While he was not one of the landed elites who had dominated Philippine politics before 1965, Marcos was aided by his attractive wife, Imelda, a member of the influential Romualdez family. During his first term in office, Marcos embarked on public works projects and urban renewal programs. He seized the opportunity provided by United States escalation of the Vietnam War to extract or extort from President Lyndon Johnson $80 million in aid for an alleged promise to commit 2,000 Philippine combat troops to Vietnam, as well as a U.S. concession for a shortened lease (from ninety-nine to twenty-five years) of military bases in the Philippines for the right to store nuclear weapons there.[11]

Marcos was reelected in 1969, with about 60 percent of the votes cast—the only president to be elected to a second term. Fueled by devaluation of the peso, inflation, and rising unemployment, unrest and violence in the Philippines had reached an alarming proportion. The lingering Huk rebellion in the countryside had by now transformed itself into the New People's Army (NPA), which had grown to a strength of 20,000, and government forces were unable to suppress it. In Mindanao, the Muslims waged guerrilla battles for independence by forming the Moro National Liberation Front with financial aid from abroad (Libya's Muammar Khaddafi).

The unrest, violence, and communist insurrection in the Philippines provided Marcos with the pretext to declare martial law on September 22, 1972. Marcos was said to have "concocted" the communist threat "as an excuse to crack down" on his political rivals as a prelude to the 1973 presidential election.[12] Terrorist bombings of a Liberal party rally in Manila in August, which caused a number of deaths and injuries, triggered Marcos's martial law decree. There was also the allegation that the U.S. Central Intelligence Agency might have played a role in the planned bombing.[13] Under the decree, Marcos authorized his martial law administrator Juan Ponce Enrile to arrest some 6,000 political rivals, journalists, and university intellectuals. Especially targeted for arrest was Senator Benigno Aquino; he languished in jail for more than seven years.

Among many other descriptions,[14] Marcos's rule from 1972 to 1985 has been characterized as a combination of military dictatorship, fascist "corporation,"[15] authoritarianism, and "kleptocracy."[16] Marcos relied on Enrile's martial law administration of the defense establishment to provide law and order. Marcos tried unsuccessfully to reorganize the Philippine society by forcing groups into an integrated organic whole: for example, all lawyers belonging to one association.[17] He engaged in systematic "plundering of the wealth of the country he governed."[18] Through patronage to elite families, he permitted, if not encouraged, the accumulation of wealth by his cronies. Marcos failed to foster labor-intensive industries and develop export industries, so that by the 1980s the Philippine total foreign debt had reached over $25 billion and inflation was up 47–50 percent per year.[19]

The 1983 assassination of an opposition leader, Benigno Aquino, who returned from exile, forced Marcos to call for a "snap" presidential election to be held in February 1986. This marked the beginning of the end for Marcos who, in spite of his rigging and other fraudulent practices lost the election to Corazon ("Corey") Aquino, widow of the murdered Ninoy Aquino.

It was with a great deal of enthusiasm and euphoria, amidst Marcos's failed attempt to foil the election with increased violence and massive fraud, Corazon Conjuangco Aquino was sworn into office on February 25, 1986, as the new president of the languid republic.[20] But after six years of Aquino's administration, the "people's revolution" stalled for lack of significant reforms to resurrect a nation that needs effective leadership both at the executive and legislative levels.

LOCUS OF POWER: POLITICAL INSTITUTIONS AND LEADERSHIP

Indonesia: Authoritarian (Presidential) Form of Government

Political institutions and power in the Indonesian government derive from the 1945 constitution, which called for a republic in a unitary form of government on a temporary basis. However, the 1945 constitution is still the fundamental legal basis for the Indonesian government of today. It has prevailed because in the mid-1950s Sukarno's attempts to draft a permanent constitution failed for a lack of agreement among members of the constituent assembly on the key questions of whether Indonesia should be a secular or Muslim state and whether a unitary or federated republic. Then on July 5, 1959, Sukarno decreed that the 1945 constitution would be Indonesia's basic constitutional instrument of government.[21]

Presidential Power   By reviewing Chapter III, Articles 4–15, of the 1945 constitution, one can see that the center of political power rests with the president. While Article 4 stipulates that the republic's president is vested with the power of government, Article 5 states that the president, with the consent of the Council of Representatives, exercises legislative powers and enacts government regulations as necessary for the proper execution of the laws. Then Article 10 states that the president is the commander-in-chief of the armed forces. Article 12 gives the president the power to proclaim martial law.

Suharto dismissed and appointed his own people to the People's Consultative Assembly, and in June 1968 he was elected to a five-year term as president; he has been reelected five times since then. He was chosen for the sixth time in March 1993. Despite public discussion of a leadership change, he has indicated that he wants to continue his leadership; this can be interpreted from his August 16, 1990, speech on the forty-fifth anniversary of Indonesia's independence where he made known his intent to be available for another five-year term.[22] Some senior leaders of the 1945 generation, such as former army chief General Nasution, have released a public letter urging limits to executive power; and some Muslim intellectuals have also urged Suharto not to seek reelection and have expressed a need for reform in the political system.[23]

The Cabinet The president is assisted by the Cabinet, currently consisting of thirty-two ministers who head the various government departments, in addition to the attorney-general, the governor of the Bank of Indonesia, and the commander-in-chief of the armed forces. The Cabinet generally meets at least once each month, presided over by the president. All major policies are discussed at the Cabinet sessions; decisions are made in the Cabinet by consensus. In the daily administration of state departments, the president designates two to three trusted aides, usually high-ranking military officers, to coordinate the various departments along functional lines of political security, economic planning, and social welfare matters. One other powerful officer, the head of the state secretariat, also attends Cabinet sessions. Elected in 1988, Vice-president Sudharmono, a former lieutenant general in the army, was once the head of the state secretariat and concurrently the chairman of the government party, Golkar. The Cabinet is a very influential body for the simple reason that it discusses and shapes policies and is presided over by the president in all of its meetings.

The Legislature: The Consultative Assembly and the Unicameral Parliament[24] Article 1 of the 1945 constitution states that sovereignty is vested in the people and exercised fully by the People's Consultative Assembly (MPR). In practice, the statement is a misnomer, for the MPR does not legislate. Its responsibility is limited to three areas: (1) consideration of constitutional changes if any are desired; (2) promulgation or endorsement by consensus of the broad outlines of state policy; and (3) the election of president and vice-president (the most important function since the 1965 coup). The MPR's membership was expanded in 1987 to a total of 1,000: 500 members in the House of Representatives (DPR), 151 appointed by the military, the rest from regional or other functional groups and political organizations. In other words, 60 percent of the MPR total membership is appointed by the president, and only 40 percent is elected by the voters. In addition to being a rather large consultative body with the majority of its membership appointed by the chief executive, the MPR meets only once in every five years (Article 2). In its 1988 meeting, the MPR devoted its entire proceedings, lasting about eleven days, to the election of president and vice president. Since Suharto controlled the appointed delegates—151 military and 548 from Golkar—his reelection was assured. However, the election of a vice president created some disagreement.

The body that exercises the normal legislative functions is the 500-member House of Representatives (DPR). It is the successor to the pre-1960s Council of Representatives under Articles 19–22. (In March 1960 the House of Representatives was created by presidential decree to replace the Council of Representatives.) Since 1987, total membership of the DPR has been 500. Of these, 100 members are appointed by the president from the military, and the remaining 400 are elected by the voters. The 1987 election for the 400-member DPR resulted in 299 seats for Golkar, the government political party, 61 for the Development Unity party, a small Muslim party known as the PPP, and 40 for the Indonesian Democratic Party (PDI).

Article 21 provides for the procedures of initiating a bill in the DPR. A bill can become law only after four separate readings. However, every bill enacted by the DPR must have presidential approval. If rejected by the president, the bill cannot be resubmitted during the same session; under Articles 20 and 21 a session meets once every year. Voting in the DPR is either by majority or by consensus where there is a two-thirds membership quorum requirement.

The Judiciary   Article 24 of the 1945 constitution states that judicial power is vested in the Supreme Court and other lesser courts established by law. Under the 1970 Basic Law on Judicial Powers the Supreme Court was designated as independent from the Justice Department in the administration of justice. However, in practice the Justice Department has considerable power over the appointments and promotion of lower court judges. The Basic Law grants the Supreme Court the power of judicial review, except over those laws enacted by the parliamentary body, the DPR. In short, the Supreme Court's judicial power of review is limited only to the administration of justice in lower courts. The chief justice for the Supreme Court is elected by the DPR from a list of nominees offered by the president. Under the Supreme Court there are high provincial courts that must handle appeals from district courts on criminal and civil cases.

Functioning alongside of the court structure described above are the religious courts in districts and municipalities. These religious courts deal with marriage or divorce and inheritance cases in accordance with Islamic law as provided in the Koran. Then there are the military courts dealing with criminal cases involving the armed forces. At the village level, the traditional mediation and arbitration process is widely utilized for settling disputes by elders in the village.

The Philippines: "Less Democracy and More Discipline"[25]

After years of abuse of power under Marcos's authoritarian rule, one of new President Corazon Aquino's first official acts was appointment of a commission to prepare a new constitution. A draft of the new constitution was completed on October 12, 1986, and submitted for voter approval in a referendum on February 2, 1987.

A key change made by the 1987 constitution was the rejection of an arbitrary and autocratic presidential system as practiced by Marcos. Instead, the new constitution opted for the American model of a presidential-congressional system with checks and balances against the executive abuse of power, as provided in the 1935 Philippine constitution. In the following sections, the key political institutions provided for in the 1987 constitution are discussed and their workings analyzed.

The President and the Cabinet In order to ensure the development of democratic institutions, the president of the republic will be elected by direct popular vote and the office shall be limited to one six-year term only. However, the vice president, also elected for a six-year term, is eligible for one immediate reelection.

President Aquino's capability of remaining in office until her term expired in 1992, despite no less than seven failed coups and mounting criticism about her as a weak leader, was an accomplishment in itself. She is said to have performed the task of "a midwife" by allowing the gradual emergence of a new "strong populist political culture" and by trying at the same time to "restore the formal pre–martial law structure of liberal democracy."[26] Other critics have variously described the political system under Aquino as "pauper democracy" for the low economic performance in terms of average annual rate of per capita income as compared to other Asian nations; as a "*cacique* democracy," a form of elite and oligarchical rule under pre-1972 martial law conditions; or simply as a "*mafiosi* democracy" run by backdoor deals made by shadowy figures.[27] These descriptions of the political system that prevailed under Aquino's presidency are perhaps oversimplification at best. What developed, at least in the early years of her presidency, was what might be called the "Corey coalition," a diverse group of political figures under the varying labels of "progressives," "nationalists," and "conservatives" or "pro-American."[28]

It was this diverse Corey coalition that gave her presidency a great deal of trouble. For one thing, as revealed by Carl Lande, the individuals whom Aquino brought into the government as Cabinet members were often political rivals with their own agendas.[29] As a consequence, disagreements over public policies surfaced. Lande pointed out the politically inexperienced Aquino's tendency to rely heavily on her Cabinet members who were encouraged to engage in debates at Cabinet meetings—a learning process for Aquino that enabled her to draw her own conclusions.[30] As argued by Lande, when these arguments leaked out in the press there emerged in the minds of the public an image of "disunity" and presidential "permissiveness" or indecision.[31]

After almost a year of slow and drifting progress, in mid-January 1991 Aquino announced her plan to reduce the size of the Cabinet and operation of the national administration. Key to the reorganization plan was a strengthening of the office of president as the command and coordinating center for the national government consisting of a total of twenty-five executive departments. Some of the department heads have been known for their mismanagement and/or conflict of interest. It has been an unwieldy setup of a corps of thirteen presidential advisors who attend Cabinet meetings at the invitation of the president, downgraded from their previous status of full Cabinet rank. The 1991 reorganization also called for reduced frequency for Cabinet meetings.[32]

These Cabinet changes and her attempt to engage in combat with her adversaries—as evidenced by the arrest of Senator Juan Ponce Enrile, Marcos's former martial law administrator, for aiding the coup plotters—seemed to strengthen her status in the final year of her controversial presidency. This was supported by the polls undertaken in 1991 that showed her performance rating falling to 48 percent in March 1990 from a high of 60 percent in May 1986, but bouncing up to 55 percent in April 1991. Her faith in "people's power" and dedication to the restoration of democratic institutions would be her legacy when she left office on June 30, 1992.

The Bicameral Legislature   Article VI of the 1987 constitution provides for a bicameral legislature for the Congress of the Philippines consisting of a Senate and a House of Representatives, following the pattern set by both the 1935 and the 1973 constitutions. Article VI states that the Senate shall be elected at large by qualified voters. Qualifications for a senator are as follows: The person must be a natural-born citizen, be at least thirty-five years of age, be a registered voter and a resident two years preceding the election, and be able to read and write. Once elected, a senator is to serve for a six-year term and can be reelected for two consecutive terms.

For the House of Representatives, Section 5 of Article VI of the 1987 constitution provides for a total of 250 members with 200 of them to be elected from single-member districts, and the other 50 elected on the basis of a limited form of proportional representation drawn up by the political parties or organizations. This is known as the "party-list system" of registered national, regional, and sectorial parties or organizations.[33] These organizations or coalitions must register with the Commission on Election (COMELEC).[34] The party-list system is designed to enable parties, organizations, or coalitions that are not strong enough to otherwise be represented under the single-member district system to obtain a seat in the lower house.[35] Thus, organizations that obtain at least 2.5 percent of the total national votes can receive one of the fifty seats allocated for that purpose. However, a party or political organization is limited to a maximum of ten seats regardless of the number of votes it receives, as opposed to the other party or organization under the party-list system.[36]

Qualifications for membership in the House of Representatives are as follows: The person must be a natural-born citizen, at least twenty-five years of age, a registered voter in the district (except party-list representatives), and must be able to read and write. Once elected members are to serve for a three-year term and can be reelected for three consecutive terms.

Legislative process for the Philippine Congress under the 1987 constitution follows mainly the traditions well established by the 1935 and 1973 constitutions. For instance, a bill may become law if it is passed by both chambers of the Philippine Congress after three readings in each house on separate days. Section 27 of Article VI grants the president of the republic the veto power on appropriations, revenues, or tariff bills. Often a proposed bill may simply stall in one chamber for considerable time. Such was the case in 1987–88 when the landlord-dominated House of Representatives was rather reluctant to move on the Comprehensive Agrarian Reform Program.[37]

THE POLITICAL PROCESS: PARTICIPATION, ELECTIONS, AND POLITICAL PARTIES

Indonesia: How a Government Party Controls the Process

Electoral Process   Since the establishment of a "New Order" in February 1967 by General Suharto, there have been four parliamentary elections in Indonesia: July 1971, May 1977, May 1982, and April 1987. The fifth election was held in March 1993. Indonesian general elections are limited to choosing 400 members of the House of Representatives, which has a total membership of 500—the remaining 100 are appointed by the president. In the 1987 election Golkar won 299 (73 percent) of the 400 elected seats, the Muslim supported United Development party (PPP) captured 61 seats (16 percent), down from its 26 percent in the 1982 election. The 1987 election was the first under which all political parties were required under the 1985 law to accept *pancasila* as the state's ideology. It was considered unlawful for a political party to adhere to any other ideology. This may serve to explain the decline of the Muslim-backed PPP in the 1987 election; it was clearly demonstrated by the PPP's inability to overtake Golkar in the province of Aceh, a stronghold of the party.[38]

Political Parties[39]   Under Suharto's New Order only "the three legitimate political organizations" were permitted to participate in the electoral process. These were the government sponsored federation of functional organizations Sekber Golkar; the Muslim backed Development Unity party (PPP), and the nationalist/Christian-oriented Indonesian Democratic party (PDI). The rationale for limiting the number of political parties in electoral contests in Indonesia has been a result of the desire of the military under Suharto to provide political stability and to lessen the ethnic, cultural, and regional conflicts that have plagued Indonesian politics since independence.

SEKBER GOLKAR   Sekber Golkar is the Indonesian acronym for Joint Secretariat of Functional Groups organized in October 1964 by sixty-one organizations. It is the final outgrowth of Sukarno's thinking during the "Guided Democracy" period in the 1950s, backed by military officers who wanted to abolish all parties. It was enacted in a bill by the DPR, known as No. 80/1958, for the establishment of a coalition entity made up of representatives from functional organizations, instead of political parties: workers, peasants, national enterprises, the armed forces, the religious leaders, intellectuals, youth, women, and regions.[40] The military must exercise the "dual function" of involving itself in politics and economic modernization as a functional group of Sekber Golkar, as well as in defense and national security. It is basically a coalition or federation of some 269 functional organizations from the armed forces to civilian bureaucrats to intellectuals, students, and women.

In the 1977 election Golkar campaigned as the government-sponsored party and on Suharto's platform of policies for development. With the military as the key instrument for mobilizing voters, Golkar again won 232 seats (62.1 percent) of the total votes cast. For by the 1977 election Golkar had become, as the military wished, the key stabilizing factor in the electoral and political process in Indonesia. In the 1982 election, Golkar performed even better than in the 1971 and 1977 elections by winning 246 seats out of a total of 364, and more than 64 percent of the total votes cast.

The 1982 election assured Suharto and the military another five years of political stability and with it economic progress—the twin goals of Suharto's New Order. Golkar's continuing victory at the polls assured the ongoing rule of the military in alliance with the technocrats in the civil bureaucracy. The 1987 election witnessed a larger landslide in which Golkar won 299 of the 400 contested seats in the DPR, and a huge 73 percent of the votes cast. Now Golkar has become a well-organized and well-financed political machine dominated by military leaders and 4 million plus civil bureaucrats at the expense of other functional associations. Small groups or associations have been co-opted by larger ones.

However, Golkar is expected to be more than a political machine designed only to win elections. President Suharto gave a significant signal in the fall of 1989, calling for Golkar to play a "central role" or "creative role" in society.[41] What this meant is not entirely clear. It could have meant Golkar should take a more independent position toward government policies. It could also have been a go-ahead signal for Golkar to move aggressively in advancing needed reform.[42] (The country was then gearing up for the April 1992 parliamentary election, the sixth since independence.) The government has prepared more restrictive campaign rules: Curtail the size of mass rallies, ban vehicle parades in urban areas, and use more radio and television. (Golkar has sent a team to the United States to study media campaign techniques.) There is some movement under foot to create a new image for Golkar in that its candidates for the 1992 parliamentary election would not be viewed as "government stooges," but more as "working politicians" who would challenge and criticize government policies.[43]

THE DEVELOPMENT UNITY PARTY (PPP)   In the 1955 parliamentary election the PPP consisted of four Muslim parties, led by Masyumi and the Nahdlatul Ulama (NU) with a combined total of 114 seats in the 257-member DPR and more than 43 percent of the total votes cast. In 1960 Sukarno ordered Masyumi dissolved for its refusal to accept the Guided Democracy. When Suharto came into power after the 1965 coup, he attempted to revive Masyumi as a Muslim political party, but met with opposition from the army. In the end a Muslim party was permitted to be formed, but prominent leaders of the Masyumi were barred from joining the new party, which was beset with internal factional disputes and repeated government intervention. Former participants of Masyumi were also barred by the government from running for office in the 1971 election. With prominent Muslim leaders becoming discouraged and disillusioned, many voted for Golkar. These setbacks prompted many Muslim leaders to question the usefulness of organizing a Muslim party for political contest in Indonesia. In the 1977 election the Muslim parties organized as the Development Unity Party (PPP) and made some respectable gains against the overwhelming popularity of Golkar-endorsed candidates for DPR. PPP captured 99 seats out of a total of 360 and over 29 percent of the votes cast.

Beginning in the 1982 election PPP went through a depression. Part of the decline as a Muslim party was due to its internal schism. The two largest factions within the PPP in the 1982 election were the Muslim Indonesia (MI) and the largest Muslim organization, the Nahdlatul Ulama (NU), the Muslim Scholar League. The two factions disagreed over the selection of candidates for the PPP slate. The matter came to a head when the Suharto government approved the list of candidates submitted by the Muslim Indonesia (MI). This led to charges by the NU that the government and the MI were working in concert to destroy the NU. In 1984 the NU decided to withdraw from politics by no longer participating in the parliamentary elections. That decision was reaffirmed at its twenty-eighth national congress, which was held at the end of 1989.[44]

The NU is Indonesia's largest Muslim organization, claiming to have the support of 20 million who are primarily rural villagers in East Java; its electoral influence has been estimated at about one-third of Indonesia's voting public.[45] As a religious and political force, it has been courted by Suharto, who addressed its November 1989 congress, held every five years and attended by more than 3,000 delegates from all twenty-six provinces. Instead of issuing warnings about religious extremism, government officials, following the tone set by Suharto, have heaped praises on the Ulama, the Muslim scholars, for their early endorsement of the state ideology, *pancasila*. Two overriding reasons serve to explain Suharto's deliberate attempts to woo the Muslim organization: his intent to seek reelection in 1993, and evident signs of Muslim religious revival. As explained by outside observers, today there is rising interest among younger Indonesians regarding religious practices and more "cultural awareness," causing Suharto and his government to pay attention to the vast majority of Indonesia's Muslim population.[46]

Despite the internal factionalism, PPP stands for the promotion of Islam. As younger Muslims in Indonesia have become more aware of socioeconomic issues, the PPP likewise has shifted its emphasis by articulating issues such as care for the poor and by demanding a ban on gambling, which has been flourishing in urban areas. All these have been interpreted as the party's strategy to gain recruits and supporters for electoral contests.[47]

THE INDONESIAN DEMOCRATIC PARTY (PDI)   In essence, the PDI is a coalition of small nationalist and Christian parties that include the Indonesian Nationalist party (PNI), founded by Sukarno in the early 1950s. For much of the 1950s the PNI was the second-largest political party in Indonesia, behind the PKI. In the 1955 election, as one of the five components of the PDI, the PNI obtained more than 8.4 million votes, or 22 percent of the total, and captured fifty-seven seats to the DPR, the House of Representatives.[48] The PNI drew its support from the "bureaucratic middle class"[49] and the professionals in central and eastern Java. The Christian element of the PDI came from the Protestant and Catholic minorities, mostly on Sumatra and other islands. As a coalition of nationalists and Christian minorities, the PDI has been beset with personality conflicts within the organization and thus has difficulty developing a coherent ideology and program. There have been attempts made by the Suharto government to use PDI as a counterweight against the PPP.

Military Politics   Immediately after independence in 1949 the national armed forces were demobilized to a size of 250,000, half of their preindependence strength. They were then reorganized as the Armed Forces of the Republic of Indonesia (ABRI—the Indonesian acronym), under the leadership of a Dutch-trained officer, Abdul Harris Nasution.

Continued internal factional disputes in the decentralized armed forces had considerably weakened the military's influence in politics. By 1955 officers from both factions came to the realization that they must be united in order to be politically influential and to prevent civilian interference in ABRI internal affairs. Their combined voices over opposition to the appointment of a new ABRI commander forced the Cabinet to resign. Now a general, Nasution was then reappointed to head the armed forces. The year 1955 was marked as a watershed when Nasution defined the military as a "social-political group" in society, and that it had a right to be involved in politics and political decision making.[50] It has been said that it was Nasution who "took the army gradually into politics."[51] He also proceeded to introduce the needed reform of a centralized command over regional units. Local authorities instigated rebellions in many outlying islands. As the nation was beset with chaos and disorder in 1956–57, ABRI became increasingly involved politically in order to put down the local uprisings. In March 1957 President Sukarno declared martial law and delegated emergency powers to ABRI, including administration and management of industrial and agricultural enterprises. By the time Sukarno had introduced the Guided Democracy in 1957, the ABRI had embraced and institutionalized Nasution's doctrine of military representation in the civilian government and the right to participate in major political decision making for the nation as a whole.[52]

SUHARTO AND THE MILITARY   Under Suharto the military's avowed mission has been to create political stability and to serve as an indispensable instrument for economic development. Thus, the ABRI is both "a military and a social force" as stipulated in the 1980 statute enacted by the DPR in which the military has 100 delegates, out of a total of 500, appointed by the president.[53] Throughout the 1970s and much of the 1980s military officers, active and/or retired, have occupied positions of power in the central government under Suharto. Management of Indonesia's economy has been under the control and supervision of the new breed of military technocrats. The military also have owned and operated their own commercial enterprises. The Dharma Putra Foundation, a *yayasan* (economic foundation that is nonprofit and tax exempt) controlled by the Army Strategic Reserve Command—a combination of the elite rapid deployment and special forces—has close ties with the Suharto family.[54]

It goes without saying that the military wanted to have a decisive say about the transition of power if Suharto did not seek reelection in 1993. But there was no consensus within the ABRI officer corps about how this might be accomplished. The lack of consensus within the ranks of the ABRI over the presidential succession issue can be attributed to the gradual disappearance of the so-called 1945 generation of officers and the emergence of a more assertive younger generation of officers who are less interested in playing "the political game."[55] General Murdani, former ABRI commander and now the defense minister, spoke recently about "a change in political attitude"; his protege, General Sutrisno, the present commander-in-chief, wants to keep a low political profile.[56] These views most likely reflect the present calibre of the new generation of military officers who are professionally trained and who lack the political experience of the older generation. It has been said that the thinking of the new generation of officers is closer to that of General Murdani, a senior officer who has tried to move away from Suharto.[57] In fact, younger officers now question the ABRI's role in politics and its dominance in the civil bureaucracy from 1965 through most of the 1980s. The new thinking emphasizes the future military role as one of reform, the reduction of appointment of ABRI officers to the civil bureaucracy, and the scaledown of their presence in provincial civil services, while still maintaining their presence in the national legislature with guaranteed appointment of 100 members to the DPR.[58] The lack of unity or consensus within the ABRI should serve as a signal of concern for Suharto and his supporters. In late August 1990 a letter signed by influential members of the 1945 generation, including General Nasution, demanded reform for a fairer election of the national legislature and limits of presidential power.[59] A more blunt letter was released and signed by Muslim intellectuals to the DPR arguing that Suharto should not seek reelection when his term expired in 1993, and that the term of president be limited to two five-year terms.[60] On the other hand, Suharto has resorted to promotion of military personnel to strengthen his control over the army. In addition other promotions, he has assigned to his close supporters the key positions of Strategic Reserve Command, one he occupied during the military countercoup in 1965, and the Jakarta garrison command.[61] After the 1993 presidential election, the question of succession remained as Suharto moved on to the decade of "takeoff." However, sooner or later Indonesia will have to make a choice between succession and smooth transition of power. In any event, if there is a power contest the ABRI and its factions will continue to play a dominant role.

The Philippines: Revival of Multiparty Competitiveness

The Electoral Process   Article V of the 1987 constitution qualifies anyone who is at least eighteen, who has resided in the country for at least one year, and who claims a local residence for voting purposes of at least six months immediately preceding the election. There are no other voting requirements in the exercise of suffrage.

THE MAY 1992 ELECTION   The May 11, 1992, election was truly a national election because, for the first time, the 31 million voters not only voted for a president and a vice president, but also for 24 senators, 200 members of the House of Representatives, 73 provincial governors and vice governors, 62 city mayors, 1,543 town mayors, and thousands of provincial and municipal council members.[62] Official campaigning for the national election began in earnest on January 12; a total of more than 70,000 candidates at all levels, including 8 candidates for president, threw their hats into the ring. The 1992 election was administered and supervised by the Commission on Elections made up of a chairperson and six commissioners with a majority of the members of the Philippine Bar and practicing attorneys.[63] The commission's responsibilities included the registration of political parties, certification of candidates' qualifications, and investigation or prosecution of violations of election laws or election fraud, offenses, and malpractices. For the 1992 election of the presidency, some candidates for that office—Mrs. Marcos, Eduardo Cojuangco, and Senator Jovito Salonga—faced challenges before the commission for not meeting the residency requirement. Strict interpretation of the 1987 constitution demanded that they must be residing in the country for at least ten years immediately preceding their filing of candidacy for president.

While the 1992 election was held on May 11, it took months to obtain the results from precincts on thousands of islands in the Philippine archipelago. By the end of June, after the Philippine Supreme Court had rejected a petition for a recount of the presidential race involving a total of eight candidates, Fidel Ramos was declared the winner and was inaugurated as the new president to succeed Aquino. The total voter turnout for the 1992 election was about 23 million from among 31 million eligible voters. The results showed that Fidel Ramos received 5.3 million votes cast, or about 23.5 percent of the total. He was followed by Santiago, who received 4.5 million popular votes, or about 20 percent of the total. The third runner-up was Cojuangco, with 4.1 million popular votes, or barely 18 percent of the total. Ramon Mitra received only 3.5 million votes, or 15.2 percent of the total.

Political Parties   It must be noted that political parties in the Philippines revolve around personality factors rather than ideological concerns. On the eve of the May 11, 1992 election the political parties lineup and profile were as follows.

LABAN NG DEMOKRATIKONG PILIPINO   In 1988, in preparation for the 1992 election, the People's party (led by Aquino's brother-in-law, Paul Aquino) merged with the Philippine Democratic party (PDP-Leban) (led by the president's brother, Jose Cojuangco, a member of the House) to become the Fight for Philippine Democracy, *Laban ng Demokratikong Pilipino*, as a major political party. LDP is pro-Corey Aquino, even though she professed herself as nonpartisan and not a candidate to a second term for president.[64] It is the largest political party in the Philippines today. The leadership of the LDP consists of supporters for the Aquino administration who occupy positions in Congress and the government bureaucracy.[65] For instance, 10 of the 23 incumbent senators and 121 of the 198 congressmen are supporters of the LDP.[66] At the local level, LDP supporters include 43 of the 73 governors, and 700 (46 percent) of the 1,538 municipal mayors to constitute a collection of *trapo* or "dirty rag," a disparaging term for the traditional politicians.[67] This is a formidable political machine based on patronage at the grass-roots level. The LDP claims to have an organized chapter in each of the country's 165,000 voting precincts—each precinct has about 300 voters—and a total membership of 700,000.

At the party's 1991 year-end annual conference, attended by more than 4,000 delegates, Ramon Mitra, then Speaker of the House and a politician skilled in the dispensing of patronage, won the LDP's endorsement as their 1992 candidate for president.[68] The party has a policymaking body, the executive committee of fifty-seven members, headed by Neptail Gonzales, the president, Jose Cojuangco, and four deputies, plus forty-seven vice presidents to represent provincial and local powers. It has been reported that there is an informal inner controlling clique of a number of congressmen and policy-media experts headed by Cojuangco and Paul Aquino, the president's brother and brother-in-law, respectively.[69]

THE LIBERAL PARTY AND THE PHILIPPINE DEMOCRATIC PARTY   Corey Aquino's husband, Ninoy, was the Liberal party's secretary-general in 1967. The party became dormant when Marcos declared martial law in 1972. Nevertheless, together with the Nacionalista party it has been one of the two traditional parties in Philippine politics. In January 1992 the Liberal party joined with the Philippine Democratic party (PDP-Laban) to form a nationalist left-of-center group: the People's Coalition, under the leadership of Senate president, seventy-one-year-old Jovito Salonga, the head of the Liberal party. The People's Coalition endorsed Salonga as a candidate for president. Led by Salonga, recently deposed from his position as Senate president, the Liberal party has leaned toward the Left in recent years and has opposed the U.S. military base agreement. The Coalition is the second largest political force to challenge the dominance by the LDP.

THE NACIONALISTA PARTY   The Nacionalista is a traditional party, but is generally characterized as conservative. Salvador Laurel was the official 1992 presidential candidate for the party. This was the organization that enjoyed the support of former Marcos officials and cronies. Vice president Laurel did not have a wide base of support. His style of shifting loyalty—he joined Aquino in 1986 and then broke away from her administration two years later—raised reliability and credibility questions with many seasoned politicians. The party was factionalized among former Marcos officials, such as Juan Enrile, who also declared as a presidential candidate, and former Marcos crony Eduardo Cojuangco, a business tycoon and recently returned exile who controls the coconut monopoly, among many other business ventures. He is the "boss" to his followers. Many businessmen fear the prospect of Cojuangco being elected president, for many of them supported Aquino during the 1986 people's revolution that deposed Marcos.[70]

THE NATIONAL DEMOCRATIC FRONT, THE RADICAL LEFT   The National Democratic Front (NDF) is the radical Left umbrella organization for the Communist Party of the Philippines (CPP) and its armed unit, the New People's Army (NPA). Having missed its opportunity by boycotting the 1986 election which put Aquino as the head of the "people's revolution," the radical Left had been weakened considerably in electoral politics. However, a more significant participation of the radical Left has been the use of the NPA to serve as poll-watchers to ensure that there is no cheating at polling stations in rural areas. The NPA had used its armed strength, estimated at 15,000–20,000, to "neutralize" the province warlords who maintain private armies that traditionally intervene in the electoral process to secure victories for the feudal barons in the countryside.[71]

Military Politics   The military's involvement in Philippine politics took place in the 1953 presidential election when the military provided protection for guarding and inspecting election ballots against illegal tampering. President Ramon Magsaysay's appointment of as many as eighty-five military officers to civil government positions marked the beginning of the practice that was followed in large scale by Marcos. After Magsaysay's death in 1957, coup attempts were made by the military to topple President Carlos Garcia.

Marcos contributed to the growth of the Armed Forces of the Philippines (AFP) and its involvement in politics in several ways. First, holding concurrently the position of defense secretary, Marcos made significant personnel changes in the AFP command to place the military under his personal control. His imposition of martial law in 1972 and the appointment of General Fabian Ver as the chief of staff for the AFP centralized control under the presidency. Thus, in the 1982–83 decade the AFP increased in size, authority, and involvement in politics. Marcos's use of the military was designed to obtain more U.S. military aid that would make possible more resources for the military and help him to build a support base. Martial law relied heavily on military officers and men for effective administration. Marcos promoted those officers who would lend support to his political objectives, retaining those officers beyond their retirement; thus, normal upward mobility for the younger officers became stagnated. By that time, the AFP had become known for its oppressive treatment of the populace and its violations of human rights, its incompetence in waging antiinsurgence measures against the NPA-CPP on the Left, and its internal factionalism.

In 1985 continued widespread dissatisfaction with the military led to a reform of the Armed Forces Movement, known as RAM. It was an informal, secret group of junior officers at the company and field levels, led by army colonel Gregoio Honasan and navy captain Rex Robles, both of whom were on the staff of the defense minister and martial law administrator Juan Enrile. The objectives of RAM were to eliminate corruption from the military and more direct involvement in national politics. The seeds of their ideas germinated in 1971 during the days when many of them were cadet officers in the Philippine Military Academy. RAM made its debut as a political force when it participated in the February 1986 anti-Marcos "People's Revolution," which deposed Marcos.

There had been seven coup attempts engineered by RAM and its more idealistic Left-oriented officers, the Young Officers Union (YOU). But from 1989 to 1992 the Aquino government survived without any further coup attempts by the military rebels. Two events explain the absence of military coups for that period. The first of these was the introduction of the needed reform, as demanded by RAM and YOU, in speedy promotion for deserving military personnel on the basis of merit and competence rather than on the basis of political loyalty. Then, conservative businessmen, who were the chief financial backers of RAM, diverted their attention and resources to the May 1992 national election. Only time will tell whether the military rebels will be succeeded by others who will engage in armed intervention in Philippine politics. In short, a Marcos legacy, the politicization of the military, is still very much in existence in Philippine politics.

POLITICAL PERFORMANCE AND PUBLIC POLICY

Indonesia: Deregulation and Privatization

Economic Performance   Indonesia's domestic growth product—growth national product minus foreign investment—totaled about $65 billion in 1989. Per capita income was more than $400 for the same period;[72] the annual growth rate was over 6 percent for 1989.[73] On the whole it has been a rapidly growing economy since 1965 when the average growth rate was less than 2 percent per annum. For most of the 1980s Indonesia's domestic growth product remained at least the 5 percent level, considering the declining 1980s oil prices.

Suharto has launched a series of five-year plans, the current one, known as Repelita V for 1989–94, has targeted a 5 percent annual domestic growth rate with greater emphasis on nonoil exports. Indonesia's oil revenue grew by 3.3 percent to almost $12 billion U.S. dollars after the Gulf

War. Repelita V ends in 1995 and would be "the last of the master plan's development periods, during which the final foundation will be laid down for takeoff"—so says the government in its advertisement in the *Asian Wall Street Journal*.[74] The "takeoff" has been preceded by economic reforms away from the traditional planned and state-owned and operated system of enterprises.

The Government Role: Deregulation and Privatization In addition to the introduction of a land and property tax and the contracting with a Swiss concern to streamline the corruption-ridden customs inspection service (the inspection service expired in 1991), a major economic reform under the current five-year plan has been the reduction of government intervention in the economy. One action taken was reduction from 209 to 20 of the number of areas in which foreign investment was not permitted to enter.[75] An export license was the only bureaucratic government control needed, and removal of the ban on items to be exported. In 1983 state banks were no longer subsidizing credit to preferred sectors, but on a "competitive commercial basis"; in addition, October 1988 legislation permitted extension of credit by private smaller banks on a competitive basis. Deregulation of the Indonesian banking system has resulted in growth of new banks, which in turn have made available credit and funds for investment and a lowering of the interest rate for lending.[76] The mushrooming of new banks—63 private ones in the first twenty-seven months since October 1988, totaling 174 by 1991—stimulated a rush in bank deposits with the consequence of new savings that could then be channeled into new economic activities. Lottery tickets were given to large deposit accounts by some of the large privately owned banks to attract new deposits, which were channeled to consumer finance and housing loans.[77]

In a 1989 government audit report two-thirds of 189 government-controlled Indonesian companies were declared financially "unhealthy."[78] The reform-minded government officials offered several alternatives to these inefficiently operated companies in which the government held a majority of shares: merger with other state firms; selling their shares on the stock exchange, another economic reform in the 1980s; private management; or liquidation.[79] In June–July 1989 some seventeen Indonesian companies were offered for sale, including banks, insurance companies, steel producers, oil services, ship repair companies, and pharmaceuticals.[80] By the end of 1989 the government decided that the state-owned enterprises (SOEs) should either reduce the government's share, sell out, or "go public" through sale in the stock market. The decision was contentious in that the business conglomerates, particularly those organized and owned by the Chinese (who by now seemed to have the backing of the military-bureaucratic leaders), appeared to have benefited most from the economic reform.

Suharto and his family members have extensive business dealings, particularly his three sons who, because of their connection to the political power, have control over multimillion-dollar business ventures in petrochemicals and plastics; the latter is a government monopoly.[81] In addition, through the cultural-economic system of social foundations known as *yayasans*—which are nonprofit, tax exempt, and free of government regulation—the Suharto family members have been able to reap substantial economic gains.[82] There have been as many as 700 such *yayasans* controlling an estimated U.S. $400–500 million in accumulated assets. Under the guise of a social-humanitarian focus, President Suharto has personally founded and controlled at least eighteen of the largest *yayasans* engaging in business ventures,[83] including monopolistic control of the clove trade and plastics. Attempts to legislate the *yayasans* have produced slow and "lowkeyed" progress, primarily because of Suharto's extensive personal involvement in the system.[84] There have been rising cries against the rapid growth of business conglomerates, and demands for sharing the wealth. It seems the obvious beneficiaries have been the wealthy businessmen, including Indonesia's wealthy Chinese.

Indonesia's continued economy growth has been spurred by foreign investment, one of the key economic reform strategies. 1990 foreign investment was close to $9 billion, an increase of more than 80 percent over 1989. Japan dominated foreign investment in 1990 with 25 percent of the total share. It was followed by Hong Kong (about 12.0 percent), South Korea (8.3 percent), and Taiwan (7.1 percent).[85]

The Philippines: Slow Growth, Budget Deficits, and Failed Land Reform

Economic Performance   When Corazon Aquino took over the government after more than twenty years of Marcos rule, the Philippine economy was in a deep recession that had sent a number of enterprises into bankruptcy and foreign investment capital into a drastic decline. The GNP for 1985 was barely 4 percent, and per capita income had declined as much as 14 percent since 1983.[86] In the early years of the Aquino presidency, economic performance improved measurably with a 6.0 percent GNP in 1987 and 6.7 percent in 1988. The economic upward swing was attributable to the government's policy of providing incentives for the growth of private sector industries and of dismantling coconut and sugar marketing monopolies. Also, as a means of bolstering Aquino's stability, international funding sources were opened up. The Aquino government also embarked on infrastructure spending to further stimulate the sluggish economy. However, as the International Monetary Fund approved a contingency fund for a balance-of-payment deficit for 1989 and 1990 and the economy was about to expand further, a number of disasters descended on the islands—the failed coup attempts to depose Aquino; the Iraqi invasion of Kuwait, which resulted in high fuel costs; the supertyphoons; and the earthquake. These misfortunes created lower rates of economic growth: 5.5 percent for 1989 and 3.4 for 1990. Meantime, the inflation rate rose from 8.1 percent in 1988 to 13.4 percent in 1989 and 15.0 percent in 1990. Unemployment for 1990 was about 9.0 percent.

Economic Problems It is possible to identify briefly some of the problems that have contributed to slow economic growth and high inflation for the Philippines in the past few years. One is the inefficiency of state- owned enterprises. At the end of 1988 there were a total of 296 state-run firms ranging from power-energy to waterworks and sewage to irrigation to housing. In 1988 the World Bank reached a loan agreement with the Aquino government, which earmarked $200 million for a three-year "rationalization program for government-owned or government-run corporations" from the number of 296 to perhaps 40 by 1990.[87] The program called for these state-run firms to institute systematic evaluation methods to improve accountability.

The budget deficit has been another problem. In 1990 President Aquino submitted a budget of $11.29 billion in order to provide the government with funds for infrastructure and land reform.[88] However, the problem is that the budget deficit has been accumulated by both domestic spending and foreign debt owed by the Philippine government. When Marcos was deposed in 1986, the Philippine foreign debt was more than $28 billion. In June 1990 the foreign debt stood at $26.1 billion with a debt service cost estimated at $3 billion, equivalent to one-third of the country's export earnings, or 17 percent of the budget for 1989.[89] The total foreign debt of $28 billion represented 65 percent of the country's GNP.

The Flawed Land Reform: Continued Struggle The land reform introduced by the Aquino administration, often touted as "the centerpiece of economic recovery and development."[90] In early June 1988, in spite of the fact that 90 percent of the House members came from landlord families, after a lengthy legislative tug of war, Congress enacted the Comprehensive Agrarian Reform; it was signed by President Aquino on June 10, 1988. Under the reform program the government planned to purchase 5 million hectares (about 12.5 million acres) and to redistribute them over a ten-year period to 2.8 million landless peasants.[91]

The 1988 Comprehensive Agrarian Reform has run into a host of problems. First, there is the question of determining the basis on which the landlords must be compensated: on the harvest value from the land or on "just compensation."The term was inserted in the 1987 constitution as a result of successful lobbying by landlords. It has been interpreted to mean "fair-market value" (25 percent in cash and the remainder in government bonds). The interpretation is subject to litigation in courts, and thus has had the effect of stymieing the implementation of land reform. Besides, if the concept of "just compensation" were applied to its fullest extent, the government would have been bankrupt while providing such compensation to the landlords.[92] Thus, this legal loophole has served as an effective barrier to land-reform implementation.

Second, the flawed land-reform measure has encouraged corruptive practices in its purchasing price procedures, which promote gouging. There has been a recent exposure of a scam by a firm that purchased less than 2,000 hectares of land and sold it to the government more than 100 times over.[93] Third, there is the lingering doubt that neither the Congress nor President Aquino is committed to land reform. The Aquino family owns a 14,500-acre sugar plantation, the Hacienda Luisita, in central Luzon, and the estate has not been put up for sale. The family has introduced a profit-sharing plan with the tenants who work on the land.[94] As argued by one scholar and supporter, she should have donated the family estate voluntarily.[95]

Fourth, the administration of land reform needs a reorganization of its own, as evidenced by the frequent turnout of the director of the Department of Agrarian Reform (DAR). Key personnel, as well as a large part of the regular staff for the department, were recruited by old officials long associated with the Marcos regime.[96]

Finally, on a comparative note with land reform in Taiwan, it may be argued that without a strong and assertive government role and a compulsory sale of surplus land owned by large landlords, land reform in the Philippines will encounter nothing but slow progress with barriers erected and to be overcome along the way. Land reform as a "centerpiece" of the Aquino administration has been a disappointment.

Education   An enduring legacy of the American occupation of the Philippines has been its stress on educational development, so that today about 90 percent of the people can read and write. There is compulsory and full education for children from ages seven to twelve, or through the sixth grade, and free high school education. In the elementary school, instruction is conducted in the local dialect for the first two years and then in English and in Filipino (Tagalog). Since 1986 students in public schools have been required to study the new constitution. As of 1989–90 enrollment in some 33,000 elementary schools was 10.3 million and enrollment in 8.8 million secondary schools was 4 million students. In short, the Philippine Republic has one of the highest school enrollment ratios: approximately 100 percent at the elementary level and 65 percent in the secondary level.[97] Add this to the impressive college or postsecondary enrollment record—26 percent of the college-age population, 5 percent above the average for most developed nations; the Philippines has been rated as a nation of "well-educated citizenry."[98] In a World Bank study Philippine higher education has been dominated by private institutions: For 1985, about 72 percent of the 1,157 institutions of higher learning was private.[99] In college enrollment, 85 percent of some 1.5 million college students attended private institutions.[100]

However, education enrollment figures in the Philippines may be illusory. First is the slim budget allocation for education from a low 1.6 percent of the GNP under Marcos to about 2.4 percent in 1988 below the average 3.7 percent for East Asia.[101] Second, teaching standards and student academic performance have been on the decline since the days of Marcos. For instance, fourteen-year-old Filipino students scored low in science, below the comparable age group from South Korea, Singapore, and Hong Kong.[102] A major area of educational reform for the Philippines must be increased budget allocations for its elementary and secondary schools.

SUGGESTED READINGS

Indonesia

Bunge, Frederica M. *Indonesia: A Country Study*. Washington, DC: U.S. Department of the Army, 1983.

Crouch, Harold. *The Army and Politics in Indonesia*. Ithaca: Cornell University Press, 1978.

Jackson, Karl D., and Lucian w. Pye, eds. *Politics, Power and Communications in Indonesia*. Berkeley: University of California Press, 1978.

Kahin, Audrey R. *Regional Dynamics of the Indonesian Revolution*. Honolulu: University of Hawaii Press, 1985.

Mackie, J. A. C., ed. *The Chinese in Indonesia*. Honolulu: University of Hawaii Press, 1976.

Mody, Nawaz B. *Indonesia under Suharto*. New York: Apt Books, 1987.

Reeve, David. *Golkar of Indonesia: An Alternative to the Party System*. Oxford and New York: Oxford University Press, 1985.

Reid, Anthony, and Oki Akira. *The Japanese Experience in Indonesia: Selected Memoirs of 1942–1945*. Athens: Ohio University, Center for International Studies, 1986.

Suryadinata, Leo. *Military Ascendancy and Political Culture: A Study of Indonesia's Golkar*. Athens: Ohio University, Center for International Studies, 1987.

The Philippines

Bresnan, John, ed. *Crisis in the Philippines: The Marcos Era and Beyond*. Princeton: Princeton University Press, 1986.

Gregor, A. James, and Virginia Aganon. *The Philippine Bases: U. S. Security at Risk.* Philadelphia: University of Pennsylvania Press, 1987.

Johnson, Bryan. *The Four Days of Courage: The Untold Story of the People Who Brought Marcos Down.* New York: Free Press, 1987.

Jones, Gregg R. *Red Revolution: Inside the Philippine Guerrilla Movement.* Boulder, CO: Westview Press, 1989.

Kessler, Richard J. *Rebellion and Repression in the Philippines.* New Haven and London: Yale University Press, 1989.

Lande, Carl H. *Rebuilding a Nation: Philippine Challenges and American Policy.* Washington, DC: Washington Institute for Values in Public Policy, 1987.

Padilla, Ambrosio B. *The 1987 Constitution of the Republic of the Philippines*, 2 vols. Caloocan City: Philippines Graphic Arts, 1986.

Seagrave, Sterling. *The Marcos Dynasty.* New York: Harper & Row, 1988.

Steinberg, David Joel. *The Philippines: A Singular and Plural Place*, 2nd ed. Boulder, CO: Westview Press, 1990.

Wurfel, David. *Filipino Politics: Development and Decay.* Ithaca: Cornell University Press, 1990.

6

Vietnam and North Korea

Changes in the Two Nations That America Fought

It may seem incongruous to compare the authoritarian regime of Vietnam with that of North Korea. The primary motivating factor for comparing the two regimes is their communist mold, now in search of an ideologically acceptable alternative, growing out of a divided nation at the end of World War II. Vietnam is now united as one political entity after decades of continuous warfare bolstered by intervention from outside foreign powers. North Korea, now deprived of generous Soviet aid as a result of the collapse of the former Soviet Union, is making overtures to South Korea, a vibrant economic powerhouse in Asia in its own right, for political and economic rapprochement.

To begin with, both Vietnam and North Korea were former colonies of the French and Japanese prior to World War II. The perpetuation of divided Vietnam and Korea were examples of communist expansion and success in the immediate postwar period. In both cases the 1954 international Geneva Conference, convened by the major contending powers in Asia, failed to resolve the Indochina conflict and the unification of the two Koreas. As a painful reminder to all of us, the United States waged war against the communist regimes in Vietnam and Korea, and in both cases the military might of America did not completely win the war.

There are other similarities when comparing Vietnam and North Korea. The Socialist Republic of Vietnam has been dominated by one faction, the Vietnamese Communist party, a Leninist party in terms of organization and decision making. For North Korea it has been the Korean Workers' party under the long-time personal control of Kim Il Sung. North Korea has embarked on a modification of its rigid ideology of "self-reliance" for joint foreign investment designed to reinvigorate its sluggish economy without abandoning the centralized planning. Vietnam's leaders, now younger and more professionally oriented, have chosen economic reform or *doi moi* in 1986, a sort of mixed economy similar to the economic reform introduced by Deng Xiaoping in China.

Finally, there is now a united Vietnam, the Socialist Republic of Vietnam. For the two Koreas, the issue of unification figures prominently in the rapidly changing configuration of relationships in East Asia. (See Chapter 2 for the case of North Korea.)

THE CASE OF VIETNAM

After more than twenty years of struggle for independence and war, the two separate entities of socialist North Vietnam and capitalist South Vietnam were finally united in 1976.

The Vietnam of today comprises a total land area of 331,688 square kilometers, or about 127,200 square miles. It stretches south like a curved letter *S* from the border of southwest China on the north, alongside Laos and Cambodia on the west, to the Gulf of Thailand on the South China Sea. Connected by the central coastal plains, two large river deltas exist at each end of the 1,000-mile stretch from North to South Vietnam: the Red River Delta and the highlands in the north, and the Mekong River Delta in the south. The Red River Delta, a densely populated region of North Vietnam, and the ancestral home of ethnic Vietnamese, had provided agricultural (rice production) and industrial life for North Vietnam before 1975. The source of the Mekong River is in Tibet; it travels over 4,000 kilometers through Laos and Cambodia and empties into the South China Sea. The Mekong River and its tributaries carry a heavy load of sediment, estimated at about 1 billion cubic meters per year.[1] The delta serves as a major rice-growing region of the world, for it is rich in alluvial soil and abundant water resources under the influence of a tropical monsoon climate. Unofficial estimates, provided by the United Nations Food and Agricultural Organization (FAO), have been over 15 million metric tons of rice per year.

The population of Vietnam ranges from 65 to 70 million, depending on the source of the statistics.[2] A population distribution shows that 52 percent live in the north and 48 percent in the south. About 90 percent of the total population are ethnic Vietnamese, related to the southern Chinese. However, there are only 2 million overseas Chinese, or Hoa, remaining in Vietnam today. There are as many as 53 different ethnic minority groups in Vietnam who inhabit the mountainous areas in the north and the central highlands. For instance, there are 3 million Moi (Montagnards), and 500,000 Khmers.

Vietnam's annual population growth rate is about 2.5 percent. It is essentially a young population with 52 percent of the total below twenty years of age. A large proportion of its people live in rural areas and about 20 percent in urbanized cities such as Hanoi, Ho Chi Minh City (formerly Saigon), Da Nang, and Hue. A family planning campaign (the goal is two per couple) launched in recent years has been unsuccessful, basically because it is voluntary. The 1986 family law that raised the legal marriageable age for women to age twenty-two has met with criticism. There is also a traditional cultural pattern in favor of large families. Government agencies in charge of family planning expect the annual birthrate to be limited to 1.7 or 1.9 percent in order to contain Vietnam's total population within 70 million by the year 2000.[3] Rapid population growth has placed a strain on food reserves.

POLITICAL CULTURE AND POLITICAL DEVELOPMENT

Vietnam: The Final Triumph of Vietnamese Nationalism and Independence

Historic Legacy   Vietnam, or Annam, had been placed under Chinese imperial administration by the third century A.D. as a protectorate. By 939, as the Tang dynasty collapsed, an independent Vietnam domain emerged as a unified Great Viet kingdom, which established tributary relations with China. Thus, for a long period of time Vietnam was exposed to continuous Chinese cultural influence and political domination. The Chinese were finally driven out by 1428. In the south and central parts of the Mekong Delta the Champa Empire (142–1471) flourished under the cultural influence of India's Hinduism through trade contacts with Bengal. Hinduism, with its religious and social customs as well as political institutions, spread over the Mekong Delta region.

The Le dynasty of the north made incursions into the Champa territory in 1306 and 1470 in retaliation for the latter's war on the north. By 1471 the north had finally conquered Champa. With its demise the cultural influence of Hinduism gave way to the Chinese influence. During the fifteenth century the Confucian culture flourished as Vietnam became "Sinicized." Meanwhile wars were waged by rulers from the north (the Great Viet) and the south (the Champa) from the beginning of the fifteenth century until 1592, when the Trinh (north) and the Nguyen (south) established a truce at the 17th parallel—the precursor of the temporary dividing line drawn at the 1954 Geneva Conference.

The French were interested in exploiting the resources of their

Indochina colonial empire by developing mining, mostly coal, in the Tonkin region, rubber plantations in the central hill areas, and rice cultivation in the south. They accomplished a piece of magnificent railroad engineering: railways along the Red River connecting Hanoi and Haiphong with China's Yunan Province, then under the French sphere of influence. By 1885 Vietnam was a French colony: Cochinchina in the south, and Tonkin and Annam in the north and central region as protectorates. By adding Cambodia in 1887 and Laos in 1893, the French were able to establish a central colonial administration by 1901 for all of Indochina, known as the Indochinese Union.

Political Belief There have been several influences that helped to shape the political belief of Vietnam. First, there is the Chinese cultural influence, particularly for North Vietnam. For as long as a thousand`years, from 111 B.C. to 907 A.D., Chinese cultural and political impact on North Vietnam was extensive; it included the assimilation of Chinese political tradition and bureaucratic institutions, as well as the Chinese religions of Confucianism and Mahayana Buddhism. Under the influence of Confucianism, the rulers were considered to derive their authority from the mandate of heaven, as long as they were virtuous, and assumed the moral obligation for the welfare of the ruled. Under this political belief system, the subjects must give the Mandarins unquestioned loyalty and obedience. The Chinese system of civil service examination was introduced for recruitment of officials who then perpetuated, as it was their counterparts in Imperial China, the basic precepts of Confucian ideology. However, the degree of the subjects' loyalty to the royalty and the Mandarin officialdom must also be based on their ability to defend the territorial integrity.[4] Even under the influence of communism, Vietnamese leaders, from Ho Chi Minh to Vo Nguyen Giap, all came from the traditional background of scholar families.

The traditional pattern of the Vietnamese social system is based on the Chinese Confucian code of ethics: an authoritarian and hierarchical society under which filial piety for the family and acceptance of superior rule are stressed. Family life is characterized as patriarchal, governed by the Confucian mode of duties and obligations for members of the family. Despite the long period of war, the traditional family system endured. Family loyalty and identification are still important in social life. However, the war years disrupted family life; in addition to deaths, families became separated and resettled. In the north, the communist regime emphasized loyalty to the state instead of to family.

With the military victory won by the north in 1975, the immediate need was to integrate two distinct societies—a socialist north and a "feudal" or "neocolonialist" south. The new regime imposed reeducation, resettlement, and ideological indoctrination through "study sessions" for the ruling elites of the south. As late as 1982 there were 120,000 southern

Vietnamese still forced to languish in reeducation camps. New economic zones were established for relocating urban dwellers in southern cities to work in fields. In one year (1975–76) more than 600,000 were forcibly relocated as exiles from Saigon (now Ho Chi Minh City) to the country-side; they live under deplorable conditions. However, efforts for the transition to a new socialist society have not been successful to say the least.

The Chinese Communist party (CCP), under the leadership of Mao Zedong, and its success in China provided inspiration for Vietnamese communists in all their years of revolutionary struggle, bolstered by Chinese material and military aid. The Soviet legal procedure and bureaucratic practices became a model for the Vietnamese in the north.[5] However, there has been no strong or indisputable evidence that the Vietnamese regime today adheres to either Chinese or Soviet communist modes; they tend to mold these influences into essentially Vietnamese patterns. Ingrained in Vietnamese political culture there has been the persistent aversion to foreign rule and colonial subjugation by the Chinese or the French or any other foreign power. Vietnamese nationalism, imbued with Marxism-Leninism and the abhorrence of outside or neighboring influences, has shaped a distinct political culture that is Vietnamese.

Ho Chi Minh and the Rise of Vietnamese Nationalism Although Vietnamese nationalism blossomed almost immediately after the French established their colonial administration in 1895–1901 and in the years during World War I and thereafter, one revolutionary stood out in his pursuit of an independent Vietnam, free from the French. Ho Chi Minh, son of a scholar from a poor peasant family, ventured to Europe as crew on board a French ship. It was in Paris in 1919 that he was attracted to Marxist literature; and in 1920 he became a founding member of the French Communist party.

In 1940 Ho Chi Minh returned to the Chinese provincial capital of Yunan, bordering North Vietnam, to reorganize Indochina Communist party (ICP) activities. He was able to cross the Sino-Vietnamese border in early 1941to organize the Vietminh front and rally the support of all Vietnamese for national independence, not a class war, with his ICP as the core. A revolutionary base was established near the border as a guerrilla zone for national liberation. By the summer of 1945 the Vietminh had gained strength against the Japanese occupation forces in Northern Vietnam; with aid from the U.S. military based in Yunan China, it had controlled the mountainous regions leading to Hanoi.

As the end of war with Japan approached, the Allied powers met in July 1945 at the Potsdam Conference and agreed that when Japan acquiesced to the unconditional surrender terms the Chinese Nationalist troops would accept the Japanese surrender north of the 17th parallel and the British south of the demarcation line. However, most of the territories north of Hanoi had been controlled by local Vietnamese forces loyal to the

Vietminh. On August 16–17, 1945, Vietminh forces entered the suburbs of Hanoi and staged a massive demonstration and general uprising inside Hanoi demanding acceptance of the Japanese surrender. Two days later Vietminh troops entered the capital city, and on August 30 Ho Chi Minh arrived in Hanoi to proclaim Vietnamese independence under the Democratic Republic of Vietnam (DRV).

Under the February 1946 agreement between the postwar French government and the Chinese Nationalists, Chinese troops withdrew to permit the entry of French forces into Tonkin in the south. Ho and the French also reached an agreement for an Indochinese federation under which the DRV was recognized as a "free state" and for further negotiation on the future national government.

After having accepted the Japanese surrender in accordance with the Potsdam Conference decision, the British passed control of the country south of the 17th parallel back to the French forces. On June 1, 1946, the French proclaimed the formation of the Republic of Cochinchina as a "counterweight" to the DRV in the north. In a desperate attempt to find an acceptable Vietnamese leader for Cochinchina, the French resorted in 1949 to reinstating former emperor Bao Dai, who had abdicated in August 1945 after opposition by the Vietminh. He was to be the head of a supposed united Vietnam, to be known as the Associated States of Vietnam—Cochinchina, Annam, and Tonkin—and also including Laos and Cambodia. This attempt never materialized. By 1949–50 Mao's forces had won the Chinese civil war; and as the Vietminh under Ho Chi Minh moved closer to China, it was inevitable that both China and the Soviet Union would recognize the DRV. Led by the United States, the Western democracies were eager to provide assistance to the French in their futile effort to unite the Vietnamese nation.

After the 1950s, a war of liberation had begun in earnest. By 1952 the Red River Delta had come under Vietminh control. In a move designed to prevent Vietminh penetration into Laos, French military strategy called for the defense of Dien Bien Phu, less than ten miles from the Laotian border. With the aid of the Chinese, Vietminh forces of over 100,000 strong made siege of the French forces of only 15,000. The supply route to the French garrison, which depended on air drops for needed supplies, was cut off by the Vietminh. On May 7, 1954, the French capitulated at Dien Bien Phu after suffering a loss of more than 1,500 against a larger loss of about 25,000 Vietnamese. Under President Dwight Eisenhower, the United States refused to provide the needed airlift at Dien Bien Phu; for this the French criticized the American policy, which contributed to their loss of Indochina.

The 1954 Geneva Conference and the Partition of Vietnam   An international conference was called in Geneva in an attempt to resolve both the Indochina conflict and the unification of the two Koreas. Key agreements reached at Geneva, a five-power (the United States, the former Soviet Union, China, France, and the United Kingdom) arrangement, included a cease fire between the French and the Vietminh, a prohibition of introduction of foreign troops, and a temporary partition of Vietnam at the 17th parallel until a national election to be held in July 1956.[6]

The election to achieve national unification of Vietnam never took place, and the two entities remained separate until 1975–76, when the United States withdrew its forces after more than a decade of military involvement in Southeast Asia. By the time the U.S. forces withdrew, the United States had provided the South Vietnamese government, the Republic of Vietnam (RVN), more than $14 billion in military aid. U.S. military involvement began in the Eisenhower and Kennedy administrations with military advisors to the RVN. By the end of 1965 there were a total of 184,000 U.S. troops in Vietnam and air strikes were launched against North Vietnam. This marked the escalation of the U.S. military involvement. The United States finally withdrew from the Indochina conflict ending the hostility in 1973, when the United States and Vietnam reached an agreement for ceasing all military operations and opted for settlement of the Indochina conflict by the Vietnamese themselves. After Saigon fell to the forces of North Vietnam on April 28, 1975, unification was achieved with the establishment of the Socialist Republic of Vietnam on July 2, 1976.

North Korea: Four Decades of "Personality Cult"

Historic Legacy   North Korea shares with South Korea its historic legacy as discussed in Chapter 2. This chapter focuses on North Korea after the partition at the 38th parallel and the Korean War, 1950–53.

When World War II ended in August 1945, the North Korean communists were not united as a cohesive group. There were Korean communists who fought alongside of the Chinese communists in Yenan, China. This included the group that had operated as guerrillas in Manchuria led by Kim Il Sung, then commander of a detachment of a division of the Soviet international unit.[7] The primary aim of the Soviet occupation was to unify these elements into a disciplined Korean Communist party.

By mid-October Kim Il Sung emerged as the Soviet choice for leadership when he became the head of the North Korean Branch Bureau of the Korean Communist party based in Seoul. In mid-December Kim consolidated his power in the north through party purges and by detaching from the Korean Communist party in Seoul. On June 22, 1946, the North Korean Branch Bureau was changed to the independent North Korean Communist party. Kim was able to accomplish his control largely as a result of help from the Soviet occupation authorities (the Soviet army) and the separation from South Korea. On November 24, 1946, Kim was chosen as the head of the newly organized Workers' party of North Korea.

The Allied attempt to solve the political and economic problems facing the Korean peninsula resulted in a declaration at the Moscow conference in December 1945 for a joint commission of two military commands north and south of the parallel to recommend the establishment of a provisional Korean democratic government, a sort of trusteeship. These efforts were met with resentment and opposition in the south and in the north. In 1947 the United States brought the matter of Korean unification to the United Nations General Assembly, which enacted a resolution calling for a UN temporary commission to supervise free elections by secret ballot to choose a national representative assembly. With Soviet opposition and North Korea's refusal to permit observers of the UN commission to enter, elections took place only in South Korea on May 10, 1948. By August 15, 1948, the Republic of Korea was founded south of the 38th parallel, followed by the establishment of the Democratic People's Republic in North Korea. While leaders on both sides of the parallel consolidated their rule and control, they were also in bitter confrontation with each other throughout most of the 1948–50 period.

THE KOREAN WAR, 1950–1953[8]   In the early morning (Korean time) on June 15, 1950, North Korean forces consisting of over 100,000 infantry soldiers, backed by more than 100 tanks and thousands of artillery pieces, crossed the 38th parallel and launched a full-scale invasion against South Korea's less than 65,000 trained troops, who were equipped with small arms. Within three days the South Korean capital city of Seoul was about to fall and the military situation was deteriorating rapidly for the Republic of Korea.

The question as to why North Korea embarked on its military invasion of South Korea has been the subject of many interpretations and remains unclear to this day. One opinion advanced the thesis that the invasion was part of a grand scheme designed by the Kremlin to dominate the Eurasian land mass after the Chinese communist victory in mainland China. This was the substance contained in the report (NSC-68) prepared by the U.S. National Security Council for President Harry Truman just a few months prior to North Korea's crossing of the 38th parallel.[9] That assumption was not valid, as subsequent events indicated otherwise. If it had been a part of Joseph Stalin's grand scheme, the Soviet Union would have been present to cast the veto when the UN Security Council met in an emergency session to order a cease fire and to authorize military action.

Another interpretation for explanation of North Korea's motive for crossing the 38th parallel might have been its miscalculation and misconception of the United States's intention to defend South Korea if attacked. In June 1949 the United States had withdrawn its forces from South Korea on the basis of a conclusion reached by the U.S. Joint Chiefs that Korea was of little strategic value.[10] North Korea might have misread Secretary of

State Dean Acheson's January 12, 1950, speech to the National Press Club stating that the U.S. defense perimeter in the Far East/Pacific was the line drawn from the Aleutians to Okinawa-Japan and the Philippines. The exclusion of the Korean peninsula from the defense perimeter could have provided encouragement for North Korea to make the move.

But there were also other internal factors that serve to provide a plausible explanation for the outbreak of hostilities. Kim Il Sung might have used the invasion to lay the claim that he was the champion for Korean unification in opposition to the rising recognition of Pak Hon Yong, the former leader of the South Korean Communist party, now exiled in North Korea.[11] The political situation in South Korea was rather chaotic as opposition to Syngman Rhee's autocratic rule was mounting. South Korea's economy was in disarray as the country faced spiral inflation and deficit spending. North Korea under Kim Il Sung might have decided then that it was the right moment to strike. I. F. Stone's hypothesis[12] that the south had invaded or provoked the north was unfounded, since the massive full-scale force mobilized by North Korea did not indicate it was merely in response to an alleged attack initiated by South Korea.

The UN Security Council adopted the first of a series of resolutions on Korea on June 25: It demanded the immediate withdrawal of North Korean forces to the 38th parallel and the cessation of hostilities.[13] Upon the report of the UN Temporary Commission on Korea in the field that North Korea had not complied with the Security Council resolution of June 25, it then adopted on June 27 the second resolution that called for "urgent military measures" in order to restore international peace and security in the Korean peninsula. The June 27 Security Council resolution also called for assistance from member nations to repel the armed attack to coincide with President Truman's ordering of U.S. land, air, and sea forces to Korea.[14] Between June 27 and July 7 a total of fifteen other nations, in addition to the United States, responded to the call for assistance to repel North Korea's armed attack. On July 7 the Security Council designated the United States as commander-in-chief for the UN forces in Korea; and the U.S. government in turn designated General Douglas MacArthur as the UN commander.[15]

The turning point in the Korean War was the successful Inchon amphibious landing near Seoul on September 5, 1950. Within two weeks the UN forces were in full pursuit of retreating North Korean forces right up to the 38th parallel. Then a crucial decision was made by Washington to pursue the fleeing North Korean forces beyond the 38th parallel, as there was no evidence of either Soviet or Chinese intervention.[16] In October and November, as the UN forces rushed to the Yalu River bordering Chinese Manchuria, the Chinese reacted on November 25 by sending the regular armed forces designated as volunteers across the Yalu and overran the UN command positions. In less than two weeks after the Chinese intervention in the Korean War, UN forces were in full retreat. As the Korean War dragged on in stalemate until July 27, 1953 when a cease fire and truce agreement was reached and a buffer known as the Demilitarized Zone was established almost along the lines of the 38th parallel. In fact, the zone provided South Korea almost an additional 1,500 square miles of territory. The Korean War cost more than $18 billion, and U.S. casualties alone amounted to more than 33,000 soldiers dead and 103,000 wounded.

   Political Belief   While both the Stalinist model and the Chinese (Maoist) model influenced the North Korean regime in terms of a highly centralized party and government structure, there has been a continuous acceptance and loyalty, unbroken for more than forty years, to one leader, Kim Il Sung, now in his eighties. In addition, North Korean ideology calls for unity at home, self-reliance, and independence, if not isolation, from the outside world. This aspect of self-reliance, known as *juche*,[17] refers to isolation—to have no or as few contacts as possible with foreigners except, at arm's length, with the Chinese and the Russians. *Juche* contains little of the basic precepts of Marxism-Leninism or Maoism. It implies Korean ideas as basic and foremost and alien ideas as secondary, but only for their usefulness to the development of North Korea as a nation.
   Together with *juche* as the basic ideology for North Korea is the adulation of Kim Il Sung as the "brain" and "body" of Korean politics, a fatherly figure whose rule is always virtuous and benevolent. The leader is always right and his ideas (note, not the ideas of Marxism-Leninism) are the will of the people and of the nation. A good follower of Kim Il Sung is the one whose thought and actions are *juche* in origin. *Juche* and Kim Il Sung became the embodiment of "North Korean national socialism."[18]

LOCUS OF POWER: POLITICAL INSTITUTIONS AND LEADERSHIP

Vietnam: The Rise of a Strong President and the Demise of Collective Leadership

The constitution for the Socialist Republic of Vietnam, the fourth since 1946, was approved by its National Assembly in April 1992. It reflects the changing circumstances brought on by the collapse of the Soviet Union and the need for some political and economic reforms in terms of continuing control by the Vietnamese Communist party (VCP). The 1992 constitution contains 148 articles, representing a major revision of the 1980 constitution, which was drafted when Vietnam was fighting a border war with China and relying heavily on aid from the Soviet Union. Key changes in the 1992 constitution include the strengthening of law-making power in the

National Assembly, advocacy of free-market principles instead of "socialist orientation," and guarantees for foreign investment.

The National Assembly   Under the 1980 constitution the National Assembly in reality served as the legislative arm of the VCP and the politburo. Its 496 delegates—249 for the north and 243 for the south—were elected every five years by the people, but in practice they were appointed or designated by the party. They met twice a year and served as a rubber-stamp parliament for the party.

The 1992 constitution emphasizes the law-making role of the National Assembly, which is to meet at least three times each year, with reduced interference from the party. A provision of the 1992 constitution states that "the National Assembly is the only body vested with constitutional and legislative powers" in domestic and foreign affairs. New powers for the National Assembly include the election of a President, who will have "real administrative responsibilities" as the head of the state, and nomination of candidates for premier and the Supreme People's Court chief justice.[19] Final appointment to these high positions must have the approval of the National Assembly.

The President   A new position was created by the 1992 constitution for a single head of state, the presidency, instead of the old Council of State, which was abolished as a collective presidency and as a standing committee of the National Assembly. Now it is the president who serves as the head of state. The president, elected by the National Assembly, is the supreme commander of the armed forces and chairs the new Council on National Defense and Security. Under the 1992 constitution, the president may issue decrees when the National Assembly is not in session. The election for the new National Assembly was conducted on July 19, 1992. There were 601 candidates for 395 seats in the assembly. About three-quarters of those elected to the new assembly were newcomers, including two independents who had no affiliation with the ruling communist party.[20]

The Prime Minister and the Cabinet   The 1992 constitution abolished the Council of Ministers and replaces it with a prime minister who in turn nominates members for his Cabinet. The prime minister has the authority to dismiss members of the Cabinet whose appointment and dismissal must be subject to approval by the National Assembly. The prime minister must be a member of the National Assembly; that requirement does not apply to members of the Cabinet, however. The major functions of the prime minister and his Cabinet remain much the same as the abolished Council of Ministers, which served as the highest administrative state agency responsible for the management of state affairs: drafting legislation for submission to the National Assembly, preparation of state plans and budgets, management of the national economy, and implementation of foreign policy.

People's Courts[21]   Vietnam follows the judicial system that prevailed in the former Soviet Union and China. It has a Supreme People's Court whose justices are now, under the new 1992 constitution, nominated by the president and approved by the National Assembly. The Supreme People's Court is the highest tribunal for the land, and as such it has the power to try cases of treason or high crimes, as well as acting as an appellate court for reviewing cases from lower courts. There are lower courts in the districts and provinces, cities, or municipalities, except at the village level, where village committees render judicial decisions.

There is also the Supreme People's Inspectorate, which exercises power of control and inspection over other government agencies at all levels. Under the 1992 constitution, the head of the Supreme People's Inspectorate is nominated by the president but subject to approval by the National Assembly.

North Korea: Power Grows out of Kim Il Sung

There have been two constitutions for North Korea, the Democratic People's Republic of Korea (DPRK): the 1948 constitution as amended, and the December 17, 1972, constitution, which replaced the former. Under Articles 1 and 3, the DPRK is an "independent socialist state" and "a revolutionary state power." One of the major features of the 1972 constitution is the continuation of a highly centralized state.

The President   In the 1972 constitution the office of the president in the DPRK was new in the sense that the instrument elevated and aggrandized Kim Il Sung as the supreme leader. It is the ultimate expression of Kim's personality cult, perhaps surpassing that of Mao or Stalin. Under the 1948 constitution, as amended, Kim Il Sung was the prime minister (*susang*) and the chairman for the standing committee of the Supreme People's Assembly. The new arrangement is said to have been modeled after the Chinese, for the new title of presidency, *Chusok*, is comparable to the Chinese *Zhu-xi (Chu-hsi)*.[22] The Kim Il Sung personality cult is so pervasive that it extends not only to his entire family, but mandates the deliberate promotion of his son, Kim Chong Il, as successor to his political dynasty.Like Mao Zedong, Kim Il Sung is fearful that the succeeding young generations will not be endowed with the necessary revolutionary fervor.

The 1972 constitution in general terms grants the executive power to the president. He is to be elected by the Supreme People's Assembly for a term of four years (Article 90). Under Article 93, he is the supreme commander of the armed forces and the chairman of the National Defense

Commission. He promulgates laws and decrees. He ratifies and abrogates treaties with foreign powers (Article 96). He has the right to grant pardons (Article 95). The formal language in the 1972 constitution merely disguises the enormous personal power wielded by Kim Il Sung, the "peerless patriot," "the greatest military strategist," and "the most profound revolutionary genius of all times."

The Supreme People's Assembly Article 73 of the DPRK's 1972 constitution states that the Supreme People's Assembly is the "highest organ of state power" and exercises the exclusive legislative power. Among the powers listed in Article 76, the Supreme People's Assembly makes laws; amends the constitution; establishes basic foreign policy principles; elects the president, the premier, president for the Central Court, and other central governmental officials; approves the state budget and state plan for national economic development; and declares war. Also, it can establish or alter provincial and local political divisions. But, in practice, the Supreme People's Assembly is merely a rubber stamp for decisions already made by the Korean Workers' party.

There are some 615 deputies, each representing 30,000 people—in the Supreme People's Assembly, elected for a four-year term. In practice it is the Korean Workers' party that selects the nominees to be elected perfunctorily. For each election district there is only one slate of candidates. Because of its size, it cannot serve as a deliberative legislative body, leaving aside the fact that it meets only twice a year for a duration of a week or less. When it is in session, an enormous amount of time is devoted to presentation of reports by the governmental administrative agencies about their programs. When the Supreme People's Assembly is not in session, its Standing Committee functions as the interim assembly on a daily basis—much in the same fashion as the Standing Committee of the National People's Congress in the Chinese case. In addition to the chairman and two vice chairmen, the Standing Committee of the Supreme People's Assembly has twelve members. There are also other key committees for the assembly: a budget committee and the bills committee. Little is known about how these committees work.

Executive and Administrative Bodies The DPRK 1972 constitution provides for two separate central government agencies for policymaking and administration. Article 100 states that the Central People's Committee will be composed of the DPRK's president and the vice presidents, a secretary, and an unspecified number of members. It is headed by the president, Kim Il Sung. Its membership is interlocked with the Politburo Bureau of the Korean Workers' party and thus serves as a link between the party and the central government, a supercabinet. Article 103 defines powers of the Central People's Committee as follows: foreign and domestic policymaking, supervising state administrative agencies, directing work of the judicial organs, controlling national defense and security, implementing laws enacted by the Supreme People's Assembly, establishing or abolishing ministries, appointing and removing deputy premiers and ministers, appointing ambassadors and conferring titles on military generals, granting general amnesties, and declaring war and mobilizing the nation in a state of emergency. In order to carry out the above-listed responsibilities, the Central People's Committee may establish functional commissions on foreign policy, national defense, and state security. As the president, Kim Il Sung personally supervises the State Political Security Department. The security agency undertakes extensive political surveillance of the populace as a whole, maintaining at least eight labor camps that house some 100,000 political prisoners for "antiparty" and counterrevolutionary activities.[23]

Article 107 states that the State Administrative Council is "the administrative and executive body of the highest organ of state power." It is supervised by President Kim Il Sung and the Central People's Committee. It is composed of the premier, deputy premiers, ministers, and other necessary members. Before 1972 this was the Cabinet. The council provides the actual administration of the government. Article 109 lists these functions and powers for the State Administrative Council: directing the work of ministries and commissions (total numbering at least thirty-three), establishing and abolishing organs directly under its authority, developing plans for the national economy, formulating the budget, taking measures on banking and the monetary system, concluding treaties, maintaining armed forces and public order, and annulling any decisions or directives of government agencies not in conformity with the decisions of the State Administrative Council. Generally, the council is headed by the premier who presides at the Cabinet meetings, the plenary sessions. Then there are also sessions or meetings of the council's permanent commission defined in Article 110 as the "kitchen cabinet." Most of these permanent commissions—each in charge of a specific industry such as mining, machine building, trade, agriculture, fisheries, light industry, and transportation—are headed by a deputy premier. As stated in Article 114, a ministry is an executive departmental body of the State Administration Council, whereas a commission may have to coordinate the works of two or more ministries.

The Judiciary The court system for the DPRK is based on the Soviet and Chinese model, which provide the judicial process of adjudication and a procurator system, a combined prosecution and public defender role, assisted by a system of lay or people's assessors.

Under Article 136 of the 1972 constitution, the highest judicial organ is the Central Court, which is empowered to protect the rights of workers and peasants in the socialist state as guaranteed under the constitution against any infringement, to guarantee that all state institutions and enterprises must observe state laws, and to execute judgments rendered by the courts. The Central Court is presided over by its president who is elected by the Supreme People's Assembly. It is the highest court of appeal. Below the Central Court, there are provincial courts or municipal courts for special cities directly under central government supervision. These are the courts of original jurisdiction on civil and criminal cases at the intermediate level. At the city, county, and district levels are the people's courts. Special courts are generally for the military and the railroads. While Article 140 states that in administering justice, the court is independent, in practice it is influenced in its decision-making by the wishes of the Korean Workers' party.

Two other aspects of the DPRK's judicial system need to be mentioned. One is the role of the people's assessors. Articles 134 and 135 of the 1972 constitution provide that court judges are assisted in their judgment by "people's assessors" who are elected by "servicemen and employees" at their work places, at the provincial or district level assemblies. At the intermediate and lower levels the court is composed of at least one judge, plus two people's assessors. In the case of the Central Court, the judges and people's assessors are elected by the Standing Committee of the Supreme People's Assembly.

The other is the system of procuratorate. Article 143 provides for the Central Procurator's Office and similar offices in the provinces, cities, counties, and districts. As mentioned previously, a procurator has the dual role of a prosecutor and a public defender. Article 144 states that the procurator's office exercises these functions: ensuring the observance of state laws by state institutions and citizens alike; seeing to it that all state organs conform to the laws enacted by the Supreme People's Assembly, the edicts of the president and the decrees and decisions of the Central People's Committee and the State Administrative Council; exposing and instituting penal proceedings against criminals; and safeguarding the power of the workers and peasants. It is the procurator who is empowered to bring a case before the courts on behalf of the state, and it is also his responsibility to see that law offenders or breakers are being properly charged and indicted.

THE POLITICAL PROCESS: PARTICIPATION, ELECTIONS, AND POLITICAL PARTIES

Vietnam: Renovation (*Doi Moi*) and Rejuvenation

The Electoral Process   As mentioned earlier, the Socialist Republic held a national election on July 19, 1992, for the new National Assembly under the 1992 constitution. While there have been scanty hard facts on voter turnout from Hanoi, the latest election has been officially called the most democratic since political reform, the *doi moi*, was introduced in 1986. Meetings were arranged during the election period between the candidates for the National Assembly and "invited voters" (retired civil servants and soldiers).[24] Campaign organizers provided free cigarettes and tea for the voters.[25] However, elections are generally controlled by the Vietnamese Communist party.

The Political Party   There is only one political party for Vietnam today—the Socialist Republic of Vietnam has been dominated by the Vietnamese Communist party since 1976. The VCP is the successor to the Indochinese Communist party formed in 1930, but dissolved in 1945. For the six-year period, from 1945 to 1951, it operated underground and reemerged in 1951 as the Vietnamese Workers' party. In 1976 it adopted its present name when North and South Vietnam were united after the collapse of the Republic of Vietnam and the withdrawal of U.S. forces from Indochina.

The highest organ of the VCP is the National Party Congress, which meets once in five years. The party Congress sets the course and direction for Vietnam's political and economic development. Its seventh congress, held from June 24 to 27, 1991, was attended by 1,176 delegates representing the party total membership of 2.1 million. As a Leninist party, such as that of the Chinese Communist party, the VCP party Congress elects a central committee of 146 members, which in turn elects an all powerful thirteen-member politburo of the party's highest-ranking members at the apex for ultimate decision making.[26] The politburo is assisted by a nine-member secretariat and a military affairs committee. Membership in the secretariat, as in the case of the CCP, interlocks with the politburo. The new politburo members were not only younger,[27] but also more "professional" or less ideology oriented.[28] These changes—the elevation of younger and more professionally oriented leaders to top party posts—reflect continued attempts by the party to strive for "renovation" (*doi moi*) and rejuvenation. Factionalism along lines of age, professionalism, and reform remain key areas of dissent and conflict within the top leadership.[29] One of the top leaders, the former party chief, Nguyen Van Linh, a key player in the 1986 reform movement, was forced to resign after the 1991 June party congress because of age and health. However, Linh probably was criticized by the younger reform-minded politburo members for his stand against political pluralism, or the multiparty system, and "bourgeois liberalization," demonstrated in his speech on August 24, 1989, as moving away from reform.[30] Rising to the top leadership ladder is Vo Van Kiet, the former chairman of the abolished Council of Ministers and now the new prime minister.[31] General Le Duc Anh, chairman of the new Council for National Defense, is slated to become the new president under the 1992 constitution.

The Role of the Military   The People's Army of Vietnam (PAVN) began in December 1944 as a collection of guerrillas organized by Ho Chi Minh. After three wars against the French, the United States, and China it grew to a size of 1.2 million, excluding millions more in related paramilitary such as border and self-defense services. It has been rated as the fourth-largest army in the world next to the United States, the former Soviet Union, and China. It is essentially a universal and compulsory conscript force that requires all men between the ages of eighteen and twenty-five to complete two years of service. Before agreement in 1989 to withdraw its forces beyond its border there were at least 15,000 PAVN troops in Laos and 60,000 in Cambodia. Currently Vietnam plans to reduce its total military strength to 600,000, or about 1 percent of its total population.

Under the 1980 constitution, the chairman of the Council of State served as overall commander-in-chief for the PAVN. However, the 1992 constitution revision now designates the president of the republic elected by the National Assembly as the supreme commander of the armed forces. The president now chairs the national council for defense.

The PAVN's role in society is more than the defense of the country; it must also contribute to the "building of socialism" by engaging in construction of roads and bridges, as well as in the running of state farms and other economic activities. The PAVN assembles its weapons through a system of ammunition factories, ordnance plants, and explosives-manufacturing facilities. However, until the beginning of 1990, the Soviet Union maintained its MIG-23 fighter planes and T4-16 bombers at the Cam Ranh Bay, which was finally shut down as a Soviet base.[32]

The Vietnam Communist party has always exercised its control over the PAVN through the party's organizational units within the military. After the model of the People's Liberation Army (PLA) in China, at every level of the military command structure, from senior to infantry company, there is a party committee headed by a party officer. In the early days young village recruits relied on the party cadres within the military for political guidance and looked up to party representatives as officers of superiority and intelligence. Party cadres within the military units conducted political discussions or indoctrination sessions. Then the party exercised its control by promoting self-criticism as a means of generating peer pressure for conformity.[33] From time to time, "emulation campaigns" were utilized to enforce or reinforce an approved standard of behavior or thinking in the military vis-a-vis its relations with the larger Vietnamese society.[34] Then there are the party membership recruitment drives in the military; since 1987 approximately 10 to 20 percent of PAVN personnel have been party members.

The PAVN has had difficulty operating under the so-called dual command system familiar to the Chinese or the former Soviet Union armed forces: a military commander sharing decision making and control with a political commissar, the party's representative. The dual command structure was not modified until 1987, when the military commander was given control of the unit in initiating decisions, but the party cadre in the unit was given the final responsibility. In short, the invasion of Cambodia and the border war with China compelled the party to relegate more autonomy to the military commanders. As did its Chinese counterpart, the PAVN had to address the conflict between military professionalism and ideological purity. In the PAVN there is still no clear solution to the conflict despite an increased demand for modern military technology and expertise. As admitted by an army journal, party-military relations have also been strained due to the privileges enjoyed by party cadres or members within the PAVN units.[35]

Corruption and lack of discipline have also been problems that strain the military-civilian relationship, as cases have been exposed of high military officers engaging in black-market operations. There has also been a lack of sufficient care for the soldier's daily living conditions.[36]

North Korea: The Monolithic Party

The Electoral Process   As discussed earlier the only election that takes place periodically is the election for the 615 deputies to the Supreme People's Assembly for the Democratic People's Republic of Korea under the 1972 constitution. However, election in DPRK means that the Korean Workers' party chooses nominees and that there is only one slate of candidates approved by the party.

The Political Party   The Workers' party of North Korea was founded in 1946 as a coalition between the North Korean Communist party and the New Democratic party.[37] The party's membership is about 1.5 to 2 million. As a Marxist-Leninist party, the supreme organ of leadership of the Korean Workers' party (KWP) is the Party Congress, convened by the Central Committee supposedly every five years. There is a standing committee of the politburo, which leads all party activities for the Central Committee. In addition to the politburo, the party has a secretariat and a military commission—all headed by Kim Il Sung and his son, the designated heir, Kim Jong Il.[38] Kim Il Sung personifies the party constitutional framework for North Korea: He is the head of the Workers' party, president of the state, and commander-in-chief of the armed forces. The party adheres to *Juche* as "the monolithic ideology," said to have been created by the supreme leader.[39] The party concentrates its efforts in organizing and controlling mass organizations, such as youth groups, trade unions, and women.

Two puppet parties have been allowed to exist under control of the KWP: the Korean Social Democratic party (formerly the Korean Democratic party) and the Young Friends' party of a religious sect.[40]

The Military Role The North Korean armed forces began as a guerrilla contingent attached to the Chinese communist forces in Manchuria. It then received Soviet military training and assistance, and the Korean People's Army was formed officially in February 1948 under Kim Il Sung months ahead of the formation of the Democratic People's Republic of Korea. The North Korean forces suffered devastating losses during the Korean War. Reorganization and rebuilding of its armed forces did not begin until 1953–58 with appreciable support from both China and the Soviet Union. By 1980 the North Korean armed forces had grown to a strength of 678,000; well equipped with modern weapons, including 2,500 tanks and 5,000–6,000 antiaircraft artillery.[41] Today North Korean armed forces have been estimated at the 1.1 million level, supported by an arsenal of fighter aircraft and missiles.[42]

The current level of North Korean defense expenditure has been estimated at $11–13 billion per year, or about 25 percent of its GNP and 12 percent of the national budget, excluding outlays for arms production by more than 100 arms factories.[43] Recent disclosure shows that North Korea will be able to produce nuclear weapons by the mid-1990s. Even though it signed the Nuclear Non-proliferation Agreement in 1985, North Korea has refused to permit international inspection of its nuclear processing facility for making weapon-grade nuclear fuel at Yongbyon, north of Pyongyang. The North Korean nuclear program adds a new threat to East Asian regional security. North Korea acquired the Scud missiles from Egypt in the mid-1970s and has been able to produce these missiles since 1987. It has been reported that in the 1980s North Korea sold Scuds valued at $500 million to the Iranians, as well as making sales of its improved model to Syria.[44] On March 12, 1993, North Korea announced that it intended to withdraw from the Nuclear Non-Proliferation treaty (NPT). The declaration created fear and tension in Northeast Asia because North Korea is known to have the capacity to produce the nuclear bomb. The United States then entered into direct bilateral negotiation with the North Koreans with the objective of forcing them to reconsider the intended move from the NPT. After four rounds of negotiations, a joint statement was issued on June 11, 1993, declaring that North Korea agreed to reverse its decision to withdraw from the NPT for the time being.

The military apparatus, similar to the Chinese PLA, has always been an indispensable and reliable instrument for the Korean Workers' party. Kim Jong Il, son of dictator Kim Il Sung, has been appointed recently as the first vice-chairman of the National Defense Commission—a move suspected by observers as a significant step for the younger Kim to climb the ladder of succession. As a successor to his father's long reign, the young Kim must have the support of the military.

POLITICAL PERFORMANCE AND PUBLIC POLICY

Vietnam: The Chinese Economic Reform Model under *Doi Moi*

Economic Performance   The Socialist Republic of Vietnam is one of the poorest nations in Asia today. Its per capita income for 1990 was about $200, and the goal of the ruling regime of reformers is the doubling of that figure.[45] The economic situation has been aggravated by the U.S. embargo and the reduction, or dry up, of Soviet economic aid, which had been estimated at over $1 billion a year.[46] As noted in a recent World Bank report, in addition to economic reform measures, the regime needs an injection of foreign capital and investment, as much as $250 million a year.[47]

The nation has faced a runaway rate of inflation, estimated at 200 percent in 1991 as compared to 64 percent in 1990 and 36 percent in 1989.[48] The unemployment rate has also risen to 20 percent, partly because of the demobilization of 600,000 military troops and the return of contract workers from the Persian Gulf. Its international debt is about $3 billion, and 30 percent of the national budget is used for government subsidies.

With this review of the current economic status of Vietnam, it is perhaps useful to look back briefly at the disastrous effects of the socialist planned economy and then the reform measures that have been introduced since 1986.

The Government Role   The model for building a unified socialist economy for all of Vietnam was the rigid orthodox Stalinist centralized plan of rapid industrialization and collectivized agriculture. This was the goal set by the party Congress which convened in December 1976 to launch the second five-year plan (1976–80). In 1982 and 1986 the succeeding party congresses endorsed the third (1981–85) and the fourth (1986–90) five-year plans, which were aimed at transforming Vietnam into the stage of industrialization by first developing increases in agriculture.Food production was to reach 22 million tons by the end of the fourth five-year plan. There were to be manifold increases in national income and industrial production in accordance with the plans.

All the above targets sounded grandiose on paper to the planners and bureaucrats in the party. By 1985–86, at the beginning of the fourth five-year plan, Vietnam ran into severe problems. Rice rationing had to be reinstituted; the inflation rate reached more than 700 percent; and the Vietnamese currency (dong) devalued by as much as 80 percent, which catapulted the country into a monetary crisis.[49] In addition, there were other economic problems: persistent peasant opposition to collectivization, low productivity in heavy industries, and inefficient production that was unable to meet consumer demands. With the exception of higher food production from the Mekong River Delta in 1985, the Vietnamese economy was as "poverty stricken" as ever.[50]

Economic Reform, or Doi Moi, 1986 *Doi moi* in Vietnamese means simply "renovation," which implies reform, a sort of Vietnamese *perestroika*. In fact, Vietnam introduced economic reform in December 1986 before the collapse of the Eastern European bloc. The reform introduced in China by Deng Xiaoping is probably its closest model. At the sixth party Congress, Nguyen Van Linh, the only party veteran who remained in the south to direct the Vietcong activities there from 1945 to 1975, was elevated to the new party chief position. When he was responsible for the south for Hanoi after 1975, Linh, considered by many to be the Vietnamese version of Mikhail Gorbachev, had advocated a "mixed economy" and was opposed to the "collectivization of agriculture."[51] In the winter of 1985–86, as a part of the criticism and self-criticism campaign, the Vietnamese press revealed a party leadership debate over the issues of centralized planning being too inflexible to solve economic problems and the cumbersome bureaucratic structure in the planning process.[52] In the end the reformers led by Linh won, and the party endorsed the reform program of renovation and openness, *doi moi*.

The Vietnamese economic reform, launched in December 1986, entailed the following changes:[53] First, it "repudiated bureaucratic management" based on state subsidies to underwrite the cost of production and artificial pricing on the sale of goods—as much as 30 percent of the state budget had been devoted to subsidies. Second, development of a free market-economy for agricultural goods was encouraged in lieu of government regulation. Third, so as to encourage accountability and businesslike management, all productive units were required to operate on the basis of loss and profit. Fourth, state subsidies on food, state-owned enterprises, and export-import trade would be eliminated. Fifth, in order to encourage private ownership and operation, entrepreneurs were permitted to form individual corporations for goods production and distribution.

What has been the result of economic reform in Vietnam? Douglas Pike writes that the enduring contribution of the reform is the party's commitment to the free-market concept.[54] Since the reform, food production, estimated at over 21 million metric tons, has increased in recent years. The inflation rate has come down to about 80 percent; and there has been as much as a 40 percent rise in imported consumer goods. While foreign investment reached U.S. $2.4 billion in 1991, about a third of it was in offshore petroleum development.[55] In 1990 Vietnam was able to export 1.3 million tons of rice—the first time since the 1930s. However, in agriculture, Vietnam faced the problems of a chemical fertilizer shortage and inadequate transportation facilities to bring the produce to market. When the Party Congress met in June 1991 to abolish subsidies in the form of cheap credits to state enterprises that operated at a loss, there was some opposition from party hardliners who feared that these state enterprises would fall into private hands.[56]

The overall economic picture is not good, as Vietnam's growth rate is only 3.5 percent per year in conjunction with a rising population rate of 2.2 percent per year. Vietnam needs foreign assistance, as Soviet aid has dried up. Pike writes that in 1990 "an estimated 80 percent of all state enterprises in Vietnam were in some degree of economic difficulty."[57]

A bright spot in Vietnam's economic development has been the potential energy exploitation by foreign oil companies—Royal Dutch-Shell Group, British Petroleum, and Broken Hill Proprietary of Australia, as well as those from Japan and South Korea—for offshore oil drilling in the South China Sea. In a 1991 study by the Hawaii based East-West Center Resource Systems Institute, this production was estimated to be 1.5 billion barrels.[58] President Clinton dispatched retired general John Vessey, Jr., to Hanoi in April 1993 to make a positive assessment of the MIA situation in the hope that a change of policy to lift the U.S. embargo on trade with Vietnam may be feasible.

Education   Despite enormous destruction to Vietnam's educational facilities, since 1975 progress has been made in rebuilding the educational system. As of 1985, there were some 12,511 primary schools with an enrollment of 8.1 million students from age six to age eleven. Most primary schools are free and compulsory. At the secondary level, from ages twelve to seventeen, total enrollment for 1985 was over 4 million, comprising 43 percent of children of that age. Higher education enrollment reached 114,701, primarily comprising students in technical education.

The above statistics do not reveal the educational crisis in Vietnam. A recent report, based on a Ho Chi Minh City newspaper finding, stated that 2.2 million Vietnamese are still illiterate and about 1.2 million in the six- to ten-year age group dropped out of school, in addition to another million in the age group from eleven to fourteen.[59] The dropout rate was said to have been caused by the nation's economic difficulties and economic reform, which relaxed enforcement for school attendance when opportunities for money making arose. There is a teacher shortage as well as a lack of teacher training. As a part of the reform and relaxation thrust, private schools are now permitted to open.[60] A private university was opened in 1989 in Hanoi following the *doi moi* movement launched in 1986. Children of former middle-class families can now be admitted to universities if they pass the entrance examinations.

For Vietnam youth in general, the problem is unemployment, as 2 million of them enter into a job market that pays only $130 per year. It is this group of jobless youth that becomes cynical about the validity of socialism based on Marxism and Leninism. If not addressed by the regime, the discontent will eventually breed unrest.

North Korea: Continued Isolation and Selective Contact with the Outside World

The North Korean economy has been anything but sluggish, but its growth has been hampered by a highly centralized and inefficient planned economy, supported for over four decades by the Soviet Union and China.

Economic Performance   The North Korean economy is on the verge of becoming a disaster. It is now on the third level of the Seven-Year Plan for 1987–93, designed to modernize production and managerial techniques. Part of the economic problem lies in the plan's emphasis in placing investment resources on heavy industry instead of consumer or light industries. These ambitious industrial projects require a constant supply of energy resources in the form of coal and electric power, which North Korea has not been able to produce in sufficient quantity to meet the enormous demands. As a consequence, most factories are running at less than half capacity.[61] The energy problem is further aggravated by the primitive state of industrial facilities. (This was the same situation that existed in China before Deng Xiaoping's economic reform.)

Another serious economic problem in the North Korean economy is the shortage of land for cultivation—only about 22 percent of its land is arable. There is a serious food shortage in North Korea, particularly in rice. In 1990 the rice harvest was only 2.28 million tons, a reduction of almost half of the 1989 harvest, which was estimated at 4.6 million tons.[62] This critical food shortage has forced North Korea to either barter or trade for emergency rice imports from Thailand and South Korea. Food rations have been cut, and there is a campaign in the country to eat only two meals per day. North Korea is also deeply in foreign debt: $2.7 billion to Western European countries (plus Japan) and $4.0 billion to the former Soviet Union and China for a total of $6.7 billion.[63] This foreign indebtedness has created a shortage of hard currency and forced North Korea to engage in counter trade.

Reform in the Face of a Faltering Economy   In order to reinvigorate the sluggish economy, North Korea has embarked in recent years on a strategy of joint venture development to attract foreign technology and investment by modifying its political ideology of *Juche*, or self-reliance, and self-imposed isolation.[64] The first such joint venture was the 1986 North Korea International Joint Venture Company between the North Korean government and pro-Pyonyang Korean residents in Japan. Its original capitalization was $1.2 million, owned equally by North Korea and the joint venture general company. The joint venture corporate entity decided which investment project was most appropriate for attracting the needed foreign capital and technology.

There have been some attempts to introduce needed economic reforms in the centralized North Korean economy. Hy Song Lee refuted the 1984–85 introduction of "free-market" experiments in cities and counties of each of the provinces.[65] These were not truly free markets, for prices were manipulated by officers managing the markets, and they merely represented "half-hearted attempts" at reforming the Soviet-style system of centralized planning.[66] However, the increasing stance of international isolation and the potential economic disaster may force North Korea to open up its closed society, including a renewed attempt at a dialogue with South Korea.

Dialogue on Unification   The issue of Korean unification figures prominently in the rapidly changing configuration of relationships in East Asia and on the Korean peninsula. The first step toward achieving the elusive, emotional, and complex issue of unification was taken by the then President Roh Tae Woo of South Korea on July 7, 1988, when he announced a package of proposals for reuniting North and South Korea by peaceful means. In the proposal, Roh called for exchange visits between the two divided nations, family reunions through an open border, free travel for some 10 million Koreans who have been separated from their families since 1945, and trade.One might add that these proposals were similar to the ones that have been advanced by South Korea since 1972. Then, after almost two years of discussion, on September 4, 1990, a North Korean delegation, led by Premier Yon Hyong Muk, arrived in Seoul for two days of formal talks with South Korean premier Kang Young Hoon and President Roh.[67] However, there has been much mistrust of each other's motives in advancing proposals for negotiation.[68] While the sessions in the second round ended with no agreement, the two sides decided to meet in Seoul in December 1990 for a third round of talks. They met on December 12 in a mood of "mutual distrust."[69] In this round of negotiation, North Korea proposed a ten-article Declaration of Non-aggression and Reconciliation, and demanded (1) that the annual joint military exercise by South Korea and the United States command be halted; (2) that Seoul cease its intent to apply for UN membership; and (3) release of those South Korean residents illegally visiting North Korea.[70] The South Korean premier countered with a ten-article proposal that included family reunion visits and trade. Former South Korean president Roh predicted a united Korea by the end of this century. This optimism may stem from the exchange of ideas at these reunification negotiation sessions. Roh was too optimistic about eventual reunification. The optimism may be influenced by rapidly changing world events and patterns of East Asian regional politics, which may hasten a normalization of relations between the South and the North on a peaceful coexistence framework. If unification does take place, South Korea will have to commit heavy investment in North Korean industries for the first five to ten years of the merger.[71] Costs by the South Korean government were estimated to be at least $200 billion.[72] However, the decision made by North Korea on March 12, 1993, to withdraw from the Nuclear Non-Proliferation Treaty, which mandates international inspections, has revived Seoul's fear and mistrust of North Korea[73]—not to mention the ill effect it would have on the 1991 historic agreement between the South and North Korean governments for the banning of nuclear weapons on both sides of the 38th parallel.

SUGGESTED READINGS

Vietnam

Brown, Frederick Z. *Second Chance: The United States and Indochina in the 1990s*. New York: Basic Books, 1989.

Cima, Ronald J. *Vietnam: A Country Study*. Washington, DC: U.S. Department of the Army, 1989.

Fitzgerald, Frances. *Fire in the Lake: The Vietnamese and the Americans in Vietnam*. New York: Vintage Books, 1972.

Harrison, James P. *The Endless War: Vietnam's Struggle for Independence*. New York: Columbia University Press, 1990.

Herz, Martin. *The Vietnam War in Retrospect*. New York: University Press of America, 1984.

Hess, Gary R. *Vietnam and the United States*. New York: Twayne, 1990.

Jones, Anthony James. The War for South Vietnam, 1954–1975. New York: Praeger, 1989.

Le Boutillier, John. *Vietnam: A Case for Normalizing Relations with Hanoi*. New York: Praeger, 1989.

Lockhart, Greg. *Nation in Arms: The Origins of the People's Army of Vietnam*;. New York: Allen & Unwin, 1990.

Olson, James S. *Where the Domino Fell: America and Vietnam, 1945–1990*. New York: St. Martin's Press, 1991.

Rotter, Andrew J. *The Path to Vietnam: Origins of the American Commitment to Southeast Asia*. Ithaca: Cornell University Press, 1990.

Rowe, John Carlos. *The Vietnam War and American Culture*. New York: Columbia University Press, 1991.

Taylor, Keith Weller. *The Birth of Vietnam*. Berkeley: University of California Press, 1983.

Van De Mark, Brian. *Into the Quagmire: Lyndon Johnson and the Escalation of the Vietnam War*. New York and London: Oxford University Press, 1991.

Zasloff, Joseph J. *Postwar Indochina: Old Enemies and New Allies*. Washington, DC: U.S. Department of State, 1988.

North Korea

Bunge, Frederica M. *North Korea: A Country Study*. Washington, DC: U.S. Department of the Army, 1987.

Kihl, Young Whan. *Politics and Policies in Divided Korea: Regime in Contest*. Boulder, CO, and London: Westview Press, 1984.

Kim, Byoung-Lo Philo. *Two Koreas in Development*. New Brunswick, NJ: Rutgers University Press, 1981.

Okonogi, Masao. *North Korea at the Crossroads*. Tokyo: Japan Institute of International Affairs, 1976.

Suh, Dae-Sook. *Kim Il Sung: The North Korean Leader*. New York: Columbia University Press.

7

Cambodia and Laos

Continued Battle
for National Independence
and against Foreign
Interference

Cambodia and Laos have many things in common. First, in ancient times, long before the arrival of the French in the 1860s, independent kingdoms— the Angkor Empire and royal Lao Kingdom of Lan Xang—had been established in both countries. Then, as part of their historic legacy, the Khmers and Laos were engulfed in wars and invasions with their neighbors, Siam (Thailand) or with each other or with the powerful Annam (now Vietnam). The Khmers fought for more than half a century against Siam, and the Laotian kingdom had served as a buffer between Siam and Annam in their continuous rivalry with neighbors.

At one time, around the 1890s, the French were able to place Cambodia, the Vietnamese regions of Tonkin, Annam, Cochinchina, and Laos into the Indochina Union—a consolidated French colonial empire that lasted until World War II.

In addition to the influence of Theravada Buddhism in their cultural life, Cambodians and Laotians have depended considerably on leadership from the royal elites who too often have been factionalized and manipulated by intervening foreign powers in the postwar period. With the advent of communism in Vietnam, in their struggle for independence both Cambodia and Laos have had to confront the problems posed by radical revolutionary forces.

Cambodia, a small Southeast Asian nation, with 70,000 square miles, about the size of Missouri, is bordered on the north and west by Thailand

and Laos and on the east by Vietnam. (*Cambodia* was the accepted name before 1975; between 1975 and 1979 it was changed to *Kampuchea* by the Khmer Rouge. The use of the name *Cambodia* was resumed after 1979, and throughout this section the name *Cambodia* is used.) For more than two decades the Thai-Cambodian border had been closed because civil war raged among various factions in Cambodia. But in 1991 the border was opened, and border trade has flourished since then.

The Mekong River flows from Laos through Cambodia before it empties into the South China Sea from South Vietnam. The river valleys have become fertile plains for agriculture, mainly rice production, for about one-third of the country. The remainder of the land consists of forest dominated by the Cardamom and the Dangrek mountains. Cambodia has a very short coastline and a natural harbor, the Kampong Saom, formerly the Sihanoukville. Basically, it is a country of flat and fertile soil under tropical monsoon influence with a plentiful supply of water, ideal for growing rice. (Cambodia produced 2.2 million tons of rice in 1989.)

For the provinces in northeastern Cambodia living has been rather hazardous; more than 400,000 land mines have been estimated to remain—the legacy of the almost two decades of war in Cambodia.[1] Another legacy of the war in Cambodia has been deforestation—estimated by one environmentalist to be 50 to 75 percent of the total forests lost due to American bombing, Khmer Rouge burning, and unrestricted logging for sale to Japan and Thailand.[2]

In 1988 the United Nations estimated the population of Cambodia to be about 7.8 million. In the late 1980s approximately 800,000 lived and worked in the nation's capital, Phnom-Penh—quite a contrast to only 20,000 during 1975–79, when the Khmer Rouge imposed a reign of terror and waged a campaign of emptying the cities in favor of forceful rural transfers.

There are also some 350,000 Cambodian refugees living in camps in Thailand waiting to be resettled to Cambodia by the United Nations, in addition to some 130,000 "internal refugees" who had been forcefully dislocated by the Khmer Rouge.[3]

On the other hand, Laos, about the size of Oregon, the only landlocked nation in Southeast Asia, contains 91,340 square miles of mostly mountainous tropical forest land bordered by China to the north, Vietnam on the east, Thailand and Burma on the west, and Cambodia on the south. The Mekong River flows from the north and forms the long natural border separating Laos from Thailand in the south and west. Only in the northern part of the country is there a stretch of flat land known as the Plain of Jars, the early 1960s battleground of government forces and the communist-inspired insurgents of the Pathet Lao. The Annamite Mountains separate southern Laos and Vietnam. Sections of these mountains were the target of intensive bombing by the United States in the early 1970s in order to prevent supplies from reaching the Vietcong via the Ho Chi Minh Trail—an unsuccessful effort that created untold human tragedy for Laos.

The population of Laos today stands at 3.9 million. The vast majority of them, more than 80 percent, live in rural villages along the Mekong River valleys and its tributaries. Urban areas center in the capital of Vientiane, the royal palaces at Luang Prabang, and Savannakhet, close to the Thai border on the Mekong River. The Indochina wars forced Laotians to seek refuge in Thailand, and many of them are living in UN refugee camps. In recent years Thailand has placed tight restrictions on refugee movements and has imposed forcible repatriation to Laos.

Known as the Tai people, Laotians originally came from the south-western areas of China; they are related to the Thai of Thailand. Their migration route followed the Mekong River; by the time of the Mongol Empire in 1253 they had moved southward to what is the Laos of today. They have been influenced by both the Chinese culture in art and rice growing, and by the Khmer culture, particularly in their written script and Buddhism.

POLITICAL CULTURE AND POLITICAL DEVELOPMENT

Cambodia: From Sihanouk's Rule to the Rise of the Khmer Rouge to the UN Peacekeeping Plan

Historic Legacy We begin a brief discussion of Cambodia's early history by focusing on the Angkor Empire, which ruled Cambodia and beyond from 820 to 1500 A.D. The world retains the legacy of the magnificent Angkor Wat stone monument and temples as an expression of the ancient Khmer civilization.[4] The Angkor Empire was ruled by a king influenced by the Hindu Brahman. He provided irrigation projects of catchments and reservoirs to enable the peasants to grow rice, and in return for their service to build the Vishnu temples at Angkor Wat. From 1181 to 1218 the Khmer rulers extended their rule to Thailand, Laos, and Burma. Then came wars against the Thai; the Khmers fought for over seventy years until 1430, when they were finally overtaken by the Thai forces.

For over 400 years thereafter Cambodia struggled for survival against incursions from Thailand, Laos, and Vietnam. By the early nineteenth century, Vietnam controlled central Cambodia; this led to rebellions until 1841, when Cambodia became a protectorate under an alliance of Thailand and Vietnam.

THE FRENCH COLONIAL ADMINISTRATION   French interest in Indochina was motivated by a desire to compete with the British in India and Burma. With gains made in Vietnam, the French ventured into

Cambodia for the purposes of exploiting its natural resources and seeking Catholic converts. In 1863 the French and the king of Cambodia signed a treaty that placed Cambodia under a French protectorate against the Thais and Vietnamese. In 1887, after having dispatched French naval forces to attack Phnom Penh, France had consolidated its control in Indochina by creating the Indochina Union of Cambodia and Vietnamese regions of Tonkin, Annam, and Cochinchina. Laos was subsequently added in 1893 to become the third major component of the union.

The French developed a central bureaucracy and manipulated the Cambodian monarchy to such an extent that the latter joined France to fight in Europe during World War I. For some four decades of the twentieth century, from 1904 to 1941, Cambodia was an obliging French protectorate behind the facade of a succession of ruling Cambodian monarchs under the names of Norodom and Sisowath. In 1941 when France fell to the invading Nazis and the Vichy regime took over French Indochina, the Cambodian throne was passed on to the great grandson of King Norodom, Prince Norodom Sihanouk; the French had installed him to be the new monarch, supposedly more pliable by the Vichy French.

Political Culture for Cambodia and Laos   In both Cambodia and Laos Theravada Buddhism has been the traditional faith for the majority of people. Buddhist monks played an important role in the lives of the people in Cambodia, and they occupied a unique position in Cambodian culture and values. The monks were the moral teachers in rural life. In Cambodia in the 1950s and 1960s there was a shift away from Buddhist influence as young Cambodian intellectuals began to stress modern statehood and government. The Khmer Rouge was on the whole antireligious in orientation and considered Buddhism incompatible with a socialist revolution.

For both Cambodia and Laos there is some considerable dependence on leadership from the royal families. People in both countries tend to accept that political power resides with the ruling nobility. Communist elements, Khmer Rouge or Pathet Lao, and the royal nobility seem to believe in one thing: that democratic institutions are only for decorative purposes. Political institutions established by modern constitutions in Cambodia and Laos must be seen in this perspective.

Karl D. Jackson speaks of the divergent political cultures—"the traditional hierarchical political culture" of Sihanouk and Lon Nol and "the authoritarian radical political culture" of the Khmer Rouge—that prevailed at the end of World War II to cause revolutions and civil wars in Cambodia.[5] Jackson's thesis is that the 1970–75 Cambodian civil war was primarily a clash between "the traditional hierarchical-bureaucratic political culture" and "the revolutionary egalitarian culture" that resulted in the Khmer Rouge's desire to "reconstruct Cambodian society from ground zero as the world's most egalitarian, and therefore revolutionary, social order."[6]

Sihanouk Rule, 1953–1970[7]   Sihanouk declared Cambodia's independence on March 12, 1945, but wished to remain tied to the French, who returned to Phnom Penh in September of that year. A treaty was signed in 1949 under which the French recognized all Indochinese states as members of the associate states of the French union, comparable to the British commonwealth concept. The new arrangement did provide Cambodia with "50 percent independence," but was opposed by the more nationalist-oriented leaders of the political parties. The dissent and unrest gave Sihanouk an excuse to impose his royal prerogative by calling new elections to a national assembly in the fall of 1951. Opposition grew as Sihanouk moved closer to French support and reliance on French forces to maintain law and order. In June 1952 Sihanouk took bold steps in his authoritarian rule by dismissing the Cabinet, suspending the constitution, and placing himself as the prime minister.

A year later, in January 1953, Sihanouk declared martial law, as dissenters for complete independence were exiled and joined an armed rebellion against Sihanouk and the French. By this time Sihanouk was caught in a bind: He must convince the French to grant Cambodia full independence or face an uprising against his rule at home if he could not bring this about. He went to Paris in March 1953 to accomplish full independence for Cambodia, but failed. Sihanouk finally won full independence for Cambodia from the French on November 3, 1953, as France faced a deteriorating military situation in Vietnam.

Sihanouk's one-man rule, from 1954 to 1970, was characterized by his personal style of vanity, flamboyance and eccentricity. He was a mixture of a nationalist, patriot, and "god king" with a common touch. He enjoyed frequent contacts with villagers and peasants. And he was a dedicated hard worker for Cambodian independence.

The 1970 Coup and the Rise of the Khmer Rouge, 1970–1975   In 1955 in the midst of a mounting challenge to his rule by the organized Left, the moderate center, and the right-wing groups, Sihanouk abdicated his throne in favor of his father in order to play a more active role in Cambodian politics. He organized the Popular Socialist Community as a political party which won election to the National Assembly, which in turn elected Sihanouk the head of state. The country was then in the throes of economic chaos and political unrest, but Sihanouk ruled with arbitrary arrests against the opposition. In mid-March 1970, while Sihanouk was visiting Moscow and Beijing, General Lon Nol, then serving as the prime minister, engineered a coup d'etat, which Sihanouk charged from Beijing was instigated by the Central Intelligence Agency. Lon Nol then headed the shaky Khmer Republic. Encouraged by mass demonstrations against the coup, Sihanouk, in a dramatic move, formed an alliance with Ho Chi

Minh's North Vietnam and the Khmer Rouge, the communist insurgent group. Fearing that the Lon Nol regime might collapse, the U.S. and South Vietnamese forces invaded Cambodia. The United States also launched a nine-month bombing campaign in 1973 and 1974 when the Khmer Rouge gained ground. On April 1, 1975, Lon Nol fled to Indonesia and then to Hawaii as the revolutionary forces approached Phnom Penh.

***Democratic Kampuchea and the Khmer Rouge, 1975–1978*[8]**   When the toughened and disciplined guerrilla forces of the Khmer Rouge, the armed units of the Communist party of Kampuchea (PKK), entered Phnom Penh on April 1975, the victory represented the culmination of a long revolutionary struggle. As pointed out by Timothy Carney, it dated back to the 1930s and 1940s. The idea of a Democratic Kampuchea had been firmly planted in the minds of a number of Khmer student leaders then studying in Paris. They included Pol Pot, Ieng Sary, Khieu Samphan and Hou Yuon— the latter two earned their doctoral degrees from the University of Paris, where they had joined the French Communist party in the early 1940s. Upon their return to Cambodia, they and other student leaders and intellectuals organized the Khmer People's Revolutionary party, which in the 1960s was renamed the Workers' party of Kampuchea, and finally the Kampuchean Communist party (KCP).

The Democratic Kampuchea, 1975–78, which the Khmer Rouge established, was led by the most radical faction of the KCP. Under the newly drafted 1976 constitution, which embraced state ownership of a collectivized peasantry and other productive forces, it installed Sihanouk upon his return from exile as the figurehead without the title of head of state. There was a national assembly of 250 deputies dominated by the peasants. Then the radical student leaders from Paris, Khieu Samphan and Pol Pot, took over control of the government. Sihanouk was forced to retire with a pension.

Thereafter, the regime under the control of the Khmer Rouge became known worldwide as one of terror and genocide in its radical policy of emptying or forcefully evacuating city residents to the countryside where they died of torture, starvation, and disease, or for lack of health care. Pol Pot, then the prime minister, turned the countryside of Cambodia into "killing fields." Estimates of the number who perished under Pol Pot's revolutionary reign of terror ranged from 1.2 million by Amnesty International to as high as 2 million for the period 1975–79[9]—Pol Pot's own estimate was between 800,000 to 1 million.[10] The system of killing by Pol Pot's Khmer Rouge was designed to exterminate internal threats to the revolutionary regime, a standard pattern of violence associated with a new totalitarian regime.[11] Suggestions have been made recently that the 1948 Convention on Genocide be invoked to hold the Pol Pot regime accountable.[12]

The new revolutionary regime of the Democratic Kampuchea under

Khieu Samphan and Pol Pot moved closer to China and was dependent upon the latter's aid to drive out the Vietnamese influence and threat. In its eagerness to transform the Cambodian backward agrarian economy, the regime embarked on a strategy of mass mobilization reminiscent of Mao's 1958 Great Leap Forward for China. The exodus of Cambodian refugees along the Thai and Vietnamese borders generated border wars with the two neighboring countries in 1977 and 1978. Vietnam also instigated internal revolts against the Khieu Samphan–Pol Pot regime by lending its support to younger dissident Khmer Rouge officers such as Heng Samrin, whose efforts to challenge Pol Pot failed, making it necessary for him to escape to Vietnam. As pointed out by John and Mae Esterline, it was a combination of factors such as historic animosity between ancient empires and Vietnam's fear of a Chinese threat in Southeast Asia that motivated the 1978 signing of the Vietnamese–Soviet Union treaty of cooperation and defense partnership. This resulted in Vietnam's resolve to invade Cambodia at the end of that year.[13]

The People's Republic of Kampuchea, 1979–1993   Supported by the Khmer dissident forces under Heng Samarin, Vietnam launched its invasion forces of five divisions. On January 11, 1979, after having smashed the Khmer Rouge and captured Phnom Penh, the People's Republic of Kampuchea was established. Soon after a treaty of friendship and cooperation with Vietnam was signed under which Vietnamese troops were allowed to be stationed in Cambodia. Khmer Rouge leaders either fled to Thailand or took off to the jungle to recoup under Chinese support.

The new Cambodian government struggled in vain to gain international recognition. China and a number of Southeast Asian nations, such as Singapore and Thailand, were opposed to the People's Republic of Kampuchea because of its close ties and dependency on the support of Vietnamese troops in Cambodia (about 100,000) as a serious threat to the peace and security of the region. China was openly rearming the defeated Khmer Rouge forces with the intent to drive out the Heng Samrin government and the Vietnam troops. China even launched a border war against Vietnam because of the latter's occupation of Cambodia. China supported a coalition government-in-exile of the remnant Khmer Rouge forces, estimated at 30,000, and Sihanouk, now exiled in China. The new regime was determined to deradicalize Pol Pot's programs and engaged in campaigns against the insurgent Khmer Rouge guerrillas. These military activities ravaged the Cambodian countryside, generating waves of new refugees to the Thai border. According to one observer, with the help of good weather, international humanitarian relief programs, and Heng Samrin's postponement of centralized planning, the Cambodian economy made some gains in 1981–82.[14]

In June 1982, at the urging of the United States, China and other Asian nations, a coalition government-in-exile was formed by guerrilla factions. The coalition government-in-exile was headed by Sihanouk and Khieu Samphan as president and vice president, respectively. In December 1987 talks were held in France between Hun Sen, prime minister for the People's Republic of Kampuchea, and Sihanouk for a political settlement of Cambodia as Sino-Soviet relations improved and as pressure increased by the Association of Southeast Asian Nations (ASEAN). These talks proved to be fruitless and the Khmer Rouge guerrilla activities persisted against Vietnam's military occupation in Cambodia. In April 1989 Vietnam declared that it would withdraw its troops from Cambodia to pave the way for a political settlement by all the factions. This move was precipitated by a rapidly changing Soviet Union and United States–China cooperation in finding a peaceful solution for Cambodia. Vietnam's intent to pull out its invading troops led to convening of the nineteen-nation Paris International Conference on Cambodia, July 30 to August 30, 1989, at the urging of the United States and the ASEAN nations. These initiatives eventually led to involvement of the UN Security Council's five permanent members— China, France, the United Kingdom, the United States, and the former Soviet Union—to produce an October 1991 agreement for ending the war in Cambodia. In the next section, "The Locus of Power," the focus is on the UN peace settlement for Cambodia, brokered by the United States, China, the former Soviet Union, and the ASEAN members.

Laos: Colonial Rule, Independence, Civil War, and the End of Monarchical Rule

The first royal Lao kingdom was founded in 1353 under the name of Lan Xang, "the land of the million elephants." It comprised not only the present-day Laos, but some northern and eastern parts of Thailand. This absolute monarchical system endured until the sixteenth century, when the kingdom became engulfed in a decade long dispute with Thailand, then Siam, and Burma over the control of Chieng Mai. For much of the seventeenth century Laos was peaceful. Then in 1694 an unsettled succession question divided the kingdom into three separate entities inviting invasions and interference from Siam and Annam. In fact, Siam occupied Vientiane in 1778 and tribute was exacted by both Siam and Vietnam for a while. In 1820 there was a disastrous war between Vientiane and Siam that practically depopulated the central Mekong area. The Laotian kingdom of Luang Prabang then served as a buffer between Siam and Vietnam in a complex game of war and conquest waged by these neighboring countries.

French Colonial Rule, 1863–1945   The year 1863 marked the beginning of French control in Indochina as it annexed Cochinchina and then by 1884 made the rest of Vietnam (Annam and Tonkin) French protectorates. Parts of Laos were then under Thai (Siamese) occupation. The

French pressured Siam to relinquish its claims over the territories east of the Mekong basin, but it held on to the area west of the Mekong River. By 1899 the French were able to merge the separate Lao territories of Luang Prabang, Xieng Khouang, Champassak, and Vientiane into a single colonial administration by relying on the local elites to exercise control. They restored the Lao throne to a crown prince who returned from studying in Paris in 1904. Other than occasional military actions to quell tribal rebellions and Chinese bandit raids, the French left Laos more or less to themselves. Through a series of diplomatic agreements with British Burma, China, and Thailand, the French were able to fix the kingdom of Laos borders in 1896–97 and 1904–05.

Independence, Civil War, and the Geneva Conferences, 1945–1962   In 1941 Japan occupied French Indochina, and in March 1945 it declared independence for Indochinese entities formerly under French colonial rule. The king of Laos proclaimed the end of French colonial rule and the formation of a free Laos. However, a few months later World War II ended and the French troops returned in October 1945 to accept the Japanese surrender. In April 1946, after some disagreement with the free Laos movement, the king accepted the newly drafted constitution and was enthroned as king of all Laos. In the meantime, French troops were ordered to enter Laos to engage in battle against free Lao guerrillas and communist Vietminh forces infiltrating into Laos. The French victory forced into exile in Thailand the small band of free Lao, led by Prince Phetsarath, who had served as prime minister for the pro-French Laotian king.

After having reestablished authority, the French were able to convince the Laotian elites to elect an assembly in January 1947 for the purpose of drafting a new constitution. In the meantime the free Laos movement exiled in Thailand developed leadership differences among the three half-brothers: Prince Phetsarath, who wanted complete independence for Laos by refusing to cooperate with the French; his half-brother Souvanna Phouma, who preferred to work with the French in order to get independence for Laos; and a third half-brother Prince Souphanouvong, who led the guerrilla band and operated under Vietminh direction.[15]

In the 1949 agreement entered into between France and the Kingdom of Laos, Laos was recognized as an associate state of the French Union. The Laotians would have control over foreign affairs and their admission to the United Nations. The free Laos movement collapsed and many of the participants returned to Laos to reenter the government.

The 1954 Geneva Conference provided that the Vietminh and Pathet Lao forces, organized in 1950 by Prince Souphanouvong with the help of Vietminh, be confined to the two northern provinces until a final political settlement was found. By 1956–57 a coalition government was formed under the leadership of Prince Souvanna Phouma and assigned the task of reintegrating the Pathet Lao after Prince Souphanouvong relinquished control of the two northern provinces and pledged his loyalty to the Kingdom of Laos. Elections were held in May 1958 for National Assembly seats for the two provinces; results favored the Lao Patriotic Front and its military arm, the Pathet Lao. On the pretext for a neutral Lao government, to be led by Souvanna Phouma, a young commander named Kong Le led a coup and seized the Lao capital. The coup and the resulting political development of installing Souvanna Phouma as the new premier were opposed by the country's military faction led by General Phoumi Nosavan, defense minister of the previous coalition government. However, the factional leaders soon temporarily patched their differences on August 31, 1960, by making Nosavan the deputy prime minister. Kong Le and his 600 paratroopers, still entrenched in Vientiane, refused to accept Nosavan. Instead, they organized an insurgent group to oppose the new government. The movement chose a southern leader, Prince Boun Oum. This provided the excuse the Pathet Lao needed to launch a retaliation against the resistance movement.

Now the Kingdom of Laos was beset with internal warfare waged by three factions: the hardliners, or rightists, led by Prince Boun Oum; the neutral government group led by Prince Souvanna Phouma, but supported by Kong Le's paratroopers; and the communist Pathet Lao, which supported Prince Souphanouvong. Somehow, out of this chaos and divisiveness in June 1962 there came an agreement to attempt once more a coalition government with the leaders of the three factions serving as premier and deputy premiers. But that peaceful interlude did not last long, for fighting soon broke out between Kong Le's forces and the Pathet Lao on the Plain of Jars, which separates Vientiane and Luang Prabang, the royal capital.

Foreign Intervention   It was during this existence of civil war waged by the disputing factions that foreign intervention entered into Laotian affairs. First, a civilian outfit, known as Air America, Inc., chartered by the United States Air Force and the CIA, air-lifted military supplies from Bangkok to the rightist faction under Nosavan. However, the official U.S. policy, along with that of the other Western powers of Great Britain and France, was to support the neutralist government coalition under Prince Souvanna Phouma.[16] As U.S. military aid poured to Nosavan in large quantities, undermining the neutralist-led coalition government, government troops began to mutiny and to defect to Nosavan, who mounted a campaign to take over Vientiane and depose the neutralist coalition government. By December the Soviets also intervened by pouring in armaments in support of the Kong Le–Pathet Lao alliance.[17] The latter, now with the support of the Soviets, Chinese, and the Vietminh, was in control of some six provinces in Laos.

On May 16, 1961, the Geneva Conference was convened by the fourteen foreign ministers who negotiated for more than a year over the question of neutrality for Laos under international guarantees. U.S. objectives at the conference were to persuade Thailand to support Laotian neutrality in return for U.S. assurance in support of Thai security and to convince the three Laotian factions to form a coalition government.[18] With regard to the first objective in July 1962 the conference produced a Declaration on the Neutrality of Laos to "respect and observe in every way the sovereignty, independence, neutrality, unity and territorial integrity of the Kingdom of Laos."[19] Article 2 of the agreement also called for withdrawal of all foreign "regular and irregular forces" from Laos; inspection was to be by the International Control Commission established by the 1954 Geneva Conference. Article 6 prohibited the introduction of all foreign military personnel and armaments into Laos. However, the communist Vietnam had increased its troop strength in Laos. At the 1962 Geneva Conference the various factions in Laos agreed to form another coalition government. But the coalition government soon failed to provide effective control over the country, so by 1963–64 fighting broke out again between the neutralist faction and the Pathet Lao, which obtained military aid from North Vietnam and the then Soviet Union. The royalist government had agreed to receive U.S. military supplies air-lifted by Air America, a front unit for the CIA. Thus, for the next nine years, 1964 to 1973, civil war in Laos was in full swing. In addition, in order to prevent the Vietcong's receiving supplies from North Vietnam via the Ho Chi Minh Trail and to eliminate the route via the Plain of Jars used by the Pathet Lao in its drive toward Vientiane, the United States undertook one of the most intensive bombing campaigns in modern history along the Lao-Vietnam border. It has been reported that by 1973, when bombing finally ceased, a total of more than 2 million tons of bombs had rained on Laos, or "one planeload of bombs every 8 minutes around the clock for 9 years."[20]

By January 1973 the royal Lao government called for a cease fire, which was accepted by the Pathet Lao under Prince Souphanouvong and by Prince Souvanna Phouma. Thus, a third coalition government in seventeen years was formed on April 5, 1974. The U.S. military advisors and the CIA withdrew in June, in addition to some 9,000 Chinese troops that had been building roads in northern Laos. But the communist forces from North Vietnam remained and supported the Pathet Lao (the Lao National People's Army), which helped to establish the Lao People's Democratic Republic on December 3, 1973, when the king abdicated after 700 years of monarchical rule.

LOCUS OF POWER: POLITICAL INSTITUTIONS AND LEADERSHIP

Cambodia: The Elusive Peace Settlement among Warring Factions

The continued existence and control of Cambodia by the People's Republic of Kampuchea (PRK) rested with Vietnam's support through its military occupation. (When Vietnam announced its troop withdrawal in April 1989, it maintained a strength of 150,000–200,000 garrison force in Cambodia. Vietnam promised that by September 1989 it would withdraw its last 26,000 from Cambodia without verification from any impartial source.) With Vietnam as its patron and protector, on June 27, 1981, the PRK made public a constitution that declared Cambodia a democratic socialist state under the leadership of the party of Democratic Kampuchea, a newly formed communist party to take the place of Pol Pot's Kampuchean People's Revolutionary party.

Under the 1981 constitution the People's Republic of Kampuchea established the following government organs.

The National Assembly   In the May 1, 1981 election a total of 117 deputies were elected for a five-year term to constitute the "supreme organ of state power." The assembly has been dominated by pro-Vietnam and anti-Khmer Rouge, or anti-Pol Pot, Cambodians. The assembly meets twice a year to enact laws for the nation. In 1986 the life of the assembly elected in 1981 was extended until 1991.

The Council of State   This has been a seven-member council representing the most influential leaders of the country. The Council of State serves as an interim assembly between sessions with legislative powers. The chairman of the Council of State serves as the head of state.

The Council of Ministers   This has been the Cabinet, which is responsible for the execution of laws enacted by the National Assembly. The Council of Ministers is headed by a prime minister, a position that has been occupied since 1985 by Hun Sen.

The Judiciary   The People's Supreme Court is the state's highest court. However, the justice system has been administered since 1979 by the People's Revolutionary Courts at Phnom Penh and in the provinces. Judges are appointed by the Council of Ministers upon recommendation from the local revolutionary committees, the villages, communes, and provincial administrative bodies.

All of the above political institutions established under the 1981 constitution are in the main in a political vacuum as the UN peace settlement provisions are being implemented for Cambodia under the October 23, 1991, UN-sponsored peace agreement. The United Nations took over administrative control of the Cambodian government until a UN-supervised election took place in 1993. The following is a brief review of the key points in the UN-enforced peace plan for Cambodia as accepted by all the warring factions in Cambodia.

The United Nations Peace Settlement for Cambodia, October 23, 1991: "Mission Impossible"?   The key to any peace settlement for Cambodia was to obtain agreement among the four warring Cambodian factions to cease their quarrels in favor of national reconciliation once the Vietnamese troops had been withdrawn. Two of the factions were the noncommunist resistance: Sihanouk's own Sihanouk National Army—a guerrilla band of 20,000 troops—and the Khmer People's National Liberation Front of 14,000 troops headed by former premier Son Sann. The United States has been politically supportive of the two noncommunist resistance groups, and wants Sihanouk's group to play an influential role in the interim coalition government. The communist group consisted of the Marxist-Leninist Khmer Rouge, whose brutal regime was overthrown by the invading Vietnamese troops in 1978–79. The Khmer Rouge has a force of about 50,000 troops. The Khmer Rouge has been led by Pol Pot in spite of his September 1985 announcement to retire as its military leader. For a number of years prior to the 1991 final agreement, negotiations were deadlocked over the issue of the continued participation of the Khmer Rouge in the new coalition government. The United States expressed its opposition to the Khmer Rouge's involvement in any future peace plan. However, Sihanouk and the ASEAN wanted the Khmer Rouge to plan a part in the future permanent government for Cambodia. The United States' opposition was softened due to guarantees of adequate safeguards in any settlement to prevent the Khmer Rouge from playing a dominant role.

As for China, the other major power-game player, its basic objectives have been its desire to rid Cambodia of Vietnamese influence or "Vietnam hegemonism" and support for an independent or neutral Cambodia.[21] During the negotiation process for a Cambodian peace settlement from 1987 to 1991, China was determined to help create a new political framework that would ensure that its ally Sihanouk and the coalition of guerrillas would play an important role instead of the Vietnam-backed government of Hun Sen and Heng Samrin. China's acceptance of the UN interim administration of Cambodia under the peace settlement has been viewed as the fulfillment of its last basic objective after having seen the withdrawal of Vietnamese troops from Cambodia and a drastically reduced Soviet influence. China's only concession in the diplomatic negotiation process was to pressure the Khmer Rouge to participate as the coalition opposed to the Heng Samrin government and therefore remove the obstacle to the eventual peace agreement. The Cambodian peace plan satisfies China's consistent demand that no outside power is to control Cambodia.

The UN peace plan was signed in Paris October 23, 1992, by a representative of the People's Republic of Kampuchea, Heng Samrin, Sihanouk for the Sihanouk National Army, Son Sann for the Khmer People's National Liberation Front, and Khieu Samphan for the Khmer Rouge, in

addition to eighteen other nations including the United Nations' five permanent Security Council members.

The Cambodian peace plan, officially titled "The Agreement on a
Comprehensive Political Settlement of the Cambodian Conflict," calls for
the following:[22]

1. An immediate cease fire by the three guerrilla forces and the government forces. It mandates demobilization of 70 percent (about 220,000)
of these forces under UN supervision. The cease-fire portion of the agreement will halt foreign military assistance to any of the factions. (As of
March and April 1992 there was still guerrilla fighting occurring in central
and north Cambodia.) The UN-supervised demobilization would establish
the "cantonment" zones where 70 percent of government soldiers and guerrillas would turn in their weapons and the remaining 30 percent would be
commanded by and utilized by the UN-Cambodian peace-keeping force.
The UN peacekeeping force will consist of about 16,000 troops; the first
250 Indonesian contingent assigned to the United Nations arrived at the
Phnom Penh airport on April 17, 1992.[23] In addition, the United Nations
would have 3,000 police and hire 6,000 bureaucrats to constitute the full
strength of its peacekeeping responsibilities in Cambodia.

2. As an interim arrangement, the government of Cambodia will in
theory be administered by the United Nations in close cooperation with the
Supreme National Council, headed by Sihanouk, to represent the various
Cambodian factions. The Supreme National Council will have eleven
members, in addition to Sihanouk as the neutral chairman, divided between
six from the State of Cambodia (the present government) and five from the
opposing or resistance factions. The 3,000 UN bureaucrats and technocrats
will manage the various Cambodian ministerial departments such as
defense, foreign affairs, economic development and finances.

3. In early 1993 there will be free elections for a constitutional assembly, which in turn will prepare a new constitution for Cambodia that would
place emphasis on human rights guarantees. This election will be administered and supervised by the UN peacekeeping force, the UN Transitional
Authority in Cambodia (UNTAC).

4. The signers pledge in the agreement not only to recognize
Cambodian sovereignty and independence, but to make financial commit-
ments toward Cambodia's reconstruction after almost two decades of war
and destruction.

5. Some 370,000 Cambodian refugees now living in camps along the
Thai border will be returned. (The first group of 527 Cambodian refugees
were returned in March 1992 and housed in temporary UN structures of
bamboo and reeds.)[24] The cost of resettling refugees will most likely reach
$100 million. Total cost for the UN peacekeeping mission in Cambodia is
estimated to be about $2 billion to be contributed by UN members on the
established UN assessment formula, which allocates 30 percent to the

United States, 12.2 percent to the former Soviet Union, and 11 percent to Japan. At the international conference held in Tokyo in late June 1992 Japan pledged $800 million in aid to help with the reconstruction of Cambodia.)

The UN peacekeeping plan for Cambodia does not remove overnight the deep suspicion and mistrust among and between the various factions. There is still some vagueness and uncertainty regarding the respective policy roles to be played by the United Nations and the Supreme National Council headed by Sihanouk, who is known for his unpredictable temperament. There is also some ambiguity in the relationship between the UNTAC and the existing government of Cambodia, for the latter still administers the territory under its control and the other territories are likewise under the control of other factions because in reality UNTAC does not administer these territories.

Another difficult task will be disarming the battle-hardened Khmer Rouge troops of 50,000 strong. This force still commands the support of at least 10 percent of Cambodia's 8 million population. There have been reports that weapons and arms for future conflicts have been stored in hidden places by the Khmer Rouge.[25] Even though the Khmer Rouge has officially pledged in favor of capitalism and multiparty democracy, it is being controlled and directed by the same radical cadres such as Pol Pot and Khieu Samphan, who are committed to "old ideals" with "new tactics," or simply biding their time for a return to power in five to ten years.[26] As of June 1992 the Khmer Rouge attempted to balk at the UN peace effort by refusing to give up arms to the UN demobilization authority established under the peace plan. There had been renewed rounds of fighting between the Khmer Rouge guerrilla forces and government troops. The Khmer Rouge claimed that there were still Vietnamese troops inside Cambodia, a claim that was denied by Yasushi Akashi, the UN chief for UNTAC.

In January 1993, as UNTAC made preparations—the registration of potential voters—for the May 1993 national election under the 1991 Paris agreement discussed earlier, prime minister Hung Sen's state government of Cambodia in Phnom Penh launched its offensive against the Khmer Rouge guerrillas. The latter has refused to cooperate and participate in the forthcoming national election. The refusal by Khmer Rouge is considered a violation of the 1991 Paris agreement; for that matter, so is the government's military offensive against the Khmer Rouge. At this writing, peace is still not possible in Cambodia. Even Sihanouk has denounced the UN peacekeeping efforts.

The United Nations at the time of the May 1993 election had provided a peacekeeping force of 22,000 (plus 16,000 civilian personnel), had played its role successfully as the "honest broker" for the warring factions by completing the national election in more than thirteen years, and had made it possible for the 120-seat Constituent Assembly to convene in October 1993[27]. In the meantime, a provisional national government had been formed at the conclusion of the May national election with the leaders of the two largest vote-getting political parties sharing the governance for the country[28]: Hun Sen of the Cambodian People's party (CPP), the political arm of the Vietnam-installed State of Cambodia regime, and Prince Norodom Ranariddh, son of the senior Sihanouk of the winning royalist party, the FUNCINPEC. Norodom Sihanouk was made king again by the New National Assembly under the new constitution in the fall of 1993.

Laos: The Abolition of the Royal Kingdom and the Post–Vietnam War Constitution

King Savang Vatthana was forced to abdicate his throne in December 1975. For over sixteen years, since the founding of the Lao People's Democratic Republic (LPDR) in 1975, Laos has been without a state constitution. After several years of preparation and drafting, a post–Vietnam War constitution for Laos was adopted on August 14, 1991. Under this constitution the Lao People's Democratic Republic is to be a united and independent state; it establishes a national assembly, the president of the state, the government in the form of a council of ministers, local governments, and a supreme judiciary.

The National Assembly   This is a unicameral national legislative body with powers to amend the constitution, and to enact or abrogate laws. It has also adopted the European parliamentary concept of expressing "no confidence" in the work of the government by calling for a vote in the sessions of the National Assembly. It is the National Assembly that elects or removes the president of the state, as well as the president of the People's Supreme Court. The National Assembly has a standing committee that can make recommendations on laws and the constitutionality of laws to the full body. It meets twice a year in ordinary sessions, but if it is deemed necessary, the standing committee may convene an extraordinary session of the National Assembly.

There are seventy-nine members elected to the National Assembly; their term of office is for five years. All present seventy-nine members were elected by the former Supreme People's Assembly on March 1989. (A new election for the National Assembly took place in 1992.) The Chairman of the National Assembly is Nouhak Phoumsavan, aged eighty, the second highest ranking officer in the politburo of the Lao People's Revolutionary party (LPRP).

The President of the State   The 1991 constitution created a position for the head of state comparable to the one for the French Fifth Republic with real, not limited to ceremonial, tasks. The presidency of the state of Laos is now held by Kaysone Phomvihan, a long-time leader, having served as the party chairman and as the former prime minister of the LPRP that once dominated the communist Lao Patriotic Front. He has been elected by the National Assembly for a five-year term. Laws enacted by the National Assembly must be approved and promulgated by the president within thirty days of passage. The president has the power to appoint or dismiss members of the national government, including the prime minister. All provincial/local government officials and military personnel are appointed by the president upon the recommendation of the prime minister.

The Prime Minister and the Cabinet Under the 1991 constitution, the old Council of Ministers responsible for government administration is now simply the government, which is composed of a prime minister, several deputy prime ministers, and a host of other ministers and chairmen of administrative committees with ministerial rank. With approval by the National Assembly the prime minister is appointed by the president of state for a five-year term. In turn the prime minister appoints his deputies and other ministers. Collectively, the government manages state affairs and implements or enforces laws enacted by the National Assembly. The prime minister serves as the supreme commander of the Lao People's Army.

Currently, the prime minister is General Khamtay Siphandone, a former defense minister, ranked number three in the LPRP politburo. General Khamtay is the youngest, now sixty-eight, of the three top-ranked LPRP leaders. He has been slated to succeed Kaysone in the position of state presidency.[29] Khamtay's experience has been exclusively with the military, and his contacts have been limited only to communist countries. He is said to be "reclusive," and it has been widely held that his soldiers have been "involved in the drug trade."[30] In addition, he has little experience with economic affairs.[31]

The Judiciary The judiciary and the judicial process are in general based on the French system of jurisprudence. The 1991 constitution establishes three levels of courts: the People's Supreme Court, the People's Provincial and Municipal Courts, and the District Courts. At the village level, it is the village headman who dispenses justice and resolves disputes. There is also the public prosecutor-general. The president of the People's Supreme Court and the public prosecutor-general are elected by the National Assembly upon recommendation by its standing committee. However, judges for courts at all levels are appointed by the National Assembly.

THE POLITICAL PROCESS: PARTICIPATION, ELECTIONS, AND POLITICAL PARTIES

Cambodia: United Nations Supervision of National Elections

The Electoral Process and Political Parties The last nationwide election in Cambodia took place in 1981, two years after the invading

Vietnamese troops chased the Khmer Rouge regime to the hills, so to speak. That election was orchestrated and controlled by the Kampuchea People's Revolutionary party, now named Cambodian People's party, successor to the Kampuchea Communist party and the Kampuchea People's Revolutionary party. There were 117 seats for the National Assembly and the KPRP monopolized the candidate slate; voter turnout was over 90 percent due to party coercion or strong pressure. A 1986 election for the National Assembly was scheduled, but was postponed.

At the UN negotiations for a peace settlement for Cambodia, Sihanouk, who exercised tight control over legislative elections when he was the authoritarian ruler, insisted on a multiparty election system under UN supervision. As pointed out earlier, the plan that was finally accepted by all four factions and signed on October 23, 1991, by all nineteen nations involved in the negotiations called for proportional representation "with seats distributed among the factions on a province-by-province basis."[32] The proportional representation plan was initially opposed as too premature by Hun Sen, prime minister for the People's Republic of Kampuchea. He preferred that the candidate who obtained the most votes should represent the legislative district, instead of allocating legislative seats on the basis of a percentage distribution among the four factions. In the end the five permanent Security Council members endorsed the proportional representation system for twenty provinces.[33] Under the UN-supervised election, which took place in 1993, the Cambodian People's party, whose membership is about 30,000 with an affiliated membership of 70,000, was in a better position to capture the legislative seats.

The UN-supervised national election was based on universal suffrage; that is, all those over age eighteen born in Cambodia or of Cambodian parentage were able to take part in the national elections for the twenty provinces.[34] This also included the Cambodian refugees returned from camps in Thailand.

The UN-supervised election system permits any political party with 5,000 registered voters to organize and take part in the national elections for the constituent assembly, which would prepare a constitution for Cambodia within three months of the elections. The following major political factions took part in the elections in 1993: the government's Cambodian People's party (CPP), led by Hun Sen for the Vietnamese-installed State of Cambodia regime; the Sihanuok royalists, known as the National United Front for an Independent, Neutral, Peaceful, and Cooperative Cambodia (FUNCINPEC), led by the senior Sihanouk's son, Prince Norodom Ranariddh; the Buddhist group known as the Liberal Democratic Buddhist party (LDBP); and the small Molinaka and Naktaorsou Khmeretor Freedom, an offshoot of the FUNCINPEC. The final popular vote distribution, based on the May 1993 election, and the 120-seat Constituent Assembly seats won by the four major groups were as follows: FUNCIN-

PEC, 45.7 percent of the votes, or 58 seats; CCP, 38.1 percent, or 51 seats; LDBP, 3.8 percent, or 10 seats; Molinaka with 1 seat. It was estimated that about 90 percent of the 4.7 million registered Cambodian voters turned out to take part in the election. The large vote turnout was for the Cambodians a national celebration and an expression of hope for a better future after decades of war and genocide.

The Role of the Military Cambodian armed development involved the formation of non-communist resistance after the Vietnamese invasion of Cambodia in 1978. With help from China, Sihanouk organized his Sihanouk National Army as a guerrilla force of resistance against the invading army. This army was the military arm of Sihanouk's drive for Cambodian independence, a longtime goal of the prince and former head-of-state for Cambodia. At the signing of the United Nations peace plan on October 23, 1991, the Sihanouk National Army claimed to be 20,000 strong. The other component of the non-communist coalition was the Khmer People's National Liberation Front, headed by former prime minister Son Sann, who claimed the strength of its guerrilla force to be at least 14,000.

As pointed out earlier, according to the United Nations peace plan, 70 percent of the armed forces controlled by the four factions, including the existing government in Phnom Penh, must be disbanded under UN supervision. This 70 percent cut includes not only armed personnel, but ammunition and weapons as well for each group or faction. The remaining 30 percent of the armed personnel would be demobilized by the United Nations and their weapons put in storage, so that as Sihanouk, the chairman of the Supreme National Council under the UN peace plan, is quoted to have said: "Nobody is allowed to fight."[35] This means 70 percent of 100,000 Cambodian government forces, plus 50,000 Khmer Rouge fighters (excluding its 50,000 militia) and about 35,000 non-communist coalition forces of Sihanouk and Son Sann for a grand total of about 185,000–200,000 troops in Cambodia. In the past the Chinese have been the major arms supplier for the Khmer Rouge and the Sihanouk fighters. The Chinese announced that they have ceased arms supply to the Khmer Rouge since September 1990.[36] However, in the spring of 1990 there were reports that the Chinese had sent "large new shipments of weapons to Khmer Rouge guerrillas," including "mortars, rifles, rocket-propelled grenades, anti-aircraft machine guns, rocket launchers, 122-millimeter howitzers, 130-millimeter field guns and other heavy artillery."[37] The Chinese also supplied arms to forces under Sihanouk and Son Sann. (In the past the United States had extended covert nonmilitary aid through the CIA, about $20 million per year, to the noncommunist insurgents until the aid was cut by Congress in the fall of 1990.)[38]

The situation following the signing of the UN peace plan seemed to indicate a number of immediate problems facing the UNTAC. One of these was resentment among the soldiers about their uncertain future when demobilization by the United Nations begins in late 1992. Unless training programs can be instituted, which take time and money, the demobilized soldier may "pose a threat to peace" in Cambodia,[39] assuming that the Khmer Rouge would grant the United Nations access to its controlled area for implementing the peace plan.[40]

In conclusion, the UN peacekeeping force will have an enormous task of demobilizing the armed forces controlled by all of the four factions, parties to the Cambodian peace plan. Only time will tell whether this crucial aspect of the peace plan can work, considering the twelve years of civil war waged by these factions in Cambodian politics. After July 1992 military demobilization under the United Nations supervision ran into some serious problems, including continued fighting waged by the Khmer Rouge in capturing a number of villages in northern Cambodia. These sporadic combat activities, involving as many as three Khmer Rouge divisions, were clear violations of the UN peace agreements discussed earlier. However, after the May 1993 election, the Khmer Rouge decided to participate in the provisional constitutional assembly and the new government under Sihanouk. The rebels plan to join a Cambodian national army.

Laos: Monolithic Party Control in the Election Process

The 1989 Election   In the March 1989 national election for the former Supreme People's Assembly there was a voter turnout of 98.4 percent of eligible voters on the basis of universal adult suffrage. There were 121 candidates competing for the 79-seat legislative body that existed before the adoption of the 1991 constitution. The 1989 election was controlled by the LPRP or its front organization, the Lao Front for National Reconstruction, as 70 percent of the candidates were members of the LPRP. Geoffrey C. Gunn has provided the following breakdown of the results of the 1989 national election for the seventy-nine members of the former Supreme People's Assembly:[41] six were from the majority ethnic Lao; nine from Lao Theung, the Khmer-speaking hill tribal people; four from Lao Sung or the Hmong (Meo). Five women deputies, as well as five high-ranking military officers, were elected. Sixty-five of the seventy-nine deputies elected were members of the LPRP. This is not surprising considering only party or front organization members were permitted to canvass votes for candidates.

The One-Party State: The Lao People's Revolutionary Party   The fact remains that there is only one political party, the LPRP, that has dominated Lao politics since 1975. The LPRP operates as the key component of the front organization, which used to be known as the Lao Patriotic Front.

It later reorganized as the Lao Front for National Reconstruction, headed from 1987 to 1990 by Souphanouvong, who recently retired. The organizational structure of the LPRP is essentially Leninist, modeled after the old Indochina Communist party, with a small but tightly knit politburo and a central committee. A large proportion of the party's politburo and central committee members were long-time students of the old Indochina Communist party. It was not until 1982 that the LPRP made its "doctrinal adjustment" from ideological rigidity to that of pragmatism insofar as economic reforms were concerned.[42] In January 1986 the party launched a serious reform within the party in order to provide the needed qualified cadres for implementing economic reforms. In addition, attempts were made, though not very successfully, to decentralize the party-state bureaucracy, improve cadre performance, apply modern managerial techniques, and eliminate waste, greed, and bribery.[43] More significant have been changes made in the party's politburo by adding younger cadres. In the party's Fifth Congress held from March 27 to 29, 1991, a momentous decision was made to retire three senior party leaders, including the "Red Prince" Souphanouvong, who had been active for the past forty years. The Congress also abolished the party's central secretariat in order to "streamline decision making," as well as to reassert the party's control over the provinces.[44]

Total party membership of the LPRP is estimated to be 40,000. There has been public admission by top party leaders that there were weaknesses in the party that included low cadre performance, a bureaucratic working style, and corruption. Purges have been conducted to weed out the unqualified party cadres.

The LPRP is also supported by a host of so-called mass organizations, a sort of transmission belt for the party, such as the Federation of Lao Women, the People's Revolutionary Youth, and the Lao Federation of Trade Unions.

The Role of the Military   The Pathet Lao, at one time the military arm of the Lao Patriotic Front of communists, became the Lao People's Liberation Army in October 1965. In 1969–70 five years before it came into power, its regular strength was estimated at 25,000, augmented by village militia and other guerrilla units to a total strength of 45,000. Its operational base before 1975 was in northern Laos. For years the Lao Liberation Army, or the Pathet Lao, received its support from the North Vietnamese and the Chinese.

Because of its original neutral guerrilla origin, but with heavy dependence on the North Vietnamese and Chinese communist influence, this military establishment in Laos operated on the political commissar system. Only very recently, in 1985, did the LPRP begin to exert more direct control by eliminating the political commissar system. Instead, party committees in the army units at all levels were instituted and strengthened to include "oversight responsibilities" for local affairs at the village level and among the masses.[45] Party cadres in the army were instructed to help fight against corruptive practices such as bribery and theft of public properties. Moreover, the army has been called upon to engage in economic activities such as running civilian industries and agricultural cooperatives.

The Lao Liberation Army is also preoccupied with fighting against the anticommunist Lao resistance movement in northern Laos on the Thai border. There have been persistent reports of government forces using chemical weapons, so-called yellow rain against the resistance guerrillas who are estimated to be more than 10,000 in strength, mostly drawn from the Hmong people.[46]

POLITICAL PERFORMANCE AND PUBLIC POLICY

Cambodia: "Planned Economy with Markets"

Economic Performance As of 1991–92, the state of the Cambodian economy is one of decay and stagnation on the eve of the warring factions' acceptance of the UN Security Council permanent-members-brokered peace plan. The per capita gross domestic product has not been more than $80; the present plan is to raise it to $150. There has been a drastic reduction of Soviet bloc aid and subsidies, which constituted 80 percent of the Cambodian state budget. Inflation has been estimated at 200 percent. There is a flourishing black market in consumer goods coming from Thailand, Taiwan, and Singapore. There is a dire need for investment capital and technology. International nonmilitary aid for 1990 was not more than $20–25 million. Imports (1986) amounted to $17 million, consisting mostly of food aid, fuel, and some consumer goods. Exports (1986) totaled barely $3 million—wood, natural rubber, and rice.[47] Of course, with the arrival of UNTAC to implement the UN peace plan for Cambodia, there would be a significant injection of money into the economy—the cost of the UN peacekeeping operation would be in the neighborhood of $1.5–2 billion.

As of 1986, Cambodia has a long-term debt of $622 million; the bulk of it is owed to the former Soviet Union. The root cause of Cambodia's sad economic state lies in the twelve years of civil war and international isolation.

Economic Reform When the Khmer Rouge ruled Cambodia from 1975 to 1979, its brutal regime carried out the concepts presented in the 1959 doctoral thesis of Khieu Samphan at the University of Paris: there must be collectivization of agriculture and complete nationalization of the economy, more radical than the Chinese or Vietnamese models in their earlier experiments. Private ownership of land was abolished and communism was forcefully implemented without adequate preparation. However, the economy remained in such a poor state that in the late 1970s it was not able to provide the daily ratio of rice for the populace. Then, when the Vietnam troops invaded Cambodia in December 1978, the economy came to a standstill; there was a food crisis in 1979.

The People's Republic of Kampuchea installed by Vietnam under Heng Samrin and his Khmer People's Revolutionary party launched a modified "planned economy with markets" by restoring banks and stressing pay for work performed. A first five-year plan (1986–90) was launched; the plan placed priority on agricultural production of rice and natural rubber farming, and 97 percent of the rural population was organized into 100,000 so-called solidarity groups of fifteen families each.[48] These groups received land that was to be cultivated collectively; the system also permitted private plots for members of the family. However, in practice only a small percentage of these "solidarity groups" functioned well, and the whole system provided no incentives for the peasants. Only in 1989 did the government begin to introduce reforms in the rural areas to consist of hereditary land tenure for individual farming families and raise the purchasing price of rice to be comparable to the free-market price.[49] These measures did not work, as 60 percent of rice procurement was by the state. As explained by Richard Vokes, the peasants began the common practice of hoarding rice as a hedge against a currency decline.[50] Industries, mostly rice mills, were revived after the ouster of the Khmer Rouge in 1979. Other state industries operated below capacity because of a shortage of raw materials and energy. In 1989 the government also announced its plans to transfer state-owned enterprises to private hands, as well as promotion of joint ventures with foreign investors. Vokes listed estimates of 12,300 private business enterprises in Phnom Penh that engaged in food processing, handicrafts, vehicle repairs, retailing, and banking. The only private bank in Cambodia opened in 1991: the Cambodian Commercial Bank, 70 percent owned by Thailand's Siam Commercial Bank and 30 percent by the Cambodian government.[51]

Free-market reform has certainly encouraged overseas Cambodians and foreign concerns doing business in Cambodia. For instance, in 1991 private firms imported about 10,000 tons of oil products each month to compensate for the fuel shortage caused by the drying up of Soviet oil supplies.[52] Foreign investors are beginning to come to Cambodia, since the prospect of civil war has diminished with acceptance of the UN peace plan. For the first six months of 1990 exports with the noncommunist bloc stood at $7 million and imports at $10 million.[53] The government has "tolerated well-organized black market trade" along the Thai border.[54]

Meantime, the most immediate urgent problems are the clearing of land mines that carpeted the country during the wars in Cambodia, and feeding of the returned refugees, estimated by one negotiator at the Paris conference to be more than 66,000 tons of food for the first year.[55]

Education   First some statistics on education as provided by the Ministry of Education:[56] The total general school enrollment in 1988–89 was 1.7 million students. Secondary school enrollment was about 20,000 for the same period. Attendance of school-aged children in 1986–87 was 95 percent. The number of school teachers for the same period was about 45,000 as compared to 5,000 during the Khmer Rouge days in 1979. Phnom Penh University was reopened in March 1988; it had enrolled about 586 students in 1982–83. All these statistics seem to indicate progress as compared to the period of 1975–79, when the Khmer Rouge brutally decimated the intellectual and educated in Cambodia—only 50 of 725 university instructors survived after the "killing fields;" they were the primary target during the wanton destruction of the elites. Many survivors ended up as refugees in border camps in Thailand.

Thus, the educated elites who remained in Cambodia after the ouster of the Khmer Rouge ended up working for the government as salaried public officials or bureaucrats. Sheila Tefft of the *Christian Science Monitor* wrote that some sixty surviving medical doctors are now top officials in the Ministry of Health.[57] The country is now relying on the various UN agencies to draw technical expertise needed to rebuild Cambodia. As UN activities expand and as foreign investments grow, it is not surprising to see these well-educated who are now employed by the government move to higher-salaried positions provided by these agencies. So there is, or is going to be, an internal brain-drain depriving the country of the needed technical personnel for rebuilding Cambodia. Worse still is the lack of trained personnel for the rural villages as workers and youth migrate to the urban areas, particularly to Phnom Penh.

Laos: "The New Thinking"

Economic Performance   Current economic status figures show that Laos, along with Cambodia, is one of the poorest nations in Southeast Asia. Its GNP for 1988, the latest statistics available, was $546 million, and per capita income for the same period was about $156, or not more than $180.[58] In 1990 inflation was about 60 percent.

When the Pathet Lao forces came into full power in 1975, they had no clear idea for a strategy of economic development except adherence to the building of a socialist state in the midst of mounting inflation and rice production failure. The new revolutionary government instituted the familiar programs of nationalization of enterprises; a small industrial base, then owned mostly by the French, Chinese, and Vietnamese; and control of agriculture via forced agricultural cooperatives. These harsh economic measures merely further aggravated the troubled economy as peasant resistance rose against forced agricultural cooperatives and the closing down of wood mill industries. In the late 1970s there was a steady exodus of Laotian refugees to Thailand—a total of 250,000 (about 10 percent) of the entire population.[59] US aid, about $50 million annually (three times the Laotian government budget) was terminated after 1975. Exchange with Thailand, its major trade partner, was interrupted because of tensions and quarreling over disputed borders. The Laotian economy would have collapsed entirely in the late 1970s if there had been no aid from China, the former Soviet Union, and neighboring Vietnam. Since there was a rice production short-fall of over 100,000 metric tons in 1978, the revolutionary government under the LPRP had to abandon its policy of agricultural cooperatives as a means of "a transition to socialism."

Economic Reform The year 1979 has been marked as the beginning of a series of new initiatives, or "new thinking," within the ruling LPRP for the purpose of correcting the ills of the economy by discarding the unwork-able Stalinist economic doctrines. By then communist Vietnam was introduc-ing major economic reforms known as *doi moi*. That reform development, perhaps more than any other, had a decisive influence on thinking at the top echelons of the LPRP's leadership, in particular Kaysone Phomvihan, son of a former Vietnamese civil servant who married an ethnic Lao and who was then prime minister and later became president of the LPDR.

As approved by the Third Congress of the LPRP and included in its first five-year plan (1981–85), economic reform contained several key provisions:[60] First, the state made a commitment to develop all economic sectors including private, mixed, cooperative and state. Second, peasants were permitted to own their land provided they paid taxes—thus decol-lectivization—and the introduction of free-market prices for their prod-ucts in the open market. Third, agricultural cooperatives, as well as state-owned enterprises, must operate on the basis of profit and loss, permitting them to make their own decisions about production and pricing. Finally, foreign investment was encouraged to improve the long stagnant econo-my.

After Kaysone's visit to Moscow, the prime minister and secretary-general of the LPRP announced in December 1985 a new plan for 1986–90, known as the New Economic Management System, for raising the overall economic growth for Laos to a new target of 5 percent. The New Economic Management System, as approved by the party's Fourth Congress in November 1986, called for several reform measures.[61]

One of the goals under the reform was to provide grass roots units such as factories, stores, and cooperatives a large measure of autonomy or "self-mastery" in decision-making areas, such as purchasing of raw materi-als and equipment, investment of funds, production timetable, and consumer demands. Later it was admitted that the autonomy scheme had generated "greed" and other corruptive practices. Also, the New Economic Management System called for changes in the banking system to allow capital formation and to encourage savings by requiring banks to pay interest on deposits. The concept of pricing based on capitalistic supply and demand was also emphasized. So was the introduction of private trading and the contract system to permit workers and cadres to acquire land, animals, and feed. In 1988, as a means of encouraging foreign investment, joint ventures were permitted to become part of the new economic reform—laws were enacted to guarantee the repatriation of profits by foreign investors, and such joint ventures were protected against nationalization. Soon Japanese and U.S. investors were found, in the latter case including the Texas Hunt Oil Company for oil exploration in southeastern Laos. Privatization also included leasing to Thai investors state-owned enterprises for cigarette manufacturing and a sheet-metal plant.[62]

What have been some of the results of economic reforms since 1986? Gunn wrote that by 1989 some 200 formerly centralized firms have been placed under the profit-and-loss managerial basis; in addition, there has been an increase in goods circulation.[63] He reported further that a "quiet revolution" has taken place in the streets and marketplaces in the towns and cities of the Mekong Valley.[64] There were more bicycles, housing projects, and an abundance of imported durable consumer goods. However, another observer comments that while the Lao currency has been stabilized by these reform measures, on the whole life in Laos has not been improved to any significant level.[65] Two areas for attracting foreign investment—mining and tourism—remain to be explored if infrastructure improvements can be made now that Laos has adopted its 1991 constitution.[66] Under the third five-year-plan for 1991–95, emphasis would be on agricultural development with expanded public expenditures and in transport infrastructure improvements. The Australians are financing the construction of a bridge over the Mekong River to connect Vientiane with roads into Thailand.

The reformers are in firm control despite some inner debate over the economic reform as evidenced by the recent leadership reshuffle and the continued stewardship of the LPRP under Kaysone Phomvihan and General Khamtay Siphandone, as discussed earlier.

Education   Despite the enormous disruption of educational development in Laos caused by decades of war, some improvements have been made since 1975. For instance, in 1987–88 general education for the first level had an enrollment of over 683,000 students (68 percent of school-aged children) in some 8,136 schools with over 20,000 teachers.[67] Officially, primary education is supposed to be compulsory for five years for those between ages seven and twelve. UNESCO figures also show that for 1987–88 there were over 6,800 students enrolled in vocational education and over 9,000 in teacher training.[68] However, these educational improvements do not obscure the glaring gap between literate and illiterate in Laos: About 50 percent of the population aged fifteen to forty-five probably cannot read or write; the gap is most likely wider in the rural areas.

Two other problems related to educational development are the low government budget allocations and the need for trained/skilled personnel for economic development. The allotment for 1990 in terms of education allocation was about 5.4 percent of a total estimated government expenditure of $21 million.[69] The other is the exodus of a large number—about 10 percent of the population—of the educated elite who fled to Thailand or to the West.[70]

SUGGESTED READINGS

Cambodia

Chandler, David P. *The Tragedy of Cambodian History: Politics, War, and Revolution since 1945*. New Haven: Yale University Press, 1991.

Esterline, John H., and Mae H. *"How the Dominoes Fell": Southeast Asia in Perspective*. Lanham, MD, and London: Hamilton Press, 1986.

Etcheson, Craig. *The Rise and Demise of Democratic Kampuchea*. Boulder, CO: Westview Press, 1984.

Jackson, Karl D., ed. *Cambodia, 1975–78: Rendezvous with Death*. Princeton: Princeton University Press, 1989.

Muskie, Edmund S. *Exploring Cambodia: Issues and Reality in a Time of Transition*. Washington, DC: University Press of America, 1990.

Picq, Laurence. *Beyond the Horizon: Five Years with the Khmer Rouge*. New York: St. Martin's Press, 1989.

Ross, Russell R., ed. *Cambodia: A Country Study*. Washington, DC: U.S. Department of the Army, 1990.

Sutter, Robert G. *The Cambodian Crisis and U.S. Policy Dilemmas*. Boulder, CO: Westview Press, 1990.

Laos

Esterline, John H., and Mae H. *"How the Dominoes Fell": Southeast Asia in Perspective*. Lanham, MD, and London: Hamilton Press, 1986.

Evans, Grant. *Lao Peasants under Socialism*. New Haven: Yale University Press, 1990.

Fox, Stuart M. *Politics, Economics and Society*. London: Francis Pinter, 1986.

Whitaker, Donald P., et al. *Laos: A Country Study*. Washington, DC: American University Press, 1979.

Zasloff, Joseph L., and Leonard Unger. *Laos: Beyond the Revolution*, New York: St. Martin's Press, 1991.

Conclusion

A Changing Asia
and the Response
of the United States

It used to be fashionable to describe Asia as a continent reluctant to change. But Asia today is undergoing rapid change. One obvious development that has taken place is the relative peace in Asia after the Korean War, the Indochina War, the wars between India and Pakistan on the Indian subcontinent, the Vietnam invasion of Cambodia, the Chinese incursion into Vietnam, and the Soviet invasion of Afghanistan. There is now an ongoing debate among policymakers in the US government, the military, and academic circles over the question of continued U.S. military presence in Asia.[1]

Second, there is no longer an ideological confrontation or contest between the Leninist-socialist system and the capitalist West. The former has failed both as a system and as an appeal in the minds of Asian people, even before the demise of the Soviet Union and the ending of the Cold War, except in China, North Korea, and Vietnam. As has been discussed in the various chapters of this textbook, even in those socialist countries there is now increasing pressure from within, as well as from without, for change and reform. The decline of communist ideological appeal is best manifested by the new economic relationship formed between traditional antagonists such as South Korea and Russia, South Korea and China, China and Taiwan (across the Formosa Strait), and South and North

Korea in their agreement on nonaggression and the ban of nuclear weapons (1991).

There is also a significant change in the power relationship and balance in Asia. Instead of the two superpower hegemony, multipower centers have developed in Asia. There has evolved a gradual "dispersion of power" between five great powers: China, India, Japan, Russia, and the United States, with none in a dominant position.[2] Added to this constellation of powers in Asia is the Association of Southeast Asian Nations (ASEAN), whose original goals were not only regional economic cooperation, but also prevention and management of regional conflicts.[3] The new power balance in post–cold war Asia is said to be more stable partly because four of the nations (China, the United States, Russia, and India) possess nuclear capabilities.[4] A potential threat to that power balance and Asia's stability is the nuclear capability being developed by Pakistan and North Korea.

The most dynamic and one of the more important changes has been the growth of Asian economies. As pointed out in the introduction to this book, the Asian Development Bank is predicting a 1993 gross domestic growth (minus foreign investment) averaging 7.3 percent for Asia's twenty-five developing nations. Post–cold war Asia is not only relatively peaceful, but also "prosperous," as summarized by Michel Oksenberg, a former staff member for the National Security Council under President Jimmy Carter and now president of the Honolulu-based East-West Center.[5] The 1993 World Labor Report, issued by the International Labor Organization, points out that Asia has "a healthy outlook for growth in jobs."[6]

Asia's economic prosperity is the result of the use by many Asian nations of a market economic strategy that includes a host of economic reforms—productivity incentives, privatization of state-run enterprises, and an open door to foreign investments and technology—that have helped to enhance rapid industrialization and the expansion of exports in an increasingly competitive world market. Japan led the march for the so-called economic miracle, and was followed by the new industrialized countries (NICs) of South Korea, Taiwan, Singapore, and Hong Kong. The NICs' success has been the model for Indonesia, Malaysia, and Thailand. Even Deng Xiaoping's economic reform, the so-called Chinese system of market economy and socialistic planning, received its origin, if not its impetus, from the NICs' success. In short, Asian economic growth continues to lead the world.

Equally significant and parallel to the success of market economy in Asia, particularly the NICs, has been the implications of opening doors to Western or foreign investment and technology. This dynamic process has fostered democratic reforms in military-authoritarian regimes such as South

Korea and Taiwan. Or to put it another way, economic growth and prosperity have been the key ingredients needed to pave the way for political changes, which have led to democratization of the military-authoritarian regimes of South Korea and Taiwan.

These changes in Asia, as briefly outlined here, require necessary responses by the new Clinton administration if this country is to meet the challenges of the twenty-first century. Specifically, there are three key areas in which the United States must respond with carefully thought out strategies in the context of a rapidly changing Asia. Collectively these issues constitute the Clinton Asia agenda.

THE ASIAN SECURITY ISSUE AND THE ROLE OF THE UNITED STATES[7]

The Asian security issue in the post–cold war era must be seen in two interrelated perspectives. One is that the U.S. military presence since the end of World War II, in addition to its involvement in the Korean and Vietnam wars, has been a major factor in providing stability in much of Asia. The military threat from China, the former Soviet Union, and/or North Korea has been the basis on which the United States has maintained its military presence and forged alliances in Asia.[8] Many have defended the concept that it has been the U.S. military presence in Asia that has served as the predictable "security environment" (to borrow a term used by Robert A. Scalapino)[9] under which economic change and growth have taken root and ultimately fostered political change in the form of democratization in South Korea and Taiwan. The other perspective is that the post–cold war era has produced relative peace in Asia, which means there is no longer a global military confrontation and competition by superpowers (the United States and Russia).[10] Instead of a continuing military presence in Asia by the only remaining superpower, the United States, there is pressure for reducing its military spending and presence in Asia in order to relieve a budgetary burden.[11] There is also the concept that the American traditional deterrence strategy to contain expansion of communism "no longer represents a guarantee for regional stability"—a contention attributed to a 1990 U.S. Defense Department document.[12]

There is still some concern over the regional instability and uncertainty despite the ending of the cold war in Asia and elsewhere in the world.[13] One area of instability and uncertainty is in East and Northeast Asia, due to the potential threat of North Korea. Recently it manifested its isolation and belligerence with an initial refusal to comply with international inspection under the Non-Proliferation Treaty, to which it is a party; the refusal was subsequently rescinded on June 11, 1993, however. There is continued friction between the United States and China over human rights. There is also uncertainty over Japan's leadership and responsibility in Asia, besides its singlemindedness in the pursuit of economic gains. Rising nationalism in many parts of Asia also constitutes an area of uncertainty as demonstrated by the vote in the Philippine Senate on September 15, 1991, not to renew leasing of the American military base at Subic Bay and Clark Air Force Base.

In South Asia continued Kashmir crises can be a battleground for another Indo-Pakistan war, with a potential for nuclear exchange in the Indian subcontinent. It seemed that so long as the Soviet invasion of Afghanistan endured for much of the 1980s, the United States was rather tolerant of Pakistan's efforts to develop a nuclear capability. In terms of Pakistan's domestic politics, the nuclear program has always been a source of national pride. With the end of the war in Afghanistan and with increased unresolved Kashmir tension, the nuclear issue has strained U.S.-Pakistan relations. A succession of Pakistan leaders have been eager to continue Pakistan's nuclear program, both as a matter of national pride and as a deterrence against India.

In October 1990 President Bush refused to certify that Pakistan "does not possess a nuclear weapon." Thus, under a law enacted by the U.S. Congress, military and economic aid to Pakistan was suspended. The aid was crucial for a financially strapped Pakistan because 42 percent of the nation's revenue needed to be set aside for debt reduction, on top of 39 percent for defense.[14]

Threats to Southeast Asian security most likely would be intraregional: rivalry between Vietnam and Thailand, besides peaceful settlement for Cambodia, maritime Southeast Asia's concern over protection of the Malaysian-Indonesia archipelago, in addition to competing claims for the Spratly and Paracel Islands in the South China Sea between China, Vietnam, Brunei, Malaysia, the Philippines, and Taiwan. As pointed out by Richard F. Ellings and Edward A. Olsen in their study, for the region as a whole, national and regional interests can become more confrontational than global concerns, which interest the United States.[15] In some instances it will be difficult to distinguish friends from foes in these national and intraregional conflicts. Scalapino also points out that in Northeast Asia the "security environment" in the post–cold war era will mean that nations in the subregion must ask the question, "Who is the enemy?"[16] This may be illustrated by Singapore's potential military confrontation with Malaysia.

Tension has always existed between the two neighbors despite the emphasis for cooperation under the regional framework of ASEAN. Much of the rationale behind Singapore's "Total Defense" strategy has been the need to develop deterrence to military threat from Malaysia. Singapore was infuriated by the Malaysian and Indonesian joint military exercise in Johore in July 1991, which was followed by the crash of two Singapore fighter planes in Johore. Thus, in the midst of closer economic relations there have been frictions between Malaysia and Singapore that might involve military intervention by either of the two neighbors.[17] In such a case Singapore might make a swift advance by seizing Johore, on which the city-state depends for its water supply.[18]

There is also another view on the probability of Malaysia-Singapore military confrontation: that "periodic low-intensity tension" between the two neighbors "is more apparent than real," and that the two nations "are prone to exploiting them for their own domestic political purposes."[19] There has been closer economic cooperation between Malaysia and Singapore—for instance, the formation in recent years of the Johore-Singapore Joint Committee on Business Cooperation—which in the future would most likely reduce suspicion and misunderstanding to enable both to feel more secure and comfortable toward each other. Then there is also the 1971 Five Power Defense Arrangement (FPDA), which provides a protective shield for the security of Malaysia and Singapore, pledged by the United Kingdom, Australia, and New Zealand in addition to the two neighbors. Under the arrangement there have been frequent joint air and naval exercises involving Malaysian and Singaporean military units.

There are a number of options available to the Clinton administration in its response to the challenges posed by the changing Asian security issue discussed here.

One alternative is to continue the three-phase withdrawal plan contained in the 1990 Department of Defense report, "The East Asia Strategic Initiative," mentioned earlier—a phased pull-out dictated by budgetary considerations and "diminishing superpower competition."[20] This alternative also calls for reliance on the mutual security pact with Japan and the latter's willingness to participate in "burden sharing."

As suggested by William T. Tow, a second alternative for Asian security, particularly for East and Northeast Asia, would be the formation of a "multilateral collaborative system" involving China, Japan, Russia, and the United States "to underwrite a series of confidence-building measures leading to eventual Korean unification."[21]

A third alternative could be the development of the concept for "common security modeled on the European experiences," as advocated by Geoffrey Wiseman.[22] The concept rests on "the development of a defensive orientation of military forces and the adoption of nonthreatening strategies."[23] In applying the "common defense security concept" to the Korean peninsula, there would need to be control of arms buildup, and improvement in political climate and stability through a bilateral relationship. Or, as applied to the six-nation dispute over the Spratly Islands in the South China Sea, the service of Indonesia as a "broker" may produce "regional cooperation rather than confrontation" based on community interests.[24]

Wiseman's common security concept leads to the alternative of placing more emphasis on regionalization of defense in Southeast Asia revolving around the regional organization ASEAN. Sheldon W. Simon argues that there is a need to emphasize "the subregionalization of security arrangements based on traditional national concerns over territorial integrity and ethnic integration."[25] In this sense, ASEAN would be a "security community" that stresses stability and security and it need not be "the base for wider military collaboration" or a Southeast Asian NATO.[26] Simon's views are shared by Amitar Acharya, who argues that ASEAN needs to be strengthened as a "security community" for the original major goals are "to prevent, manage and resolve conflicts in the region."[27]

There is still another strategic alternative for the U.S. role in Asian security: It is "the engaged balancer strategy" advocated by Ellings and Olsen.[28] The strategy calls for the United States to (1) "bolster the nations' technological, industrial and financial competitiveness"; (2) effect "maintenance of an array of bilateral ties with Asian countries with a preference for leading ad hoc coalitions...to meet threats"; (3) place Asia's economic challenges as a priority by establishing "strong ties with all the major countries of Asia and by remaining a leader—usually in coalitions—in matters of economic relations, politics and security." What the United States must do in the strategy as the "engaged balancer" is to maintain a "significant maritime presence, with air and ground support" in the region.[29]

ARMS BUILDUP AND ARMS SALES BY ASIAN NATIONS

Related to the issue of Asian security is the arms buildup in the region despite the end of the global cold war and the reduction of tension in Asia. The rate of arms buildup has been greater in East-Northeast than in Southeast Asia as measured by the combined 1990 defense budgets of Japan, China, Taiwan, and North and South Korea, which were five times higher than the major Southeast Asian states.[30] For instance, China has increased its military spending by more than 13 percent per year since 1988. Military spending increases are also found for Japan, North Korea,

Taiwan, Singapore, Pakistan, and India. Reasons for the buildup may include the Asian nations' perception of American withdrawal of its military presence in Asia; fear of the Chinese military entering the competing maritime and territorial claims for the Spratly and Paracel Islands in the resource-rich South China Sea; fear of Japanese military resurgence; the need on the part of Asian coastal nations to protect their 200-mile Exclusive Economic Zones (EEZs) under the 1982 Law of the Sea Convention; and the opportunity for hard currency-rich Asian nations to take advantage of the large post–cold war era stockpiling of weapons eager to be disposed of by many European nations, particularly the cash-strapped Russians.[31]

There is also an arms race in East Asia, which generated "35 percent of all major weapons purchases in 1991."[32] China is reported to have sold its new missiles (M-11) to Pakistan even though the former gave assurances to the Bush administration that it would not sell such weapons. At the same time, China was very upset over Bush's fall 1992 decision to sell F-16 fighters and the French sale of Mirage 2000 to Taiwan. And the Chinese have been buying advanced (MIG-31) arms from the Russian suppliers. In turn, China has been the major supplier of ballistic missiles to Third World nations, including the secret transfer of intermediate range CSS missiles to Saudi Arabia.

The Clinton administration will have to formulate some workable policy or strategy that could place arms sales in Asia under control, including U.S. arms sales. One possible action might be institution of an enforceable and effective registration system, as once suggested by former Japanese prime minister Kaifu, that would keep track of arms sales and imports by nations.[33] The Clinton administration can take a leadership role in this direction through the mechanism provided by the UN Security Council's sixteen-member Missile Technology Control Regime (MTCR). The United States can provide the needed leadership in persuading Asian nations, particularly those in East Asia, to participate in new regional arms control arrangements.

TRADE WITH ASIA: COOPERATION AND COMPETITION

The American trade pattern with Asia can be seen by the following statistics summary: In 1991 it exported $122 billion goods to Asia, about 25 percent of total U.S. exports; America imported $195 billion goods from Asia, which constituted about 40 percent of all American imports. U.S. trade with Asian nations is also troublesome because of America's continuous unfavorable trade pattern: The trade deficit with Japan reached over $50 billion in 1990–91, with China over $20 billion, and with Taiwan over $19 billion. The focus of America's chief complaint has been trade friction with Japan. For some time the solution to unbalanced trade with Japan has been the protectionist stance. Only in 1990–91 did a trade policy shift with Japan from confrontation to cooperation take place. U.S.-Japan trade frictions focus on three problem areas: the size of the U.S. trade deficit with Japan, the composition of bilateral trade, and the matter of access to Japan markets restricted by trade barriers.

The 1989 U.S.-Japan trade deficit represented about 45 percent of the total U.S. deficit. For 1989 U.S. exports to Japan had increased from the previous year of $37.7 billion to $44.6 billion and thus reduced the deficit by about $6 billion. But these figures do not detract from the enormous size of the U.S. trade deficit with Japan, over $50 billion for 1991. The size of the trade deficit has been the source of tension in U.S.-Japan relations. The total volume of Japan's imports reached $127 billion for 1986, using available figures for that year as an example for discussion here. Since Japan must import almost 99 percent of its oil, $38 billion of Japan's imports for 1986 was for energy imports or about 30 percent in terms of the total import value. The remaining $89 billion of Japan's imports for 1986 was for machinery, chemical products, metals, textiles, wood, and animal products. Again using the available figures for that year for discussion purposes, the total volume of Japan's exports for 1986 amounted to about $220 billion.[34] Over 60 percent of Japan's exports for 1986 was made up of automobiles, heavy machinery, electrical machinery (including electronics), and iron and steel. About 20 percent of the total exports was passenger cars. Japan's total trade surplus in recent years has been about $90–95 billion.[35] One other point that needs to be made in discussing the composition of U.S.-Japan trade is that Japan is still the largest importer of American farm products. Japan could buy these agricultural items elsewhere perhaps at a lower price. But it chooses not to do so now in order to protect its exports to the United States.

How to force the Japanese to open their domestic markets to U.S. products has been the key objective in American trade negotiation with Japan in recent years. For years American firms have made the standard complaint that the Japanese government, through bureaucratic "administrative guidance," has erected rules, regulations, and practices augmented by its Byzantine distribution system controlled by the conglomerates, which have made it difficult for any outsider to enter into Japanese markets. American companies complained that as a result of these unfair trade practices, fostered by the various bureaucratic ministries such as MITI, markets for telecommunications equipment, supercomputers, and satellites are closed to competitive American firms. The United States has demanded that Japan lower its trade barriers on U.S. products such as lumber and wood, which carry a tariff of 20 percent. Japan has steadfastly maintained its ban on rice imports in order to protect their domestic rice growers, a segment of the powerful National Farmers' Association, an interest group with 40,000 members who have been politically strong supporters of the LDP. Japanese consumers pay four to eight times the world price for the rice they consume. The American beef industry has objected for years to Japan's yearly quota on beef imports, which in 1988–89 was limited to about 141,000 tons.

Frustration over Japan's reluctance to open its domestic markets to American products and the mounting trade deficit with Japan in recent years have led to Japan bashing and cries for launching a trade war against Japan's protectionism. These pressures have led to intense yearly bilateral trade negotiations, which in the past two years have produced some concessions from Japan—concessions obtained only under the threat of applying sanctions by the United States, as authorized under the 1988 Omnibus Trade and Competitiveness Act. Under Section 301, known as "Super 301," sanctions could be imposed by the United States against an unfair trade partner. In 1989 the United States cited Japan for unfair trade practices in forest products (timber and lumber), satellites, and supercomputers. It demanded resolution on these and some food products or the alternative of facing sanctions against Japanese imports to, and limitation of Japanese investment in, the United States. Regarding the continuing U.S. complaints about Japan's monopolistic distribution system and the lack of open access to domestic markets, in the fall of 1989 the United States proposed the structural impediments initiative (SII) and began talks with Japan to correct "the economic imbalances" in U.S.-Japan relations.[36] It is also a goal of the United States to resolve issues of protection of intellectual property (patents and copyrights for technological inventions) and access to Japanese construction contracts, microelectronics, software, and advanced computer designs.[37] By early May 1990 the negotiations had reached agreement on three major issues. The Japanese government will buy supercomputers on the basis of both performance and price as determined in the private sector, not at a discount to the government as practiced in the past. Supercomputers must be tested and delivered on time under an agreed-on bidding system. (The Japanese government's yearly purchase of supercomputers has amounted to over $100 million.)[38] Construction of government procured satellites will now be open to the most advanced American aerospace industries in competition with domestic satellite builders in Japan.

Access to Japanese markets for American food products has improved since 1988. There have been agreements pledged by Japan to phase out import quotas on American-made processed food, fruit juice products, pineapples, dairy products such as frozen yogurt and ice cream, processed cheese, ketchup, and syrups. MITI has promised to expand Japanese imports and eliminate tariffs on 1,004 items with a projected trade surplus reduction of about $3 billion from $81 billion in 1989 to $78 billion in 1990.[39]

While there has been definitely some improvement in U.S.-Japan trade relations in the past two years, there have been some criticisms about the impact on long-range trade relations between the two nations. One critic points out that Japan must view the access to markets as a mutual benefit to the two nations, rather than simply a matter of concessions.[40] There should be more concessions by Japan for American services in Japan, such as bond underwriting, insurance and information—areas where there is more political clout from the interest groups. In these areas outside pressures must be applied to "coerce" change.[41] Other experts have considered the results under the "structural impediments initiative" as nothing but "trade charades."[42]

During the 1990 U.S.-Japan trade negotiation sessions Japanese negotiators presented to the United States a list of eighty policy suggestions on how to improve the U.S. economy.[43] One piece of advice was that the United States curb excessive consumption by restricting the use of credit cards, as well as tax exemptions for home mortgages. U.S. counterproposals included the raising of public spending by the Japanese government to 10 percent of its GNP and the repeal of the law that made it hard to open large department stores in Japanese urban areas. The United States has been in favor of implementation of restructuring the Japanese economy contained in the 1986 report prepared by Haruo Maekawa, the former governor of the Bank of Japan.[44] The Maekawa report recommended less emphasis on export as a major feature of Japan's economic growth, and more attention on meeting critical domestic demands such as housing.[45]

While current U.S.-Japan trade negotiations have been concentrating on removal of trade barriers discussed here, the long-range objective to some observers ought to be to lay a foundation of free and reciprocal trade relations between the two nations. The idea of a free-trade pact, comparable to the U.S.-Canada trade agreement, was discussed by former U.S. ambassador Mike Mansfield during former prime minister Takeshita's visit to the United States in January 1988. A skeptical view is that the free-trade pact is not a good idea because removal of trade barriers by Japan is not enough if nothing is done to change "the symbiotic relationship between government and business (including administrative guidance), the tight net relationship between affiliated companies in *keiretsu* groups, and the multi-layered and exclusive distribution system."[46] Japanese attitudes such as Japan's imperative to export, superiority of Japanese products and the uniqueness of Japan also contribute to this skepticism.[47] If a free reciprocal trade pact between Japan and the United States is not attainable or does not work in reality, then the ultimate alternative would be what James Fallows has suggested: the containment of Japan.[48] Fallows feels it would be necessary to impose limits on Japan's economy and industrial growth:

> Unless Japanese society changes fundamentally, it is hard to imagine that Mitsubishi, Matsushita and Dai-Ichi Kangyo Bank, or any of Japan's other great power centers will ever share their power with non-Japanese.[49]

Fallows argues that in a head-on competition, the "capitalist developmental states" would win.[50] However, it must be pointed out that the structural impediments initiative talks in the fourth round in April 1990 produced several concessions from Japan—these concessions were obtained only after Prime Minister Kaifu's hard battle with the bureaucratic ministries:[51] price reduction for domestic consumption to comparable competitive international pricing; exemption of urban centers from the application of the Big Stores Law by 1992 to permit foreign competition; promotion of personal consumption by relaxing rules on credit cards; increased fines against illegal cartels by revising the antimonopoly law by 1991; and a promise from Japan to review laws relating to the formation and practices of *keiretsu*, or conglomerates, in market and trading domination.[52]

However, the strained U.S.-Japan trade relationship means more than obtaining more trade concessions from the Japanese or South Korea or Taiwan. The challenge posed by Asia in economic relations is for the United States to improve and sharpen its "industrial and technological competitiveness" in the decades ahead, as urged by Ellings and Olsen.[53] Scalapino offers the same view that "the greatest challenge may come in the economic arena," and for both the United States and Japan the strategy must be to strengthen the global bargaining session under the General Agreements on Tariff and Trade (GATT).[54] He also urged that the U.S. strategy must be designed "to keep regional economic organizations accessible to all."[55] Yet this nation paid little attention to the newest regional organization, the Asia-Pacific Economic Cooperation (APEC) when it first convened in November 1989 in Australia.[56] Thus, the appropriate approach for the United States to meet the Asian challenge is both competitiveness and cooperation. The approach will be essentially multilateral rather than bilateral.

In short, the U.S. response to the overall Asian challenge is to find new ways of achieving cooperation and avoiding confrontation in solving security and economic problems. The United States must place priority on the development of an integrated multilateral security and economic policy toward a rapidly changing Asia. The Clinton administration's hosting of the Seattle APEC Forum conference in November 1993 was a positive step toward the multilateral and cooperative approach needed in dealings with Asia. The APEC conference revealed clearly that Asian nations are more self-confident than ever, and expect the United States to be less dominant and more cooperative in its dealings with Asia.

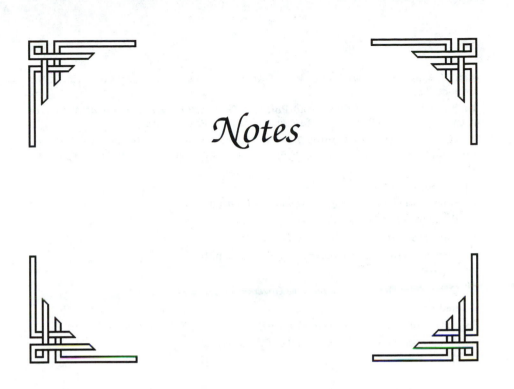

Notes

INTRODUCTION

1. Rolf H. W. Theen and Frank L. Wilson, *Comparative Politics: An Introduction to Six Countries* (Englewood Cliffs, NJ: Prentice Hall, 1986), p. 3.

2. Gabriel Almond and Bingham Powell, Jr., *Comparative Politics Today: A World View* (New York: Little, Brown, 1974), p. 2.

3. Ibid., p. 3.

4. Ibid.

5. Thomas M. Magstadt, *Nations and Governments: Comparative Politics in Regional Perspective* (New York: St. Martin's Press, 1991), p. 4.

6. Ibid., p. 6.

7. Michael Curtis, *Introduction to Comparative Government*, 2nd ed. (New York: Harper & Row, 1990), p. 2.

8. Ibid.

9. Almond and Powell, *Comparative Politics Today*, pp. 33–146.

10. Magstadt, *Nations and Governments*, pp. 6–7.

11. The list includes some of the works cited here: Magstadt, *Nations and Governments*, pp. 293–363; Curtis, *Introduction to Comparative Government*, pp. 269–325, 397–465, 469–517; Theen and Wilson, *Comparative Politics*, pp. 425–511; David Roth and Frank Wilson, *The Comparative Study of Politics* (Boston: Houghton Mifflin, 1976), pp. 35–49, 131–14, 179–85, 225–40, 287–300, 331–40; Almond and Powell, *Comparative Politics Today*, pp. 381–434; and Gabriel Almond and Bingham Powell, Jr., *Comparative Politics: Systems, Process, and Policy*, 2nd ed. (Boston and Toronto: Little, Brown and Company, 1978), pp. 25–76, 108–140, 232–280, 283–321.

12. C. I. Kim and Laurence Ziring, *An Introduction to Asian Nations* (Englewood Cliffs, NJ: Prentice Hall, 1977).

13. Lucian Pye, Asian Power and Politics: *The Cultural Dimensions of Authority* (Cambridge, MA: Belknap Press of Harvard University Press, 1985).

14. Gary Gereffi and Donald L. Wyman, *Manufacturing Miracles: Paths of Industrialization in Latin-America and East Asia* (Princeton: Princeton University Press, 1990).

15. Magstadt, *Nations and Governments*.

16. Almond and Powell, *Comparative Politics Today*, p. 42.

17. David Easton, *A System of Analysis of Political Life* (New York: Wiley, 1965).

18. Almond and Powell, *Comparative Politics Today*, p. 54.

19. Roth and Wilson, *Comparative Study of Politics*, p. 161.

20. Ibid.

21. Curtis, *Introduction to Comparative Government*, pp. 17–18.

22. Ibid., p. 17.

23. David Truman, *The Government Process*, 2nd ed. (New York: Knopf, 1971).

24. Almond and Powell, *Comparative Politics Today*, p. 71.

25. Ibid.

26. Ibid., pp. 72–73.

27. See James C. F. Wang, *Chinese Contemporary Politics: An Introduction*, 4th ed. (Englewood Cliffs, NJ: Prentice Hall, 1992), p. 209; and Roth and Wilson, *Comparative Study of Politics*, p. 200.

28. Almond and Powell, *Comparative Politics Today*, pp. 85, 86.

29. Roth and Wilson, *Comparative Study of Politics*, pp. 319–32. Also see Eric A. Nordinger, "Soldiers in Mufti: The Impact of Military Rule upon Economic and Social Change in the Non-Western States," *American Political Science Review* 64 (December 1970): 1132–33.

30. Theen and Wilson, *Comparative Politics*, p. 26.

31. Ibid.

32. James R. Townsend, "Politics in China," in *Comparative Politics Today: A World View*, Gabriel Almond and Bingham Powell, Jr. (New York: Little, Brown, 1974), p. 407.

CHAPTER 1

1. *Hawaii Tribune-Herald*, 4 October 1981, p. 9.

2. *Beijing Review*, 31 (3 August 1981), pp. 4–5.

3. Shan-yu Yao, "The Chronological and Seasonal Distribution of Flood and Droughts in Chinese History, 206 B.C.–A.D. 1911," *Harvard Journal of Asiatic Studies* 7 (1942): 275.

4. John Fairbank, *The United States and China*, (New York: Viking Press, 1962), p. 48.

5. For China's 1982 population census, see "The World's Biggest Census," *Beijing Review*, no. 32 (9 August 1982), p. 16; "The 1982 Census Results," Beijing Review, no. 45 (8 November 1982), pp. 20–21; and "Report on the Sixth Five-Year Plan," p. 18.

6. "1982 Census Results," p. 20; and "Report on the Sixth Five-Year Plan," p. 181.

7. "Report on the Sixth Five-Year Plan," p. 18.

8. See Michele Vink, "China's Draconian Birth Control Program Weighs Heavily on Its Women," *Asian Wall Street Journal Weekly*, 23 November 1981, pp. 1, 21.

9. See Jeffrey Wasserstrom, "Resistance to One Child Family," *Modern China* 10, no. 3 (July 1984): 345–72.

10. See Joyce K. Kallgren, "Politics, Welfare, and Change: The Single Child Family in China," in *The Political Economy of Reform in Post-Mao China*, ed. Elizabeth Perry and Christine Wong (Council of East Asian Studies/Harvard University), p. 151.

11. Wang Wee's statement in an interview in *Honolulu Star-Bulletin*, 17 August 1984, p. A-4.

12. *Christian Science Monitor*, 18 February 1987, p. 8.

13. See *Honolulu Advertiser*, 31 July 1987, p. A-21.

14. For results of 1990 census, see *Beijing Review*, nos. 17–23 December 1990, p. 27.

15. See Edwin O. Reischauer, *The United States and Japan*, 3rd ed. (New York: Viking Press, 1965), pp. 54–55; and Reischauer, *The Japanese* (Cambridge, MA: Belknap Press of Harvard University Press, 1978), pp. 4–5.

16. Ping-ti Ho, "Salient Aspects of China's Heritage," in *China in Crisis*, vol. 1, bk. 1, ed. Ping-ti Ho and Tang Tsou (Chicago: University of Chicago Press, 1968), p. 17.

17. "The Correct Concept of Individual Role in History," *People's Daily*, 4 July 1980, p. 1.

18. Charles Fitzgerald, *Revolution in China* (New York: Holt, Rinehart and Winston, 1952), p. 23.

19. Kung-chuan Hsiao, *Rural China: Imperial Control in the Nineteenth Century* (Seattle: University of Washington Press, 1960), pp. 253–54.

20. Lucian Pye, *China: An Introduction*, 2nd ed. (Boston: Little, Brown, 1972), p. 68.

21. Ibid., p. 71; and Fairbank, United States and China, p. 103.

22. Fred Hung, "Some Observations on Confucian Ideology," in *Moving a Mountain: Cultural Changes in China*, ed. Goodwin C. Chu and Francis L. K. Hsu (Honolulu: University Press of Hawaii, 1979), p. 423.

23. Kuang Yaming, "Appraisal of Confucius; Why? How?" *Beijing Review*, no. 22 (30 May 1983), pp. 22–24.

24. "Creating a New Situation in All Fields of Socialist Modernization," *Beijing Review*, no. 37 (13 September 1982), p. 21.

25. Franklin Houn, *A Short History of Chinese Communism* (Englewood Cliffs, NJ: Prentice Hall, 1967), p. 159.

26. George B. Sansom, *History of Japan, 1615–1867* (Stanford: Stanford University Press, 1963); and Sansom, *Japan: A Short Cultural History* (New York: Appleton-Century-Crofts, 1962).

27. Reischauer, *The Japanese*, p. 60.

28. Ibid., p. 61.

29. Ibid., p. 71.

30. Frederica A. Bunge and Donald P. Whitaker, eds., *Japan: A Country Study* (Washington, DC: U.S. Government Printing Office, 1983), p. 72.

31. Karel van Wolferen, *The Enigma of Japanese Power: People and Politics in a Stateless Nation* (New York: Knopf, 1989), p. 52.

32. Ibid., pp. 52, 165.

33. For more detailed discussion, see Frank Langdon, *Politics in Japan* (Boston: Little, Brown, 1967), pp. 76–82.

34. van Wolferen, *Enigma of Japanese Power*, p. 314; and Bunge and Whitaker, *Japan*, pp. 75–76.

35. For an interesting discussion of consensus as a myth, see van Wolferen, *Enigma of Japanese Power*, pp. 337–39.

36. Langdon, *Politics in Japan*, p. 74; and Reischauer, *The Japanese*, pp. 134–135.

37. Bunge and Whitaker, *Japan*, pp. 75–76.

38. Reischauer, *The Japanese*, pp. 146–48.

39. Laurence W. Beer, "Group Rights and Individual Rights in Japan," *Asian Survey* 21, no. 4 (April 1981): 439–45.

40. Ibid., p. 413.

41. See van Wolferen, *Enigma of Japanese Power*, p. 256.

42. Robert E. Ward, *Japan's Political System*, 2nd ed. (Englewood Cliffs, NJ: Prentice Hall, 1978), p. 11.

43. Ibid., p. 14.

44. C. I. Eugene Kim and Laurence Ziring, *An Introduction to Asian Politics* (Englewood Cliffs, NJ: Prentice Hall, 1977), p. 21.

45. Ibid., p. 573.

46. van Wolferen, *Enigma of Japanese Power*, pp. 381–82. The studies on the subject are to be found in Nakamura Takafusa, *Economic Growth in Prewar Japan* (New Haven: Yale University Press, 1983); and Mark R. Peattie, *Ishiwara Kanji and Japan's Confrontation with the West* (Princeton: Princeton University Press, 1975).

47. Ward, *Japan's Political System*, p. 19.

48. Reischauer, *The Japanese*, p. 103.

49. See Hans H. Baerwald, *The Purge of Japanese Leaders under the Occupation* (Berkeley: University of California Press, 1959), p. 59; van Wolferen, *Enigma of Japanese Power*, p. 349; *The Far East in the Modern World*, p. 614; Ward, *Japan's Political System*, p. 22.

50. van Wolferen, *Enigma of Japanese Power*, p. 390.

51. See Franze Michael and George Taylor, *Far East in the Modern World*, 3rd. ed. (Hinsdale, Illinois: The Dryden Press, 1975), p. 617.

52. See Mark Gayn, "Drafting the Japanese Constitution," in *Postwar Japan: 1945 to the Present*, ed. Jon Livingston et al. (New York: Pantheon Books, 1973), p. 20; Ward, *Japan's Political System*, p. 22.

53. See "Deputies to the 6th NPC," *Beijing Review*, no. 22 (30 May 1983), p. 5.

54. "Investigating the Causes of Oil Rig Accident," *Beijing Review*, no. 31 (4 August 1980), p. 7.

55. "The Present Economic Situation and the Principles for Future Economic Construction," *Beijing Review*, no. 51 (21 December 1981), p. 4.

56. Donald Klein, "The State Council and the Cultural Revolution," *The China Quarterly* 35 (July–September 1968): 78–95. Also see John P. Burns, "Reforming China's Bureaucracy, 1979–1982," *Asian Survey* 23, no. 6 (June 1983): 707–14.

57. A. Doak Barnett, Cadres, *Bureaucracy, and Political Power in Communist China* (New York: Columbia University Press, 1967), pp. 3–17.

58. Parris Chang, *Power and Politics in China* (University Park and London: Pennsylvania State University Press, 1974), p. 50.

59. Ibid., pp. 63–64, 106–08; and also see A. Doak Barnett, *Uncertain Passage: China's Transition to the Post-Mao Era* (Washington, DC: Brookings Institution, 1974), pp. 136–43.

60. Byron Weng, "Some Key Aspects of the 1982 Draft Constitution of the People's Republic of China," *The China Quarterly* 91 (September 1982): 492–506.

61. Deng once told Oriana Fallaci that he was purged for the first time in 1932 for lending his support to Mao in the inner-party struggle against the Moscow-trained returned Chinese group led at that time by Wang Ming. See "Deng: Cleaning Up Mao's Feudal Mistakes," *The Guardian*, September 21, 1980, p. 16.

62. Chang, "The Last of Deng's Revolution,"*Journal of Northeast Asian Studies*, vol. 1, no. 2, 1982, p. 6. Also see Michael Ng-Quinn, "Deng Xiaoping's Political Reform and Political Order," *Asian Survey* 22, no. 12 (December 1982): 1187–1205. Also see "Man of the Year: The Comeback Comrade," *Time*, 6 January 1986, pp. 42, 45; and Harrison E. Salisbury, "The Little Man Who Could Never Be Put Down," *Time*, 30 September 1985, pp. 54–57.

63. See Chang, "Chinese Politics: Deng's Turbulent Quest," Problems of Communism, xxx (January–February 1981), pp. 1–21, and "The Last of Deng's Revolution," *Journal of Northeast Asian Studies,* vol. 1, no. 2, June 1982, pp. 5–6; "A Speech at the Enlarged Meeting of the Politburo of the Central Committee," *Issues and Studies* 17, no. 3 (March 1981): 81–103; "Important Speech by Deng Xiaoping to the 1980 December 25 Central Work Conference," *Ming Pao Daily* (Hong Kong), 3–8 May 1981; and "Text of Deng Xiaoping's Speech at the Great Hall of People on January 16, 1980," *Ming Pao Daily* (Hong Kong), 2–4 March 1980. Also see Suzanne Pepper, "Can the House that Deng Built Endure?" *Asian Wall Street Journal Weekly*, 10 August 1981, p. 10; Fox Butterfield, "The Pragmatists Take China's Helm," *New York Times Magazine*, 28 December 1980, pp. 22–31; and Lowell Dittmer, "China in 1980: Modernization and Its Discontents," *Asian Survey*, vol. xx, no. 1, January 1981, pp. 31–42, and "China in 1981," *Asian Survey*, vol. xxi, no. 1, 1982, pp. 33–45.

64. Information on criticism about Li Peng is culled from the following: *Zhengming* (Hong Kong), no. 105 (July 1986), pp. 9–10; and no. 123 (January 1988), pp. 6–10; *Christian Science Monitor*, 25 November 1987, pp. 7–8; *Asian Wall Street Journal*, 25 November 1987, pp. 1, 13; *Ming Pao Daily* (Hong Kong), 16 November 1987, p. 1, and 7 November 1987, p. 12; and *Far Eastern Economic Review*, 10 September 1987, pp. 46–47.

65. See *Beijing Review*, no. 14 (6 April 1987), p. 14.

66. *Ming Pao Daily* (Hong Kong), 2 January 1988, p. 1.

67. *Renmin Ribao*, overseas ed., 25 November 1987, p. 1.

68. Information about Jiang is culled from *Zhengming* (Hong Kong), no. 141 (July 1989), pp. 6–7; no. 142 (August 1989), pp. 9–10; no. 148 (February 1989), p. 10; no. 155 (September 1990), pp. 8–9; *Far Eastern Economic Review* 23 (November 1989): 10–11; *Beijing Review*, 10–16 July 1989, pp. 21–22; *New York Times*, 25 June 1989, pp. A4-A6; 30 June 1989, p. A-4; *Wall Street Journal*, 26 June 1989, p. A-7; *China News Analysis*, no. 1394 (1 October 1989), pp. 109; and *Wen Hai Pao* (Hong Kong), 4 July 1989, p. 1.

69. *Zhengming* (Hong Kong), no. 142 (August 1989), p. 10.

70. *Zhengming* (Hong Kong), no. 141 (July 1989), p. 7.

71. *Zhengming* (Hong Kong), 28 June 1989, p. 1.

72. *Zhengming* (Hong Kong), no. 155 (September 1990), pp. 8–9.

73. See James C. F. Wang, *Contemporary Chinese Politics*, (Englewood Cliffs, NJ: Prentice Hall, 1980), p. 119. Also see Hong-Yung Lee, "Deng Xiaoping's Reform of the Chinese Bureaucracy," *Journal of Northeast Asian Studies* 1 (June 1982): 21–35. John Burns put the total cadres in China at 27 million; see his article "Chinese Civil Service Reform: The 13th Party Congress Proposal," *The China Quarterly*, no. 120, December 1989, p. 740.

74. Text of Chen Yun's speech at the CCP Central Committee Work Conference in *Issues and Studies* 16 (April 1980): 82.

75. *Ming Pao Daily* (Hong Kong), 7 July 1981, p. 1.

76. "Create a New Situation in All Fields of Socialist Modernization," *Beijing Review*, July 16–22, 1970, p. 36.

77. Ibid.

78. Peng Zhen, "Report on Work of NPC Standing Committee," *Beijing Review*, no. 39 (29 September 1980), pp. 24–25.

79. See Melanie Manion, "The Cadres Management System, Post-Mao: The Appointment, Promotion, Transfer and Removal of Party and State Leaders," *The China Quarterly* 102 (January 1985): 203–33.

80. Ibid., p. 233.

81. *People's Daily*, overseas ed., 3 February 1986, p. 1.

82. Ibid.

83. Ibid.

84. "Reforming the Cadres System," *Beijing Review*, no. 9 (1 March 1982), p. 3.

85. "Veteran Cadres Retire," *Beijing Review*, no. 7 (15 February 1982), p. 5.

86. Ibid.

87. *People's Daily*, overseas ed., 19 February 1986, p. 1.

88. See editorial in *Renmin Ribao*, 7 August 1980.

89. *Ming Pao Daily* (Hong Kong), 14 August 1981, p. 3.

90. *Ming Pao Daily* (Hong Kong), 18 August 1981, p. 1.

91. "Economic Criminals Surrender," *Beijing Review*, no. 17 (19 April 1982), pp. 7–8.

92. "Decision on Combating Economic Crimes," *Beijing Review*, no. 17 (16 April 1982); and *Hongqi*, no. 4 (16 February 1982), p. 8.

93. "Senior Cadres Support Sentences on Their Criminal Sons," *Beijing Review*, no. 20 (17 May 1982), p. 5.

94. See *China Daily*, 31 July 1986, p. 1. Also see an earlier report from *China Daily*, 10 July 1986, p. 2.

95. *Ming Pao Daily* (Hong Kong), 6 April 1980, p. 3. Translation is by this author.

96. Fox Butterfield, *China: Alive in the Bitter Sea*, (New York: Time Books, 1982), pp. 217–88; and Richard Bernstein, *From the Center of the Earth: The Search for the Truth about China*, (Boston, Little Brown and Co., 1982), pp. 104, 131, 134, 136–37, 140, for anecdotes to illustrate how Chinese bureaucracy works.

97. "A Speech at the Enlarged Meeting of the Politburo, August 18, 1980," in *Issues and Studies* 23, no. 3 (March 1981): 88; also see *Ming Pao Daily* (Hong Kong), 14 February 1982, p. 3.

98. See Frank Pestana, "Law in the People's Republic of China," *Asian Studies Occasional Report*, 1 (Tempe: Arizona State University, June 1975), p. 2; Victor Li, "The Role of Law in Communist China," *The China Quarterly* 44 (October–December 1970): 70–110; and George Gingurgs and Arthur Stahnake, "The People's Procuratorate in Communist China: The Institutional Ascendant, 1954–1957," *The China Quarterly* 34 (April–June 1968): 82–132.

99. Gingurgs and Stahnake, "People's Procuratorate," pp. 90–91.

100. For more information about China's criminal code and procedure, see *Beijing Review*,

no. 33 (17 August 1979), pp. 16–27; *Beijing Review*, no. 23 (9 June 1980), pp. 17–26; *Beijing Review*, no. 44 (3 November 1980), pp. 17–28; Hungdah Chiu, "China's New Legal System," *Current History* 459 (September 1980): 29–32; Fox Butterfield, "China's New Criminal Code," New York Times Service, as reprinted in *Honolulu Star-Bulletin*, 20 July 1979, p. A-19; Takashi Oka, "China's Penchant for a Penal Code," *Christian Science Monitor*, 3 September 1980, p. 3; and Stanley B. Lubman, "Emerging Functions of Normal Legal Institutions in China's Modernization," *China under the Four Modernization: Pt. 2. Selected Papers*, U.S. Congress, Joint Economic Committee (Washington, DC: U.S. Government Printing Office, 30 December 1982), pp. 235–85.

101. Chiu, "China's New Legal System," p. 32.

102. Ibid., p. 31.

103. John M. Maki, *Government and Politics in Japan: The Road to Democracy* (New York: Praeger, 1962:), pp. 86, 112–14. For other analyses of the role of the emperor, see Ward, *Japan's Political System*, pp. 147–48; Samson, *Japan*, pp. 86–88, 266–67; Bunge and Whitaker, *Japan*, pp. 250–51; Reischauer, *The Japanese*, pp. 244–48; and van Wolferen, *Enigma of Japanese Power*, pp. 322–25.

104. For a glimpse of Akihito's life and style, as well as his upbringing, see Edwin D. Reischauer, *The Japanese* (Cambridge, MA: The Belknap Press of Harvard University Press, 1977), p. 248.

105. See Daniel Sneider, "Stock Scandal Enmeshes Japan's Diet," *Christian Science Monitor*, 22 February 1989, p. 4

106. Maki, *Government and Politics in Japan*, pp. 100–102.

107. For information about the Recruit scandal, see the following media accounts: Urban C. Lehner, "Japan Recruits a Scandal," *Asian Wall Street Journal*, 8–9 December 1988, p. 10; *Wall Street Journal*, 13 February 1989, p. 1; *New York Times*, 25 April 1989, p. A-1, and 29 June 1989, p. A-1; *Newsweek*, 8 May 1989, p. 35. Also see Yayama Taro, "The Recruit Scandal: Learning from the Causes of Corruption," *The Journal of Japanese Studies* 16, no. 1 (Winter 1990): 93–114.

108. See *New York Times*, 9 August 9, 1989, p. A-1; *Christian Science Monitor*, 30 August 1989, p. 1; and *Wall Street Journal*, 9 August 1989, p. A-8.

109. *Christian Science Monitor*, 24 August 1989, p. 19; and *New York Times*, 9 August 1989, p. A-6.

110. Ward, *Japan's Political System*, p. 159.

111. Nathaniel B. Thayer, *How the Conservative Rule Japan* (Princeton: Princeton University Press, 1969), p. 191.

112. John Endicott and William R. Heaton, *The Politics of East Asia: China, Japan, and Korea* (Boulder, CO: Westview Press, 1978), pp. 179, 300 (fn. 30).

113. Ward, *Japan's Political System*, p. 158.

114. Peter P. Cheng, "The Japanese Cabinet, 1885–1973: An Elite Analysis," *Asian Survey* 14, no. 12 (December 1974): 1056.

115. See John Woodruff, "Takeshita Reshuffles His Cabinet," *Baltimore Sun*, as reprinted in Honolulu Advertiser, 29 December 1988, p. A-14.

116. For an interesting analysis of Kaifu's cabinet reshuffle, see *Far East Economic Review*, 8 March 1990, pp. 9–10. Also see *The Japan Times*, 12–18 March 1990, pp. 1, 4.

117. Chalmers Johnson, *MITI and the Japanese Miracle: The Growth of Industrial Policy, 1925–1975* (Stanford, CA: Stanford University Press, 1982), pp. 20–21.

118. van Wolferen, *Enigma of Japanese Power*, pp. 33, 309.

119. Ward, *Japan's Political System* 1980, p. 1.

120. van Wolferen, *Enigma of Japanese Power*, pp. 33, 309.

121. Ibid., p. 114

122. Information on the Japanese judiciary are culled from the following sources: *Japan's Political System*, pp. 171–173; John E. Endicott and William K. Heaton, *The Politics of East Asia*, pp. 181–183; *Japan*, pp. 178–184; *Government and Politics in Japan*, pp. 105–108; *Japan: A Country Study*, pp. 262–264; *The Japanese*, pp. 263–266; *The Enigma of Japanese Power*, pp. 207–226; and Mark Davies West, "The Japanese Legal System: Why Many Americans Fail," *Journal of Northeast Asian Studies*, vol. viii, no. 1, Spring 1989, pp. 20–38.

123. *The Enigma of Japanese Power*, p. 216.

124. Ibid., pp. 219–220.

125. Ibid., p. 220

126. *Japan: A Country Study*, p. 263.

127. *Japan's Political System*, p. 173.

128. *The Enigma of Japanese Power*, pp. 218–219; *Politics in Japan*, p. 182; and *Government and Politics in Japan*, p. 105.

129. *The Enigma of Japanese Power*, p. 214.

130. Ibid.

131. Ibid., pp. 221–222.

132. Ibid., pp. 223–224.

133. *The New York Times*, 29 June 1989, A-4.

134. See Jack Gray and Patrick Cavendish, *Chinese Communism in Crisis: Maoism and the Cultural Revolution* (New York: Holt Rinehart and Winston, 1958); and John W. Lewis, *Leadership in Communist China* (Ithaca, NY: Cornell University Press, 1963), p. 70.

135. Article 27 of "The Constitution of the PRC," *Beijing Review*, no. 25, 27 December 1982, p. 15.

136. See Fox Butterfield, *China: Alive in the Bitter Sea*, pp. 421–422. Laing Heng subsequently left China for the United States with his wife, Judy Shapiro. They wrote a biography, *Son of the Revolution* (New York: Knopf, 1983).

137. "Election at the County Level," *Beijing Review*, no. 5, 1 February 1982, p. 18. Also see Brantly Womack, "The 1980 County-Level Elections in China: Experiment in Democratic Modernization," *Asian Survey*, xxii, 3, March 1982, pp. 261–277.

138. For Chinese coverage of recent elections, see "Election of Deputies to a County People's Congress," *Beijing Review*, no. 8, 25 February 1980, pp. 11–19; no. 18, 4 May 1981, p. 5; and no. 5, 1 February 1982, pp. 13–19.

139. "Election of Deputies to a County People's Congress," p. 14.

140. Ibid., pp. 16–17.

141. Brantly Womack, "The 1980 County-Level Elections in China: Experiment in Democratic Modernization," *Asian Survey*, xxii, 3, March 1982, p. 269.

142. See Parris Chang, *Power and Policy in China* (University Park, PA and London: The Pennsylvania State University Press, 1974), p. 184.

143. *Renmin Ribao*, 1 March 1977 and *Ming Pao Daily* (Hong Kong), 3 March 1977, p. 3.

144. *Survey of Chinese Mainland Press*, no. 4097, 11 January 1968, pp. 1–4.

145. "Resolution on the Convening of the 12th Party Congress," *Beijing Review*, no. 10, 10 March 1980, p. 11.

146. Lo Bing, "Inside View of the Elections at the 12th Party Congress," *Zhengin ing* (Hong Kong), 60, October 1982, p. 7.

147. Houn, *A Short History of Chinese Communism*, p. 93.

148. Zhao Ziyang, "Create a New Situation in All Fields of Socialist Modernization," pp. 11–40.

149. Franklin Houn, *A Short History of Chinese Communism*, p. 87.

150. See Article 3 of "The Constitution of the Communist Party of China: Adopted by the 12th Party Congress of the CCP on September 6, 1982," in *Beijing Review*, no. 38, 20 September 1982, p. 11.

151. Franklin Houn, *A Short History of Chinese Communism*, p. 89.

152. Board of Directors, China, Inc.," *Far Eastern Economic Review*, 2 September 1977, p. 9.

153. "The Central Committee's Secretariat and Its Work," *Beijing Review*, no. 19, 11 May 1981, p. 21.

154. David Lampton, "New 'Revolution' in China's SocialPolicy," *Problems of Communism*, 22, September–December 1979, p. 30.

155. Christopher Howe, *Pattern and Wage Politics in Modern China, 1919–1972* (Cambridge University Press, 1973), pp. 50–51; and Martin King Whyte, "Inequality and Stratification in China," *The China Quarterly*, no. 64, December 1975, pp. 684–711.

156. *Beijing Review*, no. 43, 24 October 1983, pp. 23–25.

157. *Beijing Review*, no. 40, 2 October 1982, p. 8.

158. David M. Lampton, "New 'Revolution' in China's Social Policy," pp. 28–29.

159. Martin Wilbur, "Military Separatism and the ProcCs of Reunification under the Nationalist Regime, 1922–1937," in *China in Crisis*, vol. 1, bk. 1 ed. Ping-ti Ho and Tang Tsou (Chicago: University of Chicago Press, 1968), p. 203.

160. Ibid., p. 203

161. Ibid.

162. Kent. E. Calder, *Crisis and Compensation*, p. 298.

163. *The Japanese*, p. 270.

164. Curtis, *Introduction to Comparative Government*, 2nd ed., p. 294.

165. Calder, *Crisis and Compensation*, p. 493.

166. See Gerald L. Curtis, *Election Campaigning Japanese Style* (New York and London: Columbia University Press, 1971), pp. 214–215.

167. Ibid., p. 216.

168. Ibid., pp. 219–220.

169. See *Time*, 24 April 1989, p. 39.

170. See Yayama Taro, "The Recruit Scandal: Learning from the Causes of Corruption," *The Journal of Japanese Studies*, vol. 16, no. 1, Winter 1990, pp. 93–114.

171. *The New York Times*, 9 August 1989, A-6; and *The Christian Science Monitor*, 24 August 1989, p. 19.

172. *The New York Times*, 25 April 1989, A-4.

173. See the article by David E. Sanger of *The New York Times* as reprinted in *The Honolulu Star-Bulletin*, 14 October 1989, A-9. Also see *Far Eastern Economic Review*, 19 October, 1989, p. 25.

174. *The Japanese*, p. 272.

175. For an earlier, but fuller, discussion on Koenkai, see works by Nathaniel B. Thayer, *How the Conservatives Rule Japan* (Princeton, NJ: Princeton University Press, 1969), pp. 88–110; and Curtis, *Election Campaigning Japanese Style*, pp. 126–151. A brief discussion is also found in Reischauer's *The Japanese*, pp. 273–274. Also, see discussion of Koenkai in Frank Langdon's *Politics in Japan*, pp. 127–132. For an up-to-date discussion see *The Enigma of Japanese Power*, pp. 56–57, 117 and 131; and Calder, *Crisis and Compensation*, pp. 64–69.

176. Curtis, *Election Campaigning Japanese Style*, p. 128.

177. van Wolferen, *Enigma of Japanese Power*, p. 131.

178. Calder, *Crisis and Compensation*, p. 64.

179. Curtis, *Election Campaigning Japanese Style*, p. 136.

180. The quote is from Calder, *Crisis and Compensation*, pp. 64–65.

181. Basic information on the Liberal Democratic party is culled from these sources: Ward, *Japan's Political System*, pp. 88–95; Endicott and Heaton, *The Politics of East Asia*, (Boulder, CO: Westview Press, 1978), pp. 191–203; Maki, *Government and Politics in Japan*, pp. 160–65; Langdon, *Politics in Japan*, pp. 132–38; Reischauer, *The Japanese*, pp. 279–85; Bunge and Whitaker, *Japan*, pp. 275–88; van Wolferen, *Enigma of Japanese Power*, pp. 139–46; and Bill Emmott, *The Sun Also Sets: The Limits to Japan's Economic Power*, (New York: Time Books, Random House, 1989), pp. 42–44, 216–19.

182. See Murray Sayde, "The Party's (Almost) Over," *Far Eastern Economic Review*, 10 August 1989, p. 19.

183. Ward, *Japan's Political System*, p. 90.

184. *Asahi Shinbun*, 25 July 1989.

185. Calder, *Crisis and Compensation*, pp. 193–95.

186. van Wolferen, *Enigma of Japanese Power*, p. 133.

187. Ibid., p. 445 (fn. 58).

188. *Far Eastern Economic Review*, 22 February 1990, p. 11.

189. Ibid., pp. 11–12.

190. Maki, *Government and Politics in Japan*, p. 165.

191. Calder, *Crisis and Compensation*, p. 490.

192. Kazuo Nukazawa (managing director of Keidauren), "LDP Must Face up to the Future," *Asian Wall Street Journal*, 19 July 1989, p. A-10.

193. *Far Eastern Economic Review*, 7 September 1989, p. 23.

194. *Far Eastern Economic Review*, 21 September 1989, p. 12. For a brief background of JSP factions, see Endicott and Heaton, *Politics of East Asia*, pp. 205–08; and Chae-Jin Lee, "The Japanese Socialist Party and China, 1975–1977," *Asian Survey* 18, no. 3 (March 1978): 275–89.

195. See Lee, "Japanese Socialist Party and China," p. 280.

196. Ibid., p. 289.

197. Jooinn Lee, "Komeito: Sokagakkai-ism in Japanese Politics," *Asian Survey* 10, no. 6 (June 1970): 504.

198. Ibid., p. 507.

199. George M. Beckmann and Okubo Genji, *The Japanese Communist Party*, 1922–1945 (Stanford, CA: Stanford University Press, 1969), pp. 47–49.

200. See John K. Emmerson, "The Japanese Communist Party after Fifty Years," *Asian Survey* 12, no. 7 (July 1972): 565–67.

201. *Far Eastern Economic Review*, 21 December 1989, p. 26. Also see Larry A. Niksch, "Japanese Defense Policy: Suzuki's Shrinking Options," *Journal of Northeast Asian Studies* 1, no. 2 (June 1982): 80–83.

202. See Niksch, "Japanese Defense Policy," pp. 83–85. Also see Martin E. Weinstein, "Japan's Defense Policy and the May 1981 Summit," *Journal of Northeast Asian Studies* 1, no. 1 (March 1982): 23–33, and his *Japan's Postwar Defense Policy, 1947–1968* (New York: Columbia University Press, 1971).

203. Niksch, "Japanese Defense Policy," pp. 87–88.

204. See Katsuro Sakoh, "Japan, Defend Itself," *Asian Wall Street Journal*, 30 March 1987, p. 6.

205. Ibid.

206. *Christian Science Monitor*, 3 August 1989, p. 7.

207. Ibid.

208. See *Christian Science Monitor*, 13 September 1989, p. 4; and *New York Times*, 6 March 1989, p. A-1. Also see Hisahiko Okazaki, *A Grand Strategy for Japanese Defense* (New York: University Press of America, 1986), pp. 75–100; and Allen S. Whiting, *China Eyes Japan* (Berkeley: University of California Press, 1989), pp. 41–79.

209. For the published summary of the poll undertaken jointly by Asahi Shinbun and the Louis-Harris Organization on Japanese and American public opinion concerning Japan's military buildup, see *The Strait Times*, 30 May 1990, p. 4.

210. *Beijing Review*, no. 44 (2–8 November 1992).

211. *Far Eastern Economic Review*, 14 May 1992, p. 63.

212. Ibid.

213. *People's Daily*, 23 February 1992, p. 1. Also see an analysis by the *New York Times*, 24 February 1992, p. A-1.

214. See Thomas Bernstein, "Reforming Chinese Agriculture: The Consequences of Unanticipated Consequences," *China Business Review*, May–April 1985, p. 46.

215. Ibid., p. 52.

216. Jonathan Unger, "The Decollectivization of the Chinese Countryside: A Survey of Twenty-eight Villages," *Pacific Affairs*, vol. 58, no. 4 (Winter 1985–86), p. 594.

217. Ibid., p. 599. Also see *Beijing Review*, no. 44 (29 October 1984), p. vi.

218. Jan Prybyla, "China's Economic Experiment," *Asian Survey*, xxix, (November 1989), p. 34.

219. *Beijing Review*, no. 34 (24 August 1987), p. 4.

220. Prybyla, "China's Economic Experiment," p. 34.

221. Ibid., p. 38.

222. Ibid., p. 37.

223. *Beijing Review*, no. 52 (29 December 1986), p. 18.

224. Ibid.

225. *Christian Science Monitor*, 5 December 1991, p. 8.

226. Ibid. Also see *Wall Street Journal*, 8–9 January 1993, pp. 1, 3.

227. *Beijing Review*, no. 47 (24 November 1986), p. 14.

228. *Beijing Review*, no. 29 (21 July 1986), p. 4.

229. *Beijing Review*, no. 23 (10 June 1985), p. 16.

230. Ibid. Also see Austin Swanson and Zhang Zhian, "Education Reform in China," *Phi Delta Kappan*, January 1987, pp. 373–78.

231. *Wall Street Journal*, 19 March 1990, p. A-11.

232. Ibid.

233. *Business Week*, 7 August 1989, p. 51.

234. See at least two of the more popular books on Japanese management theories: William Ouchi, Theory Z: *How American Business Can Meet the Japanes Challenge* (New York: Addison Wesley, 1980); and Richard T. Pascale and Anthony G. Athose, *The Art of Japanese Management: Applications for American Executives* (New York: Warner Books, 1982).

235. See Chalmers Johnson, MITI and the Japanese Miracle; Clyde V. Prestowitz, Jr., *Trading Places: How We Allowed Japan to Take the Lead* (New York: Basic Books, 1988); and van Wolferen, *Enigma of Japanese Power*.

236. Ezra E. Vogel, *Japan as Number One: Lessons for America* (Cambridge, MA: Harvard University Press, 1979).

237. T. J. Pempel, "The Unbundling of 'Japan, Inc.': The Changing Dynamics of Japanese Policy Formation," *Journal of Japanese Studies* 13, no. 2 (Summer 1967): 271. The term was first popularized in Eugene J. Kaplan, *Japan: The Government-Business Relationship* (Washington, DC: U.S. Department of Commerce, 1972).

238. See "Lesson from Japan, Inc.," *Newsweek*, 8 September 1980, p. 63.

239. Johnson, *MITI and the Japanese Miracle*.

240. Ibid., p. 18.

241. Ibid., p. 27.

242. Ibid., p. 19.

243. Vogel, *Japan as Number One*.

244. Prestowitz, *Trading Places*.

245. Daniel Burstein, *Yen! Japan's New Financial Empire and Its Threat to America* (New York: Fawcett Columbine, 1990).

246. James Fallows, "Containing Japan," *The Atlantic Monthly*, May 1989, pp. 40–54.

247. van Wolferen, *Enigma of Japanese Power*, pp. 44–47.

248. Information about MITI is culled from the following sources: Johnson, *MITI and the Japanese Miracle*, pp. 3–26, 157–274; James C. Abegglen and George Stalk, Jr., Kaisha: *The Japanese Corportion* (New York: Basic Books, 1985), pp. 260–88; van Wolferen, *Enigma of Japanese Power*, pp. 109–58; Vogel, *Japan as Number One*, pp. 70–79; Calder, *Crisis and Compensation*, pp. 122–23, 154; Prestowitz, *Trading Places*, pp. 107–21; Pempel, "The Unbundling of 'Japan, Inc.,'" pp. 271–306; Michael Smith, Jane McLoughlin, Peter Lange, and Rod Chapman, *Asia's New Industrial World* (New York: Methuen, 1985); and Ravi Sarathy, "Japanese Trading Companies: Can They Be Copied?" *Journal of International Business Studies* 16, no. 2 (Summer 1985): 101–19.

249. Johnson, *MITI and the Japanese Miracle*, p. 194, and Appendix B on pp. 332–38.

250. Ibid. p. 26

251. Smith et al., *Asia's New Industrial World*, p. 18.

252. Ezra Vogel provides a detailed, but less critical, list of what MITI can do for the Japanese industries; see his *Japan as Number One*, pp. 70–79.

253. Abegglen and Stalk, *Kaisha*, p. 128.

254. Pempel, "The Unbundling of 'Japan, Inc.,'" pp. 281–91; and Daniel I. Okimoto, *Between MITI and the Market: Japanese Industrial Policy for High Technology* (Stanford, CA: Stanford University Press, 1990).

255. Ibid.

256. See Calder, *Crisis and Compensation*, p. 314. Also see Abegglen and Stalk, *Kaisha*.

257. van Wolferen, *Enigma of Japanese Power*, p. 171.

258. Prestowitz, *Trading Places*, p. 156.

259. Ibid., p. 157, and van Wolferen, *Enigma of Japanese Power*, p. 46.

260. Prestowitz, *Trading Places*, p. 157.

261. Ibid., p. 158.

262. Ibid., p. 160; and also see Bruce R. Scott, John W. Rosenblum, and Audrey T. Sproat, *Case Studies in Political Economy* (Cambridge, MA: Harvard Business School, 1980), pp. 229–30.

263. Prestowitz, *Trading Places*, pp. 161–62.

264. See *Far Eastern Economic Review*, 10 May 1990, p. 44.

265. van Wolferen, *Enigma of Japanese Power*, p. 46.

266. Ibid., p. 47.

267. Ibid.

268. *Time*, 6 October 1986, p. 66.

269. A study made by the University of Michigan is quoted in ibid.

270. *Far Eastern Economic Review*, 14 June 1984, p. 83.

271. Ibid.

CHAPTER 2

1. See Gary Gereffi and Donald L. Wyman, *Manufacturing Miracles: Path of Industrialization in Latin-America and East Asia* (Princeton: Princeton University Press, 1990), pp. 139–72.

2. See James C. F. Wang, *Handbook on Ocean Politics and Law* (New York: Greenwood Press, 1992), p. 198.

3. *Asia 1991 Yearbook* (Hong Kong, BCC: Review Publishing Company, Limited, 1991), p. 7.

4. Figure is taken from Robert Elegant, *Pacific Destiny: Inside Asia Today* (New York: Crown, 1990), p. 22.

5. Information about Japan's rule in Korea is culled from: Hilary Conroy, *The Japanese Seizure of Korea* (Philadelphia: University of Pennsylvania Press, 1961).

6. Dae-Sook Suh, *Kim Il-Sung: The North Korean Leader* (New York: Columbia University Press, 1988), pp. 55–60; Ilpyong J. Kim, *Communist Politics in North Korea* (New York: Praeger, 1967); Yuk-Sa Li, ed., *The Speeches and Writings of Kim Il Sung* (New York: Grossman, 1972); Robert A. Scalapino and Chong-Sik Lee, *Communism in Korea*, 2 vols. (Berkeley: University of California Press, 1972); and Koon Woo Nam, *The North Korean Communist Leadership, 1945–1965: A Study of Factionalism and Political Consolidation* (Tuscaloosa: University of Alabama Press, 1974).

7. Gregory Henderson, *Korea: The Politics of the Vortex* (Cambridge, MA: Harvard

University Press, 1968); Soon-Sung Cho, *Korea in World Politics, 1940–1950* (Berkeley: University of California Press, 1967); Joung Won A. Kim, *Divided Korea: The Politics of Development, 1945–1972* (Cambridge, MA: East Asian Research Center, Harvard University, 1975); Frederica M. Bunge, *South Korea: A Country Study* (Washington, DC: U.S. Department of the Army, 1982); Ralph N. Clough, *Embattled Korea: The Rivalry for International Support* (Boulder, CO, and London: Westview Press, 1987).

8. See Laurence Ziring and C. I. Eugene Kim, *The Asian Political Dictionary* (Santa Barbara, CA: ABC-CUO, 1985), p. 41. Also see their book *An Introduction to Asian Politics* (Englewood Cliffs, NJ: Prentice Hall, 1977), pp. 353–89.

9. See Clough, *Embattled Korea*, pp. 8–10.4.

10. John F. Copper, *Taiwan: Nation-State or Province?* (Boulder, CO: Westview Press, 1990), p. 17.

11. Ibid., p. 24.

12. Ibid., pp. 26–27.

13. *Far Eastern Economic Review*, 19 March 1992, p. 30; and the issue of 27 February 1992, pp. 48–49, on how historians rediscover the story of the massacre. In a different account of the February 28 tragedy, which seemed to absolve the KMT of responsibility, see Lai Tse-lian, Raymon H. Myers, and Wei Wou, *The Tragic Beginning: The Taiwan Uprising of February 28, 1947* (Stanford, CA: Stanford University Press, 1992).

14. *Far Eastern Economic Review*, 19 March 1992, p. 30.

15. For details, see James C. F. Wang, *Contemporary Chinese Politics: An Introduction, 4th ed.* (Englewood Cliffs, NJ: Prentice Hall, 1991), pp. 338–43.

16. Ibid., pp. 344–46.

17. See Young Whan Kihl, *Politics and Policies in Divided Korea: Regimes in Contest* (Boulder, CO, and London: Westview Press, 1984), pp. 81–85.

18. See *New York Times*, 1 January 1990, p. A-3; and *Far Eastern Economic Review*, 11 January 1990, pp. 8–9. Also see *Asian Wall Street Journal*, 2 January 1990, p. A-1.

19. *Far Eastern Economic Review*, 26 July 1990, p. 13.

20. *New York Times*, 6 February 1990, p. A-3.

21. See Copper, Taiwan, p. 56; and Ray S. Cline and Hundah Chiu, eds., *The United States Constitution and Constitutionalism in China* (Washington, DC: U.S. Global Strategy Council, 1988).

22. See Andrew J. Nathan, *China's Crisis: Dilemmas of Reform and Prospects for Democracy* (New York: Columbia University Press, 1990), p. 131.

23. See the story in *Asian Wall Street Journal*, 8 April 1991, p. 1.

24. See *Far Eastern Economic Review*, 18 June 1992, p. 23.

25. Ibid. Also see *Far Eastern Economic Review*, 26 March 1992, pp. 8–9.

26. Copper, *Taiwan*, p. 62.

27. *Far Eastern Economic Review*, 17 October, 1991, pp. 26–27.

28. See article by Lu Ya-li, professor of political science at National Taiwan University, that appeared in *Asian Wall Street Journal*, 2 April 1990, p. 8. For possible bargains with the KMT rightwing, see *Far Eastern Economic Review*, 22 February 1990, pp. 10–11.

29. See *New York Times*, 1 May 1991, p. A-6. Also see *Far Eastern Economic Review*, 9 May 1991, pp. 8–9.

30. *Far Eastern Economic Review*, 28 May 1992, pp. 18–19.

31. *Far Eastern Economic Review*, 29 August 1991, p. 15. Also see the issue of 8 March 1990, pp. 8–9.

32. Ibid.

33. Ibid.

34. Copper, *Taiwan*, p. 65.

35. Ibid., p. 64.

36. Kihl, *Politics and Policies in Divided Korea*, p. 18.

37. Ibid. p. 17.

38. Results of the survey in Chong Lim Kim and Young Whan Kihl, "The 1973 Korean Survey of the Constituents and Local Notables," are to be found in Kihl, *Politics and Policies in Divided Korea*, pp. 110–14.

39. Information about the 1988 parliamentary election is culled from Hong Nack Kim, "The 1988 Parliamentary Election in South Korea," *Asian Survey* 29, no. 5 (May 1984): 480–95; and Chan Woo Park, "The 1988 National Assembly Election in South Korea: The Ruling Party's Loss of Legislative Majority," *Journal of Northeast Asian Studies* 7, no. 3 (Fall 1988): 59–74.

40. Park, "1988 National Assembly Election in South Korea," p. 61.

41. Ibid. And also see B. C. Koh, "The 1985 Parliamentary Election in South Korea," *Asian Survey* 25, no. 9 (September 1985): 883–97.

42. See C. I. Eugene Kim and B. C. Koh, eds., *Journey to North Korea: Personal Perceptions* (Berkeley: University of California Institute of East Asia Studies, 1983), as summarized in Kihl, *Politics and Policies in Divided Korea*, p. 114.

43. Kihl, *Politics and Policies in Divided Korea*, p. 86

44. Ibid., p. 87.

45. Ibid., p. 272 (n. 11).

46. *Far Eastern Economic Review*, 25 January 1990, p. 22.

47. See *Far Eastern Economic Review*, 26 February 1987, pp. 86–88.

48. *Asia 1990 Yearbook* (Hong Kong, BCC: *Review Publishing Company, Limited*, 1989), p. 7.

49. *Asian Wall Street Journal*, 20 February 1990, p. 1.

50. Ibid.

51. Figures are from *Far Eastern Economic Review*, 9 May 1991, p. 45.

52. Ibid., p. 46.

53. See *Far Eastern Economic Review*, 14 March 1991, pp. 23–24.

54. Ibid., p. 23.

55. Ibid., pp. 25–26.

56. Ibid., pp. 30–31.

57. *New York Times*, 14 October 1989, p. 3.

58. See *Far Eastern Economic Review*, 12 November 1992, pp. 20–22.

59. Information on the 1991 election is culled from: *Far Eastern Economic Review*, 9 January 1992, p. 28; Jurgen Domes, "Taiwan in 1991: Searching for Political Consensus," *Asian Survey* 30, 1 (January 1992): 46–49; *Christian Science Monitor*, 24 December 1991, p. 4; *New York Times*, 21 December 1991, p. A-4; *Asian Wall Street Journal*, 23 December 1991, pp. 1, 7.

60. *New York Times*, 21 December 1991, p. 4.

61. *Christian Science Monitor*, 20 December 1991, p. 6. Also see Lu Ya-li, "A More Progressive Taiwan Goes to the Polls," *Asian Wall Street Journal*, 21 December 1991, p. 10.

62. See *Far Eastern Economic Review*, 9 January 1992, p. 28; and Domes, "Taiwan in 1991," p. 47.

63. *Far Eastern Economic Review*, 9 January 1991, p. 28.

64. See Hung-mao Tien, "Social Change and Political Development in Taiwan," in *Taiwan in a Time of Transition*, ed. Harvey Feldman, Michael Y. M. Kau, and Ilpyong J. Kim (New York: Paragon House, 1988), p. 13.

65. *Asia 1991 Yearbook*, p. 9.

66. Tien, "Social Change and Political Development in Taiwan," p. 12.

67. Ibid.

68. See Dennis Van Vranken Hickey, "American Technological Assistance, Technology Transfers and Taiwan's Drive for Defense and Self-Sufficiency," *Journal of Northeast Asian Studies* 12, no. 3 (Fall 1989): 45.

69. As admitted by Taiwan's defense minister in November 1988, quoted in ibid., p. 48.

70. Ibid.

71. *Far Eastern Economic Review*, 4 June 1992, pp. 18–19.

72. *New York Times*, 24 September 1991, p. A-5.

73. See *The Far East and Australia, 1990*, 21st ed. (London, U.K.: Europa Publications, Limited, 1990), p. 543. Also see *Business Week*, 13 May 1991, p. 111.

74. *Worldmark Encyclopedia of the Nations: Asia and Oceania*, vol. 4 (New York: Worldmark Press and Wiley, 1988), p. 201.

75. "South Korea in 1990," *Asian Survey* 31, no. 1 (January 1991): 68–69.

76. Ibid.

77. *Christian Science Monitor*, 26 May 1989, p. 9.

78. See Leroy Jones and Il Sakong, *Government, Business and Entrepreneurship in Economic Development: The Case of Korea* (Cambridge, MA: Harvard University Press, 1980), p. 150.

79. Paul N. Kuznets, "Government and Economic Strategy in Contemporary South Korea," *Pacific Affairs* 58, no. 1 (Spring 1985): 49.

80. The term is used by Kuznets in ibid., p. 49. For argument against the linkage or correlation between economic success and authoritarian regime, see William Dick, "Authoritarian Approaches to Economic Development," *Journal of Political Economy*, no. 82 (1974): 819.

81. Kuznets, "Government and Economic Strategy in Contemporary South Korea," pp. 49–50.

82. Ibid., p. 53. Also, for an insightful analysis of economic policy development in South Korea under Park, see the recently published volume, which contained essays by some of the policymakers during Park's rule: Lee Jay Cho and Yoon Hyung Kim, eds., *Economic Development in the Republic of Korea: A Policy Perspective* (Honolulu: East-West Center, University of Hawaii Press, 1991).

83. See *Far Eastern Economic Review*, 1 March 1990, pp. 46–50; "Korea's Powerhouses Are under Siege," *Business Week*, 20 November 1989, pp. 52, 55. Also see *Far Eastern Economic Review*, 13 May 1993, pp. 64–70.

84. *Business Week*, 20 November 1989, p. 52.

85. *Far Eastern Economic Review*, 1 March 1990, pp. 46–47; and *Business Week*, 20 November 1989, p. 52. Also see *Far Eastern Economic Review*, 16 May 1991, pp. 73–74.

86. *Far Eastern Economic Review*, 1 March 1990, pp. 48–49.

87. Ibid.

88. Ibid., p. 47.

89. *Far Eastern Economic Review*, 15 January 1987, pp. 30–31, and 18 July 1985, pp. 65–67.

90. The figure is taken from the article by Yuan-li Wu, "Taiwan in the Regional Economy of the Pacific Basin," in *Taiwan in a Time of Transition*, ed. Harvey Feldman, Michael Y. M. Kau, and Ilpyong J. Kim (New York: Paragon House, 1988), p. 47.

91. Ibid, p. 51.

92. See T. H. Shen, ed., *Agriculture's Place in the Strategy for Development: The Taiwan Experience* (Taipei: Joint Commission on Rural Reconstruction, 1974).

93. The figures are provided in Copper, *Taiwan*, p. 77.

94. See Lucian W. Pye, *Asian Power and Politics: The Cultural Dimensions of Authority* (Cambridge, MA, and London: Belknap Press of Harvard University Press, 1985), p. 229.

95. Ibid., pp. 229–30. Also see Martin M. C. Yang, *Socio-Economic Results of Land Reform in Taiwan* (Honolulu: University Press of Hawaii and the East-West Center, 1970).

96. Wu, "Taiwan in the Regional Economy of the Pacific Basin," p. 54.

97. See the section on Taiwan's economy by Raymon H. Myers in *The Far East and Australia 1991*, 23rd ed. (London: Europa, 1992), p. 240.

98. Wu, "Taiwan in the Regional Economy of the Pacific Basin," p. 58.

99. Ibid.

100. See Domes, "Taiwan in 1991," p. 42. Also see *Far Eastern Economic Review*, 18 March 1993, pp. 44–45.

101. *Christian Science Monitor*, 13 September 1990, p. 8.

102. *Far Eastern Economic Review*, 23 January 1992, p. 55.

103. Ibid.

104. Ibid.

105. As argued by Wu, "Taiwan in the Regional Economy of the Pacific Basin," p. 62.

106. *The Far East and Australia 1991*, 23rd ed., p. 243.

107. For an earlier discussion of the topic of unification, see Victor H. Li, ed., *The Future of Taiwan: A Difference of Opinion* (White Plains, NY: M.E. Sharp, 1980); and Gerald Chan, "The Two China Problem and the Dynamic Formula," *Pacific Affairs* 58, no. 3 (Fall 1985): 473–90. Also see Hungdah Chiu, ed., *China and the Taiwan Issue* (New York: Praeger, 1979); and Lai To Lee, *The Unification of China: PRC-Taiwan Relations in Flux* (New York: Praeger, 1991). For a summary of recent developments in unification, see Wang, *Contemporary Chinese Politics*, p. 346.

108. See *Beijing Review*, no. 15 (13 April 1987), p. 15. Also see *New York Times*, 10 February 1991, p. A-7. For a discussion of Beijing's dilemma over reunification, see C. L. Chiou, "Dilemmas in China's Reunification Policy toward Taiwan," *Asian Survey* 26, no. 4 (April 1986): 467–82.

109. *Far Eastern Economic Review*, 25 July 1991, p. 21.

110. Ibid.

111. Ibid.

112. Ibid.

113. See Qingguo Jia, "Changing Relations across the Taiwan Strait," *Asian Survey* 32, 3 (March 1992): 279.

CHAPTER 3

1. See Gary Gerefi and Donald Wyman, *Manufacturing Miracles: Paths of Industrialization in Latin America and East Asia* (Princeton: Princeton University Press, 1990), p. 259.

2. See *Far Eastern Economic Review*, 20 June 1991, p. 17.

3. Ibid.

4. "Decision of the National People's Congress on the Establishment of the Hong Kong Special Administrative Region," *Beijing Review*, 30 April–6 May 1990, p. xxi.

5. *Far Eastern Economic Review*, 5 December 1991, p. 11.

6. Ibid.

7. See Fred C. Shapiro, "Letter from Hong Kong," *The New Yorker*, 9 September 1991, p. 85; and *Far Eastern Economic Review*, 15 December 1991, p. 10. For a detailed description of the Walled City, see Jan Morris, *Hong Kong* (New York: Random House, 1988), pp. 293–96; and Kevin Rafferty, *City on the Rocks: Hong Kong's Uncertain Future* (New York: Viking, 1990), pp. 365–77.

8. See C. Mary Turnbull, *A History of Singapore: 1819–1975* (London and New York: Oxford University Press, 1977), p. 2.

9. See Noel Barber, *The Singapore Story: From Raffles to Lee Kuan Yew* (Glasgow: Fontana/Collins, 1978), p. 33.

10. Information on the administration of the Straits Settlements is culled from Turnbull, *History of Singapore*, pp. 34–37; and C. Mary Turnbull's section "Singapore: History," in *The Far East and Australia, 1986,* 17th ed. (London: Europa, 1985), pp. 848–50.

11. Turnbull, *History of Singapore*, pp. 34–35.

12. Ibid., p. 226.

13. Kernial Singh Sandhu and Paul Wheatley, eds., *Management of Success: The Moulding of Modern Singapore* (Boulder, CO: Westview Press, 1990), pp. 563–77.

14. Ibid., pp. 564–65.

15. See "Singaporean Identity," in Kernial Singh Sandher and Paul Wheatley, *Management of Success: The Moulding of Modern Singapore* (Boulder, CO: Westview Press, 1990), p. 569.

16. Ibid., p. 570.

17. Ibid.

18. See Trevor Ling, "Religion," *Management Success: The Moulding of Modern Singapore* (Boulder, CO: Westview Press, 1990), pp. 701–03.

19. Ibid., p. 701.

20. Ibid., p. 702.

21. Turnbull, *History of Singapore*, p. 229.

22. For detailed discussion of colonial rule in Hong Kong, consult the following works:

Morris, *Hong Kong*, pp. 68–89, 136–54, 198–216; Rafferty, *City on the Rocks*, pp. 51–145; and Ian Scott, *Political Change and Crisis of Legitimacy in Hong Kong* (Honolulu: University of Hawaii Press, 1989), pp. 39–65.

23. Morris, *Hong Kong*, p. 74.

24. Scott, *Political Change and the Crisis of Legitimacy in Hong Kong*, p. 40.

25. For text of the 1982 constitution see James C. F. Wang, *Contemporary Chinese Politics: An Introduction*, 4th ed. (Englewood Cliffs, NJ: Prentice Hall, 1991), p. 381.

26. Text of the Joint Declaration and Annexes are found in Ian Scott, *Political Change and the Crisis of Legitimacy in Hong Kong*, pp. 353–85.

27. *Far Eastern Economic Review*, 30 September 1990, p. 17.

28. Ibid.

29. Ibid., p. 18.

30. Ibid.

31. See Chan Heng Chee, "The PAP and the Structuring of the Political System," *Management of Success: The Moulding of Modern Singapore* (Boulder, CO: Westview Press, 1990), p. 86; and Lee Lai To, "Singapore in 1987: Setting a New Agenda," *Asian Survey* 28, no. 2 (February 1988): 203–04. Also see *Far Eastern Economic Review*, 26 March 1987, pp. 22–23.

32. Chee, "PAP and the Structuring of the Political System," p. 86; and To, "Singapore in 1987," p. 203.

33. *Far Eastern Economic Review*, 26 March 1987, p. 22.

34. To, "Singapore in 1987," p. 204.

35. *Asia 1991 Yearbook* (Hong Kong, BCC: Review Publishing Company, 1990), p. 205.

36. Ibid.

37. *Far Eastern Economic Review*, 24 March 1985, p. 36.

38. *Far Eastern Economic Review*, 21 March 1985, p. 38.

39. See *Asian Wall Street Journal*, 8 September 1986, pp. 1, 7. The *Far Eastern Economic Review* had published numerous accounts on the case including the following issues: 2 March 1985, pp. 36–37; 25 September 1986, pp. 12–13; 20 November 1986, pp. 12–15; and 8 January 1987, pp. 63–64.

40. See Robert O. Tilman, "The Political Leadership: Lee Kuan Yew and the PAP Team," *Management of Success: The Moulding of Modern Singapore* (Boulder, CO: Westview Press, 1990), pp. 53, 60.

41. Ibid., p. 60.

42. Ibid.

43. Ibid.

44. Ibid., pp. 62–64; and also see *Asiaweek*, 12 October 1985, p. 43.

45. Alex Josey, *Lee Kuan Yew* (Singapore: Asia Pacific Press, 1968), p. 9.

46. Ibid.

47. See *Far Eastern Economic Review*, 30 October 1986, p. 14, and 5 June 1986, p. 28. For settlement of the dispute, see *Wall Street Journal*, 4 September 1991, p. A-7.

48. *Far Eastern Economic Review*, 6 September 1990, p. 25.

49. Ibid.

50. Information about Goh Chok Tong is culled from the following sources: Stan Sesser,

"Reporter at Large: A Nation of Contradictions," *The New Yorker*, 13 January 1992, pp. 37–68; New York Times, 27 August 1991, p. A-4; *Wall Street Journal*, 5 September 1991, p. A-11; 3 September 1991, p. A-9A, 30 August 1991, p. A-3A, 22 August 1991, pp. A-1, A-14; *Asiaweek*, 18 January 1988, pp. 25–28; *Far Eastern Economic Review*, 15 November 1990, pp. 30, 35. Also see Shee Poon Kim, "Singapore in 1990: Continuity and Stability," *Asian Survey* 31, no. 2 (February 1991): 172–75.

51. See *Wall Street Journal*, 3 September 1991, p. A-9A.

52. See *Wall Street Journal*, 30 August 1991, p. A-3A.

53. See *Wall Street Journal*, 5 September 1991, p. A-11.

54. For a lengthy discourse on the legacy of the British legal system in Singapore, see G. W. Bartholomew, "The Singapore Legal System," *Management of Success: The Moulding of Modern Singapore* (Boulder, CO: Westview Press, 1990), pp. 601–33.

55. *Far Eastern Economic Review*, 25 September 1986, p. 12.

56. Rafferty, *City on the Rocks*, p. 147.

57. Scott, *Political Change and the Crisis of Legitimacy in Hong Kong*, p. 48.

58. In addition to the text of the Basic Law as approved by the Chinese National People's Congress on April 4, 1990, the following contain discussion, analysis, and criticism of the Basic Law, both in draft form and the approved version: Ian Scott, *Political Change and the Crisis of Legitimacy in Hong Kong*; *Hong Kong: A Chinese and International Concern* (Honolulu: University of Hawaii Press, 1989), particularly the chapter by George L. Hicks, "Hong Kong after the Sino-British Agreement: The Illusion of Stability," pp. 231–45; Joseph Y. S. Cheng, "The Post-1997 Government of Hong Kong: Toward a Stronger Legislature," *Asian Survey* 29, no. 8 (August 1989): 731–48; "The Basic Law and Hong Kong's Future," *Asian Wall Street Journal*, 5 April 1990, p. A-8; *New York Times*, 17 February 1990, p. A-3; Daniel R. Fung, "The Basic Law of the Hong Kong Special Administrative Region of the People's Republic of China: Problems of Interpretation," *International and Comparative Law Quarterly* 37 (July 1988): 701–14; and Hungdah Chiu, ed., *The Draft Basic Law of Hong Kong: Analysis and Documents*, Occasional papers/reprint series in *Contemporary Asian Studies*, no. 5, 1988, University of Maryland, School of Law; and *Ming Pao Daily* (Hong Kong), 14 December 1987, p. 2.

59. Text is found in "The Basic Law of the Hong Kong Special Administrative Region of the People's Republic of China," *Beijing Review*, 30 April–6 May 1990, pp. ii–xxiv, as approved by the Chinese Seventh National People's Congress at its third session on April 4, 1990, and put into effect as of July 1, 1997.

60. For text of Annex I, see *Beijing Review*, 30 April–6 May 1990, p. xix.

61. Ibid, p. vii.

62. As reported by Cheng, "The Post-1997 Government of Hong Kong," p. 734.

63. Ibid.

64. Ibid, p. 737.

65. Ibid.

66. *Far Eastern Economic Review*, 11 October 1991, p. 12.

67. *Far Eastern Economic Review*, 19 September 1991, p. 10.

68. See Thomas J. Bellows, "Singapore in 1988: The Transition Moves Forward," *Asian Survey* 29, no. 2 (February 1989): 150.

69. *Far Eastern Economic Review*, 12 September 1991, p. 11.

70. See *The New Yorker*, 13 January 1991, p. 62.

71. Information on the PAP is culled from these sources: Pang Cheng Lian, *Singapore People's Action Party: Its History, Organization and Leadership* (Singapore and Kuala Lumpur: Oxford University Press, 1971); Carolyn Choo, *Singapore: The PAP and the Problem of Political Succession* (Singapore: Asiapac Books-Pelanduk, 1985); Chee, "PAP and the Structuring of the Political System," pp. 70–87; Ch'ng Jit Koon, "Role of Grass Roots Organizations," *People's Action Party, 1954–1984* (Singapore: Central Executive Committee, People's Action Party, 1984). Throughout the years, there have been numerous articles and analyses on the PAP in the *Far Eastern Economic Review*, and the following recent articles in particular: 12 September 1991, pp. 11–12; 10 October 1991, p. 27; 29 August 1991, p. 21; 6 December 1990, p. 20; 15 November 1990, pp. 27–30; 11 July 1985, pp. 34–40; 21 March 1989, pp. 36–37; 10 January 1985, pp. 12–15. Also the following articles from the *Wall Street Journal*: 5 September 1991, p. A-11; 3 September 1991, p. A-9A; 30 August 1991, p. A-3A. *Asian Wall Street Journal,* 7 November 1990, p. A-8. Also from Shee Poon Kim, "Singapore in 1990: Continuity and Stability," *Asian Survey* 31, no. 2 (February 1991): 172–75; Thomas J. Bellows, "Singapore in 1989: Progress in Search for Roots," *Asian Survey* 30, no. 2 (February 1990): 201–06; To, "Singapore in 1987," pp. 206–09.

72. See *Wall Street Journal*, 5 September 1991, p. A-11.

73. Ibid.

74. See "A Nation of Contradictions," *The New Yorker*, 13 January 1992, pp. 37, 61; and Claudia Rosett, "Secret of Singapore's Leninist Order," *Asian Wall Street Journal*, 7 November 1991, p. A-8.

75. Ibid.

76. Ibid. Also see *Far Eastern Economic Review*, 6 December 1990, p. 20.

77. *Far Eastern Economic Review*, 6 December 1990, p. 20.

78. See Tim Huxley, "Singapore and Malaysia: A Precarious Balance?" *The Pacific Review* 4, no. 3 (1991): 205.

79. Ibid., p. 211.

80. Information on academic scholarships for military officers is taken from *Far Eastern Economic Review*, 5 December 1991, p. 15.

81. Ibid.

82. Ibid., pp. 15–16.

83. Ibid., p. 16.

84. Ibid., p. 17.

85. Ibid.

86. Ibid.

87. *New York Times*, 8 September 1991, p. A-6.

88. See *New York Times*, 17 September 1991, p. A-4; and *Christian Science Monitor*, 17 September 1991, p. 4.

89. *Ming Pao Daily* (Hong Kong), 26 August 1991, p. 4.

90. Lo Shia-King, "Decolonization and Political Development in Hong Kong: Citizen Participation," *Asian Survey* 28, no. 6 (June 1988), p. 615.

91. Ibid.

92. Ibid., p. 616.

93. See two informative articles about Hong Kong group activities: "Decolonization and Political Development in Hong Kong"; and John L. Burns, "The Structure of Communist Party Control in Hong Kong," *Asian Survey* 30, no. 8 (August 1990): 614–20, 748–65.

94. *Far Eastern Economic Review*, 20 August 1991, p. 18.

95. Ibid., p. 19.

96. Ibid., p. 20.

97. Growth figures are obtained from To, "Singapore in 1987," p. 208; Bellows, "Singapore in 1988," p. 150, and "Singapore in 1989," p. 207; Shee Poon Kim, "Singapore in 1990: Continuity and Stability," *Asian Survey* 31, no. 2 (February 1990): 175; and *Asian Wall Street Journal*, 28 August 1991, p. A-1.

98. See William and Arline McCord, "Third World Report III: Singapore's Success Story," *The New Leader*, 12–16 August 1985, p. 9.

99. Lim Chong Yah, *Economic Development in Singapore* (Singapore, Kuala Lumpur, and Hong Kong: Federal Publications, 1963), p. 10.

100. Ibid., p. 50. Also see Lim Chong Yah and You Poh Seng, "The Singapore Economy and the Vietnam War," *The Singapore Economy* (Singapore: Eastern Universities Press, 1971), pp. 352–69.

101. Yah, *Economic Development in Singapore*, pp. 19–20.

102. See McCord and McCord, "Third World Report III: Singapore's Success Story," p. 8.

103. See Linda Low, "Singapore: Economy," in *The Far East and Australia, 1986*, 17th ed. (London: Europa, 1985), p. 854.

104. See Peter Large, "Singapore," in Michael Smith, Jane McGloughlin, Peter Large, and Rod Chapman, *Asia's New Industrial World* (New York: Methuen, 1985), pp. 67–93.

105. Ibid., p. 68.

106. *Far Eastern Economic Review*, 14 March 1985, pp. 68–70.

107. See Augustine H. H. Tan, "Putting the Spark Back in Singapore," *Asian Wall Street Journal*, 11 November 1985, p. 8.

108. *Far Eastern Economic Review*, 27 March 1986, p. 72.

109. Smith et al., *Asia's New Industrial World*, p. 75.

110. Robert Elegant, *Pacific Destiny: Inside Asia Today* (New York: Crown, 1990), p. 174.

111. Lucian W. Pye, *Asian Power and Politics: The Cultural Dimensions of Authority* (Cambridge, MA: Belknap Press of Harvard University Press, 1988), p. 255.

112. See Melanie Kirkpatrick, "Singapore's Central Improvident Fund," *Asian Wall Street Journal*, 18–19 October 1985, p. 10. Also see *Far Eastern Economic Review*, 27 March 1986, p. 73, and 20 November 1986, p. 72.

113. Kirkpatrick, "Singapore's Central Improvident Fund," p. 10.

114. *Far Eastern Economic Review*, 27 March 1986, p. 73.

115. Tham Seong Chee, "The Perception and Practice of Education," *Management of Success: The Moulding of Modern Singapore* (Boulder, CO: Westview Press, 1990), p. 478.

116. Ibid., p. 481.

117. Ibid., p. 483.

118. *Far Eastern Economic Review*, 17 January 1991, p. 18.

119. Ibid.

120. *Far Eastern Economic Review*, 21 March 1991, p. 62.

121. Y.G. Yao, "The Rise of Hong Kong as a Financial Center," *Asian Survey*, vol. xix, no. 7 (July 1979), pp. 674–694.

122. Ibid., p. 684.

123. Ibid., p. 675.

124. See Victor F. S. Sit, "Dynamism in Small Industries—The Case of Hong Kong," *Asian Survey* 22, no. 4 (April 1982): 399–408.

125. *The Far East and Australia*, 1991, 23rd ed. (London: Europa, 1992), p. 265.

126. See Wang, *Contemporary Chinese Politics*, p. 363.

127. See article on the problem in the *Christian Science Monitor*, 19 December 1990, p. 6.

128. *New York Times*, 1 March 1991, p. A-3. Also see its issues for 10 January 1990, p. A-1; and 21 December 1989, p. A-3; and *Far Eastern Economic Review*, 28 December 1989, pp. 10–11.

CHAPTER 4

1. *Asia 1990 Yearbook* (Hong Kong, BCC: Review Publishing Company, Limited, 1989), p. 6. Also see Richard F. Nyrod, *Pakistan: A Country Study* (Washington, DC: U.S. Department of the Army, 1984), p. 75.

2. See Craig Baxter, Yogendra K. Malik, Charles H. Kennedy, and Robert C. Oberst, *Government and Politics in South Asia* (Boulder, CO, and London: Westview Press, 1987), p. 160; and Nyrod, Pakistan, pp. 82–83.

3. See Shahid J. Burki, "Economic Decision Making in Pakistan," in *Pakistan: The Long View*, ed. Laurence Ziring, Ralph Braibanti, and W. Howard Wriggins (Durham, NC: Duke University Press, 1977), pp. 147–84; and Khalid B. Sayeed, *Politics in Pakistan: The Nature and Direction of Change* (New York: Praeger, 1980), pp. 8–9.

4. Sayeed, *Politics in Pakistan*, pp. 56–57.

5. See Benazir Bhutto, *Daughter of Destiny* (New York and London: Simon & Schuster, 1989), pp. 39, 41.

6. Nyrod, *Pakistan*, p. 86.

7. Ibid., p. 87. Also see Akbar S. Ahmed, *Pukhtun Economy and Society: Traditional Structure and Economic Development in a Tribal Society* (London and Boston: Routledge & Kegan Paul, 1980)

8. A. L. Herman, *A Brief Introduction to Hinduism* (Boulder, CO: Westview Press, 1991).

9. Bruce R. Reichenbach, *The Law of Karma* (Honolulu: University of Hawaii Press, 1991).

10. Laurence Ziring and C. I. Eugene Kim, *The Asian Political Dictionary* (Santa Barbara, CA, and Oxford: ABC-CLIO, 1985), p. 84.

11. Information on the caste system is culled from Baxter et al., *Government and Politics in South Asia*, pp. 42–44; Richard F. Nyrod, ed., *India: A Country Study* (Washington, DC: U.S. Department of the Army, 1985), pp. 221–37; T. Walter Wallbank, *A Short History of India and Pakistan* (New York: Scott, Foresman, 1958), pp. 25–32; J. C. Heesterman, *The Inner Conflict of Tradition; Essays in Indian Ritual, Kinship and Society* (Chicago and London: University of Chicago Press, 1985), pp. 180–202.

12. Baxter et al., *Government and Politics in South Asia*, p. 42.

13. Wallbank, *Short History of India and Pakistan*, p. 12.

14. Ibid., p. 71.

15. See Charles H. Kennedy, "Islamization in Pakistan: Implementation of the Hudood Ordinances," *Asian Survey* 28, no. 3 (March 1988): 307–16.

16. Golam W. Choudbury, *Pakistan: Transition from Military to Civilian Rule* (Essex, UK: Scorpion, 1988), pp. 35–40.

17. Nyrod, *Pakistan*, p. 225.

18. Discussion on Zia's rule of Pakistan is culled from Nyrod, *Pakistan*, pp. 188–94, 213–18; Craig Baxter, ed., *Zia's Pakistan: Politics and Stability in a Frontline State* (Boulder, CO, and London: Westview Press, 1984): Eliza Van Hollen, "Pakistan in 1986: Trials of Transition," *Asian Survey* 27, no. 2 (February 1987): 143–54; Rasul B. Rais, "Pakistan in 1987: Transition to Democracy," *Asian Survey* 28, no. 2 (February 1988): 126–36; Laurence Ziring, "Public Policy Dilemma and Pakistan's Nationality Problem," *Asian Survey* 28, no. 8 (August 1988): 795–812; Kennedy, "Islamization in Pakistan," pp. 307–16; and "Pakistan in 1988: From Command to Conciliation Politics," *Asian Survey* 29, no. 2 (February 1989): 199–206.

19. Nyrod, *Pakistan*, pp. 188–94.

20. See Laurence Ziring, "Pakistan in 1989: The Politics of Stalemate," *Asian Survey* 30, no. 2 (February 1990): 129–31; *Time*, 29 January 1990, p. 56; *Far Eastern Economic Review*, 14 January 1990, pp. 12–13; and 25 June 1990, pp. 38–39; *Asian Wall Street Journal*, 25 June 1990, pp. 1, 10.

21. See *Far Eastern Economic Review*, 7 September 1990, pp. 38–39, and 4 January 1990, pp. 12–13.

22. *Far Eastern Economic Review*, 16 August 1990, p. 8.

23. *Far Eastern Economic Review*, 15 August 1991, p. 20.

24. *Far Eastern Economic Review*, 11 July 1991, p. 22.

25. *Far Eastern Economic Review*, 19 September 1991, pp. 27–28.

26. See Baxter et al., *Government and Politics in South Asia*, p. 77. Also see Nyrod, *India*, p. 387.

27. David T. Cattell and Richard Sisson, *Comparative Politics: Institutions, Behavior and Development* (Palo Alto, CA: Mayfield, 1978), pp. 121–22.

28. See Bhawan D. Dua, "Presidential Rule in India: A Study in Crisis Politics," *Asian Survey* 19, no. 6 (June 1979): pp. 611–26.

29. Nyrod, *India*, p. 388.

30. Ziring and Kim, *Asian Political Dictionary*, p. 235.

31. Baxter et al., *Government and Politics in South Asia*, p. 89.

32. Ibid.

33. Ibid.

34. Ziring and Kim, *Asian Political Dictionary*, p. 236.

35. Myron Weiner, "India's New Political Institutions," *Asian Survey* 16, no. 9 (September 1976): 898–901.

36. Ibid., p. 898.

37. Ibid., p. 900.

38. *New York Times*, 30 November 1989, p. A-1.

39. *New York Times*, 28 November 1989, pp. A-1, A-5. For an analysis of V. P. Singh, see also a report and an article by D. K. Patel in the *Asian Wall Street Journal*, 14 December 1989, p. A-10.

40. *New York Times*, 2 October 1990, p. A-3, and 8 November 1990, p. A-2.

41. See *New York Times*, 24 December 1990, p. A-2, and 28 December 1990, p. A-3.

42. For a description of the case, see Richard L. Park, "Political Crisis in India, 1975," *Asian Survey* 15, no. 11 (November 1975): 1001–10.

43. Ibid., pp. 1004–05.

44. Nyrod, *India*, p. 389.

45. See Norman Palmer, "India in 1976: The Politics of Depoliticization," *Asian Survey* 17, no. 2 (February 1977): 166–68.

46. *Far Eastern Economic Review*, 7 September 1989, p. 39, and 16 August 1990, p. 8.

47. Information on Pakistan's national legislature is culled from Richard Nyrod, ed., *Area Handbook for Pakistan* (Washington, DC: Foreign Area Studies, American University, 1974) pp. 202–11; Baxter et al., *Government and Politics in South Asia*, pp. 188–94, 205–06; Choudbury, *Pakistan*, pp. 57–73; and Ziring and Kim, *Asian Political Dictionary*, pp. 236–37.

48. Baxter et al., *Government and Politics in South Asia*, p. 208.

49. *The Constitution of the Islamic Republic of Pakistan* (as modified up to 19 March 1985) (Islamabad: Printing Corporation of Pakistan Press, 1985).

50. Choudbury, *Pakistan*, pp. 69, 66.

51. Ibid., pp. 63–65.

52. See *Baxter, Government and Politics in South Asia*, p. 206. Also see Choudbury, *Pakistan*, p. 218.

53. Choudbury, *Pakistan*, pp. 228–29; and the chapter on the process of Islamization, pp. 129–52.

54. See article from the Associated Press by Rohimullah Yusutzai, as reprinted in the *Honolulu Star-Bulletin*, 9 October 1991, p. A-16.

55. Choudbury, *Pakistan*, p. 230.

56. Asaf Hussain, *Elite Politics in an Ideological State: The Case of Pakistan* (Kent, UK: Wm. Dawson & Sons, 1979), p. 123.

57. Ibid.

58. Ibid., p. 124.

59. Bhutto, *Daughter of Destiny*, p. 171.

60. Ibid., p. 183.

61. *Far Eastern Economic Review*, 11 October 1990, p. 24.

62. See Beatrice B. Lamb, *India: A World in Transition* (New York and London: Praeger, 1963), pp. 221–24.

63. Weiner, "Congress Restored: Continuities and Discontinuities in Indian Politics," *Asian Survey* 22, no. 4 (April 1982): 342.

64. Ibid.

65. Baxter et al., *Government and Politics in South Asia*, p. 105.

66. See Jyolirindra Das Gupta, "The Junata Phase: Reorganization and Redirection in Indian Politics," *Asian Survey* 19, no. 4 (April 1979): 300–403; and Baxter et al., *Government and Politics in South Asia*, pp. 108–09. Also see Ziring and Kim, *Asian Political Dictionary*, pp. 162–66.

67. Gupta, "Junata Phase," p. 390.

68. "Congress Restored," p. 345.

69. For an analysis of the 1989 election, see Walter K. Andersen, "Election 1989 in India: The Dawn of Coalition Politics?" *Asian Survey* 30, no. 6 (June 1990): 527–40.

70. Ibid., pp. 534–35.

71. See *Far Eastern Economic Review*, 27 June 1991, p. 11, and 18 April 1991, p. 19. Also see *New York Times*, 18 June 1991, p. A-4.

72. Recent information about the Bharatiya Junata party is culled from the following sources: "The Hindu Burden," *Far Eastern Economic Review*, 27 June 1991, pp. 12–13; and "BJP Launches Its Campaign for Power: Revivalist Rally," *Far Eastern Economic Review*, 18 April 1991, p. 19; *Time*, 24 June 1991, p. 35; *Christian Science Monitor*, 30 May 1991, pp. 1–2; "Toward a Hindu Utopia," *Asian Wall Street Journal*, 30 May 1991, p. A-14; *New York Times*, 10 February 1991, p. A-9, and 8 November 1990, p. A-3; and Yogendra K. Malik and Dhirendra K. Vajpeyi, "The Rise of Hindu Militancy: India's Secular Democracy at Risk," *Asian Survey* 24, no. 3 (1984): 308–25. Also see Ziring and Kim, *Asian Political Dictionary*, pp. 103–04, 163–65; and Baxter et al., *Government and Politics in South Asia*, pp. 309–10.

73. See Malik and Vajpeyi, "Rise of Hindu Militancy," pp. 315–16.

74. *Far Eastern Economic Review*, 18 April 1991, p. 19.

75. *Far Eastern Economic Review*, 16 May 1991, p. 16, and 27 June 1991, p. 10. Also see Walter K. Andersen, "Election 1989 in India," *Asian Survey* 30, no. 6 (June 1990): 529, 531.

76. Anderson, "Election 1989 in India," p. 531.

77. *Far Eastern Economic Review*, 27 June 1991, p. 10.

78. Marguerite R. Barnett, *The Politics of Cultural Nationalism in South India* (Princeton: Princeton University Press, 1976).

79. See Baxter et al., *Government and Politics in South Asia*, p. 114; and Ziring and Kim, *Asian Political Dictionary*, pp. 153–54.

80. See Rajni Kothari, "The Congress 'System' in India," *Asian Survey* iv no. 12 (December 1964): 11–12; and a discussion on the system in James Manor, "Parties and the Party System," in *India's Democracy: An Analysis of Changing State-Society Relations*, ed. Atul Kohli (Princeton: Princeton University Press, 1988), p. 64. Also see Kothari, "The Congress 'System' in India," in *Politics and the People: In Search of a Humane India* (New York: New Horizon Press, 1989), pp. 21–35.

81. Manor, "Parties and the Party System," p. 72.

82. Ibid., p. 73.

83. Steve Cohen in *Far Eastern Economic Review*, 7 June, 1990, p. 47.

84. Nyrod, *India*, p. 511.

85. *Far Eastern Economic Review*, 5 April 1990, p. 28.

86. Ibid., and *Asia Yearbook 1989* (Hong Kong: *Far Eastern Economic Review*, 1989), p. 126.

87. *Far Eastern Economic Review*, 7 June 1990, pp. 47–50.

88. Ibid., pp. 47, 50.

89. Ibid.

90. Ibid.

91. Ibid.

92. Ibid.

93. Ibid., pp. 115–16.

94. Ibid., 117.

95. Ibid., p. 143. Also see Lloyd and Susanne H. Rudolph, "Generals and Politicians in

India," *Pacific Affairs* 27, no. 1 (Spring 1964): 5–19.

96. *Far Eastern Economic Review*, 27 February 1981; and Salamat Ali, "In Step with Tradition," *Far Eastern Economic Review*, 31 May 1984, pp. 25–29.

97. Bhutto, *Daughter of Destiny*, p. 50.

98. Baxter et al., *Government and Politics in South Asia*, p. 193.

99. See Hussain, *Elite Politics in an Ideological State*, p. 157.

100. See the accounts of their ordeal in Bhutto, *Daughter of Destiny*.

101. *Christian Science Monitor*, 14 November 1988, p. 12.

102. See Laurence Ziring, "Pakistan in 1990," *Asian Survey* 31, no. 2 (February 1991): 114.

103. See *New York Times*, 11 January 1991, p. A-4.

104. *Far Eastern Economic Review*, 31 January 1991, p. 18.

105. Ibid.

106. Hussain, *Elite Politics in an Ideological State*, pp. 126–27.

107. Ibid., pp. 130–31; and *Christian Science Monitor*, 29 August 1988, pp. 1–2; and its issue of 7 June 1990, p. 1.

108. See Edward Shils, Political Development in the New States (Gravenhages: Moaton, 1962).

109. Hussain, *Elite Politics in an Ideological State*, p. 135.

110. See Ayala Jalal, *The State of Martial Rule: The Origins of Pakistan's Political Economy of Defense* (New York: Cambridge University Press, 1990).

111. See Hussain, *Elite Politics in an Ideological State*, pp. 61–78, 93–110, 111–25.

112. *Christian Science Monitor*, 29 August 1988, p. 2

113. *Far Eastern Economic Review*, 4 October 1990, p. 27.

114. Ibid.

115. *New York Times*, 8 August 1990, p. A-4.

116. See *Far Eastern Economic Review*, 16 August 1990, p. 8.

117. See Raghar Gaiha, "On Estimates of Rural Poverty in India: An Assessment," *Asian Survey* 29, no. 7 (July 1989): 669–86.

118. Figures are taken from an article by Pramit Chandhuri in *The Far East and Australasia, 1991* (London, U.K.: Europa Publications, Limited, 1990), p. 393.

119. See Raj Krishna, "The Economic Outlook for India," in *India 2000: The Next Fifteen Years*, ed. James R. Roach (Riverdale, MD: Riverdale Company), p. 172.

120. Ibid.

121. *New York Times*, 29 June 1991, p. A-5.

122. See *Far Eastern Economic Review*, 8 August 1991, p. 49. Also see *Asian Wall Street Journal*, 2 August 1990, p. A-8.

123. Ibid.

124. *Far Eastern Economic Review*, 8 August 1991, p. 49.

125. Nyrod, *India*, p. 286.

126. Summary of the various goals of India's five-year plans is culled from ibid., pp. 292–96.

127. John W. Mellor, "The Indian Economy: Objectives, Performances and Prospects," *India: A Rising Middle Power* (Boulder, CO: Westview Press, 1979), p. 86.

128. See C. T. Kurien, "Paradoxes of Planned Development: The Indian Experience," in *India 2000: The Next Fifteen Years*, ed. James R. Roach (Riverdale, MD: Riverdale Company, 1986), pp. 185–90.

129. Nyrod, *India*, p. 288.

130. *Far Eastern Economic Review*, 8 August 1991, p. 48.

131. *Far Eastern Economic Review*, 21 March 1991, p. 63.

132. Ibid., p. 64.

133. *New York Times*, 23 June 1991, p. A-3.

134. See *Asia 1990 Yearbook* (Hong Kong, BCC: Far Eastern Economic Review, 1990), p. 6.

135. *Far Eastern Economic Review*, 26 April 1990, p. 27.

136. Ibid., p. 96.

137. Ibid., pp. 94–96.

138. See Nyrod, *Pakistan*, p. 138.

139. Ibid.

140. Ibid.

141. For a brief summary of Zia's economic policy see Nyrod, *Pakistan*, pp. 139–42.

142. *Far Eastern Economic Review*, 21 December 1989, p. 52.

143. Ibid.

144. Ibid.

145. *Far Eastern Economic Review*, 28 August, 1991, p. 42.

146. Ibid., pp. 42–43.

147. *Far Eastern Economic Review*, 20 June 1991, p. 94.

148. *Far Eastern Economic Review*, 27 December 1990, p. 34.

149. *Far Eastern Economic Review*, 20 June 1991, p. 93.

CHAPTER 5

1. Definition is taken from Article 46 of the 1982 Law of the Sea Convention; see James C. F. Wang, *Handbook on Ocean Politics and Law* (New York and London: Greenwood, 1982), pp. 45–46.

2. For a brief discussion of the "Cultural System," see George McTurnan Kahin, ed., *Major Governments of Asia*, 2nd ed. (Ithaca: Cornell University Press, 1963), pp. 544–45; C. I. Eugene Kim and Laurence Ziring, *An Introduction to Asian Politics* (Englewood Cliffs, NJ: Prentice Hall, 1977), pp. 314–15. For a fuller treatment of Dutch rule, see L. H. Palmier, Indonesia and the Dutch (London: Oxford University Press, 1962); and Amy Vandenbosch, *The Dutch East Indies* (Berkeley: University of California Press, 1942).

3. Kim and Ziring, *Introduction to Asian Politics*, p. 324.

4. Kahin, *Major Governments of Asia*, p. 561.

5. See ibid., pp. 590–91; and Richard Butwell, *Southeast Asia Today and Tomorrow: A Political Analysis* (New York: Praeger, 1961), pp. 35–36.

6. Ibid., pp. 637–38.

7. *A Diplomatic History of the American People*, p. 515.

8. See Tewis Gluck, Jr., *American Institutions in the Philippines, 1898–1941* (Manila: Historical Conservation Society, 1976).

9. Theodore Friend, "Philippine-American Tensions in History," in *Crisis in the Philippines: The Marcos Era and Beyond*, ed. John Bresnan (Princeton: Princeton University Press, 1986), p. 11.

10. For a full treatment of the Huks, see Benedict J. Kerkvliet, *The Huk Rebellion: A Study of Peasant Revolt in the Philippines* (Berkeley: University of California Press, 1977).

11. See Stanley Karnow, *In Our Image: America's Empire in the Philippines* (New York: Random House, 1989), pp. 376–78.

12. Ibid., p. 355.

13. Ibid., p. 358.

14. The Marcos regime has been conceptualized by Ross Marlay, "The Political Legacy of Marcos; The Political Inheritance of Aquino," in *Rebuilding a Nation: Philippine Challenges and American Policy*, ed. Carl H. Landé (Washington, DC: Washington Institute for Values in Public Policy, 1987), pp. 313–16.

15. Robert Stauffer, "Philippine Corporation: A Vote on the 'New Society,'" *Asian Survey* 17, no. 4 (April 1977): 393–407.

16. Description used by Rep. Stephen Solarz in an interview with the Associated Press on 23 March 1986.

17. Marlay, "Political Legacy of Marcos," p. 314.

18. Ibid., p. 316, as quoted from the Associated Press dispatch on 23 March 1986.

19. David A. Rosenberg, "The Changing Structure of Philippine Government from Marcos to Aquino," in *Rebuilding a Nation: Philippine Challenges and American Policy*, ed. Carl H. Landé (Washington, DC: Washington Institute for Values in Public Policy, 1987), p. 339. Also see John H. and Mae H. Esterline, *How the Dominoes Fell: Southeast Asia in Perspective* (Lanham, MD: Hamilton Press, 1986), p. 349.

20. See Guy J. Pauker, "President Corazon Aquino: A Political and Personal Assessment," in *Rebuilding a Nation: Philippine Challenges and American Policy*, ed. Carl H. Landé (Washington, DC: Washington Institute for Values in Public Policy, 1987), pp. 291–311; and Bernardo M. Villegas, "The Philippines in 1986: Democratic Reconstruction in the Post-Marcos Era," *Asian Survey* 27, no. 2 (February 1987): 194–99.

21. For a discussion of the drafting of the 1945 constitution, see David Reeve, Golkar of *Indonesia: An Alternative to the Party System* (Oxford and New York: Oxford University Press, 1985), pp. 65–75. For the text of the 1945 constitution, see Daniel S. Lev, *The Transition to Guided Democracy: Indonesian Politics, 1957–1958* (Ithaca, N.Y.: Cornell University Press, 1966).

22. See *Far Eastern Economic Review*, 30 August 1990, p. 10.

23. Ibid., p. 11.

24. Information on the 1988 MPR session is culled from the following issues of *Asian Wall Street Journal*: 14 March 1988, pp. 1, 4; 11–12 March 1988, p. 3; 10 March 1988, pp. 1, 7; 2 March 1988, pp. 1, 8.

25. Former Singapore prime minister Lee Kwan Yew made a speech to a conference held in Manila in 1992 during which he made the statement that what the Philippines needed was more discipline and less democracy. See the article by Robert H. Reid of the Associated Press as reprinted in the *Honolulu Star-Bulletin*, 25 February 1993, p. A-10.

26. *Far Eastern Economic Review*, 5 September 1991, p. 16.

27. Ibid.

28. Landé, *Rebuilding a Nation*, pp. 32–33. Carl Landé used a Philippine news magazine, Ang Katipunan, for a description of those who accompanied Corey Aquino's visit to the United States in September 1986.

29. Ibid., p. 32.

30. Ibid., p. 33.

31. Ibid.

32. *Asian Wall Street Journal*, 15 January 1991, p. A-3.

33. See Jose Agaton R. Sibal, *The Constitution of the Republic of the Philippines, 1981* (Quezon City, PH: Central Lawbook, 1988), p. 34.

34. Ibid., pp. 34–35.

35. Ibid., pp. 35–36.

36. Ibid., p. 36.

37. *Asian Wall Street Journal*, 3 July 1989, p. A-3. Also see *Asian Wall Street Journal*, 24 March 1988, p. A-1.

38. See Dwight Y. King and M. Ryass Rasjid, "The Golkar Landslide in the 1987 Indonesian Elections," *Asian Survey* 28, no. 9 (September 1988): 916–25.

39. See Reeve, *Golkar of Indonesia*, pp. 140–49, 185–86. Also, see Leo Suryadinata, *Military Ascendancy and Political Culture: A Study of Indonesia's Golkar* (Athens: Ohio University, Center for International Studies, 1987).

40. Reeve, *Golkar of Indonesia*, pp. 125–26.

41. See *Far Eastern Economic Review*, 9 November 1989, p. 38. Also see Suryadinata, *Military Ascendance and Political Culture*, a more recent study.

42. See Suryadinata, *Military Ascendance and Political Culture*.

43. See *Far Eastern Economic Review*, 7 February 1991, pp. 17, 51.

44. *Far Eastern Economic Review*, 14 December 1989, p. 34.

45. Ibid.

46. Ibid.

47. Frederica M. Bunge, *Indonesia: A Country Study* (Washington DC: U.S. Department of the Army, 1983), p. 201.

48. See Kahin, *Major Governments of Asia*, p. 614.

49. Ibid. Also see Bonner, "A Reporter at Large: The New Order II," *New Yorker Magazine*, September 12, 1989, pp. 75–77.

50. See Ulf Sundhanssen, "The Military: Structure, Procedures and Effects in Indonesian Society," in *Political Power and Communications in Indonesia*, ed. Karl D. Jackson and Lucian W. Pye (Berkeley: University of California Press, 1978).

51. Ibid.

52. *Indonesia: A Country Study*, p. 228.

53. Ibid., p. 231.

54. Ibid, p. 233.

55. For a discussion of the generational difference, see John B. Haseman,"The Dynamics of Change: Regeneration of the Indonesian Army, "*Asian Survey* 26, no. 8 (August 1986): 885–91; and *Far Eastern Economic Review*, 18 January 1990, pp. 24–25.

56. *Far Eastern Economic Review*, 18 January 1990, p. 24. Also see *Far Eastern Economic Review*, 5 July 1990, p. 16.

57. See *Far Eastern Economic Review*, 16 August 1990, p. 19.

58. *Far Eastern Economic Review*, 8 March 1990, pp. 18–19.

59. *Far Eastern Economic Review*, 30 August 1990, pp. 10–11.

60. Ibid., p. 11.

61. *Far Eastern Economic Review*, 16 August 1990, pp. 18–19.

62. See *New York Times*, 13 November 1991, p. A-7.

63. See Jose Agaton R. Sibal, *The Constitution of the Republic of Philippines* (Quezon City, PH: Central Lawbook, 1988), 1987, pp. 113–22.

64. See *New York Times*, 1 December 1991, p. A-3, and *Far Eastern Economic Review*, 16 January 1992, p. 15.

65. *Far Eastern Economic Review*, 16 January 1992, p. 15.

66. The count was revealed in *Far Eastern Economic Review*, 19 March 1992, p. 24.

67. Ibid., p. 28.

68. *New York Times*, 1 December 1991, p. A-3.

69. *Far Eastern Economic Review*, 19 March 1992, p. 22.

70. *Far Eastern Economic Review*, 20 February 1992, p. 19.

71. *Far Eastern Economic Review*, 12 March 1992, p. 18.

72. See *Asia 1990* by *Far Eastern Economic Review*, p. 8.

73. See "Indonesia" in the special advertising section of the *Wall Street Journal*, 21 May 1990, p. 8.

74. *Asian Wall Street Journal*, 21 May 1990, p. 7.

75. See Geoffrey B. Hainsworth, "Indonesia: On the Road to Privatization?" *Current History*, March 1990, p. 124.

76. See *Far Eastern Economic Review*, 12 October 1989, pp. 72–73.

77. See *Far Eastern Economic Review*, 18 April 1991, p. 44.

78. *Far Eastern Economic Review*, 23 November 1989, p. 72.

79. Ibid.

80. For the list to go public, see *Far Eastern Economic Review*, 29 June 1989, p. 56.

81. See editorial in *Asian Wall Street Journal*, 31 March 1988, p. 6.

82. *Far Eastern Economic Review*, 4 October 1990, pp. 62–63.

83. Ibid., p. 62.

84. Ibid., p. 64.

85. *Far Eastern Economic Review*, 10 January 1991, p. 52.

86. See Bernardo M. Villegas, "The Philippines in 1985: Rolling with the Political Punches," *Asian Survey* 26, no. 2 (February 1986): 135.

87. *Asian Wall Street Journal*, 30 September–1 October 1988, p. 3. Also see *Far Eastern Economic Review*, 6 July 1989, pp. 54–55.

88. *Asian Wall Street Journal*, 5–6 January 1990, p. 3.

89. *Asia 1991 Yearbook* (Hong Kong: Review Publishing Company, 1991), p. 202.

90. *Christian Science Monitor*, 27 April 1989, p. 2.

91. *Asian Wall Street Journal*, 20 August 1990, p. 1.

92. *Christian Science Monitor*, 25 April 1990, p. 8.

93. *Far Eastern Economic Review*, 13 July 1989, p. 15.

94. See Robert H. Reid's Associated Press report reprinted in the *Honolulu Star-Bulletin*, 10 April 1990, p. A-18.

95. Belinda A. Aquino, "Corey Aquino Must Enforce Land Reform and End Corruption," *Honolulu Star-Bulletin*, 31 March 1988, p. A-15.

96. *Far Eastern Economic Review*, 13 July 1989, p. 15.

97. *Far Eastern Economic Review*, 6 July 1989, p. 37.

98. Ibid.

99. Ibid., p. 38.

100. Ibid.

101. Ibid., p. 37.

102. Ibid.

CHAPTER 6

1. Ronald J. Cima, ed., *Vietnam: A Country Study* (Washington, DC: U.S. Department of the Army, 1989), p. 89.

2. *The Far East and Australia Yearbook 1991*, 22nd ed. (London, U.K.: Europa Publications, Limited, 1990) gives 64.4 million for 1989. *The Asia 1991 Yearbook* (Hong Kong: Review Publishing Company, Ltd., 1990) lists 70.2 million for Vietnam.

3. Cima, *Vietnam*, p. 92.

4. Ibid., pp. 200–204.

5. Ibid.

6. See James P. Harrison, *The Endless War: Vietnam's Struggle for Independence* (New York: Columbia University Press, 1990).

7. Dae Sook Suh, Kim Il Sung: *The North Korean Leader* (New York: Columbia University Press, 1988), pp. 55–60.

8. Information and analysis on the Korean War are culled from the following published studies: Richard Whelan, *Drawing the Line: The Korean War, 1950–1953* (Boston: Little, Brown, 1990); Glenn D. Paige, *The Korean Decision, June 24–30, 1950* (New York: Free Press, 1968); Burton I. Kaufman, *The Korean War: Challenges in Crisis, Credibility and Command* (Philadelphia: Temple University Press, 1986); Allen S. Whiting, *China Crosses the Yalu* (Stanford, CA: Stanford University Press, 1960); Bruce Cummings, *The Origin of the Korean War: Liberation and Its Emergence of Separate Regimes, 1945–1947* (Princeton: Princeton University Press, 1981); Trumbull Higgins, *Korea and the Fall of MacArthur* (Cambridge, UK: Oxford University Press, 1960); Suh, Kim Il Sung, pp. 111–57; Trumbull Higgins, *War in Korea* (Garden City, NY: Doubleday, 1951); Robert Leckie, *Conflict: The History of the Korean War* (New York: Putnam's, 1962); Oliver T. Robert, *Why War Came in Korea* (New York: Fordham University Press, 1950); I. F. Stone, *The Hidden History of the Korean War* (New York: Monthly Review Press, 1952); and Robert C. Thomas, *The War in Korea, 1950–1953* (Aldershot, UK: Gale and Bolden, 1954); *Yearbook of the United Nations, 1950* (New York: UN Department of Public Information, 1951); U.S. Department of State, *Events Prior to the Attack on June 25, 1950: The Conflict in Korea* (Washington, DC: U.S. Government Printing Office, 1951).

9. See Kaufman, *Korean War*, p. 28; and *Foreign Relations of the United States, 1950*, 1 (Washington, DC: U.S. Department of State, 1982), pp. 237–57.

10. Ralph N. Clough, *Embattled Korea: The Rivalry for International Support* (Boulder, CO, and London: Westview Press, 1987), p. 20; and Kaufman, *Korean War*, pp. 22–23.

11. Kaufman, *Korean War*, p. 33.

12. Stone, *Hidden History of the Korean War*.

13. See text of resolution (S/1501) adopted on June 25, 1950, in *Yearbook of the United Nations, 1950,* pp. 221–22.

14. See UN Security Council resolution (S/1511) adopted on 27 June 1950 in *ibid.*, pp. 223–24.

15. Text of the enabling Security Council resolution, adopted on July 7, 1950 (S/1588) regarding provision of UN forces to Korea, is found in ibid., pp. 223–24. In the end, fifteen other nations besides the United States contributed forces to constitute the UN command: Australia, Belgium, Canada, Colombia, Ethiopia, France, Greece, Luxembourg, the Netherlands, New Zealand, the Philippines, Union of South Africa, Thailand, Turkey, and the United Kingdom. For the U.S. decision to take the matter to the United Nations, see Paige, *Korean Decision*, pp. 79–272.

16. See *Foreign Relations of the United States*, 1950, VII, pp. 826–27. Also see Dean Acheson, *Present at the Creation: My Years in the State Department* (New York: Norton, 1969), pp. 453–55.

17. See Bruce Cummings, *The Two Koreas: On the Road to Reunification* (New York: Foreign Policy Association, 1991), p. 56.

18. Ibid., p. 58.

19. See *Far Eastern Economic Review*, 30 April 1992, p. 20.

20. See *Far Eastern Economic Review*, 30 July, 1992, p. 10.

21. See Cima, *Vietnam*, pp. 209–10.

22. See B. C. Koh, "The Impact of the Chinese Model on North Korea," *Asian Survey* 18, no. 6 (June 1978): 628–29.

23. Tai Sung An, *North Korea: A Political Handbook* (Wilmington, DE: Scholarly Resources, 1983), p. 52.

24. See *Far Eastern Economic Review*, 30 July 1992, p. 10.

25. Ibid.

26. *New York Times*, 1 April 1990, p. A-5.

27. *Asian Wall Street Journal*, 21 June 1991, p. A-10.

28. See Douglas Pike, "Vietnam in 1991: The Turning Point," *Asian Survey* xxxii, no. 1 (January 1992): 79.

29. Ibid. Also see *New York Times*, 28 June 1991, p. A-3; and 1 April 1990, p. A-5.

30. See *Far Eastern Economic Review*, 14 September 1989, pp. 28–30.

31. For a discussion on Vo Van Kiet's views, see *Asian Wall Street Journal*, 15 August 1991, pp. 1, 8.

32. *New York Times,* 19 January 1990, p. A-8.

33. Cima, *Vietnam*, p. 272.

34. Ibid., pp. 272–73.

35. *Christian Science Monitor*, 14 December 1988, p. 18.

36. Ibid.

37. Suh, *Kim Il Sung*, pp. 75–94.

38. Masao Okonogi, *North Korea at the Crossroads* (Tokyo: Japan Institute of International Affairs, 1976), pp. 39–40.

39. Frederica M. Bunge, *North Korea: A Country Study* (Washington, DC: U.S. Government Printing Office, 1987), p. 175.

40. An, *North Korea*, pp. 38–39.

41. Bunge, *North Korea*, p. 231.

42. *Far Eastern Economic Review*, 2 May 1991, p. 18.

43. *Far Eastern Economic Review*, 23 May 1991, p. 16.

44. Ibid., p. 17.

45. *New York Times*, 4 December 1990, p. A-6.

46. *Asian Wall Street Journal*, 6 June 1991, p. A-1.

47. Ibid.

48. Ibid., p. A-6.

49. John H. Esterline, "Vietnam in 1986: An Uncertain Tiger," *Asian Survey* 27, no. 1 (January 1987): 93.

50. Ibid., p. 94, as quoted from an *Asiaweek* report of 8 April 1986.

51. See Neil and Susan Sheehan, "Reporter at Large in Vietnam," *The New Yorker*, 18 November 1991, p. 81.

52. Lewis M. Stern, "The Scramble toward Revitalization: The Vietnamese Communist Party and the Economic Reform Program," *Asian Survey* 27, no. 4 (April 1987): 481–82.

53. Information on doi moi is culled from Stern, "Scramble toward Revitalization," pp. 477–93; Ronald J. Cima, "Vietnam's Economic Reform: Approaching the 1990s," *Asian Survey* 29, no. 8 (August 1989): 786–99; and Charles A. Joiner, "The Vietnam Communist Party Strives to Remain the 'Only Force,'" *Asian Survey* 30, no. 11 (November 1990): 1053–65. Also see Pike, "Vietnam in 1991," pp. 74–78; John H. Esterline, "Vietnam in 1987: Steps toward Rejuvenation," *Asian Survey* 28, no. 1 (January 1988): 79–89; *Far Eastern Economic Review*, 19 December 1991, p. 22.

54. Pike, "Vietnam in 1991," p. 77.

55. Ibid., p. 78.

56. *Far Eastern Economic Review*, 19 December 1991, p. 22.

57. Douglas Pike, "Vietnam in 1990: The Last Picture Show," *Asian Survey* 31, no. 1 (January 1991): 82–83.

58. *Far Eastern Economic Review*, 7 May 1992, pp. 64–66.

59. *Far Eastern Economic Review*, 19 October 1991, p. 20.

60. Ibid.

61. *Far Eastern Economic Review*, 30 May 1991, p. 38.

62. Ibid.

63. Ibid., p. 37.

64. Hy-Sung Lee, "North Korea's Closed Economy: The Hidden Opening," *Asian Survey* 28, no. 12 (November 1988): 1264–79.

65. Lee, "North Korea's Closed Economy," pp. 1268–71.

66. Ibid., p. 1269.

67. *Far Eastern Economic Review*, 13 September 1990, p. 11, and 20 September 1990, pp. 24–25. Also, *Asian Wall Street Journal*, 3 September 1990, p. A-1.

68. *New York Times*, 18 October 1990, p. A-3, and 19 October 1990, p. A-5.

69. *Far Eastern Economic Review*, 27 December 1990, pp. 6–7.

70. Ibid., p. 6.

71. For a discussion on unification policy issues and differences of plans advocated by North and South Korea, see Young Whan Kihl, *Politics and Policies in Divided Korea: Regimes in Contest*, pp. 205–30.

72. *Far Eastern Economic Review*, 28 March 1992, pp. 56–59. Also see *Honolulu Star-Bulletin*, 3 February 1993, p. A-12.

73. *Far Eastern Economic Review*, 11 March 1993, pp. 10–11.

CHAPTER 7

1. A Reuters release as reprinted in the *Honolulu Star-Bulletin*, 7 December 1991, p. A-10.

2. See Susan Manuel's article in the *Honolulu Star-Bulletin*, 27 February 1990, p. B-1.

3. *New York Times*, 9 August 1990, p. A-3, and 25 March 1990, p. A-3. For a background look at the migration and refugees problem for Cambodia, see Russell R. Ross, ed., *Cambodia: A Country Study* (Washington, DC: U.S. Department of the Army, 1990), pp. 85–87.

4. Information on historical development of Cambodia is culled from Ross, Cambodia, pp. 6–61; John H. and Mae H. Esterline, eds., "How the Dominoes Fell": *Southeast Asia in Perspective* (Lanham, MD, and London: Hamilton Press, 1986), pp. 67–99; Laura Summers, "Cambodia: History," in *The Far East and Australia, 1991,* 23rd ed. (London: Europa, 1992), pp. 268–72; David P. Chandler and Ben Kiernan, eds., *Revolution and Its Aftermath in Kampuchea: Eight Essays* (New Haven: Yale University Press, 1983); Michael Vickery, *Cambodia: 1975–82* (Boston: South End Press, 1984); and Milton E. Osborne, *Before Kampuchea: Preludes to Tragedy* (London: George Allen & Unwin, 1979).

5. Karl D. Jackson, ed., *Cambodia 1975–78: Rendezvous with Death* (Princeton: Princeton University Press, 1989), pp. 4–5.

6. Ibid., p. 7.

7. See Esterline and Esterline, "How the Dominoes Fell," pp. 86–87.

8. For discussion of the Khmer Rouge, see Jackson, *Cambodia 1975–1978*; Ben Kiernan, *How Pol Pot Came to Power* (London: Verso, 1984); and William Shawcross, *Sideshow: Kissinger, Nixon, and the Destruction of Cambodia* (New York: Simon & Schuster, 1979).

9. Ross, *Cambodia*, pp. 38–40.

10. Ibid., p. 51. Also see John Barron and Anthony Paul, *Murder of a Gentle Land* (New York: Reader's Digest Press, 1976).

11. See Kenneth M. Quinn, "The Pattern and Scope of Violence," in *Cambodia 1975–78*, ed. Jackson, pp. 179–208.

12. See the article by Ben Kiernan in *Far Eastern Economic Review*, 1 March 1990, pp. 18–19.

13. Esterline and Esterline, "How the Dominoes Fell," p. 93.

14. Ibid., p. 97.

15. See Donald P. Whitaker, Helen A. Barth, Sylvan M. Berman, Judith M. Heimann, John E. MacDonald, Kenneth W. Martindale, and Rinn-Sup Shinn, eds., *Laos: A Country Study* (Washington, DC: American University Press, 1979), p. 34. Also see Esterline and Esterline, "How the Dominoes Fell," pp. 112–13.

16. Esteline and Esterline, "How the Dominoes Fell," pp. 118–19; and Arthur J. Dommen, *Conflict in Laos* (New York: Praeger, 1965), p. 154.

17. Esterline and Esterline, "How the Dominoes Fell," p. 119.

18. Ibid., p. 121.

19. See text of the 1962 Geneva Agreement as appended to Whitaker et al., *Laos: A Country Study*, pp. 289–90.

20. Stan Sesser, "A Reporter at Large: Forgotten Country," *The New Yorker*, 20 August 1990, p. 40.

21. See Robert S. Ross, "China and the Cambodian Peace Process," *Asian Survey* 31, no. 12 (December 1991): 1170–85; Steven J. Hood, "Beijing's Cambodia Gamble and the Prospects for Peace in Indochina: The Khmer Rouge or Sihanouk?" *Asian Survey* 30, no. 10 (October 1990): 977–91; and Charles McGregor, "China, Vietnam, and the Cambodian Conflict: Beijing's End Game Strategy," *Asian Survey* 30, no. 3 (March 1990): 266–83. Also see China's reaction to U.S. policy shift of withdrawing support for the Cambodian guerrillas coalition that included the Khmer Rouge; see *New York Times*, 20 July 1990, p. A-2.

22. Information on the Cambodian peace agreement is culled from: *New York Times* 24 October 1991, pp. A-1, A-6; *Christian Science Monitor*, 28 October 1991, p. 19; and *Far Eastern Economic Review*, 7 November 1991, pp. 27–35, and 27 February 1992, pp. 22–28. Also see Frederick Z. Brown, "Cambodia in 1991: An Uncertain Peace," *Asian Survey* 32, no. 1 (January 1992): 88–96.

23. *New York Times*, 18 April 1992, p. A-3.

24. *New York Times*, 20 January 1992, p. A-2; and *The Honolulu Advertiser*, 31 March 1992, p. B-1.

25. *Far Eastern Economic Review*, 7 November 1991, p. 28.

26. Ibid., p. 34. Also see *Far Eastern Economic Review*, 27 February 1992, pp. 27–28.

27. See *Far Eastern Economic Review*, 24 June 1993, pp. 27–28.

28. Ibid.

29. See Stephen T. Johnson, "Laos in 1991: Year of the Constitution," *Asian Survey*, xxxii, 1, January 1992, p. 83; and *Far Eastern Economic Review*, 18 April 1991, p. 18.

30. Johnson, "Laos in 1991," p. 83.

31. *Far Eastern Economic Review*, 18 April 1991, p. 18.

32. See *New York Times*, 21 September 1991, p. A-3.

33. Ibid.

34. See Brown, "Cambodia in 1991," pp. 92–93.

35. *New York Times*, 28 August 1991, p. A-3.

36. *New York Times*, 1 January 1991, p. A-2. The Chinese agreement to halt its military aid to the Khmer Rouge was revealed by Richard H. Solomon, former assistant secretary of state for East Asia under President Bush. See *New York Times*, 21 July 1990, p. A-2.

37. *New York Times*, 1 May 1990, p. A-6.

38. *New York Times*, 24 October 1990, p. A-4.

39. See *Far Eastern Economic Review*, 27 February 1992, pp. 26–27.

40. *Far Eastern Economic Review*, 23 April 1992, pp. 12–13.

41. Geoffrey C. Gunn, "Laos in 1989: Quiet Revolution in the Marketplace," *Asian Survey* 31, no. 1 (January 1990): 83.

42. See Charles A. Joiner, "Laos in 1986: Administrative and International Partially Adopted Communism," *Asian Survey* 27, no. 1 (January 1987): 104–14. Also see Carlyle A. Thayer, "Laos in 1982: The Third Congress of the Lao People's Revolutionary Party," *Asian Survey* 23, no. 1 (January 1983): 84–93.

43. See Charles A. Joiner, "Laos in 1987: New Economic Management Confronts the Bureaucracy," *Asian Survey* 28, no. 1 (January 1988): 96–97.

44. See *Far Eastern Economic Review*, 18 April 1991, p. 18.

45. Joiner, "Laos in 1986," pp. 107–08.

46. See two articles on the resistance movement in northern Laos by Claudia Rosett: "Yellow Rain in Laos: New Reports," *Asian Wall Street Journal*, 14 June 1990, p. A-14; and "A Lonely Lao Fight for Freedom," 13 June 1990, p. A-14. For a fuller treatment of resistance groups fighting against the government, see Geoffrey C. Gunn, "Resistance Coalition in Laos," *Asian Survey* 23, no. 3 (March 1983): 316–40.

47. *Christian Science Monitor*, 27 November 1991, p. 10.

48. Ross, *Cambodia*, p. 160.

49. See *Far East and Australia*, 1991, p. 274. (The article on economy was written by Richard Vokes.)

50. Ibid. Also, Justus M. Van der Kroef, "Cambodia in 1990: The Elusive Peace," *Asian Survey* 31, no. 1 (January 1991): 99.

51. Ibid.; and Barron's, 9 December 1991, p. 14.

52. *Far Eastern Economic Review*, 20 June 1991, p. 84.

53. Ibid., p. 85.

54. H. D. S. Greenway, "Report from Cambodia: The Tiger and the Crocodile," *The New Yorker*, 17 July 1989, p. 76.

55. See the article by Tommy Koh, Singapore's representative to the Paris Peace Conference, in *The International Herald-Tribune*, 1 November 1991, p. 4.

56. *Far East and Australia*, 1991, p. 282.

57. *Christian Science Monitor*, 16 January 1992, p. 5.

58. See Sesser, "A Reporter at Large," p. 44. Also see Johnson, "Laos in 1991," p. 85.

59. Esterline and Esterline, "How the Dominoes Fell," p. 132.

60. See Thayer, "Laos in 1982," pp. 88–89; Sesser, "Reporter at Large," pp. 48–49; and Richard Vokes, *Far East and Australia, 1991*, 23rd ed., p. 509.

61. See Joiner, "Laos in 1987," pp. 96–98; and his "Laos in 1986," pp. 108–09; and *Far East and Australia, 1991*, p. 509.

62. Sesser, "Reporter at Large," p. 50.

63. See Gunn, "Laos in 1989," p. 81.

64. Ibid., p. 82.

65. Johnson, "Laos in 1991," p. 85.

66. Ibid.

67. *Far East and Australia, 1991*, pp. 519, 522.

68. Ibid.

69. *Asia 1991 Yearbook* (Hong Kong: Review Publishing Company, 1990), p. 8.

70. See Jinny St. Goar, "Economic Reform in Laos Falls Short," *Asian Wall Street Journal*, 5 March, 1990, p. A-8.

CONCLUSION

1. See Joseph S. Nye, Jr., "America's Asian Agenda: Coping with Japan," *Foreign Policy*, no. 89 (Winter 1992–93): 96–115; William T. Tow, "Post-Cold War Security in East Asia," *The Pacific Review* 4, no. 2 (1991): 97–108.

2. Richard F. Ellings and Edward A. Olsen, "A New Pacific Profile," *Foreign Policy*, no. 89 (Winter 1992–93): 119.

3. Amitar Acharya, "The Association of Southeast Asian Nations: 'Security Community' or 'Defence Community'?" *Pacific Affairs* 64, no. 2 (Summer 1991): 159–77.

4. Ellings and Olsen, "New Pacific Profile," p. 119.

5. *Hawaii Tribune-Herald* (Hilo), 24 January 1993, p. 24.

6. An Associated Press release as reprinted in the *Hawaii Tribune-Herald* (Hilo), 22 March 1993, p. 2.

7. There are a number of books that have been published recently on the issue of Asian security and the role of the United States (listed in order of the most recent publication): Thomas W. Robinson, ed., *Asian Security* (New York: University Press of America, 1993); Bernard K. Gordon, *New Directions for American Policy in Asia* (New York: Routledge, 1990); Janos Radvani, *The Pacific in the 1990s: Economic and Strategic Change* (New York: University Press of America, 1990); Robert A. Scalapino and Gennady Chafrim, *Asia in the 1990s: American and Soviet Perspectives* (Berkeley: Institute of East Asian Studies, 1990); and K. Holly Maze Carter, *The Asian Dilemma in United States Foreign Policy: National Interest vs. Strategic Planning* (New York: M.E. Sharpe, 1989).

   Also in recent years *The Pacific Review* has published a number of articles on the Asian security issue in addition to those cited so far: Andrew Mack and Desmond Ball, "The Military Build-up in Asia-Pacific," *The Pacific Review* 5, no. 3 (1992): 197–208; Patrick M. Cronin, "Pacific Rim Security: Beyond Bilateralism?" *The Pacific Review* 5, no. 3 (1992): 209–20; Gary Klintworth, "Asia-Pacific: More Security, Less Uncertainty, New Opportunities," *The Pacific Review* 5, no. 3 (1992): 221–31; Robert A. Scalapino, "Northeast Asia: Prospects for Cooperation," *The Pacific Review* 5, no. 2 (1992): 101–11; Sheldon W. Simon, "The Regionalization of Defence in Southeast Asia," *The Pacific Review* 5, no. 2 (1992): 112–24; Geoffrey Wiseman, "Common Security in the Asian-Pacific Region," *The Pacific Review* 5, no. 1 (1992): 42–59; Tow, "Post-Cold War Security in East Asia," pp. 97–108; Byung-joon Ahn, "Strategic Trends in East Asia," *The Pacific Review* 4, no. 2 (1991): 109–15.

8. Ellings and Olsen, "New Pacific Profile," p. 117.

9. See Scalapino, "Northeast Asia: Prospects for Cooperation," pp. 107–10.

10. Klintworth, "Asia-Pacific: More Security, Less Uncertainty, New Opportunities," p. 221.

11. Ibid.

12. The document by the U.S. Department of Defense entitled *A Strategic Framework for Asian Pacific Rim: Looking toward the 21st Century* (Washington, DC, 19 April 1990), revealed in an article by Tow, "Post-Cold War Security in East Asia," pp. 97–98.

13. Klintworth, "Asia-Pacific," pp. 223–25; and Tow, "Post-Cold War Security in East Asia," pp. 100–103. Also see Ellings and Olsen, "New Pacific Profile," pp. 126–27.

14. See *New York Times*, 1 October 1990, A-3; and *Far Eastern Economic Review*, 20 December 1990, p. 13.

15. Ellings and Olsen, "New Pacific Profile," p. 119.

16. Scalapino, "Northeast Asia," p. 107.

17. See Tim Huxley, "Singapore and Malaysia: A Precarious Balance?" *The Pacific Review* 4, no. 3 (1991): 204–05. Also *Far Eastern Economic Review*, 17 October 1991, pp. 37–38.

18. Huxley, "Singapore and Malaysia," p. 208.

19. *Far Eastern Economic Review*, 17 October 1991, p. 208.

20. Tow, "Post-Cold War Security in East Asia," p. 98.

21. Ibid., p. 103.

22. Wiseman, "Common Security in the Asia-Pacific Region," pp. 42–59.

23. Ibid., p. 48.

24. Ibid., p. 55.

25. Simon, "Regionalization of Defense in Southeast Asia," p. 113.

26. Ibid., pp. 122–23.

27. Acharya, "Association of Southeast Asian Nations," p. 159. Also see "Debating Asian Security: Michael Leifer Responds to Geoffrey Wiseman," *The Pacific Review* 5, no. 2 (1992): 167–69.

28. Ellings and Olsen, "New Pacific Profile," pp. 129–33.

29. Ibid., p. 130.

30. See Mack and Ball, "The Military Build-up in Asia-Pacific," p. 197.

31. Ibid., pp. 203–06.

32. See Leslie H. Gelb's article from the New York Times Service as reprinted in the *Hawaii Tribune-Herald* (Hilo), 26 March 1993, p. 10. Also see Amita Gupta, "Third World Militaries: New Suppliers, Deadlier Weapons," *ORBIS: A Journal of World Affairs* 37, no. 1 (Winter 1993): 57–68.

33. *New York Times*, 3 July 1991, A-4.

34. See Bruce Babock, "The Japanese Economy after Endaka," *Journal of Northeast Asian Studies* 6, no. 3 (Fall 1987): 54.

35. *Christian Science Monitor*, 5 January 1989, p. 3.

36. See speech made by Robert M. Kimmitt, under-secretary for political affairs, "The U.S. and Japan: Defining Our Global Partnership," Current Policy No. 1221 (Washington, DC: Bureau of Public Affairs, U.S. Department of State, 9 October 1989), pp. 2–3. Also see *Wall Street Journal*, 27 April 1990, p. A-12, and 14 March 1990, p. A-3; *Christian Science Monitor*, 26 June 1989, p. 6; *Far Eastern Economic Review*, 12 April 1990, pp. 56–57.

37. *New York Times*, 2 March 1990, p. C-1.

38. See *Wall Street Journal*, 26 March 1990, p. A-6. Cray Research of Minneapolis is the world's largest supercomputer producer and has cornered one-third of the private sector market in Japan, but was unable to break into the government purchases.

39. See *Honolulu Star Bulletin*, 28 December 1989, pp. A-1, A-3.

40. Comment made by Gerald L. Curtis, director of the East Asian Institute, Columbia University, at an East-West Center Symposium on "U.S.-Japan Relations in the 1990s," *Centerviews* 7, no. 5 (September–October 1989): p. 4.

41. See Peter F. Drucker, "U.S.-Japan Trade Needs a Reality Check," *Asian Wall street Journal*, 12 January 1989, p. 6.

42. See Bill Emmott and Clyde Prestowitz, "Trade Charade: U.S.-Japan Pact Is Just More of the Same," Los Angeles Times, as reprinted in *The Honolulu Advertiser*, 4 May 1990, p. A-23.

43. See Glenn S. Fukushima, "United States-Japan Free Trade Area: A Skeptical View," *Cornell International Law Journal* 22, no. 3 (September 1989): 457–61; and David E. Sanger, "Japan's Ideas for Strengthening U.S. Economy," *New York Times*, as reprinted in *The Honolulu Star-Bulletin*, 28 March 1990, p. A-14. Also see *Wall Street Journal*, 27 March 1990, p. A-17.

44. See Kimmitt, "U.S. and Japan," p. 3.

45. See Karel van Wolferen, *The Enigma of Japanese Power: People and Politics in a Stateless Nation* (New York: Knopf, 1989), pp. 412–13. Also see a summary of the Maekawa report, *Far Eastern Economic Review*, 11 July 1988, p. 12.

46. Fukushima, "United States-Japan Free Trade Area," p. 462.

47. Ibid., p. 463.

48. James Fallows, "Containing Japan," *The Atlantic Monthly*, May 1989, pp. 41–54.

49. Ibid., p. 54.

50. Ibid.

51. See *Far Eastern Economic Review*, 12 April 1990, p. 56.

52. Ibid.

53. Ellings and Olsen, "New Pacific Profile," p. 134.

54. Scalapino, "Northeast Asia," p. 110.

55. Ibid.

56. Ibid. Also see Nye, "America's Asian Agenda," p. 108; and Barry Wain, "Asia Toys with Trade Blocs," *Asian Wall Street Journal*, 18 March 1991, p. A-8.

Index